Bloom's Period Studies

BLOOM'S PERIOD STUDIES

Modern American Drama

Edited and with an introduction by
Harold Bloom
Sterling Professor of the Humanities
Yale University

CHELSEA HOUSE
P U B L I S H E R S
A Haights Cross Communications Company ®
Philadelphia

©2005 by Chelsea House Publishers, a subsidiary of
Haights Cross Communications.

A Haights Cross Communications ⟋ Company ®

www.chelseahouse.com

Introduction © 2005 by Harold Bloom.

Printed and bound in the United States of America.

10 9 8 7 6 5 4 3 2 1

Library of Congress Cataloging-in-Publication Data

Modern American drama / [edited and with an introduction by] Harold Bloom.
    p. cm. — (Bloom's period studies)
  Includes bibliographical references and index.
  ISBN 0-7910-8238-5
  1. American drama—20th century—History and criticism. I. Bloom, Harold. II.
Series.
  PS350.M63 2005
  812'.509—dc22
                                    2005005343

Contributing editor: Pamela Loos

Cover design by Keith Trego

Cover: Assocate Press, AP

Layout by EJB Publishing Services

Contents

Editor's Note

My Introduction works its way through some of the major plays of O'Neill, Wilder, Williams, Miller, Simon, Albee, Shepard, and August Wilson, before concluding with David Mamet. At the close of this volume, I both celebrate and worry about Tony Kushner. All theater, according to Benjamin Bennett, is revolutionary theater, but he astutely means that the mixed form of dramatic literature and public performance is more of a genre problem than it is a political phenomenon. Like the late Arthur Miller and August Wilson, Kushner is a politically oriented playwright, and I entertain doubts as to the long-range aesthetic validity of obsessive political concerns in our America.

Lionel Trilling, the exemplar of the liberal imagination in the United States, grants Eugene O'Neill his genius, yet wonders at the quasi-religious nature of O'Neill's dramatic quest, which the critic shrewdly compares to Pascal's wager on an existent God to meet the heart's need.

Edward Albee is seen as a dramatic allegorist of the homoerotic by Gerald Weales, while Anne Paolucci praises Albee for artistic arrogance or disciplined allegory.

Arthur Miller's social perspective, which sets the individual against organized society, is examined by Leonard Moss, after which Gilbert Debusscher shows how Tennessee Williams brilliantly molded the great poet Hart Crane into the dramatist's powerful alter ego.

The major plays of Thornton Wilder are interpreted as parables of survival by David Castronovo, while Robert A. Martin turns to the later work of Arthur Miller, from *After the Fall* onwards, in order to find that "commitment is not something one dies for, it is something one survives for."

David Mamet's superbly savage *Sexual Perversity in Chicago* finds an accurate exegete in Anne Dean who commends his linguistic control, after which Jane Palatini Bowers illuminates Gertrude Stein's *Four Saints in Three Acts*.

History in August Wilson's work is shown by John Timpane to be a rivalry of readings by audiences and the characters on stage, while David Mamet receives an impressively nuanced reading from Michael L. Quinn, who is particularly fine on *Oleanna*, where whatever actual truth exists is altogether deferred.

Sam Shepard's experimentalism is extolled by Stephen J. Bottoms, who feels that fragmentation is good for audiences, after which Elinor Fuchs discovers in Maria Irene Fornes a firm realist in all matters relating to the tragedy of gender.

Christopher Bigsby meditates upon the apparent artistic decline of the later Tennessee Williams, and finds in it a continued "public power."

I conclude this volume with a brief coda on Tony Kushner, urging upon him a further inward turn into this fecund religious imagination, since political activism in the United States of 2005 courts, in my judgment, a self-crippling of any art that engages too directly with our national banality.

Introduction

Eugene O'Neill

Eugene O'Neill's judgment upon his country was: "We are tragedy." Nearly a half-century after the playwright's death, I would be inclined to revise that into: "We are farce." O'Neill's despair of American illusions was constant and impressive, but can it be called a vision of America, in the antithetical senses in which Tennessee Williams and Arthur Miller dramatically achieve visions of our nation? In the literary sense, O'Neill had little to do with American tradition. Partly this is because we had no important playwright before O'Neill. His resort to Henrik Ibsen, and even more to Ibsen's rival, August Strindberg, was crucial for his art. *The Iceman Cometh* owes much to Strindberg's *The Dance of Death*, and something to Ibsen insofar as Hickey authentically is a deidealizer. Schopenhauer, Nietzsche, and Freud hover in the intellectual background of *Iceman*, Schopenhauer in particular. Of American intellectual or literary tradition, O'Neill was either hostile or ignorant. Without much knowing Emerson, O'Neill can be said to destroy, where he can, the American credo of Self-Reliance.

An unbelieving Irish Catholic, who yet retained the puritanism of his religious heritage, O'Neill judged that the United States had failed to achieve spiritual reality. The judgment is peculiar, partly because O'Neill knew nothing about the American Religion, which is Evangelical, personal, and both Gnostic and Orphic. Hickey, O'Neill's nihilistic protagonist, comes to destroy hope because he judges it to be more pernicious than despair. What makes Hickey dramatically interesting is his clashing realizations that the derelicts need to be divested of their hope, but also that they need their "pipe dreams" or illusions if they are to survive. O'Neill's "pipe dream" was to believe that any nation could achieve spiritual "reality" as such.

Did Hickey murder his wife because of love, or hatred? Is he too motivated by hope, or by despair? We never know, and this is all to the good, since our ignorance augments drama. Larry Slade, in contrast, is one of Neill's major failures in characterization. His condemnation of the mother-betraying Parritt to a suicide's death is persuasive neither as action nor as reflection. O'Neill's own spiritual incoherence emerges clearly in his surrogate, Slade, who thinks himself a convert to Hickey's Will-to-Die, yet remains a lapsed Catholic, yearning for grace. We are left with stirring theater, but with a spiritual enigma.

THORNTON WILDER

Rereading *Our Town* and *The Matchmaker* in 2002 provides a very mixed literary experience. One sees the past glories, but does not feel them. It is rather like—for me anyway—reseeing Fellini movies I had enjoyed immensely several decades ago. Time's revenges are inexorable, and all debates about canonical survival are resolved pragmatically by the grim process in which popular works become Period Pieces.

Aside from a few of his shorter plays, Wilder's only prospect for survival is *The Skin of Our Teeth*, again in my wavering judgment. I remember participating in occasional seminars on *Finnegans Wake* led by Wilder when I was a graduate student at Yale in the early Fifties. Genial and well-informed, Wilder particularly moved one by his clear love for Joyce's great, always-to-be-neglected Book of the Night. Rereading *The Skin of Our Teeth*, the charm of those seminars returns to me. Wilder emphasized Joyce's skill in rendering different eras of time simultaneously, which is his principal debt in the Antrobus family saga to Joyce.

It is not that the play can hold up when read too closely against the impacted mosaic of *Finnegans Wake*, but then what could? The Earwickers are obviously larger and more multivalent than the Antrobuses: they are also more Shakespearean, because of Joyce's deliberate *agon* with "the Englishman." Great "Shapesphere" puns his way through the *Wake*, where the generational struggles and family romances overtly remake *Hamlet*. One might wish that Wilder had taken even more from *Finnegans Wake*: an overtone of *Hamlet* might help to relieve the banality of the Antrobus children or the eternally unfailing goodness of Mrs. Antrobus, who would be enlivened by a touch of that sexual magnet, Queen Gertrude.

Doubtless *The Skin of Our Teeth* still stages better than it reads, but I fear that its simplifications are not intensifications but reductions. Theatrically, we are now in the Age of Sam Shepard and Tony Kushner. *Their* intensifications yet may prove to lack permanence: our theater is still Artaud's, with his angry motto: "No more masterpieces."

TENNESSEE WILLIAMS

As a lyrical dramatist, Tennessee Williams manifests the formal influence of Chekhov, yet his principal precursors were the great American lyrical poet, Hart Crane (1899–1932) and the English visionary poet-novelist, D.H. Lawrence (1885–1930). Though his own life-span was more substantial (1911–1983) than those of his forerunners, Williams underwent terrible depressions and breakdowns, and the image of Hart Crane's turbulent career emerges frequently in his plays. It is a tribute to Williams's dramatic genius that aspects of Crane vitally inform three of the playwright's very diverse major characters: Tom Wingfield in *The Glass Menagerie*, Blanche in *A Streetcar Named Desire*, and Sebastian Venable, deceased before *Suddenly Last Summer* opens, yet the central character of the play.

Hart Crane, the most Orphic and self-destructive of all American poets, is of the aesthetic eminence of Walt Whitman, Emily Dickinson, Wallace Stevens, and T.S. Elliot, his own precursors. Williams, perhaps our most gifted dramatist, burned out by his early forties, and his last three decades produced essentially inadequate work. Ever since I first fell in love with Hart Crane's poetry, almost sixty years ago, I have wondered what the poet of *The Bridge* and "The Broken Tower" would have accomplished, had he not killed himself at thirty-two. One doesn't see Crane burning out; he was poetically strongest at the very end, despite his despair. Williams identified his own art, and his own despair, with Crane's. Tom Wingfield, Blanche Du Bois and even Sebastian Venable are closer to self-portraits than they are depictions of Hart Crane, but crucial images of Crane's poetry intricately fuse into Williams's visions of himself.

The aesthetic vocation and homosexual identity are difficult to distinguish both in Crane and in Williams, though both poet and playwright develop stratagems, rhetorical and cognitive, that enrich this difficulty without reducing it to case histories. Tom Wingfield's calling will become Williams's, though *The Glass Menagerie* presents Wingfield's quest as a flight away from the family romance, the incestuous images of the mother and the sister. Blanche Du Bois, much closer to Williams himself, risks the playwright's masochistic self-parody, and yet her defeat has considerable aesthetic dignity. More effective on stage than in print, her personality is a touch too wistful to earn the great epitaph from Crane's "The Broken Tower" that Williams insists upon employing:

> And so it was I entered the broken world
> To trace the visionary company of love, its voice
> An instant in the wind (I know not whither hurled)
> But not for long to hold each desperate choice.

One of the oddities of *Suddenly Last Summer* is that Catharine is far closer to an accurate inner portrait of Hart Crane than is the poet Sebastian Venable, who lacks Crane's honesty and courage. Williams's obsession with Crane twists *Suddenly Last Summer* askew, and should not prevent us from seeing that Williams's self-hatred dominates the depiction of Sebastian. For all his gifts, Williams was a far more flawed artist than Crane, whose imaginative heroism was beyond anything Williams could never attain.

ARTHUR MILLER

"A man can get anywhere in this country on the basis of being liked." Arthur Miller's remark, made in an interview, has a peculiar force in the context of American political and social history. One reflects upon Ronald Reagan, a President impossible (for me) either to admire or to dislike. Miller, despite his palpable literary and dramatic limitations, has a shrewd understanding of our country. *Death of Salesman* is now half a century old, and retains its apparently perpetual relevance. The American ethos is sufficiently caught up by the play so that Miller's masterwork is clearly not just a period piece, unlike *All My Sons* and *The Crucible*, popular as the latter continues to be.

Arthur Miller is an Ibsenite dramatist, though his Ibsen is mostly a social realist, and not the visionary of the great plays: *Peer Gynt, Brand, Hedda Gabler,* and *When We Dead Awaken*. That Ibsen is himself something of a troll: obsessed and daemonic. Imaginative energy of that order is not present in Miller, though *Death of a Salesman* has an energy of pathos very much its own, the entropic catastrophe that Freud (with some irony) called "Family Romances."

Family romances almost invariably are melodramatic; to convert them to tragedy, you need to be the Shakespeare of *King Lear*, or at least of *Coriolanus*. Miller has a fondness for comparing *Death of a Salesman* to *King Lear*, a contrast that itself is catastrophic for Miller's play. Ibsen, at his strongest, can sustain some limited comparison to aspects of Shakespeare, but Miller cannot. Like Lear, Willy Loman needs and wants more familial love than anyone can receive, but there the likeness ends.

Does Miller, like Eugene O'Neill, write the plays of our moral climate, or have we deceived ourselves into overestimating both of these dramatists? American novelists and American poets have vastly surpassed American playwrights: there is no dramatic William Faulkner or Wallace Stevens to be acclaimed among us. It may be that day-to-day reality in the United States is so violent that stage drama scarcely can compete with the drama of common events and uncommon persons. A wilderness of pathos may be more fecund matter for storyteller and lyricists than it can be for those who would compose tragedies.

Perhaps that is why we value *Death of a Salesman* more highly than its actual achievement warrants. Even half a century back, an universal image of American fatherhood was very difficult to attain. Willy Loman moves us because he dies the death of a father, not of a salesman. Whether Miller's critique of the values of a capitalistic society is trenchant enough to be persuasive, I continue to doubt. But Loman's yearning for love remains poignant, if only because it destroys him. Miller's true gift is for rendering anguish, and his protagonist's anguish authentically touches upon the universal sorrow of failed fatherhood.

NEIL SIMON

At his best, Neil Simon moves towards a Chekhovian controlled pathos, but only rarely does he approach close to it. His comedy essentially is situational, though the overtones of Jewish traditional folk humor sometimes allow him to suggest a darker strain. He is a popular playmaker of enormous skill, and certainly persuades more easily on the stage and the screen than he does in print. If all aesthetic criteria were indeed societal, as our debased academies now tell us, then Simon would be more than an eminent hand. His plays are honorable period pieces, and will have the fate of Pinero and Odets, dramatists of their moment. And yet, there is a normative quality in his work that is heartening, and that always promises a touch more than he needs to give.

Writing what is essentially Jewish comedy after the Holocaust is not exactly an unmixed enterprise, and there is a deft quickness in Simon's rhetoric that is admirably sustained, doubtless reflecting his training as a television gag-writer. Though *Lost in Yonkers* is his sharpest and most mature play, it is marred by a forced, relatively happy ending, which has the effect of rendering the entire drama rather questionable.

The Odd Couple has entered popular consciousness, but is perhaps too overtly psychological to endure beyond our era. *Plaza Suite* can cause one to wince, in tribute to its truth-telling, but its fundamental slightness is too apparent. It is *The Sunshine Boys*, for all its sentimentality, that may last longest. Willie Clark and Al Lewis are nowhere as funny as Joe Smith and Charlie Dale, probably the greatest Jewish vaudevillians, but their ambivalent relationship is rendered as precisely representative of the complex feelings evoked by Yiddish popular culture as it transformed into the entertainment industry of American Jewry.

Neil Simon is the most popular contemporary American playwright, with a larger audience than Arthur Miller, Edward Albee, August Wilson, Tony Kushner and other real talents. It would be difficult to compare him favorably to any of them, because his range is narrow, and his mode is so deliberately restrictive. He fades away absolutely if we invoke *Death of A Salesman, The Zoo Story, Joe Turner's Come and Gone*, or *Angels in America*. And yet he is a grand entertainer, and at least in *The Sunshine Boys*, something more than that. Yiddish theater, on which I was raised, goes on more absolutely in Kushner and in David Mamet, but it finds a nostalgic echo, ebbing but sometimes poignant, in Neil Simon's comedies.

EDWARD ALBEE

Edward Albee is the crucial American dramatist of his generation, standing as the decisive link between our principal older dramatists—Eugene O'Neill, Thornton Wilder, Tennessee Williams, Arthur Miller—and the best of the younger ones—Sam Shepard and David Mamet, among others. Though Albee's best work came at his beginnings, with *The Zoo Story, The American Dream*, and *Who's Afraid of Virginia Woolf?*, he is hardly to be counted out. A way into his aesthetic dilemmas is provided by the one-scene play *Fam and Yam: An Imaginary Interview*, written and staged in 1960, the year of *The American Dream*. Fam, a Famous American Playwright, is called upon by Yam, a Young American Playwright, in what is clearly an encounter between a precursor, say Tennessee Williams, and a rising latecomer, say Edward Albee. Yam is the author of an off-Broadway play, *Dilemma, Dereliction and Death*, which sounds rather like a three-word summary of *The Zoo Story*. The outer, single joke of *Fam and Yam* is that the Famous American Playwright is tricked into an interview by the Young American Playwright, but the meaning of the skit, uneasily riding its surface, is a dramatic version of the anxiety of influence (to coin a phrase).

Haunted by Williams, Albee was compelled to swerve from the master into a lyrical drama even more vehemently phantasmagoric than *The Glass Menagerie* and even more incongruously fusing realism and visionary illusion than *A Streetcar Named Desire*. The force of Albee's initial swerve was undeniable; *The Zoo Story*, his first play (1958), still seems to me his best, and his most ambitious and famous drama remains *Who's Afraid of Virginia Woolf?* (1961–62). After *Tiny Alice* (1964), Albee's inspiration was pretty well spent, and more than twenty years later, he still matters for his intense flowering between the ages of thirty and thirty-six. The shadow of Williams, once held off by topological cunning and by rhetorical gusto, lengthened throughout all of Albee's plays of the 1970s. Hart Crane, Williams's prime precursor, can give the motto for Albee's relationship to Williams:

> Have you not heard, have you not seen that corps
> Of shadows in the tower, whose shoulders sway
> Antiphonal carillons launched before
> The stars are caught and hived in the sun's ray?

SAM SHEPARD

Incest, according to Shelley, is the most poetical of circumstances. This brief prelude to Sam Shepard centers upon *Fool for Love*, which I like best of his several dozen plays. Walt Whitman, an authentic forerunner of Shepard, denied being influenced by anyone, though without Ralph Waldo Emerson one can doubt Whitman would have happened. Shepard similarly denies all literary and dramatic indebtedness, insisting he emanates from Jackson Pollack and the Who. Plays however are written with words, and Shepard, if your perspective is long enough, is another Expressionist dramatist, a very good one, with a definite relation to "Brecht"! The quotation marks are there because we know that most of "Brecht" was written by two very talented women whom the rascal exploited.

Shepard also shows some touches of Pinter, and even of Pinter's precursor, Beckett. There seems no clear American lineage in dramatic tradition for the very American Shepard. I find a touch of Tennessee Williams in Martin, May's date in *Fool for Love*, and dimly in the background are the Strindbergian asperities of Eugene O'Neill's destructive family romances. Yet no one can dispute that Sam Shepard is an American Original. Emerson, everyone's American grandfather, told us: "The originals are not original." Rock and roll performers, whom Shepard so envies, all have their formative phases, in which their ancestry is quite clear, the Who included. Shepard, who battles so fiercely against categorization, resembles a tradition in American literature that R.W.B. Lewis has called Adamic. Like Walt Whitman, Sam Shepard seeks to be Adam early in the morning, but a Western American Adam.

Fool for Love has four characters, all American archetypes. The incestuous lovers are half-siblings, May and Eddie, who is a dead-end cowboy. May, a drifter, is caught up with Eddie in a hopelessly ambivalent relationship, always about to end but unable to do so. Their common father, the Old Man, is dead, but highly visible, at least to us in the audience. He too is a cowboy, rocking away and consuming whiskey beyond the grave. That leaves only Martin, May's would-be date, who appears to be a surrogate for the audience.

Everything about *Fool for Love* suggests a controlled hallucination. Nothing is certain, least of all incest; since the Old Man insists he sees nothing of himself in either of the lovers. Nor can we believe anything that May and Eddie say about one another. We can be certain that they inspire obsessiveness, each in himself or herself and in the (more-or-less) beloved.

The paradox in Shepard is why any of his people matter, to us or to him. The answer, which confers aesthetic dignity, is altogether Whitmanian. *Song of Myself* anticipates Shepard: his burned-out Americans were Whitman's before they were Shepard's. Walt Whitman, the true American shaman, would have been at home in *Fool for Love*, *Buried Child*, and *True West*.

Shepard's people are lyrical selves, desperately seeking a stable identity. They are not going to find it. Their dramatist remains our major living visionary, stationed at the edge of our common abyss.

AUGUST WILSON

I recall attending a performance of *Joe Turner's Come and Gone* at Yale in 1986, and came away more moved than I had been by *Ma Rainey's Black Bottom* and *Fences*. *Two Trains Running* I have never seen, and have just read for the first time, after rereading three earlier plays in the University of Pittsburgh Press's very useful *Three Plays* (1991), which has a stern Preface by the dramatist, and a useful Afterword by Paul Cater Harrison. Returning to the text of *Joe Turner's Come and Gone* after a decade is a remarkable experience in reading, since few plays by American dramatists hold up well away from the stage. As a literary work, *Joe Turner's Come and Gone* is authentically impressive, particularly in its spiritual insights. August Wilson's political stance as a black nationalist is present in *Joe Turner's* (to give it a short title), but his art as a dramatist surmounts the tendentiousness that elsewhere distracts me. Whether or not his other celebrated plays may prove to be period pieces (like those of Bullins and Baraka), I am uncertain, but there is a likely permanence in *Joe Turner's*, perhaps because of its profound depiction of the African American roots of what I have learned to call the American Religion, the actual faith of white Protestants in the United States.

The summer of 2001 is hardly a good time anyway to argue nationalist stances among African Americans, now that the full extent of black disenfranchisement in Jeb Bush's Florida is being revealed. It is clear that if there had been an unimpeded African American vote in Florida, the Supreme Court would not have been able to appoint George W. Bush as President. Since August Wilson's project is to compose a play for every decade of the black experience in twentieth century America, one wryly awaits what he might choose to do with the Florida Outrage of November 2000.

Wilson, in his Preface to *Three Plays*, offers a powerful reading of his masterwork:

> There is a moment in *Joe Turner's Come and Gone* at the end of the first act when the residents of the household, in an act of tribal solidarity and recognition of communal history, dance a Juba. Herald Loomis interrupts it to release a terrifying vision of bones walking on the water. From the outset he has been a man who has suffered a spiritual dislocation and is searching for a world that contains his image. The years of bondage to Joe Turner have disrupted his lie and severed his connection with his past. His vision is of bones walking on water that sink and wash up on the shore as fully fleshed humans. It is not the bones walking on the water that is the terrifying part of the vision—it is when they take on flesh and reveal themselves to be like him. "They black. Just like you and me. Ain't no difference." It is the shock of recognition that his birth has origins in the manifest act of the creator, that he is in fact akin to the gods. Somewhere in the Atlantic Ocean lie the bones of millions of Africans who died before reaching the New World. The flesh of their flesh populates the Americas from Mississippi to Montevideo. Loomis is made witness to the resurrection and restoration of these bones. He has only to reconcile this vision with his learned experiences and recognize he is one of the "bones people." At the end of the play he repudiates the idea that salvation comes from outside of himself and claims his moral personality by slashing his chest in a bloodletting rite that severs his bonds and demonstrates his willingness to bleed as an act of redemption.

Spiritually, this is both greatly suggestive and not unconfusing. Why does Loomis slash himself? There is a deep pattern of African gnosticism in the colonial black Baptists, who carried on from their heritage in affirming "the little me within the big me," the spark of the Alien God that was the best and oldest part of them, free of the Creation-Fall. Michal Sobel has shown how this pattern recurs in African American religion, and I suspect it was transmitted by the African Baptists to the original Southern Baptists. If Loomis slashes himself as a parody of and against Christian blood atonement, I could understand it more readily, but Wilson violates African tradition by the chest-slashing that is a bloodletting, bond-severing act of redemption. Perhaps Wilson felt he needed this self-violence as a dramatic gesture, and yet it may detract from the rebirth of Loomis. If this is a flaw, it is a small one in so strong a play.

DAVID MAMET

Very few contemporary dramas of authentic eminence depress me quite so much as does *Sexual Perversity in Chicago*, whether I see it at a theater, or reread it in my study. Doubtless, Mamet wants that affect in auditor or reader. I have encountered only one photograph of Mamet, the Brigitte Lacombe shot of the playwright as Groucho Marx that adorns the paperback of *SPC* (a short version of the title). One could argue that Groucho is more of an influence upon Mamet than are Beckett, Pinter, and Albee, since *SPC* seems (to me) best acted as parodistic farce. T.S. Eliot, still the major poet who makes me most uneasy, had a great regard both for Groucho and for Marlowe's Jew of Malta, Barabbas. I cannot read *The Jew of Malta* without casting Groucho in the role, and sometimes I wish I could direct *SPC* with Groucho playing Bernie and Chico as Danny.

The epigraph to *SPC* might be Marlowe's Mephistophiles cheerfully answering: "Why this is Hell, nor am I out of it." Though Douglas Bruster usefully compares Mamet to Ben Jonson of the City Comedies, I suspect that Mamet actually resembles Marlowe more than Jonson. The savagery of Mamet's stance towards his protagonists, particularly in *SPC*, is Marlovian, as is Mamet's fierce obsession with hyperbolical rhetoric. Here is Bernie, wildly prevaricating, and approaching the vaunting terms of Sir Epicure Mammon in *The Alchemist*:

> BERNIE: So wait. So I don't know what the shot is. So all of a
>   sudden I hear coming out of the phone: "Rat Tat Tat Tat
>   Tat. Ka POW! AK AK AK AK AK AK AK *Ka Pow!*" So fine. I'm
>   pumping away, the chick on the other end is making

airplane noises, every once in a while I go BOOM, and the broad on the bed starts going crazy. She's moaning and groaning and about to go the whole long route. Humping and bumping, and she's screaming "Red dog One to Red dog Squadron" ... all of a sudden she screams "Wait." She wriggles out, leans under the bed, and she pulls out this five-gallon jerrycan.

DANNY: Right.

BERNIE: Opens it up ... it's full of gasoline. So she splashes the mother all over the walls, whips a fuckin' Zippo out of the Flak suit, and WHOOSH, the whole room is in flames. So the whole fuckin' joint is going up in smoke, the telephone is going "Rat Tat Tat," the broad jumps back on the bed and yells "Now, give it to me *now* for the love of Christ." (*Pause.*) So I look at the broad ... and I figure ... fuck this nonsense. I grab my clothes, I peel a sawbuck off my wad, as I make the door I fling it at her. "For cab fare," I yell. She doesn't hear nothing. One, two, six, I'm in the hall. Struggling into my shorts and hustling for the elevator. Whole fucking hall is full of smoke, above the flames I just make out my broad, she's singing "Off we go into the Wild Blue Yonder," and the elevator arrives, and the whole fucking hall is full of *firemen.* (*Pause.*) Those fucking firemen make out like bandits. (*Pause.*)

Bernie is confidence man rather than gull, so that we dislike him, whereas the outrageous Sir Epicure Mammon is weirdly endearing. And yet Bernie's obsessive rhetoric has an hallucinatory quality that is more than Jonsonian enough. No audience easily tolerates Bernie, whose final tirade manifests what could be called a negative pathos, which involuntarily expresses a desperate sense of damnation:

BERNIE: Makes all the fucking difference in the world. (*Pause.*) Coming out here on the beach. Lying all over the beach, flaunting their bodies ... I mean who the fuck do they think they are all of a sudden, coming out here and just flaunting their bodies all over? (*Pause.*) I mean, what are you supposed to think? I come to the beach with a friend to get some sun and watch the action and ... I mean a fellow comes to the beach to sit out in the fucking sun, am I wrong? ... I

mean we're talking about recreational fucking space, huh?
... huh? (*Pause.*) What the fuck am I talking about?

The fear of female sexuality hardly could be more palpable, and a new kind of Inferno beckons in: "What the fuck am I talking about?" Hell, according to Jean-Paul Sartre's *No Exit*, is Other People. Like Rimbaud's Hell, Bernie's Inferno is not less than the existence of women as such.

LIONEL TRILLING

Eugene O'Neill

Whatever is unclear about Eugene O'Neill, one thing is certainly clear—his genius. We do not like the word nowadays, feeling that it is one of the blurb words of criticism. We demand that literature be a guide to life, and when we do that we put genius into a second place, for genius assures us of nothing but itself. Yet when we stress the actionable conclusions of an artist's work, we are too likely to forget the power of genius itself, quite apart from its conclusions. The spectacle of the human mind in action is vivifying; the explorer need discover nothing so long as he has adventured. Energy, scope, courage—these may be admirable in themselves. And in the end these are often what endure best. The ideas expressed by works of the imagination may be built into the social fabric and taken for granted; or they may be rejected; or they may be outgrown. But the force of their utterance comes to us over millennia. We do not read Sophocles or Aeschylus for the right answer; we read them for the force with which they represent life and attack its moral complexity. In O'Neill, despite the many failures of his art and thought, this force is inescapable.

But a writer's contemporary audience is inevitably more interested in the truth of his content than in the force of its expression; and O'Neill himself has always been ready to declare his own ideological preoccupation. His early admirers—and their lack of seriousness is a reproach to American criticism—were inclined to insist that O'Neill's content was unimportant as

---

From *Essays in the Modern Drama*, edited by Morris Freedman. © 1964 by Lionel Trilling.

compared to his purely literary interest and that he injured his art when he tried to think. But the appearance of *Days Without End* has made perfectly clear the existence of an organic and progressive unity of thought in all O'Neill's work and has brought it into the critical range of the two groups whose own thought is most sharply formulated, the Catholic and the Communist. Both discovered what O'Neill had frequently announced, the religious nature of all his effort.

Not only has O'Neill tried to encompass more of life than most American writers of his time but, almost alone among them, he has persistently tried to *solve* it. When we understand this we understand that his stage devices are not fortuitous technique; his masks and abstractions, his double personalities, his drum beats and engine rhythms are the integral and necessary expression of his temper of mind and the task it set itself. Realism is uncongenial to that mind and that task, and it is not in realistic plays like *Anna Christie* and *The Straw* but rather in such plays as *The Hairy Ape*, *Lazarus Laughed* and *The Great God Brown*, where he is explaining the world in parable, symbol and myth, that O'Neill is most creative. Not the minutiae of life, not its feel and color and smell, not its nuance and humor, but its "great inscrutable forces" are his interest. He is always moving toward the finality which philosophy sometimes, and religion always, promises. Life and death, good and evil, spirit and flesh, male and female, the all and the one, Anthony and Dionysus—O'Neill's is a world of these antithetical absolutes such as religion rather than philosophy conceives, a world of pluses and minuses; and his literary effort is an algebraic attempt to solve the equations.

In one of O'Neill's earliest one-act plays, the now unprocurable "Fog," a Poet, a Business Man and a Woman with a Dead Child, shipwrecked and adrift in an open boat, have made fast to an ice berg. When they hear the whistle of a steamer, the Business Man's impulse is to call for help, but the Poet prevents him lest the steamer be wrecked on the fog-hidden berg. But a searching party picks up the castaways and the rescuers explain that they had been guided to the spot by a child's cries; the Child, however, has been dead a whole day. This little play is a crude sketch of the moral world that O'Neill is to exploit. He is to give an ever increasing importance to the mystical implications of the Dead Child, but his earliest concern is with the struggle between the Poet and the Business Man.

It is, of course, a struggle as old as morality, especially interesting to Europe all through its industrial nineteenth century, and it was now engaging America in the second decade of its twentieth. A conscious artistic movement had raised its head to declare irreconcilable strife between the creative and the possessive ideal. O'Neill was an integral part—indeed, he became the very symbol—of that Provincetown group which represented the growing rebellion of the American intellectual against a business civilization. In 1914 his revolt was simple and socialistic; in a poem in *The Call* he urged the workers of the world not to fight, asking them if they wished to "bleed and groan—for Guggenheim" and "give your lives—for Standard Oil." By 1917 his feeling against business had become symbolized and personal. "My soul is a submarine," he said in a poem in *The Masses*:

> My aspirations are torpedoes.
> I will hide unseen
> Beneath the surface of life
> Watching for ships,
> Dull, heavy-laden merchant ships,
> Rust-eaten, grimy galleons of commerce
> Wallowing with obese assurance,
> Too sluggish to fear or wonder,
> Mocked by the laughter of the waves
> And the spit of disdainful spray.
>
> I will destroy them
> Because the sea is beautiful.

The ships against which O'Neill directed his torpedoes were the cultural keels laid in the yards of American business and their hulls were first to be torn by artistic realism. Although we now see the often gross sentimentality of the S.S. *Glencairn* plays and remember with O'Neill's own misgiving the vaudeville success of "In the Zone," we cannot forget that, at the time, the showing of a forecastle on the American stage was indeed something of a torpedo. Not, it is true, into the sides of Guggenheim and Standard Oil, but of the little people who wallowed complacently in their wake.

But O'Neill, not content with staggering middle-class complacency by a representation of how the other half lives, undertook to scrutinize the moral life of the middle class and dramatized the actual struggle between Poet and Business Man. In his first long play, *Beyond the Horizon*, the dreamer destroys his life by sacrificing his dream to domesticity; and the practical creator, the farmer, destroys his by turning from wheat-raising to wheat-gambling. It is a conflict O'Neill is to exploit again and again. Sometimes, as in "Ile" or *Gold*, the lust for gain transcends itself and becomes almost a creative ideal, but always its sordid origin makes it destructive. To O'Neill the acquisitive man, kindly and insensitive, practical and immature, became a danger to life and one that he never left off attacking.

But it developed, strangely, that the American middle class had no strong objection to being attacked and torpedoed; it seemed willing to be sunk for the insurance that was paid in a new strange coin. The middle class found that it consisted of two halves, bourgeoisie and booboisie. The booboisie might remain on the ship but the bourgeoisie could, if it would, take refuge on the submarine. Mencken and, Nathan, who sponsored the O'Neill torpedoes, never attacked the middle class but only its boobyhood. Boobish and sophisticated: these were the two categories of art; spiritual freedom could be bought at the price of finding *Jurgen* profound. And so, while the booboisie prosecuted *Desire Under the Elms*, the bourgeoisie swelled the subscription lists of the Provincetown Playhouse and helped the Washington Square Players to grow into the Theatre Guild. An increasingly respectable audience awarded O'Neill no less than three Pulitzer prizes, the medal of the American Academy of Arts and Sciences and a Yale Doctorate of Letters.

O'Neill did not win his worldly success by the slightest compromise of sincerity. Indeed, his charm consisted in his very integrity and hieratic earnestness. His position changed, not absolutely, but relatively to his audience, which was now the literate middle class caught up with the intellectual middle class. O'Neill was no longer a submarine; he had become a physician of souls. Beneath his iconoclasm his audience sensed reassurance.

The middle class is now in such literary disrepute that a writer's ability to please it is taken as the visible mark of an internal rottenness. But the middle class is people; prick them and they bleed, and whoever speaks sincerely to and for flesh and blood deserves respect. O'Neill's force derives in large part from the force of the moral and psychical upheaval of the middle class; it wanted certain of its taboos broken and O'Neill broke them. He was the Dion Anthony to its William Brown; Brown loved Dion: his love was a way of repenting for his own spiritual clumsiness.

Whoever writes sincerely about the middle class must consider the nature and the danger of the morality of "ideals," those phosphorescent remnants of a dead religion with which the middle class meets the world. This had been Ibsen's great theme, and now O'Neill undertook to investigate for America the destructive power of the ideal—not merely the sordid ideal of the Business Man but even the "idealistic" ideal of the Poet. The Freudian psychology was being discussed and O'Neill dramatized its simpler aspects in *Diff'rent* to show the effects of the repression of life. Let the ideal of chastity repress the vital forces, he was saying, and from this fine girl you will get a filthy harridan. The modern life of false ideals crushes the affirmative and creative nature of man; Pan, forbidden the light and warmth of the sun, grows "sensitive and self-conscious and proud and revengeful"—becomes the sneering Mephisthophelean mask of Dion.

The important word is *self-conscious*, for "ideals" are part of the "cheating gestures which constitute the vanity of personality." "Life is all right if you let it alone," says Cybel, the Earth Mother of *The Great God Brown*. But the poet of *Welded* cannot let it alone; he and his wife, the stage directions tell us, move in circles of light that represent "auras of egotism" and the high ideals of their marriage are but ways each ego uses to get possession of the other. O'Neill had his answer to this problem of the possessive, discrete personality. Egoism and idealism, he tells us, are twin evils growing from man's suspicion of his life and the remedy is the laughter of Lazarus—"a triumphant, blood-stirring call to that ultimate attainment in which all prepossession with self is lost in an ecstatic affirmation of Life." The ecstatic affirmation of Life, pure and simple, is salvation. In the face of death and pain, man must reply with the answer of Kublai Khan in *Marco Millions*: "Be proud of life! Know in your heart that the living of life can be noble! Be exalted by life! Be inspired by death! Be humbly proud! Be proudly grateful!"

It may be that the individual life is not noble and that it is full of pain and defeat; it would seem that Eileen Carmody in *The Straw* and Anna Christie are betrayed by life. But no. The "straw" is the knowledge that life is a "hopeless hope"—but still a hope. And nothing matters if you can conceive the whole of life. "Fog, fog, fog, all bloody time," is the chord of resolution of Anna Christie. "You can't see vhere you vas going, no. Only dat ole davil, sea—she knows." The individual does not know, but life—the sea—knows.

To affirm that life exists and is somehow good—this, then, became O'Neill's quasi-religious poetic function, nor is it difficult to see why the middle class welcomed it. "Brown will still need me," says Dion, "to reassure him he's alive." What to do with life O'Neill cannot say, but there it is. For Ponce de Leon it is the Fountain of Eternity, "the Eternal Becoming which is Beauty." There it is, somehow glorious, somehow meaningless. In the face of despair one remembers that "Always spring comes again bearing life! Always forever again. Spring again! Life again!" To this cycle, even to the personal annihilation in it, the individual must say "Yes." Man inhabits a naturalistic universe and his glory lies in his recognition of its nature and assenting to it; man's soul, no less than the stars and the dust, is part of the Whole and the free man loves the Whole and is willing to be absorbed by it.

In short, O'Neill solves the problem of evil by making explicit what men have always found to be the essence of tragedy—the courageous affirmation of life in the face of individual defeat.

But neither a naturalistic view of the universe nor a rapt assent to life constitutes a complete philosophic answer. Naturalism is the noble and realistic attitude that prepares the way for an answer; the tragic affirmation is the emotional crown of a philosophy. Spinoza—with whom O'Neill at this stage of his thought has an obvious affinity—placed between the two an ethic that arranged human values and made the world possible to live in. But O'Neill, faced with a tragic universe, unable to go beyond the febrilely passionate declaration, "Life is," finds the world impossible to live in. The naturalistic universe becomes too heavy a burden for him; its spirituality vanishes; it becomes a universe of cruelly blind matter. "Teach me to be resigned to be an atom," cries Darrell, the frustrated scientist of *Strange Interlude*, and for Nina life is but "a strange dark interlude in the electrical display of God the father"—who is a God deaf, dumb and blind. O'Neill, unable now merely to accept the tragic universe and unable to support it with man's whole strength—his intellect and emotion—prepares to support it with man's weakness: his blind faith.

For the non-Catholic reader O'Neill's explicitly religious solution is likely to be not only insupportable but incomprehensible. Neither St. Francis nor St. Thomas can tell us much about it; it is neither a mystical ecstasy nor the reasoned proof of assumptions. But Pascal can tell us a great deal, for O'Neill's faith, like Pascal's, is a poetic utilitarianism: he needs it and will have it. O'Neill rejects naturalism and materialism as Pascal had rejected Descartes and all science. He too is frightened by "the eternal silence of the infinite spaces." Like Pascal, to whom the details of life and the variety and flux of the human mind were repugnant, O'Neill feels that life is empty—having emptied it—and can fill it only by faith in a loving God. The existence of such a God, Pascal knew, cannot be proved save by the heart's need, but this seemed sufficient and he stood ready to stupefy his reason to maintain his faith. O'Neill will do no less. It is perhaps the inevitable way of modern Catholicism in a hostile world.

O'Neill's rejection of materialism involved the familiar pulpit confusion of philosophical materialism with "crass" materialism, that is, with the preference of physical to moral well-being. It is therefore natural that *Dynamo*, the play in which he makes explicit his anti-materialism, should present characters who are mean and little—that, though it contains an Earth Mother, she is not the wise and tragic Cybel but the fat and silly Mrs. Fife, the bovine wife of the atheist dynamo-tender. She, like other characters in the play, allies herself with the Dynamo-God, embodiment both of the materialistic universe and of modern man's sense of his own power. But this new god can only frustrate the forces of life, however much it at first seems life's ally against the Protestant denials, and those who worship it become contemptible and murderous.

And the contempt for humanity which pervades *Dynamo* continues in *Mourning Becomes Electra*, creating, in a sense, the utter hopelessness of that tragedy. Aeschylus had ended his Atreus trilogy on a note of social reconciliation—after the bloody deeds and the awful pursuit of the Furies, society confers its forgiveness, the Furies are tamed to deities of hearth and field: "This day there is a new Order born"; but O'Neill's version has no touch of this resolution. There is no forgiveness in *Mourning Becomes Electra* because, while there is as yet no forgiving God in O'Neill's cosmos, there is no society either, only a vague chorus of contemptible townspeople. "There's no one left to punish me," says Lavinia. "I've got to punish myself."

It is the ultimate of individual arrogance, the final statement of a universe in which society has no part. For O'Neill, since as far back as *The Hairy Ape*, there has been only the individual and the universe. The social organism has meant nothing. His Mannons, unlike the Atreides, are not monarchs with a relation to the humanity about them, a humanity that can forgive because it can condemn. They act their crimes on the stage of the infinite. The mention of human law bringing them punishment is startlingly incongruous and it is inevitable that O'Neill, looking for a law, should turn to a divine law.

Forgiveness comes in *Ah, Wilderness!* the satyr-play that follows the tragedy, and it is significant that O'Neill should have interrupted the composition of *Days Without End* to write it. With the religious answer of the more serious play firm in his mind, with its establishment of the divine law, O'Neill can, for the first time, render the sense and feel of common life, can actually be humorous. Now the family is no longer destructively possessive as he has always represented it, but creatively sympathetic. The revolt of the young son—his devotion to rebels and hedonists, to Shaw, Ibsen and Swinburne—is but the mark of adolescence and in the warm round of forgiving life he will become wisely acquiescent to a world that is not in the least terrible.

But the idyllic life of *Ah, Wilderness!* for all its warmth, is essentially ironical, almost cynical. For it is only when all magnitude has been removed from humanity by the religious answer and placed in the Church and its God that life can be seen as simple and good. The pluses and minuses of man must be made to cancel out as nearly as possible, the equation must be solved to equal nearly zero, before peace may be found. The hero of *Days Without End* has lived for years in a torturing struggle with the rationalistic, questioning "half" of himself which has led him away from piety to atheism, thence to socialism, next to unchastity and finally to the oblique attempt to murder his beloved wife. It is not until he makes an act of submissive faith at the foot of the Cross and thus annihilates the doubting mind, the root of all evil, that he can find peace.

But the annihilation of the questioning mind also annihilates the multitudinous world. *Days Without End*, perhaps O'Neill's weakest play, is cold and bleak: life is banished from it by the vision of the Life Eternal. Its religious content is expressed not so much by the hero's priestly uncle, wise, tolerant, humorous in the familiar literary convention of modern Catholicism, as by the hero's wife, a humorless, puritanical woman who lives on the pietistic-romantic love she bears her husband and on her sordid ideal of his absolute chastity. She is the very embodiment of all the warping, bullying idealism that O'Neill had once attacked. Now, however, he gives credence to this plaster saintliness, for it represents for him the spiritual life of absolutes. Now for the first time he is explicit in his rejection of all merely human bulwarks against the pain and confusion of life—finds in the attack upon capitalism almost an attack upon God, scorns socialism and is disgusted with the weakness of those who are disgusted with social individualism. The peace of the absolute can be bought only at the cost of blindness to the actual.

The philosophic position would seem to be a final one: O'Neill has crept into the dark womb of Mother Church and pulled the universe in with him. Perhaps the very violence of the gesture with which he has taken the position of passivity should remind us of his force and of what such force may yet do even in that static and simple dark. Yet it is scarcely a likely place for O'Neill to remember Dion Anthony's warning: "It isn't enough to be [life's] creature. You've got to create her or she requests you to destroy yourself."

GERALD WEALES

Edward Albee:
Don't Make Waves

Something tells me it's all
happenin' at the zoo.

—Simon and Garfunkel

Edward Albee is inescapably *the* American playwright of the 1960's. His first play, *The Zoo Story*, opened in New York, on a double bill with Samuel Beckett's *Krapp's Last Tape*, at the Provincetown Playhouse on January 14, 1960. In his Introduction to *Three Plays* (1960), Albee tells how his play, which was written in 1958, passed from friend to friend, from country to country, from manuscript to tape to production (in Berlin in 1959) before it made its way back to the United States. "It's one of those things a person has to do," says Jerry; "sometimes a person has to go a very long distance out of his way to come back a short distance correctly."

For Albee, once *The Zoo Story* had finished its peregrinations, the trip uptown—psychologically and geographically—was a short one. During 1960, there were two other Albee productions, largely unheralded—*The Sandbox*, which has since become a favorite for amateurs, and *Fam and Yam*, a *bluette*, a joke growing out of his having been ticketed as the latest white hope of the American theater. These were essentially fugitive productions of occasional pieces. In 1961, one of the producers of *The Zoo Story*, Richard Barr, joined by Clinton Wilder in the producing organization that is always

From *The Jumping-Off Place: American Drama in the 1960s.* © 1969 by Gerald Weales.

called Theater 196? after whatever the year, offered *The American Dream*, first on a double bill with William Flanagan's opera *Bartleby*, for which Albee and James Hinton, Jr., did the libretto,[1] and later, when the opera proved unsuccessful, with an earlier Albee play *The Death of Bessie Smith*. During the next few years, there were frequent revivals of both *Zoo* and *Dream*, often to help out a sagging Barr-Wilder program, as in 1964 (by which time Albee had become a co-producer) when first *Dream* and later *Zoo* were sent in as companion pieces to LeRoi Jones's *Dutchman*, after Samuel Beckett's *Play* and Fernando Arrabal's *The Two Executioners*, which opened with Jones's play, were removed from the bill. Albee had become an off-Broadway staple.

By that time, of course, Albee had become something else as well. With *Who's Afraid of Virginia Woolf?* (1962), he had moved to Broadway and had a smashing commercial success. By a process of escalation, he had passed from promising to established playwright. After *Woolf*, Albee productions averaged one a year: *The Ballad of the Sad Café* (1963), *Tiny Alice* (1964), *Malcolm* (1966), *A Delicate Balance* (1966) and *Everything in the Garden* (1967). None of these were successes in Broadway terms (by *Variety*'s chart of hits and flops), but except for *Malcolm*, a gauche and imperceptive adaptation of James Purdy's novel of that name, which closed after seven performances, all of them had respectable runs and generated their share of admiration and antagonism from critics and public alike.

Although favorable reviews helped make the Albee reputation, critics have consistently praised with one hand, damned with the other.[2] If Harold Clurman's "Albee on Balance" (*The New York Times*, January 13, 1967) treats Albee as a serious playwright and if Robert Brustein's "A Third Theater" (*The New York Times Magazine*, September 25, 1966) seems to dismiss him as a solemn one, only Broadway serious, the recent collections of their reviews—Clurman's *The Naked Image* and Brustein's *Seasons of Discontent*—indicate that both critics have had the same kind of reservations about Albee from the beginning. Albee, contrariwise, has had reservations of his own. From his pettish Introduction to *The American Dream* to the press conference he called to chastise the critics for their reactions to *Tiny Alice*, he has regularly used interviews and the occasional nondramatic pieces he has written—to suggest that the critics lack understanding, humility, responsibility.

In spite of (perhaps because of) the continuing quarrel between Albee and his critics—a love–hate relationship in the best Albee tradition—the playwright's reputation has grown tremendously. It was in part the notoriety of *Who's Afraid of Virginia Woolf?* that turned Albee into a popular figure, and certainly the publicity surrounding the making of the movie version of *Woolf* helped to keep Albee's name in the popular magazines. Whatever the cause,

Albee is now the American playwright whose name has become a touchstone, however ludicrously it is used. Thus, Thomas Meehan, writing an article on "camp" for *The New York Times Magazine* (March 21, 1965), solicits Andy Warhol's opinion of *Tiny Alice* ("I liked it because it was so empty"), and William H. Honan, interviewing Jonathan Miller for the same publication (January 22, 1967), manages to get Miller to repeat a commonplace criticism of Albee he has used twice before.

All this is simply the chi-chi mask over a serious concern with Albee. According to recent reports of the American Educational Theatre Association, Albee has been jockeying for second place (after Shakespeare) in the list of playwrights most produced on college campuses. In 1963–64, he held second place; in 1964–65, he was nosed out by Ionesco. The attractiveness of short plays to college dramatic groups—as Ionesco's presence suggests—helps explain the volume of Albee productions, but, with *The Zoo Story* invading text anthologies and *Virginia Woolf* climbing onto reading lists, it is clear that the interest in Albee in colleges is more than a matter of mechanics. More and more articles on Albee turn up in critical quarterlies—always a gauge of academic fashions—and those that are printed are only the tip of a happily submerged iceberg; Walter Meserve, one of the editors of *Modern Drama*, estimated in 1966 that 80 per cent of the submissions on American drama were about four authors: O'Neill, Williams, Miller, and Albee. The interest abroad is as intense as it is here. This is clear not only from the fact that the plays are translated and performed widely, but in the desire of audiences to talk or to hear about the playwright. Clurman, in that article in the *Times*, reporting on lecture audiences in Tokyo and Tel Aviv, says that there was more curiosity about Albee than any other American playwright. Albee's position, then, is analogous to that of Tennessee Williams in the 1950's. He recognizes this himself. When he wrote *Fam and Yam* in 1960, he let Yam (the Young American Playwright) bunch Albee with Jack Gelber, Jack Richardson, and Arthur Kopit. In an interview in *Diplomat* (October, 1966) he suggested that playwrights should be hired as critics; it was now Williams and Arthur Miller that he listed with himself.

In "Which Theatre Is the Absurd One?" (*The New York Times Magazine*, February 25, 1962), Albee wrote that "in the end a public will get what it deserves and no better." If he is right, his work may finally condemn or justify the taste of American theater audiences in the 1960's. More than likely, a little of both.

"I consider myself in a way the most eclectic playwright who ever wrote," Albee once told an interviewer (*Transatlantic Review*, Spring, 1963), and then he went on to make an elaborate joke about how he agreed with the critics that twenty-six playwrights—three of whom he had never read—had influenced him. Critics do have a way of getting influence-happy when they write about Albee—particularly Brustein, who persists in calling him an imitator—but they have good reason. There are such strong surface dissimilarities among the Albee plays that it is easier and in some ways more rewarding to think of *The Zoo Story* in relation to Samuel Beckett and Harold Pinter and *A Delicate Balance* in terms of T.S. Eliot and Enid Bagnold than it is to compare the two plays, even though both start from the same dramatic situation: the invasion (by Jerry, by Harry and Edna) of private territory (Peter's bench, Tobias's house). Yet, the comparison is obvious once it is made. Each new Albee play seems to be an experiment in form, in style (even if it is someone else's style), and yet there is unity in his work as a whole. This is apparent in the devices and the characters that recur, modified according to context, but it is most obvious in the repetition of theme, in the basic assumptions about the human condition that underlie all his work.

In *A Delicate Balance*, Tobias and his family live in a mansion in the suburbs of hell, that existential present so dear to contemporary writers, in which life is measured in terms of loss, love by its failure, contact by its absence. In that hell, there are many mansions—one of which is Peter's bench—and all of them are cages in the great zoo story of life. Peter's bench is a kind of sanctuary, both a refuge from and an extension of the stereotypical upper-middle-class existence (tweeds, horn-rimmed glasses, job in publishing, well-furnished apartment, wife, daughters, cats, parakeets) with which Albee has provided him—a place where he can safely not-live and have his nonbeing. This is the way Jerry sees Peter, at least, and—since the type is conventional enough in contemporary theater, from avant-garde satire to Broadway revue—it is safe to assume that the play does, too. Although Albee intends a little satirical fun at Peter's expense (the early needling scenes are very successful), it is clear that the stereotyping of Peter is an image of his condition, not a cause of it. Jerry, who plays "the old pigeonhole bit" so well, is another, a contrasting cliche, and it is the play's business to show that he and Peter differ only in that he does not share Peter's complacency. Just before Jerry attacks in earnest, he presents the play's chief metaphor:

> I went to the zoo to find out more about the way people exist with animals, and the way animals exist with each other, and with people too. It probably wasn't a fair test, what with everyone separated by bars from everyone else, the animals for the most

part from each other, and always the people from the animals. But, if it's a zoo, that's the way it is.

"Private wings," says Malcolm in the play that bears his name. "Indeed, that is an extension of separate rooms, is it not?" In a further extension of a joke that is no joke, Agnes, in *A Delicate Balance*, speaks of her "poor parents, in their separate heavens." *Separateness* is the operative word for Albee characters, for, even though his zoo provides suites for two people (*Who's Afraid of Virginia Woolf?*) or for more (*A Delicate Balance*), they are furnished with separate cages. "It's sad to know you've gone through it all, or most of it, without ...," says Edna in one of the fragmented speeches that characterize *A Delicate Balance*, as though thoughts too were separate, "that the one body you've wrapped your arms around ... the only skin you've ever known ... is your own—and that it's dry ... and not warm." This is a more restrained, a more resigned variation on the Nurse's desperate cry in *Bessie Smith*, "... I am tired of my skin.... I WANT OUT!"

Violence is one of the ways of trying to get out. The Nurse is an illustration of this possibility; she is an embryonic version of Martha in *Virginia Woolf*, with most of the venom, a little of the style, and practically none of the compensating softness of the later character, and she hits out at everyone around her. Yet, she never escapes herself, her cage. The other possibility is love (that, too, a form of penetration), but the Albee plays are full of characters who cannot (Nick in *Virginia Woolf*) or will not (Tobias, the Nurse) make that connection. The persistent images are of withdrawal, the most graphic being the one in *A Delicate Balance*, the information that Tobias in fact withdrew and came on Agnes's belly the last time they had sex. Although failed sex is a convenient metaphor for the failure of love, its opposite will not work so well. Connection is not necessarily contact, and it is contact—or rather its absence, those bars that bother Jerry—that preoccupies Albee. He lets Martha and George make fun of the lack-of-communication cliché in *Virginia Woolf*, but it is that cultural commonplace on which much of Albee's work is built. Jerry's story about his landlady's vicious dog—although he over-explains it—is still Albee's most effective account of an attempt to get through those bars, out of that skin (so effective, in fact, that Tobias uses a variation of it in *Balance* when he tells about his cat). Accepting the dog's attacks on him as a form of recognition, Jerry tries first to win his affection (with hamburger) and, failing that, to kill him (with poisoned hamburger: it is difficult to differentiate between the tools of love and hate). In the end, he settles for an accommodation, one in which he and the dog ignore each other. His leg remains unbitten, but he feels a sense of loss in the working arrangement: "We neither love nor hurt because we do not try to reach each other."[3]

"Give me any person ..." says Lawyer in *Tiny Alice*. "He'll take what he gets for ... what he wishes it to be. AH, it is what I have always wanted, he'll say, looking terror and betrayal straight in the eye. Why not: face the inevitable and call it what you have always wanted." The context is a special one here, a reference to Julian's impending martyrdom to God-Alice, who comes to him in the form or forms he expects. I purposely dropped from the Lawyer's speech the references to "martyr" and "saint" which follow parenthetically after the opening phrase, for as it stands above, the speech might serve as advertising copy for the Albee world in which his characters exist and—very occasionally—struggle. The too-obvious symbol of *The American Dream*, the muscle-flexing young man who is only a shell, empty of love or feeling, is, in Mommy's words, "a great deal more like it." *Like it*, but not *it*. Appearance is what she wants, for reality, as Grandma's account of the mutilation of the other "bumble" indicates, is dangerous.

The American Dream is a pat example of, to use Lawyer's words again, "How to come out on top, going under." Whether the accommodation is embraced (*Dream*) or accepted with a sense of loss (Jerry and the dog), it is always there, a way of coping instead of a way of life. It can be disguised in verbal trappings—comic (the games in *Virginia Woolf*) or serious (the religiosity of *Tiny Alice*, the conventional labels of *A Delicate Balance*). In the absence of substance, it can be given busy work; Girard Girard spells everything out in *Malcolm*: "You will move from the mansion to the chateau, and from the chateau back. You will surround yourself with your young beauties, and hide your liquor where you will. You will ... go on, my dear." The unhidden liquor in *A Delicate Balance* (even more in *Virginia Woolf*, where it serves the dramatic action, as lubricant and as occasional rest) provides an example of such busyness: all the playing at bartending, the weighty deliberation over whether to have anisette or cognac, the concern over the quality of a martini. The rush of words (abuse or elegance) and the press of activity (however meaningless) sustain the Albee characters in a tenuous relationship (a delicate balance) among themselves and in the face of the others, the ones outside, and—beyond that—the nameless terror.

Implicit in my discussion of the separateness of the Albee characters and the bogus forms of community they invent to mask the fact that they are alone is the assumption that this is Albee's view of the human condition. The deliberate refusal to locate the action of his most recent plays (*Tiny Alice*, *Malcolm*, *A Delicate Balance*) strengthens that assumption. In fact, only two of Albee's settings can be found in atlases—Central Park (*The Zoo Story*) and

Memphis (*Bessie Smith*). Even these, like the undifferentiated Southern town he borrowed from Carson McCullers for *The Ballad of the Sad Café* and the fictional New England college town of *Virginia Woolf*, might easily serve as settings for a universal drama. Yet, in much of his work, particularly in the early plays, there is a suggestion, even an insistence, that the problem is a localized one, that the emptiness and loneliness of the characters are somehow the result of a collapse of values in the Western world in general, in the United States in particular. *The American Dream*, he says in his Preface to the play, is "an attack on the substitution of artificial for real values in our society." Such an attack is implicit in the depiction of Peter in *The Zoo Story*.

It is in *Virginia Woolf* that this side of Albee's "truth" is most evident. He is not content that his characters perform an action which carries implications for an audience that far transcend the action itself. He must distribute labels. George may jokingly identify himself, as history professor, with the humanities, and Nick, as biology professor, with science, and turn their meeting into a historical-inevitability parable about the necessary decline of the West, but Albee presumably means it. Calling the town New Carthage and giving George significant throwaway lines ("When I was sixteen and going to prep school, during the Punic Wars ...") are cute ways of underlining a ponderous intention. I would not go so far as Diana Trilling (*Esquire*, December, 1963) and suggest that George and Martha are the Washingtons, or Henry Hewes (*The Best Plays of 1962–1963*) that Nick is like Nikita Khrushchev, but Albee is plainly intent on giving his sterility tale an obvious cultural point. Martha's joke when Nick fails to "make it in the sack" is apparently no joke at all: "But that's how it is in a civilized society."

My own tendency is to brush all this grandiose symbol-making under the rug to protect what I admire in *Virginia Woolf*. If we can believe Albee's remarks in the *Diplomat* interview, however, all this comprises the "play's subtleties"; in faulting the movie version of his play, he says, "the entire political argument was taken out, the argument between history and science."[4] The chasm that confronts the Albee characters may, then, be existential chaos or a materialistic society corrupt enough to make a culture hero out of ... (whom? to each critic his own horrible example, and there are those would pick Albee himself), or a combination in which the second of these is an image of the first.

There is nothing unusual about this slightly unstable mixture of philosophic assumption and social criticism; it can be found in the work of Tennessee Williams and, from quite a different perspective, that of Eugene Ionesco. The differentiation is useful primarily because it provides us with insight into the shape that Albee gives his material. If the lost and lonely

Albee character is an irrevocable fact—philosophically, theologically, psychologically—if all that *angst* is inescapable, then his plays must necessarily be reflections of that condition; any gestures of defiance are doomed to failure. If, however, the Albee character is a product of his societal context and if that context is changeable (not necessarily politically, but by an alteration of modes of behavior between one man and another), then the plays may be instructive fables. He has dismissed American drama of the 1930's as propaganda rather than art, and he has disavowed solutions to anything. Still, in several statements he has suggested that there are solutions—or, at least, alternatives. Surely that possibility is implicit in his description of *The American Dream* as an "attack." In the *Transatlantic Review* interview, he said that "the responsibility of the writer is to be a sort of demonic social critic—to present the world and people in it as he sees it and say 'Do you like it? If you don't like it change it.'" In the *Atlantic*, he said, "I've always thought ... that it was one of the responsibilities of playwrights to show people how they are and what their time is like in the hope that perhaps they'll change it."

Albee, then, shares with most American playwrights an idea of the utility of art, the supposition not only that art should convey truth, but that it should do so to some purpose. There is a strong strain of didacticism in all his work, but it is balanced by a certain ambiguity about the nature of the instructive fable. In interviews, he harps on how much of the creative process is subconscious, how little he understands his own work, how a play is to be experienced rather than understood. Insofar as this is not sour grapes pressed to make an aesthetic (his reaction to the reviews of *Tiny Alice*), it may be his way of recognizing that there is a conflict between his attitude toward man's situation and his suspicion (or hope: certainly *conviction* is too strong a word) that something can, or ought, to be done about it; between his assumption that this is hell we live in and his longing to redecorate it.

Whatever the nature of the chasm on the edge of which the Albee characters teeter so dexterously, to disturb the balance is to invite disaster or—possibly—salvation. If the conflict that I suggest above is a real one, it should be reflected in the plays in which one or more characters are willing to risk disaster. *The American Dream* and *The Sandbox* can be passed over here because, except for the sentimental death of Grandma at the end of the latter, they are diagnostic portraits of the Albee world, not actions performed in that setting. *The Death of Bessie Smith* and *The Ballad of the Sad Café* are more to the point, but they are also special cases. Although risks are taken (the Intern goes outside to examine Bessie; Amelia takes in Cousin Lymon in Ballad), the plays are less concerned with these acts than they are with the kind of expositional presentation—not particularly satirical in this case—that we get in *Dream*. Even so, the Intern's risk is meaningless since the woman is already dead; and Amelia's love is necessarily doomed by the doctrine the McCullers novella expounds—that it is difficult to love but almost impossible to be loved—and by the retrospective form the play took when Albee saddled it with a maudlin message-giving narrator. *Tiny Alice* and *Malcolm* are two of a kind, particularly if we consider them as corruption-of-innocence plays, although there is also a similarity of sorts between Malcolm's attempt to put a face on his absent father and Julian's attempt to keep from putting a face on his, abstracted Father. They are even similar in that Albee, sharing a popular-comedy misconception about what that snake was up to in the Garden, uses sex as his sign of corruption—ludicrously in *Alice*, snickeringly in *Malcolm*. Traditionally, one of two things happens in plays in which the innocent face the world: either they become corrupted and learn to live with it (the standard Broadway maturity play) or they die young and escape the corruption (Synge's *Deirdre of the Sorrows* or Maxwell Anderson's *Winterset*). In the Albee plays, both things happen. Julian dies after accepting the world (edited to fit his preconceptions about it) and Malcolm dies, muttering "I've ... lost so much," and loss, as the plays from *The Zoo Story* to *A Delicate Balance* insist, is what you gain in learning to live with it. There are extenuating circumstances for the deaths in these plays (Julian's concept of God is tied in with his desire to be a martyr; Malcolm's death is borrowed from Purdy, although Albee does not seem to understand what Purdy was doing with it in the novel), but these plays, too, are illustrations of the Albee world, and the deaths are more sentimental than central. *Everything in the Garden* is such an unlikely wedding of Albee and the late Giles Cooper, whose English play was the source of the American adaptation, that it is only superficially characteristic of Albee's work.

It is in *The Zoo Story*, *Who's Afraid of Virginia Woolf?* and *A Delicate Balance* that one finds dramatic actions by which the ambiguity of Albee's attitudes may be tested. In *The Zoo Story*, so goes the customary reading, Jerry confronts the vegetative Peter, forces him to stand his ground, dies finally on his own knife held in Peter's hand. In that suicidal act, Jerry becomes a scapegoat who gives his own life so that Peter will be knocked out of his complacency and learn to live, or LIVE. Even Albee believes this, or he said he did in answer to a question from Arthur Gelb (*The New York Times*, February 15, 1960): "Though he dies, he passes on an awareness of life to the other character in the play." If this is true, then presumably we are to take seriously—not as a dramatic device, but for its content—Jerry's "you have to make a start somewhere" speech in which he expounds the steps-to-love doctrine, a soggy inheritance from Carson McCullers ("A Tree. A Rock. A Cloud.") and Truman Capote (*The Grass Harp*). That the start should be something a great deal less gentle than the McCullers-Capote inheritance might suggest is not surprising when we consider that violence and death became twisted life symbols during the 1950's (as all the kids said after James Dean's fatal smashup, "Boy, that's living") and, then, turned literary in the 1960's (as in Jack Richardson's *Gallows Humor* and all the motorcycle movies from *The Wild Angels* to *Scorpio Rising*).

The problem with that reading is not that it is awash with adolescent profundity, which might well annoy some of the audience, but that it seems to be working against much that is going on within the play. Although Albee prepares the audience for the killing, it has always seemed gratuitous, a melodramatic flourish. The reason may be that it tries to suggest one thing (salvation) while the logic of the play demands something else. Except for a couple of expositional lapses, Jerry is too well drawn a character—self-pitying and aggressive, self-deluding and forlorn—to become the conventional "hero" (Albee uses that word in the Gelb interview) that the positive ending demands. He may well be so aware of his separation from everyone else that he plans or improvises ("could I have planned all this? No ... no, I couldn't have. But I think I did") his own murder in a last desperate attempt to make contact, but there is nothing in the play to indicate that he succeeds. At the end, Peter is plainly a man knocked off his balance, but there is no indication that he has fallen into "an awareness of life." In fact, the play we are watching has already been presented in miniature in the dog story, and all Jerry gained from that encounter was "solitary but free passage." "There are some things in it that I don't really understand," Albee told Gelb. One of them may be that the play itself denies the romantic ending.

Virginia Woolf is a more slippery case. Here, too, the play works against the presumably upbeat ending, but Albee may be more aware that this is happening. According to the conventions of Broadway psychology, as reflected, for instance, in a play like William Inge's *The Dark at the Top of the Stairs*, in a moment of crisis two characters come to see themselves clearly. Out of their knowledge a new maturity is born, creating an intimacy that has not existed before and a community that allows them to face their problems (if not solve them) with new courage. This was the prevailing cliché of the serious Broadway play of the 1950's, and it was still viable enough in the 1960's to take over the last act of Lorraine Hansberry's *The Sign in Sidney Brustein's Window* and turn an interesting play into a conventional one. *Virginia Woolf* uses, or is used by, this cliché.

Although the central device of the play is the quarrel between George and Martha, the plot concerns their nonexistent son. From George's "Just don't start on the bit, that's all," before Nick and Honey enter, the play builds through hints, warnings, revelations until "sonny-Jim"[5] is created and then destroyed. Snap, goes the illusion. Out of the ruins, presumably, new strength comes. The last section, which is to be played "very softly, very slowly," finds George offering new tenderness to Martha, assuring her that the time had come for the fantasy to die, forcing her—no longer maliciously—to admit that she is afraid of Virginia Woolf. It is "Time for bed," and there is nothing left for them to do but go together to face the dark at the top of the stairs. As though the rejuvenation were not clear enough from the last scene, there is the confirming testimony in Honey's tearful reiteration "I want a child" and Nick's broken attempt to sympathize, "I'd like to...." Then, too, the last act is called "The Exorcism," a name that had been the working title for the play itself.

As neat as Inge, and yet there is something wrong with it. How can a relationship like that of Martha and George, built so consistently on illusion (the playing of games), be expected to have gained something from a sudden admission of truth? What confirmation is there in Nick and Honey when we remember that she is drunk and hysterical and that he is regularly embarrassed by what he is forced to watch? There are two possibilities beyond the conventional reading suggested above. The last scene between Martha and George may be another one of their games; the death of the child may not be the end of illusion but an indication that the players have to go back to GO and start again their painful trip to home. Although there are many indications that George and Martha live a circular existence, going over the same ground again and again, the development of the plot and the tone of the last scene (the use of monosyllables, for instance, instead of their customary rhetoric) seem to deny that the game is still going on. The other possibility is that the truth—as in *The Iceman Cometh*—brings not freedom but death. To believe otherwise is to accept the truth-maturity cliché as readily as one must buy the violence-life analogy to get the positive ending of *The Zoo Story*. My own suspicion is that everything that feels wrong about the end of *Virginia Woolf* arises from the fact that, like the stabbing in *Zoo*, it is a balance-tipping ending that conventional theater says is positive but the Albee material insists is negative.

In *A Delicate Balance*, the line is clearer. The titular balance is the pattern of aggression and withdrawal, accusation and guilt which Tobias and his family have constructed in order to cope with existence. Agnes suggests that Tobias's "We do what we can" might be "Our motto." When Harry and Edna invade the premises, trying to escape from the nameless fears that have attacked them, they come under the white flag of friendship. Tobias must decide whether or not to let them stay, knowing that the "disease" they carry is contagious and that infection in the household will likely upset the balance. His problem is one in metaphysical semantics, like Julian's in *Tiny Alice*, although *God* is not the word whose meaning troubles him. "Would you give friend Harry the shirt off your back, as they say?" asks Claire, before the invasion begins. "I *suppose* I would. He *is* my best friend," answers Tobias, and we hear echoes from *The American Dream*: "She's just a dreadful woman, but she is chairman of our woman's club, so naturally I'm terribly fond of her." *Dream*'s satirical fun about the emptiness of conventional language becomes deadly serious in *Balance*, for Tobias must decide whether the meaning of friendship is one with substance or only surface—whether friendship is a human relationship implying the possibility of action and risk, or simply a label, like marriage or kinship, to be fastened to a form of accommodation. As Pearl Bailey sang in *House of Flowers*, "What is a friend for? Should a friend bolt the door?" Tobias (having failed with his cat as Jerry failed with the dog) decides to try doing more than he can; in his long, broken speech in the last act, he displays his fear, indicates that he does not want Harry and Edna around, does not even like them, "BUT BY GOD ... YOU STAY!!" His attempt fails because Harry and Edna, having decided that they would never risk putting real meaning into *friendship*, depart, leaving a depleted Tobias to rearrange his labels. He will have the help of Agnes, of course, which—on the balance—is a great deal, for she finds the conventional words of goodbye: "well, don't be strangers." Edna, who not many lines before made the "only skin" speech, answers, "Oh, good Lord, how could we be? Our lives are ... the same." And so they are.

Thematically, *A Delicate Balance* is Albee's most precise statement. The gesture toward change, which seemed to fit so uncomfortably at the end of *The Zoo Story* and *Virginia Woolf*, has been rendered powerless within the action of *Balance*. Not only are Albee's characters doomed to live in the worst of all possible worlds; it is the only possible world. The impulse to do something about it can end only in failure. Yet, Albee cannot leave it at that. He cannot, like Samuel Beckett, let his characters turn their meaninglessness into ritual which has a way, on stage, of reasserting the meaning of the human being. He almost does so in *Virginia Woolf*, but his suspicion that games are not enough—a failure really to recognize that games are a form of truth as much as a form of lying—leads to the doubtful exorcism. Although the *angster* in Albee cannot let Tobias succeed, the latent reformer cannot help but make him heroic in his lost-cause gesture. He becomes an older, wearier, emptier Jerry, with only the unresisting air to throw himself on at the end.

"Better than nothing!" says Clov in *Endgame*. "Is it possible?" Out of the fastness of his wasteland, and against his better judgment, Albee cannot keep from hoping so.

In my critical and psychological naivety, I assume—as the paragraphs above show—that Albee's plays are really about the accommodations forced on man by his condition and his society. It is impossible, however, to get through a discussion of Albee without facing up to what might be called—on the analogy of the fashionable critical term *subtext*—his sub-subject matter. That is the "masochistic-homosexual perfume" that Robert Brustein found hanging so heavily over *The Zoo Story*. It is a perfume of little importance except insofar as it throws the audience off the scent of the play's real quarry.

A student stopped me on campus a few years ago, hoping I would be able to confirm the story that *Who's Afraid of Virginia Woolf?* was first performed by four men in a little theater in Montreal. When I expressed my doubt, he went off to call a friend in New York who knew someone who knew the man who had been stage manager ... although somehow he never got the confirmation he wanted. Except for the circumstantiality of this account (why Montreal?), it was a familiar rumor. Albee, in the *Diplomat* interview, explained that it was a letter to the *Times* that started the whole thing, that from there it passed into print elsewhere, first as rumor, then as fact. "I know the difference between men and women," he said, "and I write both characters." The more sophisticated interpreters simply step over Albee's denials and assume that the play, whoever it was written for, is really about a homosexual marriage. The reasoning here is that homosexual marriages, lacking the sanctions of society, are extremely unstable and that to survive at all they must create fantasy devices to bind the couple together. Hence, the imaginary child—for what other kind of child could come from the union of two men? There is a kind of specious logic in operation here. The flaw in it, however, is the refusal to recognize how much fantasy is a part of any relationship, how two people who are close (husband and wife, lovers of whatever sex, good friends) invent private languages, private rituals, private games which set them off from the others. Jimmy and Alison play at squirrels-and-bears in John Osborne's *Look Back in Anger*, and Sid and Iris play wild-mountain-girl in *The Sign in Sidney Brustein's Window* without either couple being taken as surrogate homosexual unions. My own inclination would be to let Martha and George have their "little bugger," as they call the nonexistent child, without insisting that they have a big one.

I have heard the play praised for the clarity with which it presented a homosexual couple, but, for the most part, such readings are based on a rejection of the possibility that George and Martha may have a representative heterosexual marriage. A similar rejection takes place when the play is dismissed as a kind of homosexual denigration of conventional marriage. Surely the castrating female and the dominated male are such commonplace psychological stereotypes—on and off stage—that their appearance need not be taken as an indication of a perverse attempt to do in all the Darbys and Joans who provide America's divorce statistics. Besides, Martha and George do not really fit those stereotypes. They appear to at the beginning, but as the play goes on it becomes clear that they are really very evenly matched in a battle that has been going on seriously since Strindberg's *The Dance of Death* and comically since *The Taming of the Shrew*. Albee's male wins, as in Shakespeare, but only tentatively, as in Strindberg. Not that Albee is particularly interested in the battle of the sexes as such. He has his own use for it, which is not to attack heterosexuality, but to present one of his many accommodation images: a well-matched pair of antagonists form a balance of sorts.

If a play like *Virginia Woolf* could call up the homosexual echoes, it is not surprising that *Tiny Alice* set them roaring. The opening scene between Cardinal and Lawyer is an exercise in bitchiness, primly nasty and insinuating, a marked contrast to the verbal exchanges between Martha and George. It passes from Lawyer's sneering comment on the caged cardinals ("uh, together ... in conversation, as it were") to a variation on the old joke about the suitability of a boy or a clean old man, to hints of a schoolboy affair between the two men (Lawyer: "I'll have you do your obeisances. As you used to, old friend"), to mutual accusations in which Lawyer becomes an anus-entering hyena and Cardinal a mating bird. The business of the scene is apparently expositional, setting up the donation that will send Julian to Alice, so the tension between the two characters and the implication of their past relationship is gratuitous. So, too, is Lawyer's calling Butler "Darling" and "Dearest." The homosexual overtones in Julian (his attraction to the Welsh stableman, his kissing Miss Alice's hand "as he would kiss a Cardinal's ring," and the sensuality of his martyrdom dream in which the lion seems to mount him and he lingers over the entrance of the gladiator's prongs) might be more legitimate, a suggestion of the ambiguity of celibacy. Still, since he is sacrificed to heterosexuality—in that ludicrous scene in which he buries his head in Miss Alice's crotch, a cunnilingual first for the American stage— there is justice in Philip Roth's celebrated attack on "The Play that Dare Not Speak Its Name" (*New York Review of Books*, February 25, 1965). Roth accused Albee of writing "a homosexual daydream" about the martyrdom of the celibate male and disguising it as a metaphysical drama. Several weeks later (April 8, 1965), a letter to the editor insisted that there was no disguise at all in the play because a "tiny alice" is homosexual jargon for, as the writer so coyly put it, "a masculine derrière." Acting on this information, Bernard F. Dukore added an ingenious footnote to an article in *Drama Survey* (Spring, 1966) in which he considered that Julian, Butler, and Lawyer, all lovers of Miss Alice, might really be lovers of "tiny alice" and the opening doors at the end an anus symbol, but—as he went on to complain—a play that depends on a special argot for its symbolism is lost on a general audience. If "tiny alice" really is a gay word for anus and if Albee is using it consciously, he may be making an inside joke which has some relevance to his presumed serious play. If one of the points of the play is that all concepts of God (from Julian's abstraction to the mouse in the model) are creations of the men who hold them, a sardonic joke about God as a "tiny alice" is possible. Certainly, Albee has made that joke before, casually in *Virginia Woolf* (where George speaks of "Christ and all those girls") and more seriously in *The Zoo Story* (where one of the suggestions in Jerry's where-to-begin-to-love speech is "WITH GOD WHO IS A COLORED QUEEN WHO WEARS A KIMONO AND PLUCKS HIS EYEBROWS ..."). On the other hand, the phrase could turn the play into an audience put-down such as the one described by Clay in *Dutchman*, in which he says that Bessie Smith, whatever the audience thought she was doing, was always saying, "Kiss my black ass."

This kind of speculation, hedged in as it is by *ifs* and *maybes*, is finally pointless. I almost wrote *fruitless*, but I stopped myself, assuming that my use of "inside joke" earlier is contribution enough to a silly game. How cute can a critic get without his tone corrupting his purpose? This question has relevance for the playwright, too. The problem about *Tiny Alice* is not whether there is a hidden homosexual joke and/or message, but that the obvious homosexual allusions seem to have little relevance to the plot device (the conspiracy to catch Julian), the play's central action (the martyrdom of Julian), or its presumed subject matter (the old illusion–reality problem). Unless Roth is right, the homosexual material is only decoration, different in quantity but not in kind from the additions and emphases that Albee brought to the already campy (old style) surface of Purdy's *Malcolm*.

The Zoo Story is the only Albee play in which a homosexual reading seems possible and usable in terms of what else the play is doing. It is, after all, the account of a meeting between two men in Central Park ("I'm not the gentleman you were expecting," says Jerry), in which one lets himself be impaled by the other, who has a phallic name. Jerry, dying, says, "I came unto you (*He laughs, so faintly*) and you have comforted me. Dear Peter." Jerry's casual references to the "colored queen" and the police "chasing fairies down from trees" on the other side of the park; his story of his one real love affair with the park superintendent's son, whom Otto Reinert (in *Modern Drama*) identifies with Peter by virtue of Peter's "proprietary claim" to the park bench; the implications in Jerry's "with fury because the pretty little ladies aren't pretty little ladies, with making money with your body which is an act of love and I could prove it"—all contribute to the possibility of this being a homosexual encounter. If it is, then much of the verbal and physical business of the play—Jerry's teasing, his wheedling, his tickling, the wrestling struggle for the bench—can be seen as an elaborate seduction which, since Jerry forces his partner to hold the knife, can only be summed up as getting a rise out of Peter. The dramatic fable can be read this way and still be relevant to the thematic material discussed earlier in this chapter. The problem comes when we consider the end of the play. If it is the positive ending that Albee suggested in the Gelb interview, if Jerry has passed on his "awareness of life," it must be Peter's initiation, and that, as Jerry says earlier, is "jazz of a very special hotel." On the other hand, as John Rechy keeps insisting in his seemingly endless novel, *City of Night*, a homosexual pickup in a park is a particularly workable image for the failure of contact between people.

"You know, I almost think you're serious," says Nick about something other than drama criticism, and George answers, "No, baby ... you almost think you're serious, and it scares the hell out of you."

I feel a little that way about my very plausible reading of *The Zoo Story* in the section above. For if I am willing to accept the possibility of Peter as phallus, how can I deny all the interpreters who insist on seeing Jerry as Christ and Peter as the rock upon which to build his church? At least, the analogy of the homosexual pickup works comfortably within the action of the play and, less comfortably, with the thematic material. Despite the Biblical echoes ("I came unto you" again), the Christ–Jerry analogue is possible only to the extent that every sacrificial victim is a Christ figure, but that is a tautology which contributes nothing to an understanding of the play. If we see Jerry's suicidal finish as a sacrifice, we learn precious little about his action by nodding wisely and saying: oh, ho, Christ. We might as well say: oh, ho, Sydney Carton. Still, writers will use mythic and historical identifications for their characters (Tennessee Williams in *Orpheus Descending*), and critics will go myth-hunting and trap the slippery beasts. It has now become customary to dive into the underbrush of each new Albee play and bring them back alive.

Albee is partly to blame. He uses obvious symbols such as the muscular young man who is *The American Dream* and the athletic death figure in *The Sandbox*. He asks Julian and Miss Alice to form a pietà in *Tiny Alice* and the dying Julian to spread his arms to "resemble a crucifixion." In some notes prepared for a press conference, later printed in *The Best Plays of 1964–1965*, Albee said of *Tiny Alice*: "The play is full of symbols and allusions, naturally, but they are to be taken as echoes in a cave, things overheard, not fully understood at first." I take this to mean that they have no functional use in the play, in relation to either character or action, and that at best they provide a texture as allusive words do in some poetry. In a play, as in a poem, an allusion may uncover another realm of possibility (for instance, the ironies that keep emerging in *Peer Gynt*), but it can do so only if it does not wreck itself on the dramatic facts of the play. Take that pietà, for instance. It must either make clear something in the relationship between Julian and Miss Alice that has been implicit all along, or it must seem—as it did on stage— an exercise in literary pretentiousness.

Tiny Alice is the most blatant, but all the Albee plays insist on suggesting that there is more there than meets the eye and ear. This can be seen in the way Albee appears to be playing with the significance-seekers. In Agnes's "We become allegorical, my darling Tobias, as we grow older." In George's "Well, it's an allegory, really—probably—but it can be read as straight, cozy prose." Of course, Albee may mean this, too. In either case, he deserves to have the significant-name game played in his dramatic front yard. So Jerry becomes not only Christ but Jeremiah, and Julian not only Christ but Julian the Apostate. The Washingtons and the Khrushchevs get into *Virginia Woolf*. When Agnes, commenting on how much Claire has seen, says, "You were not named for nothing," she is presumably making a nasty crack about *claire* as an adjective meaning *bright*.[6] Yet audiences came out of the theater asking questions about St. Clare, St. Agnes, the Apocryphal Tobias, and even Miss Julie.

Albee may be fond of symbols and allusions, echoes and things overheard, but he plainly does not work—as the search for mythic analogies suggests—with dramatic images that come from outside his plays. This does not mean that he is the naturalist he occasionally claims to be, as when he told a *New York Times* interviewer (September 18, 1966) that even *Tiny Alice* was naturalistic. Even in *Virginia Woolf*, which is certainly the most naturalistic of his plays, the situation is basically unrealistic; the drinking party is a revelatory occasion, not a slice of life in a small New England college. For the most part, his characters have neither setting nor profession, and when they are defined by things, the process is either conventionally (Peter's possessions) or unconventionally (the contents of Jerry's room) stereotypical, so obviously so that realism is clearly not intended. Nor do the characters have biographies, at least of the kind one has come to expect from the psychological naturalism of the Broadway stage. *Virginia Woolf*, harping as it does on the parental hang-ups of its two principals, comes closest to that pattern, but it is never very clear in this play how much of the memory is invention, which of the facts are fantasy. If *Virginia Woolf* and *The Zoo Story* are, at most, distant cousins of naturalistic drama, how much more remote are Albee's plainly absurdist plays (*The Sandbox*, *The American Dream*), his "mystery" play with its label-bearing characters (*Tiny Alice*), his drawing-room noncomedy (*A Delicate Balance*).

A close look at Albee's language provides the clearest indication of the nonrealistic character of his plays. *A Delicate Balance* is the most obvious example. The lines are consciously stilted, broken by elaborate parenthesis ("It follows, to my mind, that since I speculate I might, some day, or early evening I think more likely—some autumn dusk—go quite mad") or pulled up short by formal negative endings ("Must she not?"; "is it not?")—devices that call for inflections which stop the natural flow of speech. There are lines that are barely comprehensible ("One does not apologize to those for whom one must?"), which cannot be read without great deliberation. The verbal elaboration has particular point in this play since the language itself becomes a reflection of the artificiality of the characters and the setting, a pattern in which form replaces substance. This can best be seen in the play's most intricate digression. "What I find most astonishing," Agnes begins as the play opens, only to interrupt herself with her fantasy on madness. Her thought meanders through Tobias's practical attempt to get the after-dinner drinks, and we are fifteen speeches into the play, past two reappearances of the "astonish" phrase, before her opening sentence finally comes to an end. Seems to end, really, for the phrase recurs just before the final curtain, as Agnes goes her placidly relentless way—"to fill a silence," as the stage direction says—as though the intrusion of Harry and Edna and Tobias's painful attempt to deal with it were an easily forgotten interruption of the steady flow of nonevent.

In the *Atlantic* interview, explaining why he felt that English actors were needed for *Tiny Alice*, Albee said that he had moved from the "idiomatic" language of *Virginia Woolf* to something more formal. *A Delicate Balance* is a further step in elaboration. Yet, the language of the earlier plays, however idiomatic, is plainly artificial. Albee has used three main verbal devices from the beginning: interruption, repetition, and the set speech, the last of which makes use of the first two. The set speeches are almost formal recitations, as the playwright recognizes in *The Zoo Story* when he lets Jerry give his monologue a title: "THE STORY OF JERRY AND THE DOG!" There are similar speeches in all the plays: Jack's "Hey ... Bessie" monologue which is the whole of Scene 3 of *Bessie Smith*; the Young Man's sentimental mutilation speech in *The American Dream*; George's "bergin" story and Martha's "Abandon-ed" speech in *Virginia Woolf*; the narrator's speeches in *Ballad*; Julian's dying soliloquy in *Tiny Alice*; Madame Girard's Entre-Scene monologue in *Malcolm*; Jack's direct address to the audience in *Garden*. Although Albee does not direct the speaker to step into a spotlight—as Tennessee Williams does with comparable speeches in *Sweet Bird of Youth*—he recognizes that these are essentially solo performances even when another character is on stage to gesture or grunt or single-word his way into the uneven but persistent flow of words. Of Tobias's big scene at the end of *Balance*, Albee says "This next is an aria."[7] In *The Zoo Story*, Jerry does not use a simple narration; his story is momentarily stopped for generalizing comments ("It always happens when I try to simplify things; people look up. But that's neither hither nor thither") and marked with repeated words ("The dog is black, all black; all black except ...") and phrases ("I'll kill the dog with kindness, and if that doesn't work ... I'll just kill him"). The word *laughter* punctuates the "bergin" story the way laughter itself presumably broke the cocktail-lounge murmur of the bar in which the boys were drinking.

It is not the long speeches alone that are built of interruption and repetition; that is the pattern of all the dialogue. On almost any page of *Virginia Woolf* you can find examples as obvious as this speech of George's: "Back when I was courting Martha—well, don't know if that's exactly the right word for it but back when I was courting Martha...." Then comes Martha's "Screw, sweetie!" followed by another attempt from George, more successful this time, "At any rate, back when I was courting Martha," and off he goes into an account which involves their going "into a bar ... you know, a *bar* ... a whiskey, beer, and bourbon *bar*...." Sometimes the repetitions become echoes that reach from act to act as when Martha's "snap" speech in Act Two is picked up by George in the snapdragon scene in Act Three. From *The Zoo Story* to *Everything in the Garden*, then, Albee has consciously manipulated language for effect; even when it sounds most like real speech—as in *Virginia Woolf*—it is an exercise in idiomatic artificiality.

At their best, these artifices are the chief devices by which Albee presents his dramatic images. Neither naturalist nor allegorist, he works the great middle area where most playwrights operate. He puts an action on stage—an encounter in a park that becomes a suicide-murder, a night-long quarrel that ends in the death of illusion, an invasion that collapses before the defenders can decide whether to surrender or to fight—which presumably has dramatic vitality in its own right and from which a meaning or meanings can emerge. The central situation—the encounter, the relationship implicit in the quarrel, the state of the defenders and the invaders—is defined almost completely in verbal terms. There is business, of course, but it is secondary. Jerry's poking and tickling Peter is only an extension of what he has been doing with words; George's attempt to strangle Martha is a charade not far removed from their word games. When events get more flamboyant—the shooting of Julian, Julia's hysterical scene with the gun—they tend to become ludicrous. The most obvious example in Albee of physical business gone wrong is the wrestling match between Miss Amelia and Marvin Macy in *The Ballad of the Sad Café*; the fact that it is the dramatic climax of the play does not keep it from looking silly on stage. Ordinarily, Albee does not need to ask his characters to do very much, for what they say is dramatic action. "The old pigeonhole bit?" says Jerry in *The Zoo Story*, and although it is he, not Peter, who does the pigeonholing, the accusation and the mockery in the question is an act of aggression, as good as a shove for throwing Peter off balance.

In the long run, Albee's reputation as a playwright will probably depend less on what he has to say than on the dramatic situations through which he says it. The two Albee plays that seem to have taken the strongest hold on the public imagination (which may be a way of saying they are the two plays I most admire) are *The Zoo Story* and *Virginia Woolf*. The reason is that the meeting between Jerry and Peter and the marriage of George and Martha, for all the nuances in the two relationships, are presented concretely in gesture and line; they take shape on the stage with great clarity. *Tiny Alice*, by contrast, is all amorphousness. It may finally be possible to reduce that play to an intellectual formulation, but the portentousness that hovers over so many lines and so much of the business keeps the characters and the situation from attaining dramatic validity. *The Zoo Story* is more successful as a play, not because its dramatic situation is more realistic, but because it exists on stage—a self-created dramatic fact.

A Delicate Balance is a much stronger play than *Tiny Alice*. As the discussion early in this chapter indicates, it is probably Albee's most perfect combination of theme and action, and its central metaphor—the balance—is important not only to the play but to Albee's work as a whole. Yet, compared to *Virginia Woolf*, it is an incredibly lifeless play. The reason, I think, is that the Martha–George relationship has dramatic substance in a way that the Tobias–Agnes household does not. Too much has been made—particularly by casual reviewers—of the violence, the hate, the anger in the Martha–George marriage. It is just as important that the quarrel be seen in the context of the affection they have for one another and the life—even if it is a long, sad game—which they so obviously share. One of the best inventions in all of Albee is the gun with the parasol in it, for what better way of seeing the relationship of Martha and George than in terms of a murderous weapon that is also a sheltering object; the instrument is a metaphor for the marriage, and its use is a preview of what will happen in the last act.

From the moment the play opens, from Martha's challenge, "What a dump. Hey what's that from?" it is clear that Martha and George play the same games. He may be tired at first, not really in the mood for a session of name-the-movie, or he may be faking indifference because he cannot remember that the "goddamn Bette Davis picture" Martha has in mind is *Beyond the Forest* (1949), but there is companionship in the incipient quarrel that will not disappear as the argument grows more lethal. It can be seen directly in several places. Near the beginning of the play, after a mutual accusation of baldness, they go into a momentary affectionate scene in which his "Hello honey" leads to her request for "a big sloppy kiss." Almost the same phrase, "C'mon ... give me a kiss," is her compliment for his having been clever enough to introduce the parasol-gun into the game room. Much more important than the grand games to which he gives labels—Humiliate the Host, Get the Guests, Hump the Hostess—are the small games that they play constantly—the play-acting routines, the little-kid bits, the mock-etiquette turns, the verbal games. The whole force of the play depends on their existence as a couple, a relationship made vivid in moments such as the one in Act III when Nick, humiliated at his sexual failure, begins angrily, "I'm nobody's houseboy ..." and Martha and George shout in unison, "Now!" and then begin to sing, "I'm nobody's houseboy now...." Their closeness is important if we are to recognize that George can be and is cuckolded. This event takes place on stage in Act II when Martha and Nick dance together sensuously and, speaking in time to the music, she tells about George's abortive attempt to be a novelist. It is at this moment that their marriage is violated, that George's anger shows most plainly, that he initiates a game of Get the Guests. "Book dropper! Child mentioned" accuses George, and we see—perhaps before he does—the connection that forces him to carry "the bit about the kid" to its murderous conclusion. One may come away from *Virginia Woolf* suspicious of the end of the play and its presumed implications but never in doubt about the dramatic force of either characters or situation.

A Delicate Balance provides a marked contrast. We learn a great deal about the antipathy between Agnes and Claire, the sexual life of Agnes and Tobias, the marriage problems of Julia, the nameless fears of Edna and Harry, but the situation is explained more than it is presented. Some of the language is witty, some of it—particularly Agnes' lines—is quietly bitchy, but speeches do not pass from one character to another, carving out a definition of their relationship; lines fall from the mouths of the characters and shatter on the stage at their feet. Thematically, this is fine, since separateness is what Albee wants to depict, and he is ingenious in the way he lets the artificiality of his language contribute to the general sense of empty façade. Unfortunately, the characters are defined only in terms of their separateness, their significance as exemplary lost ones. Not so indeterminate as *Tiny Alice, A Delicate Balance* still lacks the kind of concreteness that comes from a dramatic image fully realized on stage. The characters are given a little biography, a few mannerisms, a whisper of depth, but they remain highly articulate stick figures moving through a sequence of nonevents to a foregone conclusion.

Unless Edward Albee is on some unannounced road to Damascus, there is not much doubt about what he will be saying in the plays that lie ahead of him. It is how he chooses to say it that will be important. In the face of his most recent work, in which significance seems to be imposed from the outside instead of meaning rising from within, we have every reason to be afraid, not of, but for *Virginia Woolf*.

NOTES

1. According to a letter from Albee (October 13, 1966), Hinton, who was writing the libretto, fell ill and Albee finished the work; as he remembers it, he wrote the Prologue, the last scene, and did "considerable revision" on the other three scenes. The title page of the vocal score lists Flanagan with Hinton and Albee as one of the authors of the libretto. The opera, of course, is based on Herman Melville's "Bartleby the Scrivener." My responses are highly suspect since I did not see the opera in production; I read the libretto and listened to at least two of my friends—unfortunately, not at the same time—make piano assaults on the score. I would guess that the most effective scene, musically and dramatically, is Scene 2 in which Mr. Allan (the name given to Melville's nameless lawyer-narrator) goes to his office on Sunday morning and finds Bartleby there; his aria carries him from complacent Sunday-morning ruminations (mostly to slightly doctored lines from Melville) through the confrontation with Bartleby to his attempt to make sense of this clerk who will not do his work and will not go away. Bartleby's one-note "I would prefer not to" echoes in variations all through Allan's confusion in this scene. Less happy moments musically are church bells which chime in the piano part after they have been mentioned in the libretto and the calculated contrast at the end of Scene 3 when beyond the huffing-puffing violence can be heard the soprano of the office boy singing his way back on stage with the ballad-like song that identifies him. For the most part, the libretto is a softening of Melville's story. Since the Bartleby of the story makes a claim on the lawyer which cannot be (or is not) fulfilled, Melville's work has an obvious thematic relevance to Albee's. What is missing in the dramatization is Melville's superb ambiguity; there is not even an attempt in the opera to get the effect that Melville achieves when his

narrator, who believes that "the easiest way of life is the best," manages to comfort himself by pigeonholing Bartleby when the clerk is no longer alive and mutely accusing. The "Oh, Bartleby, Oh, humanity" that ends the opera is sentimental although it probably means to be something more exalted. The "Ah, Bartleby! Ah, humanity!" that ends Melville's story is ironic. Flanagan, to whom Albee dedicated *The Zoo Story*, did the music for *The Sandbox*, *The Ballad of the Sad Café*, and *Malcolm*. Flanagan's music for The Sandbox is printed with the play in Margaret Mayorga's *The Best Short Plays, 1958–1960*.

2. My own reviews, from *The Zoo Story* (*The Reporter*, February 16, 1961) to *Everything in the Garden* (*The Reporter*, December 28, 1967), have suggested with a decreasing amount of flippancy that there is less to Albee than meets the eye. Although my review of *Virginia Woolf* (*Drama Survey*, Fall, 1963) now seems unnecessarily condescending, my general misgivings about Albee as a playwright have not disappeared. What has disappeared, alas, is a letter that Albee sent to *The Reporter* to straighten me out after my review of *The Zoo Story*.

3. One of the persistent—and, I think, unfortunate—ways of reading Albee is to assume that the animals and the animal imagery which figure in so many of the plays are being used to make some instructive point about man's nature. For instance, John V. Hagopian, in a letter to the *New York Review of Books* (April 8, 1965), insisted that the point of *Tiny Alice* is that "man must embrace his animal nature." It is true that Brother Julian has an abstraction problem in that play, but his acceptance of the world (and all the animals and birds that wander through the lines in *Alice*) is not—as the ambiguity in his death scene indicates—a sure sign of either health or reality. There is a certain amount of sentimentality in such a reading of the play, at least if the "embrace" is taken as positive rather than factual. In Albee's work there is a general equation between man and animal. This can be seen in *The Zoo Story*, not only in Jerry's dog tale and the zoo metaphor, but in the confusion of Peter's children with his cats and parakeets. Perhaps there is something ennobling, an up-the-chain-of-being slogan, in Jerry's comfort to Peter, "you're not really a vegetable; it's all right, you're an animal," but as Mac the Knife would say, "What's the percentage?" Albee's animals reflect the predicament of his men. There are still bars to look through, accommodations to be made.

4. Perhaps we cannot believe him. In an article on the making of the movie (*McCall's*, June, 1966), Roy Newquist quotes Albee: "They had filmed the play, with the exception of five or ten minutes of relatively unimportant material." Although I quote from a number of interviews in this chapter, I am aware that interviews, at best, are doubtful sources of information and opinion. There are the obvious dangers of misquotation and spur-of-the-moment remarks which are untrue (is *The Ballad of the Sad Café* an earlier play than *Virginia Woolf*, as Albee told Thomas Lask in a *Times* interview, October 27, 1963, or are we to believe the dates accompanying the Atheneum editions of his plays?) or only momentarily true (the conflicting opinions about the movie version of *Woolf*). Beyond that, it is clear that Albee, when he is not on his high horse, likes to kid around. I am not thinking of an occasion like the joint interview with John Gielgud (*Atlantic*, April, 1965), where the chummy inside jocularity masks what must have been a major difference of opinion over *Tiny Alice*, but of an interview like the one in *Transatlantic Review*, in which Albee is very solemn and still sounds as though he is putting Digby Diehl on. Or the one in *Diplomat* that got me into this footnote in the first place, for in that one Albee uses what I assume is a running gag, of which Otis L. Guernsey, Jr., never seems aware. In three variations on a single line, he ponders whether or not *Woolf*, *Alice*, and *Balance* are comedies

on the basis of whether or not the characters get what they want or think they want. The joke, of course, is that the line comes from Grandma's curtain speech from *The American Dream*: "So, let's leave things as they are right now ... while everybody's happy ... while everybody's got what he wants ... or everybody's got what he thinks he wants. Good night, dears."

5. One of the "echoes"—to use Albee's word (*The Best Plays of 1964–1965*) for the unanchored allusions in *Tiny Alice*—must surely be a song that little boys used to sing: "Lulu had a baby, / Named it Sonny Jim, / Threw it in the piss-pot / To see if it could swim."

6. According to my French dictionary, *claire*, as a feminine noun, means "burnt bones or washed ashes used for making cupels." Chew on that.

7. Albee's one attempt at fiction—the beginning of a novel which *Esquire* (July, 1963) printed as one of a group of works-in-progress, a fragment that was probably written for the occasion—is essentially a long speech like the ones in the plays. *The Substitute Speaker*, a play that Albee has been announcing since 1963, will contain the granddaddy of the solos if it really has in it the forty-minute speech Albee once promised.

ANNE PAOLUCCI

The Discipline of Arrogance

All art, said Goethe, is a gesture of arrogance. When it is new it must have the nerve, the sheer brazenness, the courage even, to make room for itself in a crowded tradition. It must come on with a confident sweep, asserting its own superiority, insisting that yesterday has had it and must give ground.

Of course, what is announced as an inspired novelty often proves, in the working out, a pitiful stammering. The defiant gesture that breaks with the past too often carries the artist ahead of his talent so that his own chief resource of strength is lost in the gesture. Which is to say that while art must be arrogant in the confidence of its inspiration, that inspiration cannot be fittingly embodied without the skill and fluency that comes with practice in an art form (what Dante called *usus*), without the knowledge of the medium itself (*ars*), and without the innate talent which gives the stamp of personality to the result (*ingenium*). Without these three prerequisites, the arrogance of inspiration collapses into something foolish and inarticulate. History bears witness to this. The avant-garde exists in every age; and in every age it has had a foolish and inarticulate fringe, whose arrogance, nevertheless, provides the self-confident atmosphere conducive to art. Such a fringe clears the way ahead, but the true artist pauses to look back before taking possession of the ground thus cleared. Today's avant-garde theater has such a fringe in those who see the future of dramatic art as spontaneous expression, with or without words, "happenings" (recent "demonstrations" might be included here),

From *Tension to Tonic: The Plays of Edward Albee.* © 1972 by Southern Illinois University Press.

dramatizations which defy form and make no distinction between audience and spectator, meaning and non-meaning, words and sounds. There is a place—or, rather, a place has obviously been made—for happenings, for "open" theater, for political confrontations and dramatic marches punctuated by symbolic gestures and prepared slogans; but if theater is to remain theater, such impulses must be harnassed and controlled. They cannot ever replace what T.S. Eliot called "the third voice of poetry."

But the threat is not really serious; theater will not be destroyed, no matter how popular happenings or spontaneous dramatizations become. The worst that can happen is that avant-garde critics will make a fetish of novelty for a while, mistaking arrogance (the initial thrust) for greatness and relevancy, condemning ordered genius for its adherence to the standard prerequisites of theater. The avant-garde, for example, may blast the author of *Who's Afraid of Virginia Woolf?* and *Tiny Alice* as old-fashioned for submitting to the traditional conventions of a proscenium stage and a printed text; but such criticism will not hurt Albee in the long run, any more than it has hurt Shakespeare or Pirandello. Albee will survive the craze even as he has survived criticism leveled at him from the opposite extreme, by steady playgoers who find his work difficult and abstract.

Passing between Scylla and Charybdis, at once new and traditional, Albee has succeeded in giving repeatable theatrical expression on many levels to experiences that have for him as well as for his audience all the arrogance of inexplicable happenings. He has often been asked to *explain* his plays and has consistently refused to do so, with insolent assurance in his own worth; he has gained a kind of notorious popularity, but has not given in to the conventions of big-money theater. If anything, his plays get more difficult and his self-confidence more irritating—not because he enjoys frustrating his audience or is contemptuous of them, but because he is exploring, with the brazenness of the confident innovator, new areas of human experience with totally new dramatic means.

Albee is the only playwright, after O'Neill, who shows real growth, the only one who has made a serious effort to break away from the "message" plays which have plagued our theater, since O'Neill. Experimentation, for Albee, is a slow internal transformation of the dramatic medium, not an arbitrary exercise in expressionism, or Freudian symbolism, or stream of consciousness. His arrogance is not an empty gesture. He is the only one of our playwrights who seems to have accepted and committed himself to serious articulation of the existential questions of our time, recognizing the incongruity of insisting on pragmatic values in an age of relativity. Dramatic "statement," as Ibsen defined it, through realism, is no longer effective in such an age as ours. Albee has taken on the challenge as no one else in the American contemporary theater has. His work is a refreshing exception to John Gassner's judgment that our theater—with its message plays and its outgrown realism—is in a state of "protracted adolescence" which gives it a "provincial air."

"Happenings" are the extreme reaction to our fossilized theater and play an important role in trimming away the deadwood; Albee represents the first sober attempt to effect a transformation at the core. He has given arbitrary experimentation direction and purpose.

Even in his one-act plays, Albee is avant-garde only in the most serious sense of the word. He brings to our theater something of the poetic experience of Beckett and Ionesco—the same striving for a new dramatic language to fit the shifting scene, the same concern with making use of the stage as an articulate medium which reflects the contemporary condition— in the way, for example, that Italian film makers (Fellini and Antonioni especially) have revolutionized film techniques and raised their medium to a new art. Albee's arrogance as an innovator is prompted by profound artistic instincts which are constantly at work reshaping dramatic conventions. He does not discard such conventions altogether, but restructures them according to the organic demands of his dramatic themes. For Albee there is no a priori commitment to either a specific content or form. His early plays, for instance, reflect simultaneously the fascination of social drama and the effort to overcome that fascination. The later plays struggle head-on with the existential dilemma of our day and the frustrating search for meaning. The effort to define new content corresponds on every level to the search for original and adequate form.

Albee's procedure may be summed up as a kind of *dialectic*, an oscillation between the prosaic and the absurd, obvious and mysterious, commonplaces and revelation. What holds these extremes together as fluid, articulate reality is Albee's refusal to settle for "facts" as we know them, or experience as we have grown accustomed to defining it. A lesser artist might have been tempted to insert the latest "gimmicks" to create an impact; but Albee, with the arrogance and certainty of genius, starts confidently from scratch each time, searching out the spontaneous particular idiom that will do justice to the particular idea. He is the best product to date of the "theater of the absurd" (not excluding the French dramatists who launched it). He has absorbed from the French playwrights all there is to absorb—the Ionesco- like fragmentation of a language no longer functional, the Beckett-like economy of plot, the symbolic suggestions of Adamov, the raw exposures of Genet, the sensitive portraits of Giraudoux. His real master is not O'Neill, who provided the initial impulse for better things in our theater (without the organic principle which would guarantee his innovations, unfortunately), but Pirandello. Like the author of *Six Characters in Search of an Author* and *Right You Are!*, Albee has caught the feverish contradictions of the modern spirit, building from the inside out. And like the best representatives of the absurd tradition, he has discovered that the stage itself must be made articulate, often as a contrast against which the spoken word derives its meaning. His search for a new dramatic language is part of a deep-rooted instinct to find adequate expression for the existential dilemma at the heart of the modern experience.

In this context, social drama and the absolutes it insists on are hopelessly dated. O'Neill himself saw the danger early in his career and abandoned The Provincetown Players when he realized that they were out to "preach" social and political reform. Today that kind of theater serves a sophisticated propaganda program which has much else besides art on its agenda.

Albee's daring techniques and novel language go beyond social commentary to the disease of contemporary life. He has probed deeper than most other American playwrights for the implications of our moral and spiritual exhaustion; and if his originality has not been properly appreciated, it is because American audiences have not been properly trained to recognize either the new idiom or the pessimistic conclusion it tries to articulate. I do not suggest that the burden of dramatic communication lies with the audience; but an audience trained in humanitarian platitudes is not prepared to make the minimal effort required. The difficulty of the content must be accepted before one can begin to appreciate the extraordinary appropriateness of the way it has been portrayed on stage.

From the point of view of the conventional "concerned human being," repudiation of *assertion* and *statement* may seem to be a narcissistic self-indulgence; but in fact what appears atomistic and arbitrary in Albee is simply the organic restructuring of a reality which is no longer effective. The transformation is difficult but not new; it caught on long ago in painting, music, and poetry. In drama, the French alone have explored its rich possibilities deliberately and with success. This exploration is long overdue in the American theater.

Albee is the first playwright in the American theater to capture the feverish contradictions of our age, translating communication as commonly understood and accepted into a polarization of opposites, a skeptical questioning of "facts," substituting irony for statement and paradox for simplistic optimism. His cutting sarcasm is, understandably, one of his greatest achievements.

The main difficulty in this kind of theater lies in finding the proper balance, on stage, between dialogue and inanimate objects made articulate, between conscious awareness and unconscious suggestion. Antonioni's films are perhaps the extreme expression of the attempt to make the details surrounding conscious life speak out. The camera moves among objects like an insistent voice, underscoring, denying, outlining, setting up a silent opposition to conventional and recognizable events. Whatever the ultimate value of his technique, it serves extremely well to point up the *kind* of language demanded by an existential premise. On the stage, such a technique naturally must be corrected; drama has its own special demands. The playwright is restricted by the physical, immediate unity of the stage and the impossibility of using close-ups or of letting the camera move instead of the protagonists. He must find other ways to make the physical surroundings speak for him. O'Neill was the first of our dramatists to sense the need for such contrasts. In *All God's Chillun' Got Wings*, for example, his stage directions call for a contracting set—an ambitious design for any dramatist! Albee has turned the very limitations of the stage to his advantage. The most impressive example of the creation of a new *absurd* dimension on stage is the giant replica of the mansion in *Tiny Alice*, the most effective use to date of backdrop as dramatic script—not excluding Ionesco's empty chairs, his expanding creature of dead love, the recording machine in Beckett's *Krapp's Last Tape*. Albee has surpassed his teachers in this technique. His use of stage props—from *Tiny Alice* to *Box*—is intimate and discursive, not mere background or sheer experimentation, but living dialogue which expands as awareness increases. Perhaps the most intriguing and ambitious of these "props" is the dying man in *All Over*. The Unseen Patient, who had been kept alive in the hospital with tubes and transfusions (but who seemed, instead, to be keeping the medical gadgets alive), is the source of life for the people gathered in the room where he lies. He is the heartbeat of the dramatic action; the others nearby are "wired" into him like the TV cameras downstairs and the audience itself are "wired" into the action. This simple but expanding conceit more than makes up for the dialogue of the play, which in its lines is perhaps the least suggestive of all Albee's works; the dying man pumps meaning and unity into the larger scenes, giving them added literary dimension. As originally staged, the backstage apparatus of ropes and wires was left visible on both sides of the isolated set to extend the range of the conceit still further.

It is not without significance that, in spite of his personal commitment to certain popular causes, Albee has resisted the lure of social drama and the language of assertion. He seems to sense the artistic danger of indulging in the kind of writing which O'Neill described as "beyond theater," and which Ionesco labeled in his notebooks on drama as "one dimensional." The political and social realities of any age will find their way into art, of course; but the artist cannot indulge in personal crusades. If we still enjoy Aristophanes's *Clouds*, it is not because we identify with the social critic of Athens and side with him against this or that man, but because the dramatist in him was stronger than the reformer and produced a masterpiece.

Part of the trouble here lies with our critics, who encourage the *committed* play. According to one such critic, theater must be "subversive" to have dramatic impact. Even Arthur Miller, who is as much critic as playwright, is convinced that greatness in drama is the direct result of ethical commitment and of the playwright's acceptance of his role as moral arbiter and judge. Miller has said time and again that the tragic view of life is all-important, but that it is possible only where individual responsibility is recognized. Right and wrong, moral order, *blame*, are the values on which tragedy is built. We must struggle, says Miller, to insist on such values because where no order is believed in, no order can be breached—and thus all disasters of man will strive vainly for moral meaning. For Miller, "a true tragic victory may be scored"[1] once again, provided we recover the notion of a "moral law"[2] of individual responsibility as opposed to "the purely psychiatric view of life" or "the purely sociological." He insists that "if all our miseries, our indignities, are born and bred within our minds, then all action, let alone the heroic action, is obviously impossible.[3]

The principle is commendable in itself—and when a true artist is inspired by it (as Miller unquestionably was in the early plays), it cannot fail to produce commendable results. Unfortunately, the committed writer is often too ready to mold his medium to suit his compelling message and to identify with one side against the other. Where the audience is committed in the same way, such a play may even take on the semblance of artistic success. But, as Eric Bentley has keenly observed, innocence—especially for an artist—is suspect and misleading. The dramatist must be constantly alert to the dangers of simplistic moral extremes. The guilty may indeed be black with guilt, but the innocent are never wholly free from the burden of responsibility. In any case, the stage is not the place for such judgments, especially when they threaten to force the dramatic medium to serve an end which is something other than art.

Albee has never succumbed to the temptation of using the stage for indignant social commentary. Even in his early plays (the external "frame" of *The Death of Bessie Smith* is a fine example of such temptation to moralize), he never actually betrays his characters by reducing them to expressions of *guilt* and *innocence*. His most negative portrayals are handled with sympathetic insight into the complex totality of human motivation. In his hands, the polemic against the American family becomes a commentary on all human relationships, his violent anti-clericalism turns into a provocative question about salvation and faith, his biting criticism of racial intolerance is transformed into a subtle analysis of human insufficiency. The social problems he has inherited from our one-dimensional dramatic tradition are never resolved as dogmatic confrontations. In spite of his insolence, his harsh and often puerile judgments, his bitter sarcasm, Albee is irresistibly drawn to the profound skepticism of the absurd.

This skepticism reaches its limits, on the stage, in the tendency toward dissolution of character. Like all the other difficulties connected with the theater of the absurd, it rests on a paradox and a contradiction. Drama is action (though not necessarily plot as commonly understood), and action presupposes characters to carry it out, and characters must make themselves understood if the audience is to share in the experience the dramatist has articulated. The theater of the absurd has struggled to find ways of redefining these essentials, juxtaposing internal *landscape* and external events, facts and fantasy, reshaping language to suit the splintered action, using everything the stage offers to do so. But the kind of protagonist that emerges within this new medium is forever threatening to dissolve into a voice, a mind, a consciousness; a strange creature without identity or personality. Dramatists like Sartre and Camus have skillfully shifted attention away from the difficulty; their characters remain organically whole, integrated and unified by the internal law of individuality. The problem, however, does not cease to exist because it is masked. It is, without a doubt, the most immediate and pressing problem of the contemporary theater, but its history is at least as old as *Hamlet*.

In the most modern of his heroes, Shakespeare almost lets go of dramatic personality as understood from the time of the Greeks, threatening to destroy it at the core. Character is reduced to irreconcilable levels of consciousness—as the unusual effect of the soliloquies makes clear. These stand out from the surrounding action like islands of an internal life which seems often unrelated to the intentions professed by the hero and the actions which result from such intentions. What emerges is a surrealistic mosaic of human impulses, an in world which remains inviolate in spite of tumultuous external events. The sensitive Hamlet of the soliloquies and the Machiavellian prince capable of sending his best friends to death on mere suspicion is a double image which is never sharpened into a single focus. The audience's response is strangely dependent on the soliloquies; it is detached from the facts of the action. We remember the character as seen from *within*, and the action of the play remains somewhat distant and unreal. We follow the play through the paradoxical psychology of the strange hero who strips his consciousness bare before us.

Modern psychoanalysis and the popularization of Freud have made the notion of unresolved impulses and the subconscious a commonplace; its implications for the stage, however, have yet to be explored meaningfully—although the history of dramatic innovation clearly points to such an examination. To grasp something of what has taken place, one need only compare the sculpturelike creations of Greek drama—exquisitely molded according to their fixed purpose—with the characters of Pirandello or Beckett or even the partly realized, rough-hewn attempts of O'Neill in such plays as *Strange Interlude* (Nina) or *The Great God Brown* (Dion, Brown), or the Greek-inspired figures in *Mourning Becomes Electra* (Lavinia, Orin, Ezra).

Hamlet marks the turning point; and it is not far-fetched to say that Goldoni first showed the possibilities of modern character delineation in his whimsical and wholly arbitrary treatment of secondary figures. But the first to assume the challenge as an important and conscious innovation, and to succeed in the attempt, was Pirandello. His characters are indeed *maschere nude*—stripped semblances of what is commonly called "character." What makes the Pirandellian experience a giant step forward, dramatically, is not simply the playwright's insistence on the fragmentation of personality at the core, but his way of, going about it. We see the integrated or seemingly integrated character collapse in slow stages before our eyes through an ever more intense oscillation between what *is* and what *appears to be*; between acknowledged purpose and hidden intentions; between the outer shell of life and the living truth which resists all *facts*. Human personality is subtly transformed, even as we watch, into instinct, revelation, doubt, confession, assertion, denial. Action is translated into shifting points of motivation, contradictory statements arranged into a spiral of events, each somehow containing the life of the whole, like the seed which contains the physical potential of the human being. Naturally, action too will appear fragmented in this sort of scheme; the immediate moment is everything. It's hard to say, after seeing or reading a Pirandello play, just what this or that person really is; but we know quite well what he thinks, feels, suffers. We seem to be inside looking out. To concentrate on the *facts* of the action is to lose the heartbeat of the Pirandellian world, the living mask.

In more recent drama—Ionesco might be cited as an example—the dangers of this tendency begin to make themselves felt. The dissolution of character, if carried far enough, must destroy the very notion of character—

just as the destruction of conventional language threatens to destroy the possibility of dramatic communication. Pushed to extremes, the dissolution of character takes on the appearance of *types*, on one hand, and *symbols*, on the other—ready-made clichés and enigmatic representations. The protagonists of *The Sandbox* and *The American Dream* point up the danger in Albee's plays—but even in these "experimental" pieces the crotchety old women, the submissive males, the frighteningly efficient females, have their own individual charm as dramatic characters. In *Tiny Alice* Albee proves that he has overcome the danger. Like the Dantesque figures who express themselves simply and directly in the characteristic act which sums up their existence, Albee's protagonists are beautifully realized in their single purpose as independent creations made infinitely suggestive through a shocking and utterly transparent allegory. *Box* is, in this respect, a transcendent tour de force.

In his genial answer to the dissolution of character, as in his bold new techniques to reduce action to a transparency and language to ironic paradox, Albee has given ample evidence of his mastery of the dramatic medium. He is the arrogant newcomer who has challenged our seemingly impregnable commitment to social drama and forced us to terms, stripping familiar pragmatic conclusions to provocative questions and the mask of personality down to its mysterious pulse. Not since the time of O'Neill has the American theater witnessed such a confident assertion of artistic arrogance.

NOTES

1. Robert Hogan, *Arthur Miller* (Minneapolis: University of Minnesota Press, 1964), p. 9.

2. Arthur Miller, "Tragedy and the Common Man," *Modern Drama*, ed. Anthony Caputi (New York: W.W. Norton, 1966), pp. 329–30.

3. Ibid. See also Alan Downer, *Recent American Drama* (Minneapolis: University of Minnesota Press, 1961), pp. 34–35.

LEONARD MOSS

The Perspective of a Playwright

I THESIS

Arthur Miller has focused upon a single subject—"the struggle ... of the individual attempting to gain his 'rightful' position in his society" and in his family. Miller's chief characters, whether they eventually revise their objectives or remain rigidly defensive, are motivated by an obsession to justify themselves; they fix their identities through radical acts of ego-assertion.[1] "However one might dislike this man, who does all sorts of frightful things," the dramatist comments of Eddie Carbone, "he possesses or exemplifies the wondrous and humane fact that he too can be driven to what in the last analysis is a sacrifice of himself for his conception, however misguided, of right, dignity, and justice" (*C.P.*, 51). High rank or noble status does not distinguish such figures. "The commonest of men," Miller states in "Tragedy and the Common Man" (1949), "may take on [tragic] stature to the extent of his willingness to throw all he has into the contest." "The closer a man approaches tragedy the more intense is his concentration of emotion upon the fixed point of his commitment, which is to say the closer he approaches what in life we call fanaticism" (*C.P.*, 7).

Fanatical self-assertion may bring an individual into violent opposition with his society. Tragic antagonism arises because the "unchangeable [social] environment" often "suppresses man, perverts the flowing out of his love and

---

From *Arthur Miller*. © 1980 G.K. Hall & Co.

creative instinct" ("Tragedy and the Common Man"). According to Miller, in "The Shadows of the Gods" (1958), conflict between father and son prefigures tragedy's "revolutionary questioning" when the child affirms his independence after confronting an intolerant parental authority. Later the mature hero, in life and in art, directs his protest against restrictive forces more potent than the father's, for "in truth the parent, powerful as he appears, is not the source of injustice but its deputy" (43).

Society, however, is not the sole tragic villain. Miller admires his hero's obsessive claim to a given "right," and he sorrows at its frustration. At the same time, he realizes that total self-concern can lead to total self-defeat; "conscience," if not tempered by humility and informed by reason, may degenerate into a savagely destructive faculty. When opposed by "forces of disintegration," Miller's major figures react in either of two ways, depending upon the flexibility of their ethical posture. They may reexamine their criteria, as in the case of David Frieber, Lawrence Newman, Chris Keller, Biff Loman, John Proctor, Gay Langland, Quentin, Prince Von Berg, and Victor Franz. Or they may persist in their assertion even though persistence brings catastrophe to themselves and to those for whom they care. That is the course chosen by Joe Keller, Willy Loman, Eddie Carbone, Maggie, and Cain, each of whom arrives at "the end of his justifications."[2] In the first instance, accommodation is directed by realistic self-knowledge; in the second, "constancy" to an ideal of self-love remains the paramount value. The fanatic rejects "truth," which he fears will undermine his "power," alienate him from others, and negate his longing for "respect" and "peace." Despite the nagging pressure of guilt-feelings, he commits the grossest acts, even suicide, in order to maintain the sanctity of his "name"—pride in his adequacy as a father or lover, citizen or businessman—and to prevent the exposure of his secret weakness, dependence, malice, or shame. "To perceive somehow our own complicity with evil is a horror not to be borne."[3]

The author's moral bias is clearly evident in these divergent reactions. Individuals can buttress their own and society's stability by resisting "hatred" and "exclusiveness." Or individuals can upset social equilibrium by enforcing the exaggerated demands of a narrow egoism. Lawrence Newman and John Proctor (among others) strengthen their communities even though they defy popular standards; Willy Loman and Joe Keller adopt popular standards but become estranged from both family and society because of their uncompromising self-will. Extreme egocentrism inevitably thwarts a man's constructive energies: the only way to acquire dignity is to respect the dignity of others.

Miller has proposed his version of the Golden Rule in many essays. He has denounced writers who conform to commercial specifications, businessmen and politicians who exploit other men's insecurities, informers who betray friends in order to preserve their own reputations, civilians who passively tolerate wartime atrocities, and veterans who quickly forget the comradeship they knew during combat. He encountered the last while gathering material in American army camps for a movie. In his journal of the tour, *Situation Normal* (1944), he reports that soldiers, after sharing a common purpose in battle, lose their "unity of feeling" on returning to the United States: "civilian life in America is private, it is always striving for exclusiveness" (158).

Whatever the specific situation, his point on the necessity for communication between individuals and their institutional sources of value remains the same. He repeatedly stresses the idea that the proper business of serious drama is to demonstrate the feasibility of such communication and the disastrous results of its absence. The protagonist of this drama must enter into meaningful social relationships, if only to challenge conventional norms. He should possess "the worth, the innate dignity, of a whole people asking a basic question and demanding its answer" ("On Social Plays," 1955, 8). The "identity" he molds within the intimate bonds of his family must be tried in an inhospitable world. Society as a whole, Miller explains in "The Family in Modern Drama" (1956), is "mutable, accidental, and consequently of a profoundly arbitrary nature to us." A limited theater will therefore restrict its scope to the family, which symbolizes what is "real" and abiding in human affairs. But a writer "cannot hope to achieve truly high excellence short of an investigation into the whole gamut of causation of which society is a manifest and crucial part." He must answer the essential question, "how may man make for himself a home in that vastness of strangers and how may he transform that vastness into a home?" (37, 40–41).

Ibsen, Miller believes, conducted this evaluation, but dramatists after Ibsen have been unable to "bridge the widening gap between the private life and the social life." They usually precipitate one or the other component from the tragic equation: "our lack of tragedy may be partially accounted for by the turn which modern literature has taken toward the purely psychiatric view of life, or the purely sociological" ("Tragedy and the Common Man"). This fragmented literature reflects contemporary experience: the complexity of society militates against a tragic configuration of its irrationality. "We are so atomized socially that no character in a play can conceivably stand as our vanguard, as our heroic questioner.... To think of an individual fulfilling his subjective needs through social action ... is difficult for us to imagine" ("On Social Plays," 6). Great drama will not be produced until "a play mixes 'I' with 'we' in a significantly original way.... The only materials for a possible new trend in the U.S. are new insights into social and psychological mechanisms; the next original interpretation of these elements, one with the other, will establish a new form."[4]

The task of creating this "new form" has presented Miller—and most notable dramatists of this century—with the severest challenge. How does a writer introduce a social milieu so that its "codes" assume a recognizable and influential presence? How does he show "indignation" as a function of personality—whether the indignation of a rebellious son, a betrayed father, a downtrodden worker, a persecuted citizen, or some combination of these and other identities—rather than as an intellectual abstraction? In short, how does a playwright translate his "way of looking" into a character's way of acting? A character may discuss public issues fluently, but the job of depicting those issues in concrete terms is a formidable one; he may easily exclaim "I know who I am," but the difficulties involved in giving that self-awareness an emotional content are immense. The solutions Miller proposes in his essays and in his plays supply the index to his achievement as a dramatist. His lifelong effort to integrate the radical "I" with the reactionary "we" has been an impressive one. His shortcomings may well verify his opinion that, given the facts of contemporary life, total success in such an enterprise is inconceivable.

II The Search for "a New Form"

Miller has never seemed to be particularly intimidated by the problem of finding a dramatic means to interrelate "social and psychological mechanisms." In 1947 he said, "my development is toward an ever-greater examination of human nature. So many people are talking about new form. This to me is an evasion of the problem of playwriting, which is a revelation of human motives regardless of form."[5] A decade later he added, "however important considerations of style and form have been to me, they are only means, tools to pry up the well-worn, 'inevitable' surfaces of experience behind which swarm the living thoughts and feelings whose expression is the essential purpose of art" (*C.P.*, 52). The words "regardless" and "only" belie the tremendous concern Miller has shown for his "tools" throughout his career. If his "examination of human nature" has centered on a single subject, his methods have certainly undergone much modification. In several analyses of his own plays he illuminates those changing artistic strategies and his continuous struggle with the technical questions entailed by his thematic interests.

The most penetrating and comprehensive analysis is his long Introduction to the *Collected Plays*. In it he indicates his involvement with three stylistic modes prevalent in modern drama, which may be labeled the realistic, the expressionistic, and the rhetorical.[6] "I have stood squarely in conventional realism" (52), he declares, and an acknowledgment of a major debt to Ibsen supports the statement. Although he had gained an appreciation for the power of "hard facts" from Dostoyevsky's *The Brothers Karamazov*, he learned how "to make the moral world ... real and evident" by observing Ibsen's "ability to forge a play upon a factual bedrock. A situation in his plays is never stated but revealed in terms of hard actions, irrevocable deeds" (19). More specifically, Ibsen helped Miller answer the "biggest single [expository] problem, namely, how to dramatize what has gone before":

> If his plays, and his method, do nothing else they reveal the evolutionary quality of life. One is constantly aware, in watching his plays, of process, change, development.... It is therefore wrong to imagine that because his first and sometimes his second acts devote so much time to a studied revelation of antecedent material, his view is static compared to our own. In truth, it is profoundly dynamic, for that enormous past was always heavily documented to the end that the present be comprehended with wholeness, as a moment in a flow of time, and not—as with so many modern plays—as a situation without roots. (21)

"What I was after," Miller recalls, "was the wonder in the fact that consequences of actions are as real as the actions themselves" (18).

While he embraced words, gestures, and shapes of the familiar world, however, he "tried to expand [realism] with an imposition of various forms in order to speak more directly ... of what has moved me behind the visible façades of life" (52). He expanded in two directions. From the start of his career he wished to enrich the realistic style with an "evaluation of life"—a conscious articulation of ethical judgment. Quite early that wish led to a vexing predicament: in *The Man Who Had All the Luck*, he realized soon after completing the work, he had not been able to avoid a rhetorical, or discursive, presentation of his theme. With the next play he determined to "forego" any sentiments that did not arise naturally from the action. The plan in *All My Sons* was "to seek cause and effect, hard actions, facts, the geometry of relationships, and to bold back any tendency to express an idea in itself unless it was literally forced out of a character's mouth" (15–16). In this way Miller thought he would find it possible to elicit a "relatively sharp definition of the social aspects" (22) without resorting to the discursiveness of the earlier play.

Then he saw that the most significant consequences composing a character's inheritance from past decisions might be emotional, not physical. In *Death of a Salesman*, therefore, he introduced an "expressionistic element" to get at the "passion" residing "behind the visible façades." "From the theatrical viewpoint that play ... broke the bounds, I believe, of a long convention of realism.... I had willingly employed expressionism but always to create a subjective truth.... I had always been attracted and repelled by the brilliance of German expressionism after World War I, and one aim in *Salesman* was to employ its quite marvelous shorthand for humane, 'felt' characterizations rather than for purposes of demonstration for which the Germans had used it" (39).[7] This "shorthand" reproduced the psychological immediacy of past events: "the *Salesman* image was from the beginning absorbed with the concept that nothing in life comes 'next' but that everything exists together and at the same time within us" (23).

All My Sons represented a compromise between an explicit moralism and a realistic "geometry" of causation; *Death of a Salesman* represented a compromise between rhetorical, realistic, and expressionistic modes. After *Death of a Salesman*, a "preference for plays which seek causation not only in psychology but in society" (36) compelled Miller to curtail his exploration of subjective processes and to return to a more objective frame of reference. In writing *The Crucible* he was still bemused by "a kind of interior mechanism," but he hoped to "lift" his study "out of the morass of subjectivism" (40–41) with historical data and with evaluative declamation. "It seemed to me then," he writes in a 1960 Introduction to *A View from the Bridge*, "that the theater was retreating into an area of psycho-sexual romanticism, and this at the very moment when great events both at home and abroad cried out for recognition and analytic inspection" (vi).

Having "taken a step toward a more self-aware drama" with *The Crucible*, Miller continues in this preface, he decided to advance further into the realm ruled by "codes and ideas of social and ethical importance": the fanaticism of Eddie Carbone can be measured by his willingness to violate "the code of his culture" (vi, viii). In another essay, "On Social Plays," Miller states that by the time he wrote *A View from the Bridge* he had abandoned his theory of "interior" causation in favor of "bare" facts and rational commentary. At an earlier stage he probably would have told the story in temporal depth; now he did not want to write "a slowly evolving drama through which the hero's antecedent life forces might, one by one, be brought to light" (18). Without subjective clinical detail interrupting "that clear, clean line of [Eddie's] catastrophe," the "events themselves" could be related swiftly, and the breach of social law would reverberate with "mystery" and "wonderment" (17–18).[8] In *After the Fall*, again, Miller intended to objectify the "psychological question"—to "present the psychology of men not for its own sake.... but primarily as it issues forth in its public importance."[9]

Miller's experimentation with expressionistic, realistic, and rhetorical styles, then, has been conditioned by his overriding desire to declare objective truths about man in society: "our standards of right and wrong, good taste and bad, must in some way come into either conflict or agreement with social standards" (*C.P.*, 10–11). A playwright's goal should be to merge "surfaces of experience" (the objective) with "cogent emotional life" (the subjective) and "philosophically or socially meaningful themes" (the analytic) so as to make known the public significance of private engagements. "Drama is akin to the other inventions of man in that it ought to help us to know more, and not merely to spend our feelings. The ultimate justification for a genuine new form is the new and heightened consciousness it creates and makes possible—a consciousness of causation in the light of known but hitherto inexplicable effects" (*C.P.*, 8, 13, 52–53). Miller's aim as a craftsman has been to "make real on stage as in life that part of man which, through passion, seeks awareness. There is no contradiction between the two."[10]

III THE PROBLEM OF PERSPECTIVE

Arthur Miller and Eugene O'Neill have done more than other American dramatists to "relate the subjective to the objective truth":[11] *Death of a Salesman* and O'Neill's *Long Day's Journey into blight* are two of the finest works in the American theater.[12] Contrary to Miller's assertion, however, there is in his plays a contradiction between passion and awareness, between irrational impulse and rational concept. His best dialogue mirrors psychological conditions, yet he constantly returns to the formal generalization; he can skillfully manipulate emotional tension, yet he seeks esthetic detachment; his figures act most intelligibly in a family context, yet he feels obliged to make explicit their connection with a social "environment." Miller sees his principal subject—the drive for self-justification—primarily as an *internal* process activated by "mechanisms" that repress or involuntarily recall shameful memories and motives, that effect rapid transitions between taut and relaxed moods. When his characters fervently defend egocentric attitudes, their futility evokes a genuine sense of terror and pathos that indirectly but powerfully reinforces his thesis on the necessity for "meaningful" accommodation in society. When, on the other hand, his characters intelligently reform, their self-knowledge remains only a rhetorical promise. After their fall and recovery the mature new-men—Lawrence Newman, David Frieber, Chris Keller, Biff Loman, John Proctor, Gay Langland, Quentin, Leduc, Von Berg, and the Franz brothers—predicate rather than model their liberating insights. A tendency to impose judgment upon action—the tendency Miller worried about after writing his first Broadway play, *The Man Who Had All the Luck*—has prevented him from achieving the harmony of styles he has long sought. His attempt to enlarge the "interior psychological question" with "codes and ideas of social and ethical importance" has distorted his subjective perspective and so compromised his exceptional talent.

A review of his symbolic, structural, and verbal techniques substantiates this conclusion. Miller has been relatively fortunate in finding apt metaphors to signify the implications of a "gap between the private life and the social life." Most of his symbolic images, it is true, are drawn along simple lines—a carousel that conceals hatred (*Focus*); a fruitful tree destroyed in its prime (*All My Sons*); "green leaves" blotted out by the hard outlines of apartment buildings, a flute song displaced by childish nonsense from a wire recorder, a wife's praise erased by a whore's laugh (*Death of a Salesman*); a dingy warehouse harboring hopeless inmates (*A Memory of Two Mondays*); a herd of mustangs moving toward extinction (*The Misfits*); a ruined tower that memorializes horrors committed by "ordinary" men (*After the Fall*); feathers and a broken pot guarded as if they were life itself (*Incident at Vichy*); a "massive," discarded armchair (*The Price*).

Just as obviously, many of Miller's workers—a fearful personnel manager in an anti-Semitic corporation (*Focus*) and an unscrupulous industrialist (*All My Sons*), a frustrated salesman (*Death of a Salesman*) and a dispirited policeman (*The Price*), dehumanized laborers (*A Memory of Two Mondays*) and displaced cowboys (*The Misfits*)—find little spiritual "sustenance" in their trades.[13] Men who look for a satisfying social role in a productive occupation—Chris Keller, Biff Loman, Kenneth and Bert, Gay Langland, Quentin, and Walter Franz—are disappointed; even the reborn Lawrence Newman faces a future as a "glorified usher to salesmen." In *Incident at Vichy*, one of only two plays set in a foreign locale, the situation is worse: none of the prisoners—from Leduc, a psychiatrist, to Von Berg, an aristocratic non-worker, to the Gypsy, who does odd (or illegal) jobs—can possibly make positive use of his abilities in his country. Despite his acquaintance with a wide variety of trades as a youth, Miller never envisioned a profession—except, perhaps, his own—that could unite its practitioner with his society in mutually beneficial labor.

Taken symbolically, these vocations and images could be said to indicate the misuse of natural talent brought about by an incongruity between personal and social objectives in contemporary urban culture. As such, they are rather facile indications. A subtler, more extended occupational metaphor that objectively represents the individual's malaise in society is the pursuit of justice through law. In Miller's plays, with their rhythm of accusation and defense, the defendant invariably fails to obtain equity and must resort to extralegal means to protect his rights.

Lawrence Newman forges a new code of conduct after he perceives the inadequacy of the mores to which he had subscribed and the inability of the law to relieve racial discrimination. In *All My Sons*, a courtroom drama in essence if not in setting, the trial metaphor assumes greater importance. Joe Keller commits fraud and involuntary homicide, conspires to incriminate his partner, and evades detection until his son (with the help of George, a lawyer) prosecutes, finds him guilty, rejects his appeal, and delivers what amounts to a death sentence. Both Chris and his father call upon principles beyond the jurisdiction of formal law; each defends his principle with a fierceness that makes the legal question seem petty in comparison. In *Death of a Salesman*, again a minor character, Bernard, chooses law as his profession, and again a father stands accused, then condemned by his son for a breach of trust far more serious than, though associated with, his technical transgression (adultery).

Eddie Carbone brings on disaster by upholding a statute (against illegal immigration), not by violating one, but—as with Joe Keller, Willy Loman, and Eddie's accuser, Marco—his justification transcends the realm of jurisprudence. Institutional procedures are powerless to secure for him his paternal "rights" or to prevent Rodolpho from "stealing" his niece. "The law is not interested in this," his impassive attorney tells him; "you have no recourse in the law." Victor Franz, retiring from police work, sees his career as "a little unreal," and in *The Creation of the World* man comes out guilty even when God argues for him. Miller's central metaphorical statement of the law's insufficiency occurs in *After the Fall*, whose protagonist rejects the legal profession after having adopted its mode of operation in his personal life.[14] Quentin learns (as does Eddie Carbone) that the great limitation of the legal mode is an incapacity to account for, much less to deal with, emotional needs. Although his original outlook persists—he continues to discuss human behavior in terms of moralistic formulas ("this pointless litigation of existence before an empty bench")—he gives up his practice in the hope of arriving at more humane knowledge.

In these works the legal system for redress of grievance is seen to be almost irrelevant to the protagonist's defense of a "conception, however misguided, of right, dignity, and justice." In *Incident at Vichy*, in *The Crucible*, and in Miller's adaptation of Ibsen's *An Enemy of the People*, the system of public morality becomes, through agents acting in its name, the active perpetrator of injustice. The trial of integrity is consequently tied more closely to a courtroom or jail terminology. *Incident at Vichy* deals with the supreme perverters of law in recent times. As in Kafka's *The Trial*, the rationale that justifies political murder ("there are no persons anymore") appears bizarre and irrational to those victimized by it. Only Von Berg penetrates the ethical obscurity by reasserting, in an act of self-sacrifice, the responsibility of individual conscience. Similarly, John Proctor gives up his life to confirm a principle of enlightened self-determination intolerable to the Salem judges. (Before the hearing and the ordeal in jail, Proctor suffered a private trial at home: "I come into a court when I come into this house!" he complained to his wife, who would not forgive his liaison with Abigail.)[15]

In his adaptation of Ibsen's *An Enemy of the People* (1950), Miller reiterated with an abundance of legalistic set-speeches his belief that public antipathy can provide a grueling test for a nonconformist who dares question social standards. As in *Focus*, *The Crucible*, and *Incident at Vichy*, a community's insanity arouses indignation in a "lonely" battler. The issue is almost allegorical in its polarization of good and evil: Honesty, personified by brave Dr. Stockmann, debates (again in a trial setting) with Evil, personified by smug middle-class materialists—the "people." During the debate Stockmann exposes the bourgeois immorality, self-interest, and blindness that had masqueraded as communal justice, enterprise, and wisdom. "The majority," he declares, "is never right until it *does* right."[16] The fact that Stockmann, in common with most of Miller's chief figures, is forced to look beyond juridical criteria for a tenable standard of justice calls into question the social order founded upon those criteria. "There doesn't seem to be much of a law," a character laments in All My Sons; "all the law is not in a book," Marco states in *A View from the Bridge*. Where law is superfluous or malign, the trial process becomes an ironic metaphor for the pursuit of self-respect.[17]

Miller incorporated the accusation–defense rhythm of a trial into almost all his major plays. Despite his wide-ranging experiments with form, the narrative schemes of *All My Sons*, *Death of a Salesman*, *The Crucible*, *A View from the Bridge*, and *After the Fall* are remarkably alike."[18] In each work hidden guilt is first referred to covertly, then bared in a climactic revelation— a scheme based upon Ibsen's exhibitions of the inescapable causal movement from past action to present reaction. The secrets and the methods with which they are brought to light vary. Eddie Carbone obstinately suppresses *two* secrets—betrayal of the immigrants (an objective fact) and ardor for his niece (a "cast of mind"). Joe Keller and Willy Roman also conceal both their crimes and their moral frailty; John Proctor *confesses* his sins; Quentin concludes that *all* men are guilty. In *All My Sons*, in *The Crucible*, and in *A View from the Bridge*, the sin is suggested by verbal allusions and by the protagonist's behavior; *Death of a Salesman* and *After the Fall* modify that procedure with memory-surveys. Since the protagonist fears discovery—he usually hesitates to admit his offenses even to himself—gradual exposition generates suspense by exploiting the discrepancy between inward reality and outward appearance. "Who can ever know what will be discovered?" Alfieri muses.

Revelation ensures a surprising transition from one issue to another. As the secret comes into view, an antagonism developed at the beginning of each play gives way to a more urgent opposition. Thus attention is transferred from an argument between Chris and Kate to an argument between Chris and Joe (*All My Sons*); from a present to a past father–son dilemma (*Death of a Salesman*); from a struggle between the Proctors and Abigail to one between John Proctor and the judges who have condemned him (*The Crucible*); from the Eddie-Rodolpho to the Eddie-Mareo duel (*A View from the Bridge*); and from Quentin's dialogue with Louise to that with Maggie (*After the Fall*). Both before and after the transfer, dramatic interest centers on only one of the combatants: Keller's fear replaces his wife's as the crucial subject; Willy's failures in the past, his failures in the present; Proctor's final decision, Abigail's machinations; Eddie's response to Marco, the response to Rodolpho; Quentin's self-justification in the second marriage, that in the first.

This complex format has an outstanding weakness: the resolution of the second issue tends to occur after the emotional climax, an outcome that is likely to reduce the impact and coherence of the primary progression of character in the preceding action. Chris Keller's first engagement with his father was emotionally climactic but ethically inconclusive. The subsequent rematch forfeits excitement generated by the gradual development of Joe Keller's anxiety; during the last act Chris diverts attention from the protagonist's standpoint with speeches on social responsibility. Although the focus of interest belatedly shifts from the harried father to the outraged son, however, the decisive conflict is at least confined to a single set of opponents. In *The Crucible*, contrarily, the public problem of witchcraft (which supersedes the private problem of love-jealousy) splits into two relatively separate power struggles: one involves Abigail, Proctor, and the girls during the hearing; the other, Proctor and his jailors after it. These struggles, loosely joined by Miller's implied theory that society can be saved by its morally mature citizens, come to *independent crises* ending respectively in mass hysteria (the melodramatic highpoint) and personal honesty (Proctor's refusal to confess to witchcraft). Until the fourth act, the social implications of the play arise directly from psychological origins; then the causal connection is abruptly severed. *A View from the Bridge* displays another anticlimactic resolution. The emergence of a second antagonist moves the battle for respect from a family to a community arena, but it blurs "that clear, clean line" of the original (and critical) confrontation, a result compounded by the narrator's propensity for myth-making.

Eager to advance his concept of social "relatedness," Miller fails to honor in these plays the structural rule he observed in Ibsen, Beethoven, and Dostoyevsky: "above all, the precise collision of inner themes during, not before or after, the high dramatic scenes.... The holding back of climax until it was ready, the grasp of the rising line and the unwillingness to divert to an easy climax until the true one was ready" (*C.P.*, 16).[19] He avoids anticlimax in *After the Fall* by unfolding Quentin's problem and solution concurrently, allowing only a summary statement of the solution at the ending. Unfortunately, the skeletal, poorly integrated memory sequences inhibit the movement toward significant climax. The double-issue design is wholly successful only in *Death of a Salesman* because there the articulation of value does not become narratively (or verbally) intrusive. Like Chris Keller, Biff Loman goes home again to clarify his "revolutionary questioning," and others also offer interpretive comments. But this activity, far from redirecting attention from one character or issue to another after the play's tensional peak, merely expedites the outcome already predicted by the Salesman's spiritual collapse and makes possible a measured transition from the chaos of the climax to the numbed calm of the denouement. Willy Loman consistently channels the flow of tension; his "fanaticism" unifies psychological and sociological sources of tragedy.

Miller's construction, if rarely flawless, is never formless. His metaphors, if sometimes obvious, are sometimes subtle. It is the dialogue that swings between extremes of brilliance and insipidity. Colloquial speech may be heard in an amazing variety of accents—Irish, Swedish, German, Sicilian, Slavic, Barbados, Yiddish, Puritan, Brooklyn, Southwestern, and Midwestern. *After the Fall* and *Incident at Vichy*, in fact, were the first works that did not make extensive use of subliterate English (except for Maggie's New York locutions and childish inanities, which convey a certain charm and a certain mental barrenness). Whether in historical, regional, or foreign dialect, Miller's dialogue is most telling when it works by implication, not by explication.

Explicit analyses of motivation may, of course, serve a legitimate and even commendable purpose by establishing a rational perspective. Thus Biff Loman and Charley reflect on the meaning of Willy's existence; the misfits as philosophers explain the misfits as doers; Quentin during his psychoanalysis contemplates Quentin before; Leduc and Von Berg answer the question puzzling the other prisoners; the debates in *The Price* and *The Creation of the World* propose policies to secure deliverance from guilt. Rhetorical differences corresponding to differences in perceptiveness are often pronounced: the abstruseness of Shory, Hester, and David Frieber contrasts with the folksiness of their friends in *The Man Who Had All the Luck*; the incisiveness of Newman's thoughts contrasts with the triteness of his conversation; Chris Keller's abstractness, with his father's solidity; Proctor's eloquence, with the girls' incoherence; Alfieri's fluency, with Eddie's awkwardness; the lyricism of *A Memory of Two Mondays* with the slanginess; Gay's pretentiousness, with Roslyn's naiveté; Walter's formality, with Solomon's simplicity. Too often in these instances, however, "analytic inspection" receives disproportionate emphasis, produces artificial wisdom, and unbalances the interplay between idiomatically authentic, emotionally intense, and ethically rational language styles.

At other times, trivial homespun talk, unable to bridge the "gap" separating passion from formal communication, dumbly masks unspeakable humiliation, wrath, or sorrow. Then Miller's writing attains its greatest power. Joe Keller's bluff words resound with increasing apprehension: "because it's good money, there's nothing wrong with that money.... What have I got to hide? What the hell is the matter with you?" Interrogating his son with driving insistence, Keller harshly answers each question he raises:

> Jail? You want me to go to jail? If you want me to go, say so I ... I'll tell you why you can't say it. Because you know I don't belong there. Because you know I ... Who worked for nothin' in that war? When they work for nothin', I'll work for nothin'. Did they ship a gun or a truck outa Detroit before they got their price? Is that clean? It's dollars and cents, nickels and dimes; war and peace, it's nickels and dimes, what's clean? Half the Goddam country is gotta go if I go! That's why you can't tell me.

The conviction ringing in these rhetorical questions derives less from a businessman's self-righteousness than from a father's desperation.[20]

In a similar way Willy Loman's commonplace locutions define uncommon motives. "He won't starve. None a them starve," Charley advises concerning Biff, "forget about him." Willy answers with the poignantly simple sentence, "then what have I got to remember?"[21] Longer passages touch upon, rather than belabor, specific ideas exposed by the action. In her concluding remark Linda alludes quite laconically to her financial insecurity, to her efforts to keep the "home" intact, and above all to her inability to comprehend her husband's strange compulsion: "why did you do it? I search and search and I search, and I can't understand it, Willy. I made the last payment on the house today. Today, dear. And there'll be nobody home.... We're free and clear. We're free."

The Crucible, like *Death of a Salesman* (and all of Miller's plays), contains some self-conscious oratory. In neither work does this detract from the dynamics of character, theme, and tension (perhaps the long historical footnotes in *The Crucible* helped assuage Miller's speculative bent). The Puritan dialect may sound archaic and formal to a present-day audience, but it can be as impressive in its monosyllabic directness as contemporary English.[22] "It were a fearsome man," Rebecca eulogizes over one of the witch-hunt victims. "Spite only keeps me silent," Proctor says; "it is hard to give the lie to dogs." A few fanciful metaphors relieve the verbal plainness ("I see now your spirit twists around the single error of my life, and I will never tear it free!"), and Tituba's exotic, faintly humorous Barbados inflection contributes additional color.

Like Tituba, Joe Keller, and Willy Loman, Eddie Carbone in *A View from the Bridge* expresses fearfulness through a comfortably ungrammatical, sometimes comic idiom. "Listen," he warns Catherine, "I could tell you things about Louis which you wouldn't wave to him no more." His contorted syntax registers sharper pain as, ashamed and embarrassed, he tries to dissuade his niece from marriage. In one passage his words wander about in a sobbing rhythm before stumbling to their apologetic petition:

> I was just tellin' Beatrice ... if you wanna go out, like ... I mean I realize maybe I kept you home too much. Because he's the first guy you ever knew, y'know? I mean now that you got a job, you might meet some fellas, and you get a different idea, y'know? I mean you could always comeback to him, you're still only kids, the both of yiz. What's the hurry? Maybe you'll get around a little bit, you grow up a little more, maybe you'll see different in a couple of months. I mean you be surprised, it don't have to be him. [Miller's ellipses]

When suppressed feeling threatens to burst the everyday verbal "façade" in lines such as these, the common man's language becomes emotionally resonant. That resonance marks the distinctive quality of Arthur Miller's achievement.

NOTES

1. As previously noted, "the one exception among [Miller's] plays is *A Memory of Two Mondays*" (*C.P.*, 8): its characters establish their identities in acts of ego-subordination.

2. This classification is necessarily somewhat arbitrary. Joe Keller is grouped with the unreformed because he resigns his egocentric position in word only, not in spirit. Quentin, on the other hand, has been placed in the category of the reformed because his contrition, though questionable, directs the movement of the play. While both modes of conduct occur in almost every work, sometimes the morally rigid are only minor characters who act as a foil to the protagonist. Thus, the dogmatic Shory disagrees with an impressionable David Frieber; the inflexible Carlson, with an awakened Newman; the unregenerate Guido, with Gay Langland; Lebeau and his benighted associates, with Leduc and Von Berg.

3. Arthur Miller in "With respect for her agony."

4. Arthur Miller quoted in "American Playwrights Self-Appraised," ed. Henry Hewes, *Saturday Review* 38 (Sept. 3, 1955): 19.

5. Quoted in Stevens, p. 56.

6. This last style, well exemplified in the works of George Bernard Shaw, has also been called "discursive" and "classical"; it is described under the latter classification, in *The Reader's Companion to World Literature*, ed. L.H. Hornstein et al. (New York, 1956), as "social, formal, intellectual, and static."

7. The expressionistic techniques in *Death of a Salesman* are reminiscent more of Strindberg's late plays (*A Dream Play*, for example), than of "German expressionism." Strindberg (like Miller) projects the irrational inner life of characters through abrupt transitions and juxtapositions in time, place, mood, and theme; through hallucination, nightmare, and fantasy; and through generalized characters and symbolic images. See Seymour L. Flaxman, "The Debt of Williams and Miller to Ibsen and Strindberg," *Comparative Literature Studies* (Special Advance Issue, 1963): 51–59.

8. Miller's rationale here is almost identical with that expressed by Jean-Paul Sartre in remarks on the post-war theater in France, "Forgers of Myths" (1946), trans. Rosamond Gilder, in *The Modern Theatre*, ed. Robert W. Corrigan (New York, 1964), pp. 782, 784:

> "... we are not greatly concerned with psychology.... For us psychology is the most abstract of the sciences because it studies the workings of our passions without plunging them back into their true human surroundings, without their background of religious and moral values, the taboos and commandments of society, the conflicts of nations and classes, of rights, of wills, of actions.... We do not take time out for learned research, we feel no need of registering the imperceptible evolution of a character or a plot.... To us a *play* should not seem too familiar. Its greatness derives from its social and, in a certain sense, religious functions: it must remain a rite."

9. Arthur Miller, "Lincoln Repertory Theater—Challenge and Hope," *New York Times*, Jan. 19, 1964, Sec. II, p. 3.

10. Arthur Miller quoted in Barry Hyams, "A Theatre: Heart and Mind," *Theatre: Annual of the Repertory Theatre of Lincoln Center* 1 (1964): 61. Miller's American audience has not always been receptive to discursive analysis in drama, a fact that has greatly annoyed the author: "for a variety of reasons I think that the Anglo-Saxon audience cannot believe the reality of characters who live by principles and know very much about their own characters and situations, and who say what they know. Our drama ... is condemned, so to speak, to the emotions of subjectivism, which, as they approach knowledge and self-awareness, become less and less actual and real to us" (*C.P.*, 44–45). Europeans, Miller states in "The Playwright and the Atomic World," *Colorado Quarterly* 5 (1956): 117–37, are more philosophical and therefore maintain a higher regard for professional thinkers, particularly artists who arise "to articulate if not to immortalize their age." But Americans distrust ideas. They do not lack awareness; they simply do not care "to rationalize how [they] feel" (122). This pragmatic tendency, Miller warns, can be a great disadvantage in international politics, for if Americans "are content to appear solely as businessmen, technicians, and money-makers, [they] are handing to the Russian, who appears to make so much of culture, an advantage of regiments" (127).

11. Miller's phrase, quoted in Huftel, p. 196.

12. Interestingly (though coincidentally), the two plays have much in common in respect to theme, character, and technique. *Long Day's Journey into Night*, completed in 1940, was not published and produced until 1956; in that year Miller called the work, in "Concerning the Boom," *International Theatre Annual* 1 (1956): 88, "the most enthralling dramatic experience I have had since I first read Ibsen." For another expression of Miller's admiration for O'Neill, see "Eugene O'Neill: An Evaluation by Fellow Playwrights," ed. Edward T. Herbert, *Modern Drama* 6 (1963): 239–240.

13. Referring to *All My Sons*, *Death of Salesman*, and *The Misfits*, Popkin in "Arthur Miller Out West," p. 434, comments that Miller "likes to play with symbolic vocations."

14. The importance of the "legal metaphor" in *After the Fall* was brought to my attention by Mr. Paul Klamer.

15. As Henry Popkin writes, in "Arthur Miller's 'The Crucible,'" *College English* 26 (1964): 142, "like other works by Miller, *The Crucible* has something of the quality of a trial, of a court case, even before the formal hearings begin."

16. Quotations are taken from the Viking edition (1951). Besides simplifying Ibsen's polarity between a defiant individual and an oppressive community, Miller "modernized" the dialogue, shortened some speeches, and de-emphasized Ibsen's poisoned water symbolism (in his Preface to the Viking edition, 1951, he stated that his major change was simply to expedite continuity by reducing the number of scene and act divisions).
Miller's modifications have been variously interpreted. Robert Brustein, *The Theatre of Revolt* (Boston, 1964), p. 72, claimed that Miller "watered down" Ibsen's aristocratic bias. In the same vein, Alan Thompson, "Professor's Debauch," *Theatre Arts* 35 (March 1951): 27, found the protagonist of the adaptation "a Hollywoodish-heroical Champion of Democracy, too serious and wise to descend to horseplay or to delight in making a rumpus." However, Welland, p. 47, saw the adapter "increasing the element of humour." According to Benjamin Nelson, *Arthur Miller* (London, 1970), pp. 142–44, Miller mistakenly glorified an "ambivalent" protagonist, who in Ibsen's work is "both heroic rebel and fool," unable to separate a noble cause "from his inflated and bruised ego." And

according to Martin Dworkin, in "Miller and Ibsen," *Humanist* 11 (June 1951): 110–15, Ibsen and Miller are both attacking irrationality, whether it be found in a democratic majority, an aristocratic elite, or an idiosyncratic individual. See also Arthur Miller, "Ibsen's Message for Today's World," *New York Timers*, Dec. 24,1950, Sec. II, pp. 3–4; and David Bronson, "An Enemy of the People: A Key to Arthur Miller's Art and Ethics," *Comparative Drama* 2 (1968): 229–47.

17. Miller has protested against injustice in the United States and abroad in many essays and interviews (see the Selected Bibliography). Most recently, as he reports in his long essay, "In China," *Atlantic* 243 (March 1979): 97, 98, he found a striking absence of legal principles in Communist China. "The law [is] a subject in which no one in China seems to have the least interest.... Certain things have surely been learned, among them that under socialism, no less than capitalism, the human being is unsafe without the protection of his rights by law, and a law that the state is obliged to obey." Robert A. Martin, in his introduction to *The Theater Essays of Arthur Miller* (New York, 1978), p. xxxiii, points out the recurrence in Miller's writing of "law, lawyers, a policeman, courtrooms, or judges as representatives of truth, justice, and morality.... *After the Fall*, although very different thematically and structurally, also places the protagonist on trial in much the same way that Joe Keller in *All My Sons*, Willy Loman in *Death of a Salesman*, John Proctor in *The Crucible*, and Eddie Carbone in *A View from the Bridge* had also undergone moral and legal litigation."

18. The confrontation between Victor and Walter in *The Price* composes a simpler structure.

19. His structural principles reflect the teaching, as presented in *Write That Play*, of his instructor in playwriting at the University of Michigan, Kenneth Thorpe Rowe, who is probably the source of his interest in Ibsen. Some apparently influential observations made by Professor Rowe are the following: "Complications may also be interwoven by the introduction of a new complication while an earlier complication is still in suspense. The answer to each minor dramatic question points toward an answer to the major dramatic question" (58). In *A Doll's House*, "the antecedent material is no longer introductory, but the center of the immediate conflict, the past coming to life in the present and creating drama" (203). "Expressionism, although it has the appearance of fantasy, is an extension of realism inward to the areas of psychological experience and of abstract ideas.... Expressionism is an attempt to lift the skullcap and look inside at the brain and see how it works [Miller, *C.P.*, 23: "we would see the inside of a man's head"], or to X-ray human life in society and see the forces at work underneath the external phenomena" (358–59). "Man is capable of no great goodness without the energy of passion, and passion misguided is proportionately destructive" (404). "The exaltation of tragedy, whether Creek, Shakespearean, or modern, is a response to the spectacle of man's power to maintain the integrity of his own mind and will in the face of the utmost life can inflict" (406).

To point out Rowe's influence is not to denigrate in any way Miller's inventiveness; indeed, Rowe himself referred (in 1939) to a "brilliant young man" (presumably Miller) who came to him with "a new method for revision": "his last rewriting was for the purpose of eliminating every superfluous word, and especially to eliminate expository analysis for direct revelation of the character" (343–45). Miller recognized his central problem quite early.

20. "The speeches in *All My Sons*," John Prudhoe writes in "Arthur Miller and the Tradition of Tragedy," *English Studies* 43 (1962): 436, "frequently remind me off

Elizabethan and Jacobean patterned language in their balance of phrases and conscious repetition of words and ideas."

21. A similar exchange takes place later in the play. "But sometimes, Willy, it's better for a man just to walk away," Bernard says. Willy responds, "but if you can't walk away?"

22. Albert Hunt, "Realism and Intelligence," *Encore* 7 (May 1980): 12–17, makes the same point. But Weales, p. 179, believes that "the lines are as awkward and as stagily false as those in John Drinkwater's *Oliver Cromwell*." It is true that the language of *The Crucible*, supposedly patterned after the dialect spoken by Salemites at the end of the seventeenth century, is often anachronistic, especially insofar as the frequent use of the subjunctive ("it were sport"; "there be no blush"; "he have his goodness now"). The actual testimony recorded at the Salem trials, reprinted in *What Happened in Salem?*, ed. David Levin (New York, 1980), is far less archaic.

GILBERT DEBUSSCHER

"Minting their Separate Wills": Tennessee Williams and Hart Crane

Although unusually talkative and candid about his private life, Tennessee Williams was always comparatively reticent about his work. In fact he expressed strong feelings about the need for secrecy in order to protect "a thing that depends on seclusion till its completion for its safety."[1] Those who expected his *Memoirs* of 1975 to shed light on his writing were therefore disappointed.[2] However, he alluded repeatedly over the years to other writers who had deeply influenced him. When pressed for names he never failed to mention Hart Crane, D.H. Lawrence, and Anton Chekhov.

The influence of Lawrence and Chekhov has been examined extensively, but that of Hart Crane has been largely neglected by critics. This essay deals first with the indisputable traces of influence: the biographical evidence; the "presence" of Crane in titles, mottoes, and allusions; the note Williams wrote in 1965 for the slipcover of his recording of Crane's poems. Second, it develops a case suggesting that *The Glass Menagerie*, traditionally considered predominantly autobiographical, owes more to Crane than hitherto suspected. Last, an analysis of the one-act *Steps Must Be Gentle* provides new perspectives on the influence of Crane in *Suddenly Last Summer*.

I

The evidence of Crane's importance to Williams is overwhelming. Fist introduced to the slim volume of Crane's *Collected Poems* by Clark Mills

From *Modern Drama* 26, no. 4 (Winter 1983). © 1983 by University of Toronto.

McBurney, a poet whom he had befriended in St. Louis in 1935, Williams himself acknowledged his debt in 1944 in the "Frivolous Version" of his "Preface to My Poems": "It was Clark who warned me of the existence of people like Hart Crane and Rimbaud and Rilke, and my deep and sustained admiration for Clark's writing gently but firmly removed my attention from the more obvious to the purer voices in poetry. About this time I acquired my copy of Hart Crane's collected poems which I began to read with gradual comprehension."[3]

In this early mention Williams already reserved a special place for Crane, associating him—as he will throughout his career—with "the purer voices in poetry." "Acquired" was, however, a euphemism. In reality Williams had pilfered the copy from the library of Washington University in St. Louis, because it did not, in his opinion, get the readership it deserved. In the "Serious Version" of the same "Preface" that single book is presented as Williams's whole permanent library: "Symbolically I found a lot of books inconvenient to carry with me and gradually they dropped along the way— till finally there was only one volume with me, the book of Hart Crane. I have it with me today, my only library and all of it." And he says further: "... I am inclined to value Crane a little above Eliot or anyone else because of his organic purity and sheer breathtaking power. I feel that he stands with Keats and Shakespeare and Whitman."[4]

Shortly after coming into possession of the *Poems*, Williams further "acquired" a portrait of his favorite poet from a book in the Jacksonville Public Library. He had it framed and took it with him, along with the poems, wherever his bohemian career led him. Out of the sixteen allusions to Crane in the *Letters to Donald Windham*, three are to that treasured portrait.[5]

In addition to these two tangible reminders of Crane in Williams's surroundings, clear traces of the poet's presence can be found in the plays. In *You Touched Me!*, the dramatization of a D.H. Lawrence story which Williams wrote in collaboration with Donald Windham in the early forties, there is already a passing reference to Crane. When Hadrian reads at random from Matilda's book of verse, he comes across the lines "How like a caravan my heart—Across the desert moved towards yours!," and he wonders "Towards whose? Who is this H.C. it's dedicated to?"; Matilda shyly replies "Hart Crane. An American poet who died ten years ago."[6] Besides the explicit reference, the two lines read by Hadrian recall the "speechless caravan" in the fifth stanza of "To Brooklyn Bridge," the piece with which Crane's epic of America opens.[7]

The motto of *A Streetcar Named Desire*[8] (1947) comes from the fifth stanza of Crane's "The Broken Tower," a poetic farewell and a densely

compressed account of his own career, completed barely a month before his
suicide in the Caribbean near Florida:

> And so it was I entered the broken world
> To trace the visionary company of love, its voice
> An instant in the wind (I know not whither hurled)
> But not for long to hold each desperate choice. (pp. 139–140)

These four lines describe Blanche DuBois's dramatic march to oblivion
which began with her fateful entrance into the Vieux Carré. They reveal the
playwright's conception of not one, but two "broken world[s]"[9]: that of faded
illusions (the crumbled plantation in the past), and that of disheartening
reality (the dingy apartment of the present); "one gone with the wind, the
other barely worth having."[10]

This motto, then, introduces the first of the strong polarities from
which the play derives much of its tension. It reveals in the playwright an
attitude of deliberateness and detachment from the material of his plays with
which Williams is rarely credited by his commentators. The motto signals
that, since both Belle Reve and Elysian Fields are stamped as "broken
world[s]," and since life is defined as the making of "desperate choice[s]," the
existential itineraries of both Stanley and Blanche—not of one to the
exclusion of the other—lead to final disaster."[11] It is a measure of the
playwright's artistic control that the balance—or ambiguity—introduced by
the preliminary warning of the motto is maintained to the very end of the
play.

In the following year, 1948, Williams published *Summer and Smoke*.
This title comes from Crane's "Emblems of Conduct." The alliterative
phrase appears in the only two lines—the first two of the three quoted
below—that are Crane's own (p. 68), inserted between fragments gleaned
from the then unpublished manuscripts of Samuel Greenberg:

> By that time summer and smoke were past.
> Dolphins still played, arching the horizons,
> But only to build memories of spiritual gates.

The peaceful autumnal image sums up the general mood of the poem, "a
sadly beautiful appraisal of a world no longer animated by a genuine religious
or visionary consciousness...."[12]

This title from Crane's work evokes the nostalgia of a world long past
its apogee and now declining.[13] Williams's clear intent is further reinforced

in the only passage where Crane's phrase is echoed, when Alma describes her former "Puritan" self (and by inference all those who lived by this code), late in the play, as having "died last summer—suffocated in smoke from something on fire inside her."[14]

To those who perceive this variation of the title words and are aware of the nostalgic message of Crane's poem, Williams is suggesting through Alma that the South and its traditional way of life have collapsed under the burden of a code of morals emphasizing spiritual values and repressing the claims of man's physical nature. The title is, in fact, Williams's poetic statement of his theme of fading civilization and the disappearance of the Old South, a theme which is to be found not only here, but also in *The Glass Menagerie* and *A Streetcar Named Desire*.

Although Williams's letters mention Crane in following years as often as before, it is only in 1959, with the publication of *Sweet Bird of Youth*, that Crane regains his former prominence in the plays. The motto here comes from Crane's *White Buildings* collection, where it appears in a piece entitled "Legend" (p. 65):

> Relentless caper for all those who step
> The legend of their youth into the noon.

These two lines are pressed into service by Williams as a warning.[15] R.W.B. Lewis describes the poem: "It was as one who had learned the danger of moral despair and who had embodied the lesson in song that Crane offered his example to the young: as a 'relentless caper'—a playfully serious and morally unrelenting and impenitent model—for those who will in turn move through youthful experience toward maturity. Crane presents his own life as allegory to those who have yet to live theirs."[16]

The selection by Williams of this particular passage introduces one of the play's main motifs, the attaining of maturity and the danger of trying to extend the ideal fiction of youth, its "legend," into the heart of middle age. It thus establishes Williams's definitely moralistic intentions. Like Crane's poem, his play relates an experience which instructs us about the nature of good and evil, and from which rules can be deduced to govern the conduct of life. The dramatic itinerary of the characters, their "[r]elentless caper," is presented as a warning; their "legend," in both meanings of "key" and "exemplary life," is meant to convey a message of moral import. Chance's final speech about recognizing "the enemy, Time, in us all," however clumsily tacked on, confirms the seemingly paradoxical ambition of *Sweet Bird of Youth* to be a modern morality play,[17] as implicitly announced in the motto from Crane.

Whether they appear as motto or title, the lines from Crane are important, less as reminders of the poems from which they are lifted, than for their intrinsic meanings which provide a particular viewpoint on the material, a perspective suggested by the author on the play's events and characters. Because they constitute a standard by which the play must be measured, they are an integral and indispensable part of it.

In 1962, in *The Night of the Iguana*, Williams again alludes to Crane. A reference to the portrait of Crane painted by the Mexican artist David Siqueiros in 1931 appears in the dialogue between Shannon and Hannah, a painter who is also the play's amateur psychoanalyst. She is trying to sketch a picture not so much of Shannon's outward appearance as of a deeper reality hidden within him:

> HANNAH ...You're a very difficult subject. When the Mexican painter Siqueiros did his portrait of the American poet Hart Crane he had to paint him with closed eyes because he couldn't paint his eyes open—there was too much suffering in them and he couldn't paint it.
>
> SHANNON Sorry, but I'm not going to close my eyes for you. I'm hypnotizing myself—at least trying to—by looking at the light on the orange tree ... leaves.
>
> HANNAH That's all right. I can paint your eyes open."[18]

The reference constitutes an invitation to compare Shannon and Crane, but the lady's curt remark firmly establishes the discrepancy between her subject and that of Siqueiros. Shannon's self-indulgent histrionics are deflated by this deliberate comparison with the suffering experienced by Crane and registered in the painting. Like the submerged contrast between Shannon and his patron, St. Lawrence,[19] the allusion to Crane reveals the blend of compassionate understanding and irony with which Williams regards his character.

Williams's continued preoccupation with the poet culminated in 1965, when he agreed to read a selection of poems by Crane for Caedmon Records and to provide a note for the slipcover.[20] In the note Williams reveals his familiarity with the facts of Crane's life and mentions two early scholarly works devoted to the poet: the "superb" biography written by Philip Horton (1937), and the "marvelous" collection of letters edited by Brom Weber (1952). The particular incidents on which Williams concentrates are illustrations of themes and motifs basic to his own creative work. He focuses with characteristic dramatic flair on the most intense moments of Crane's life, the day of his suicide and the emotionally charged night immediately preceding it. Of the latter we are told that Crane "had visited the sailors' quarters and the visit had turned out badly. They had treated him mockingly and violently." Regarding the day itself, Williams describes how Peggy Cowley, the woman with whom Crane was traveling back to the United States, "had ... suffered, that same night before, the pointless accident of a book of matches blowing up in her hand and burning her hand severely. She was not in a state to sympathize much with her friend, and so what happened happened."

Crane's confrontation with the outside world is presented here as similar to that of many of the more sensitive characters in Williams's work, particularly the artists and poets. Wherever they turn in their search for understanding or togetherness, in their quest for "the visionary company of love," they meet with rejection, hostility, or indifference. The slipcover note further mentions the writing block Crane experienced in the last two years of his life, after adverse criticism of *The Bridge* had reawakened self-doubt:

> ... Crane had lived and worked with such fearful intensity—and without fearful intensity Crane was unable to work at all—that his nerves were exhausted and for many months he had been able to produce only one important poem, *The Broken Tower*, a poem that contains these beautiful and ominous lines:

> > *The bells, I say, the bells*
> > *Break down their tower.*[21]

"By the bells breaking down their tower," Williams goes on to say, Crane "undoubtedly meant the romantic and lyric intensity of his vocation." That Williams considers the lines "ominous" indicates that he views the creative process here, as elsewhere in his own work, as a consuming experience.[22] The production of poetry, and more generally of art, leaves the artist ultimately exhausted, spent as a runner and broken in body.

One cannot help noting the parallel with Williams's own career, which went into a prolonged eclipse in the early 1960's—at the time he recorded the Crane poems—when he doggedly rewrote *The Milk Train Doesn't Stop Here Anymore*, and relied more and more heavily on alcohol and drugs to alleviate doubts about his artistic future. His remarks about Crane's state of mind could therefore apply equally to himself: "He lived in a constant inner turmoil and storm that liquor, which he drank recklessly, was no longer able to quieten, to hold in check."

Finally, the Caedmon note contains a quotation whose gloss points to one of the fascinations Crane's life held for Williams. The short passage from

"For the Marriage of Faustus and Helen" (erroneously identified by Williams as belonging to "The Broken Tower") reads: "There is the world dimensional for those untwisted by the love of things irreconcilable" (p. 98). Williams interprets these lines as follows: "[T]he meaning ... is more open to varying interpretations. Could he have meant that his vocation as a poet of extraordinary purity, as well as intensity, was hopelessly at odds with his night-time search for love in waterfront bars?" The homosexual Williams of the *Memoirs* is here clearly identifying with that facet of Crane's personality which he detects in the cryptic lines.[23]

Although obviously devoted to Crane, the record note reveals, beyond the sketched portrait of the poet, a figure that is modeled after Williams himself and all the poet-characters in whom he had projected himself up to 1965. It strongly suggests, further, that if Crane enduringly captured Williams's imagination, the cause was biographical as well as poetic. Williams was aware, as he later stated in an interview with Cecil Brown,[24] of the truly stunning similarity of his and Crane's formative years, family situations, and aspirations. Crane's small-town origins, his family life, torn between egotistical parents who turned him into the battlefield of their marital strife; his fervent attachment to both his neurotic mother (with whom he was later to fall out) and his indulgent, doting grandmother; his early aversion to and later reconciliation with a father who opposed his aspirations as a poet and insisted that he enter the family business; the bohemian wanderlust that prevented him from settling down permanently;[25] his bouts of ill health which were often psychosomatic in origin; and finally his uphill fight fur artistic integrity in an uncomprehending world, his torment by spells of self-doubt and despair that led him to suicide—all of these conditions, together with a sexuality unfocused but predominantly homoerotic, were traits of Crane's life and personality in which Williams must have recognized himself as in a mirror. I submit, therefore, that Hart Crane contributed forcefully to Williams's perception of himself as revealed by the semiautobiographical characters who populate his plays: the figure of the wandering poet, the doomed artist who haunts the published work, appearing as early as *Battle of Angels* (1938); a figure who finds his most surprising incarnations in Tom Wingfield in *The Glass Menagerie* (1944) and Sebastian Venable in *Suddenly Last Summer* (1958).

II

The Glass Menagerie belongs to the period of Williams's greatest involvement with the poetry of Hart Crane, a time when the playwright quotes from

Crane repeatedly both in the correspondence with Donald Windham and in the plays. Although at first sight Crane appears to be totally absent from this particular play, in fact it is only the mode of Crane's "presence" in *The Glass Menagerie* which is different. Whereas in *A Streetcar Named Desire* and *Summer and Smoke* he is emphatically visible through motto or title, in this case he pervades the texture of the play without being explicitly mentioned.

There is nevertheless one objective clue (perhaps there are even two, as I shall point out) that attests to Williams's use of Crane. In Scene Six, Amanda appears in her "resurrected" yellow dress for the "jonquil scene," a moment of great intensity whose special quality Williams describes in the stage direction: "*the legend of her youth is nearly revived.*"[26] One recalls again the passage from Crane's poem "Legend" which was to serve as motto for *Sweet Bird of Youth*. This stage direction is a clear hint for the reader and the director aware of the Crane–Williams crosscurrents that Amanda, in her pathetic attempt to recapture her past glory, is to experience the disillusionment of those who force themselves into a "[r]elentless caper," ceaselessly reliving their pasts. The borrowing further confirms that the Southern background recollected by Amanda is actually a "legend," that is, both a key to understanding her character and motivations, and a story, a fable, even perhaps a lie. It suggests that the past was never as idyllic as she would like to remember it, but at the same time—to those who are aware of Crane's poem, and beyond it, of John Donne's "The Canonization"[27]—it indicates that this is a cautionary tale for all those who must turn their backs on their youthful pasts and move forward to maturity and decline. The borrowing relegated to a stage direction is a muted reminder at this crucial moment that Amanda's fate is intended as a model, a "legend" for consideration and enlightenment.

A more cryptic reminder of Crane may be found later in the same scene, again in a stage direction. In the course of a conversation with Jim, Tom rhapsodically describes a future that involves neither his mother and sister, nor the shoe factory. As the image of "the sailing vessel with the Jolly Roger again" is projected on a screen in the background, Tom leans over the rail of the fire escape on which he stands, which has now become the rail of an imaginary ocean liner, and the stage direction reads: "*He looks like a voyager*" (201). Williams's use of "voyager" cannot fail, for someone familiar (as the playwright was) with the Crane canon, to evoke the "Voyages" poems. Indeed the word so fittingly limns Hart Crane that John Unterecker entitled his monumental 1969 biography of the poet, *Voyager: A Life of Hart Crane*.

The short scene in which Tom leans on the rail may be, then, a dramatic reconstruction of the last minutes of the poet's life before he escaped, as Tom is planning to do, from a world that had become too oppressive to bear.[28] What we may have, therefore, is a shadowy portrait in Tom Wingfield of Hart Crane himself, at a most critical moment of his life. Just as Williams's own face could be glimpsed behind his portrait of Crane in the record note, so the figure of Crane shows through Tom Wingfield's portrait in *The Glass Menagerie*, providing it with tantalizing shadows.

Moreover, although there is by now a long tradition, supported by declarations of the playwright himself, that the figure of Amanda Wingfield is a portrait of Williams's own mother, one could make a convincing case for Grace Hart Crane, the poet's mother, as the model for some aspects of the high-strung, possessive Amanda. One should recall, in this connection, the anecdote of Mrs. Williams's visit to Chicago for a performance of *The Glass Menagerie*, at the end of which she was appalled to hear that Laurette Taylor might have considered her the real-life model for the character she portrayed in the play. Furthermore, a growing number of commentators have noticed, again following the playwright's indications,[29] that the play is hardly a faithful picture of the Williamses' circumstances around 1935/1936, and that the three characters supposedly modeled on the author and his family have all undergone important changes in the process of dramatization.

If one remembers the picture of Crane's mother as it emerges from the accounts of Philip Horton and John Unterecker, however, one realizes not only that the relationships of the sons with their respective mothers are comparable, but also that the two women show a remarkable degree of resemblance even in details. For example, Mrs. Crane, suddenly deprived of the financial security that had thus far seemed assured, contemplated taking a job as "hostess in a restaurant perhaps, assistant in one of the city's hotels, anything that would let her draw on the only assets she had, her charm and her beauty."[30] Of this situation more than an echo can be found in the job Amanda actually holds (she being a more practical-minded woman) "at Famous-Barr ... demonstrating those ... (*She indicates a brassiere with her hands*)" (154). In Williams's conception the job—which his own mother never had to envisage—capitalized on Amanda's physical appeal; one of the early drafts sent to Audrey Wood reads: "(Amanda has been working as a model for a matron's dresses at downtown depart. store and has just lost the job because of faded appearance)."[31] The picture of Mrs. Crane painted by Unterecker in the following paragraph is exactly like that of Amanda, with her reminiscences about the carefree Blue Mountain girl courted by seventeen gentlemen callers: "As she and Hart would talk through her problems, both of them would look back fondly to Hart's childhood, to the days when financial security seemed limitless—the good times of gardeners, maids, cooks, chauffeurs, handymen, tutors—until, magnifying the past out of all proportion, they would make the present unbearable."[32]

These glimpses of Grace Crane cohere into a prototype for Amanda as plausible as the playwright's own mother. But the resemblance between Mrs. Crane and Amanda is never more convincing than in the following passage: "For Grace's real problem—and to a considerable extent, Hart's—was the memory of former affluence.... Each of them found it easier to eat badly than to dress badly. 'Keeping up appearances' was for Grace not just a casual compulsion but a life-and-death matter."[33] Such a portrait anticipates Amanda's DAR outfit, her compulsive refurbishing of the apartment, the purchase of new clothes for Laura, her metamorphosis into a Southern belle in her own "resurrected" dress, and her evocation of the past for the benefit of the bewildered Jim O'Connor.

Let me now advance a further argument: beyond these strong biographical parallels with Crane and his mother, the play also reflects the influence of Crane as a poet and, in particular, of one poem, "The Wine Menagerie," from the collection *White Buildings*. To begin with, there is the striking similarity of the titles. The present title of the play was arrived at only after various other possibilities—such as "Portrait of a Girl in Glass," "The Gentleman Caller," and "if You Breathe It Breaks or Portrait of a Girl in Glass"—had been discarded.[34] I suggest, therefore, that only after growing aware of the correspondences between his play and Crane's poem, presumably late in the process of fashioning the final version, Williams hit upon this felicitous title for the play that was to establish his reputation throughout the world. It is my guess that at some point during the rehearsals—perhaps well into December 1944, when Eddie Dowling and George Jean Nathan "advised" him to introduce the drunk scene finally included at the beginning of Scene Six[35]—Williams was reminded of "The Wine Menagerie" and used this as the spark for his final title. The first two lines of the poem could have served, in fact, as a reasonable starting frame for the whole scene:

> Invariably when the wine redeems the sight
> Narrowing the mustard scansions of the eyes.... (p. 92)

Regarding these lines, R.W.B. Lewis comments that "[t]he consumption of much wine ... suddenly clarified the poet's vision and greatly increased his interpretive and creative powers."[36] Tom's drunkenness in the play is a source of similar vision, and even the "faint Eucharistic overtone" that Lewis discerns in the association of "wine" and "redeems" finds a parallel—though perhaps a sardonic one—in the Easter symbolism that pervades Tom's speech.

In his conversation with Laura, Tom presents the stage show he has just seen in terms that leave little doubt of its symbolic connection to his own fate: "... There was a big stage show! The headliner on this stage show was Malvolio the Magician. He performed wonderful tricks [...] But the wonderfullest trick of all was the coffin trick. We nailed him into a coffin and he got out of the coffin without removing one nail [...] There is a trick that would come in handy for me—get me out of this two-by-four situation!" (167). Through Tom's report we come to realize that escaping the social and emotional web in which he is entangled without hurting anyone and hence without feeling guilty is a trick that only a magician could bring off. This truth revealed in drunkenness helps justify Tom's final action in the play; it helps make the audience accept the fact that "to escape from a trap he has to act without pity" (129).

The second stanza of the poem introduces the idea that the whole should be seen as the intoxicated musing—"a sort of boozy approximation of direct statement"[37]—of the poet, who also figures as a character in the bar scene which the lines evoke. This double role of writer and protagonist is paralleled in the play, where Tom is both the narrator and a character in the story he tells. Moreover, several Crane commentators have noticed that—like the play—"The Wine Menagerie" supports a reading in terms of the poet's biography.[38] And there are further similarities: Crane's poem suggests, as Sherman Paul has emphasized, that "[t]he man and woman, whose combat [the narrator-actor] witnesses ... are father and mother seen from the 'distance' of childhood."[39] This is essentially the point of view of Tom, whose "distance in time" (236) provides him with a perspective akin to, although not identical with, that of the poet in Crane's work.[40] The seasonal setting and atmosphere of the two works present additional affinities. The bleak early winter landscape of the poem, which contributes to the Eliotian atmosphere of the whole, is traceable also in the general mood of the play. It informs the urban setting common to play and poem, and presides over the play's description of the "[c]ouples ... [in] the alley ... kissing behind ash pits and telephone poles" (179), who could have been lifted by Williams from the context Crane had earlier devised for them.

Thematically, too, the poem offers a basis for comparison with the play. Uncharacteristically for Crane, "[l]oss is the primary emotion the poem reaches into...."[41] Now "loss" is a key concept in Williams's vision, a feeling that he finds inseparable from the human condition. "[T]he monosyllable of the clock is Loss, loss, loss, unless you devote your heart to its opposition," he has said.[42] Surveying the isolation of the derelict "menagerie" assembled in the bar. Crane's poem ends in sadness, or—as Paul has aptly put it—on "a low plateau of resolve."[43] This again is a perfect description of the final moment of *The Glass Menagerie*. The mood of melancholy and nostalgia suffusing the play may therefore owe as much to Hart Crane as to Anton Chekhov, who has long been thought its primary source.

The nostalgia at the end of the play is poignantly enhanced by Tom's ultimate departure, by his painful act of tearing himself away from his family and the guilt associated with this emotional and physical exile. Tom's basic motivation—a determination to be true to his own self—and his final summoning up of courage are clearly foreshadowed in the poem, where the young man is exhorted to:

> Rise from the dates and crumbs. And walk away ....
> ....
> Beyond the wall ....
> ....
> And fold your exile on your back again .... (p. 94)

Both characters come in the end to accept, not without second thoughts, that freedom and its corollary, loneliness, are essential to the activity which they see as their fundamental reason to live.

The situation of Tom in the epilogue may have been suggested by that of the speaker in the poem, a solitary man in a bar looking at a display of multicolored bottles which reflect the movements and attitudes of patrons, images encompassing the past as much as the present. Peering in drunken fascination at the changing surfaces of the "glozening decanters," the poet manages to focus on essentials, "[n]arrowing the mustard scansions of the eyes." He thus sees through or beyond the chaotic reality that otherwise claims his attention, and through vision he imposes an order on it, "asserts a vision in the slumbering gaze" (p. 92).

Tom looks not at bottles on display in a bar, but at delicately colored vials in the window of a perfume shop. The vials too present an informal, unpatterned reality, "like bits of a shattered rainbow" (237). They reflect, far beyond the drab winter of the city, the past of Tom's family life, "conscript[ing]" him (to use Crane's word) to the shadowy glow of the menagerie.[44] In Williams's case, the play itself is the vision that imposes order and exorcises—if only temporarily—the conflicting feelings of relief and guilt stirred in Tom by memory.

Finally, poem and play have a further point of confluence. Crane's poem establishes a number of mythic parallels for its central incident, a confrontation between a man and a woman in a bar. Evoking the violent meetings of Judith and Holofernes, Salome and John the Baptist, and Petrushka and his "valentine," it presents the experience as one of dismemberment and decapitation. The figurine central to the glass collection, the unicorn, undergoes a comparable mutilation when its little horn is accidentally broken off. This interpretation is particularly apt if one recalls that the glass animal represents Rose, the playwright's sister, and that the loss of the horn is probably an attenuated echo of her prefrontal lobotomy—a modern surgical version of decapitation—which alleviated her schizophrenia but left her maimed for life.

Both poem and play can rightfully be seen, then, as "an actual incident, in a clear setting, with visible characters, and progressing from a meandering meditation to a moment of clear decision—a decision, needless to say, about the exercise of the poet's visionary power and touching upon his creative resolve."[45] Rather than being considered an indulgent wallowing in sentimental reminiscences, *The Glass Menagerie* may be viewed through a Cranean glass as a dramatic statement about the artist and his predicament. This perspective may lead to a further conclusion, again constituting a warning for all who would limit the play to a faithful account of Williams's early days in St. Louis, that *The Glass Menagerie* is as much literature as confession, as much imaginative reading as autobiography, as much Crane as Williams.

III

The publication in 1980 of a short play entitled *Steps Must Be Gentle*[46] shed new light not only on Williams's familiarity with the facts of Crane's biography, but also on the pervasive influence of Crane, both as man and poet, on Williams's writing and particularly on the play *Suddenly Last Summer*. Specifically described in the subtitle as "A Dramatic Reading for Two Performers," *Steps Must Be Gentle* presents an imaginary dialogue between Hart Crane and his mother. Although the play takes place in an unspecified location,[47] sea sounds constantly remind us that the poet is speaking from the bottom of the ocean, presumably immediately after Grace Hart Crane's death on 30 July 1947.[48] There is virtually no plot. The tenuous "connection" is interrupted several tunes, threatened with extinction; sentences are left unfinished, and Hart feigns to misunderstand or not to hear what his mother is so eager to tell him.

The short piece concentrates entirely on the reproachful reminiscences of the protagonists. Grace cannot, even after death, forgive her son for his four-year-long silence. Hart, who wants nothing more than to be left in peace at the bottom of the ocean, remembers in icy tones how both his parents turned him into a human misfit, how his father made him beg for the little money he doled out to him, and his mother, for recognition of the sexual deviancy he had confessed to her. Grace counters by pointing out that the last fifteen years of her life were devoted to preserving and enhancing Hart's posthumous reputation, to gathering the poetry that she now considers, over his protestations, as much hers as his. From the outset she appears to be on the verge of telling her son how she managed to survive without friends or money, dedicating herself totally to this work of love. When his mother broaches the subject of his deviant sexuality again, Hart changes the conversation by insisting on the question of her occupation, and she finally reveals, "I've been employed at nights as a scrubwoman, Hart" (326).

The revelation of the degrading of his once beautiful and elegant mother profoundly upsets the dead poet; his jealously preserved rest is disturbed forever, one assumes, since he is heard at the end of the play calling out her name "(*more and more faintly but with anguish*)" (327) in an ironic echo of her own insistent "Hart?—Hart?—Son?" "(*repeated a number of times in various tones, from tenderly beseeching to desperately demanding*)" (317) at the start of the play. The outcome makes it clear that Grace has reached her aim: she has broken through the willful indifference with which her son had surrounded himself. She has imposed her emotional blackmail on him; he is again, and now forever, dependent on her.

The title itself is from Crane's poem "My Grandmother's Love Letters," in the collection *White Buildings*. It expresses with painful irony the perception that to reach a balanced understanding of sorts, to bridge the distance—physical, temporal, and emotional—that separates them, Hart and Grace must proceed cautiously. "Over the greatness of such space / Steps must be gentle," the poet warns (p. 63). The characters in the play are unable, however, to heed the warning implicit in the title.

At the start of their impossible conversation, Hart reminds his mother that "[i]t's been a long while since we have existed for each other" (320), that death has severed the blood tie that once bound them together. Using a metaphor from the poem "At Melville's Tomb," where the "dice of drowned men's bones.... /.../ Beat on the dusty shore" (p. 104), he says: "There is no blood in bones that were cast and scattered as gambler's dice on the sea's floor ..." (321). This borrowing and the poem from which it comes throw an interesting light on the relationship of Williams to Melville, a relationship that might possibly involve a third presence. Although there is no doubt that Williams was acquainted firsthand with the novelist,[49] it is equally clear that he was often reminded of Melville through Crane's direct or oblique references to him, as he states in a letter of 25 March 1946: "... I was reminded of that work [*Billy Budd*] recently while reading over Crane's 'Cutty Sark.'"[50] The quotation from Melville that we shall find in *Suddenly Last Summer* may therefore be, paradoxically, another indirect reference to Crane.

A further allusion to Crane's poetry emerges in the poet's punning reminder that "'Sundered parentage,' Grace, is that from which I chose to descend to the sea's floor ..." (321). The irony is bitter and manifold. In his evocation of "the curse of sundered parentage" in his poem "Quaker Hill" (p. 51), the poet is talking about personal experience, as commentators have recognized, but he transcends this immediate context to indicate symbolically the "cleavage between present and past,"[51] "the sundering of Pocahontas and Maquokeeta."[52] In the play, however, the phrase "sundered parentage" is brought back to its literal sense, as is the verb "to descend," which refers metaphorically both to genealogical origin ("'Sundered parentage,' Grace, is that from which I ... descend") and to actual movement ("I chose to descend to the sea's floor"). The pun, reminiscent of Crane's verbal strategies elsewhere,[53] thus implies a barbed reproach that his parents' marital feud and the psychic consequences it entailed for him were the curse which presided over Crane's suicide.

This reproach is followed by another, related allusion, again to stanza five of "The Broken Tower," the passage of Crane's poetry frequently mentioned by Williams. In this context the lines regain a literal meaning. After referring to his antagonistic progenitors as his "Sundered parentage," the poet naturally thinks of his birth, his "enter[ing] the broken world" (321), a reality whose fragmentation he would seek to overcome through poetry. Grace later echoes these and earlier lines of the same poem when she reveals to Hart that she has had no occupation since his death other than the preserving of his reputation: "... I have carried the stones to build your tower again" (326). The comment is fraught with poignant irony. The metaphorical tower had all too painful and unpoetic a literalness for the mother who, having contributed definitely, though perhaps unintentionally, to the fragmentation of the world of her poet-son, then devoted the last fifteen years of her miserable life as a scrubwoman to gathering material on which his posthumous fame would firmly rest.

In this play more than anywhere else in Williams's work, the elements selected from Crane's biography reveal a parallelism with the playwright's own life which could not fail to have been recognized by Williams. The contrast between an elegant, charming mother and a mercantile, obtuse father, the tortured love–hate relationship with both of them, the pathetic and painful acknowledgment of homosexuality[54]—all of these factors must have struck a deeply responsive chord.

In 1947, *Steps Must Be Gentle* contained the seeds of what was to develop into *Suddenly Last Summer* (1958).[55] Nancy M. Tischler has already suspected that the figure of Hart Crane may have served as a model for Sebastian Venable,[56] but much more than a simple identification between the two poets can now be traced to Crane's biography. Central to the resemblance between *Steps Must Be Gentle* and *Suddenly Last Summer* is the motivation ascribed to the two mothers, Grace Hart Crane and Violet Venable: their determination to preserve their sons' posthumous reputations. In the early play Grace describes this ambition in words that might equally well have been spoken by Violet: "I have made it my dedication, my vocation, to protect your name, your legend, against the filthy scandals that you'd seemed determined to demolish them with. Despite my age, my illness ..." (325–326).

In *Suddenly Last Summer* the real-life traits of Hart Crane appear splintered, divided up among three characters: first, the dead Sebastian, the homosexual author of a limited, practically unknown body of work reserved for a coterie, who travels restlessly in pursuit of "vision"; second, the "glacially brilliant" Dr. Cuckrowicz with his "icy charm"[57] (350), in whom both Mrs. Venable and Catharine recognize a number of Sebastian's features, and who represents an aspect of Crane seen in *Steps*, where Grace reproaches her son for his "icy language" (319) and frigid attitude; finally, Catharine, whose uncompromising insistence on the truth threatens the Sebastian myth, and who embodies the self-destructive tendencies that led to Crane's suicide.

The tortured relationship between Hart and Grace, the pattern of a genteel but domineering mother and a submissive son, the figure of an absent, despised, or otherwise negligible father, and the use of emotional blackmail are all aspects of *Steps Must Be Gentle* clearly foreshadowing the complex bonds between Sebastian and Violet. Grace's claim that "I exist in your blood as you exist in mine—" (321) and her appropriation of her son's poetry ("... I have defended your poetry with my life, because— ... It was mine, too" [321]) postulate a complete, intimate symbiosis of mind and body between mother and son that is reflected in Violet's exultant affirmation of almost incestuous unity: "We were a famous couple. People didn't speak of Sebastian and his mother or Mrs. Venable and her son, they said 'Sebastian and Violet, Violet and Sebastian....'" (362); and in her claims that "[w]*ithout me*, [the poem was] impossible [to deliver], Doctor" (354) or that "[h]e was *mine!*" (408).[58]

Further echoes of *Steps* can be found. For example, there is the memorial foundation that Mrs. Venable promises to establish for the young doctor if he agrees to cut out part of Catharine's brain: the financial equivalent of the lofty poetic tower Grace claims to have rebuilt.

The end of *Suddenly Last Summer*, in which it is revealed that Sebastian was eaten alive by the young boys, was shocking material in 1958, not only because it describes cannibalism—however metaphorically this may have been meant—but also because it blasphemously endows Sebastian with the status of a Eucharistic sacrificial victim. This characteristic blend of religious ritual and sex, a trademark of Williams's since *Battle of Angels* (1938), was foreshadowed in *Steps* in a similarly startling equation of Communion with a cannibalistic version of fellatio. Grace exclaims there: "Feed you with *what*, Hart? ... the—sex of sailors picked up in Brooklyn, dockside bars, as if they were the thin bits of bread that symbolized Christ's flesh at Holy Communion, and their seed as if it were His—blood!" (322).

The new perspective on the relationship between the Venables provided by the early play about the Cranes[59] prompts me to identify the vague but definitely "tropical" locale of Sebastian's last day as Mexico, a country dear to both Crane and Williams.[60] Further, it raises a question as to Mrs. Venable's character and actions: can we be so sure that Mrs. Venable is unaware of her son's sexual deviancy? In the most recent full-length study devoted to Williams, the author still maintains serenely that "Catharine ... eventually realized that [Sebastian] was a homosexual and was using her to make contacts for him. He had used his mother in the same way without Mrs. Venable's realizing it...."[61] And it is true that Catharine seems to believe, perhaps genuinely, that if Mrs. Venable procured for her son, she did so "*Not consciously!* She didn't *know* that she was procuring for him in the smart, the fashionable places they used to go to before last summer!" (412).

Yet how could Mrs. Venable have failed to see the truth, when she herself reports to Cuckrowicz: "My son, Sebastian, was chaste. Not c-h-a-s-e-d! Oh, he was chased in that way of spelling it, too, we had to be very fleet-footed I can tell you, with his looks and his charm, to keep ahead of pursuers, every kind of pursuer!" (361). It would take a particularly obtuse character—quite unlike Mrs. Venable—not to see the light after twenty-five years of this kind of life. The new Cranean viewpoint on *Suddenly Last Summer*—notice the pun on chased–chaste—may suggest that, contrary to Catharine's belief (too readily accepted as the truth by some critics), Violet does know but cannot accept the sexual nature of her son. Her actions in the play are an attempt to hide from the outside world this unaccepted and, in her eyes, unacceptable truth. When the attempt fails, she takes refuge from that truth in death ("I won't speak again. I'll keep still, if it kills me" [411]) or in madness, as suggested by her erratic outburst at the end of the play. *Steps Must Be Gentle* and the new light it throws on *Suddenly Last Summer* allow us another glimpse of the complex artistry of the later play, further justifying, in my opinion, its reputation as one of Williams's best works.

* * *

The poet-wanderer, the romantic quester in search of purity, the nonconformist faced with hostile surroundings has haunted the world of Tennessee Williams from the beginning. And from the beginning too, commentators have been misled—not least by the playwright himself—into believing that this figure was a hardly disguised self-portrait. In retrospect, however, it appears that if the plays are to be trusted more than the playwright, they may tell a different tale and provide us with signposts that point in a new, hitherto little heeded direction.

The evidence accumulated in this essay spans Williams's entire public career from 1938 to 1980, and takes such forms as titles or mottoes; direct or submerged allusions; quotations of various lengths appearing in plays, short stories, introductions, and essays. It strongly suggests that in the process of "minting [his] separate will," of creating his character of the artist, Williams had been referring, almost systematically, not solely to his own experience, but to that of Hart Crane.

In his effort to rise from the intensely personal to the general, in his attempt to "[snatch] the eternal out of the desperately fleeting,"[62] Williams molded Hart Crane, both as a man and as a poet, into a heightened image of himself, an idealized alter ego and a tutelary power. Through Crane, Williams succeeded in "looking out, not in," in transcending his immediate self and formulating a compelling statement about the artist in the modern world.

NOTES

1. Henry Hewes, "American Playwrights Self-Appraised," *Saturday Review*, 3 September 1955, pp. 18–19.

2. The best gathering and piecing together of available evidence on Williams's artistic practice is to be found in J. William Miller's *Modern Playwrights at Work* (New York,

1968), I, 375–385. See also Marvin Spevack, "Tennessee Williams: The Idea of the Theater," *Jahrbuch für Amerikastudien*, 10 (1965), 221–231.

3. Rpt. in *Where I Live: Selected Essays by Tennessee Williams*, ed. Christine R. Day and Bob Woods (New York, 1978), pp. 2–3.

4. Ibid., p. 6.

5. *Tennessee Williams's Letters to Donald Windham, 1940–1965*, ed. Donald Windham (New York, 1977). It is interesting to note, for what statistics are worth, that Crane is the writer most frequently mentioned in this collection; Lawrence is mentioned thirteen times, Chekhov eight times.

6. Tennessee Williams and Donald Windham, You *Touched Me! A Romantic Comedy in Three Acts* (New York, 1947), p. 19.

7. *The Complete Poems of Hart Crane*, ed. Waldo Frank (New York, 1958), p. 3. Quotations of the poetry throughout are from this edition; page references appear parenthetically in my text.

8. In their article on epigraphs to the plays of Tennessee Williams (*Notes on Mississippi Writers*, 3 [Spring 1970], 2–12), Delma E. Presley and Hari Singh erroneously comment on the poem as a whole rather than on the particular lines Williams selected as epigraph.

9. Leonard Quirino, "The Cards Indicate a Voyage on *A Streetcar Named Desire*," in *Tennessee Williams: A Tribute*, ed. Jac Tharpe (Jackson, Miss., 1977), p. 80.

10. Thomas E. Porter, *Myth and Modern American Drama* (Detroit, 1969), p. 176.

11. Blanche's destruction is physical and mental; Stanley's, although less immediately apparent, is equally real, as Bert Cardullo has argued convincingly in his essay "Drama of Intimacy and Tragedy of Incomprehension: *A Streetcar Named Desire* Reconsidered," in *Tennessee Williams: A Tribute*, ed. Tharpe, p. 153, n. 5.

12. R.W.B. Lewis, *The Poetry of Hart Crane: A Critical Study* (Princeton, 1967), p. 180.

13. A different interpretation is suggested by Norman J. Fedder in *The Influence of D.H. Lawrence on Tennessee Williams* (The Hague, 1966), p. 89: "The title of this play signals immediately the nature of its major conflict: the Lawrencean sex duel between the hot passion of Summer epitomized in the figure of the lusty John and that 'immaterial something—as thin as smoke—' which the spiritual Alma (soul) represents." Such an interpretation finds support in the play, and the critic himself points out that the dichotomy of the title is immediately reflected in the symmetry of the set. But Fedder seems to have been unaware that the title is a borrowing from Crane.

14. *The Theatre of Tennessee Williams*, II (New York, 1971), 243.

15. Sherman Paul points to the rich ambiguity of the title "Legend": "the legend named in 'Legend' is of two kinds. The title of the poem may be construed as designating nothing more than the key to a chart or map; here, the poet says, is an inscription (as in Whitman's *Leaves of Grass*), the key to the kind of reality the book contains. But the key itself is a legend ('The legend of their youth'), a legend in the sense of fable, or a story of the past—old and romantic, unverifiable, *legendary*—that we must nevertheless carefully attend to because it is, in Emily Dickinson's meaning, the poet's letter to the world" (*Hart's Bridge* [Urbana, Ill., 1972], p. 98).

16. Lewis, p. 139.

17. Arthur Ganz ("The Desperate Morality of the Plays of Tennessee Williams," *The American Scholar*, 31 [1962], 278–294) and William M. Roulet ("*Sweet Bird of Youth*: Williams' Redemptive Ethic," *Cithara*, 3 [May 1964], 31–36) have argued, not quite convincingly, for a consistent morality inherent in all of Tennessee Williams's plays. Both

critics are forced to admit the somewhat paradoxical nature of their argument. Ganz characteristically acknowledges in his first paragraph: "'Moralist,' desperate or not, may seem a perverse appellation for a playwright whose works concern rape, castration, cannibalism and other bizarre activities" (278); whereas Roulet concludes (feebly in my opinion): "One might quarrel with Tennessee Williams' moral code, but not about it; it cannot be denied that he has one operative—a very straightforward one it is, too: the acceptance of life on its own terms" (p. 36).

18. *The Theatre of Tennessee Williams*, IV (New York, 1972), 302.

19. See my article, "Tennessee Williams as Hagiographer: An Aspect of Obliquity in Drama," *Revue des Langues Vivantes*, 40 (1974), 449–456; rpt. as "Tennessee Williams' Lives of the Saints: A Playwright's Obliquity," in *Tennessee Williams: A Collection of Critical Essays*, ed. Stephen S. Stanton (Englewood Cliffs, N.J., 1977), pp. 149–157.

20. "Tennessee Williams Reads Hart Crane," *TC* 1206 (1965).

21. In the original the two lines quoted by Williams form a single line.

22. For a fictional treatment of this view, the reader should turn to Williams's neglected short story "The Poet," which contains a disguised portrait of Hart Crane and constitutes at the same time—perhaps for that very reason—the quintessential portrait of the Williams artist. Published in the collection *One Arm* in 1948, the period of Williams's most intense involvement with Crane, the short story is almost contemporary with a little-known preface Williams wrote in August 1949 for Oliver Evans's *Young Man with a Screwdriver* (Lincoln, Nebr., 1950). Evans's collection of poems contains a piece entitled "For Hart Crane" (p. 23), which deals with the circumstances of Crane's suicide at sea and ends with an allusion to Baudelaire's *L'Albatros* and its depiction of the poet alienated in a hostile world. In the preface Williams inevitably mentions Crane and provides, by contrast with Evans, a definition *a contrario* of his favorite poet and a succinct view of what the short story presents in fictional form. "Although flashes of poetic genius are not absent from this volume, it is not of a tortured compulsive kind. Speaking of that demon, I think invariably of Hart Crane, at the very center of whose life it exploded, and destroyed. The dynamics of this work are, of course, less intense, but also more benign. It is illuminated without a sense of violence. The poet himself is not ravaged. He lives *with* his art instead of *by* or *for* it, which is happier for him and even, somehow, more comforting for his listeners. The poetry contained in this volume is not of the explosive nor compulsive kind, nor is it the work of a deliberately and self-consciously professional man of letters" (pp. 1–2).

23. This is not the only instance in which Williams identifies with Crane. In the "Serious Version" Williams describes the difficulties encountered by young artists, stating that he had known some who had found "the struggle too complex and exhausting to go on with." He adds, "Hart Crane wasn't the only one. I have lived in the middle of it since I was released from the comparative cocoon of schools and colleges" (*Where I Live*, p. 5). Moreover, the dichotomy established here between purity and sensual gratification reminds us of all the early heroines who are rent by the conflict between demanding sensuality and an aspiration toward the ideal. It is interesting in this respect to remember that Williams has repeatedly claimed, "I am Blanche DuBois."

24. "Interview with Tennessee Williams," *Partisan Review*, 45 (1978), 276–305.

25. Nancy M. Tischler strongly emphasizes this aspect of Crane's appeal to Williams: "More than anything else, Hart Crane must have appealed to Williams on a purely personal level. He must have felt a kinship with this lonely, Dionysian poet—a homeless wanderer like himself" (*Tennessee Williams: Rebellious Puritan* (New York, 1961], p. 65).

26. *The Theatre of Tennessee Williams*, I (New York, 1971), 193. All quotations of the play are from this edition; page references appear parenthetically in my text.

27. Lewis, p. 139, n. 13.

28. I want to thank Professor Brian Parker of the University of Toronto for carefully reading through an early version of this essay, making valuable suggestions throughout and drawing my attention to the filmscript of *The Glass Menagerie*. It was written by Williams in collaboration with Peter Berneis and is discussed in Gene D. Phillips's *The Films of Tennessee Williams* (Philadelphia, 1980), pp. 43–64; it was published in synopsis form in *Screen Hits Annual*, 5 (1950). The opening paragraph there reads: "It was the hour before dawn when the world itself stands death watch for the night. Silent as a phantom, the ship rode through tatters of ghostly fog in which Tom Wingfield's suddenly thrown cigarette became a glowing comet in miniature" (46). The arching glow of the cigarette flung down to the water may constitute an unemphatic and aptly filmic reminder of Crane's suicidal jump into the Caribbean Sea.

29. See in this connection, among others, the interview-article "Broadway Discovers Tennessee Williams," *New York Times*, 21 December 1975, p. 4: "There is, he insists, 'very little' autobiography in his plays, 'except that they reflect somehow the particular psychological turmoil I was going through when I wrote them. The early ones are relatively tranquil, like "Menagerie."' But aren't there certain similarities between Laura, the physically and emotionally crippled daughter in 'Menagerie,' and Williams's mentally ill sister, Rose? 'In a sense, although my sister was a much more vital person than Laura. Terribly vital!'"

30. John Unterecker, *Voyager: A Life of Hart Crane* (New York, 1969), p. 236. See also the account of the same period in Philip Horton, *Hart Crane: The Life of an American Poet* (New York, 1957), pp. 117–118.

31. The draft is reprinted in *The World of Tennessee Williams*, ed. Richard F. Leavitt (New York, 1978), p. 52.

32. Unterecker, p. 236.

33. Ibid., p. 533.

34. It is surprising that *The Glass Menagerie* acquired its final title only a few months before its Chicago premiere. In the correspondence with Windham it is referred to repeatedly in 1943 and 1944, but always as "The Gentleman Caller" or "Caller" or "The Caller" (*Letters*, pp. 59, 60, 94, 140, 148). Rehearsals began in December 1944, first in New York and then in Chicago, where the play opened on 26 December 1944 as *The Glass Menagerie*. Exactly when after 25 August 1944 (the date of the last mention of the old title to Windham) the play acquired its definitive title is not, at this point, ascertainable. Ellen Dunlap, Research Librarian at the Humanities Research Center of the University of Texas at Austin, where Williams's papers are deposited, was unable to locate any letters on file that contain references to the final title. I want to express my gratitude to her for her patience and cooperation.
Brian Parker's recent article "The Composition of *The Glass Menagerie:* An Argument for Complexity," *Modern Drama*, 25 (September 1982), 409–422, based on his thorough examination of the Williams collection at the University of Texas, reveals that the genesis of the play, and therefore the precise origin of its title, are far more complex than supposed up to now.

35. On this episode, see *Letters*, pp. 154–155.

36. *Hart Crane*, p. 195.

37. Ibid., p. 193.

38. See, among others, Herbert A. Leibowitz, *Hart Crane: An Introduction to the Poetry* (New York, 1968), pp. 3–4, and Paul, p. 128.

39. *Hart's Bridge*, p. 123.

40. The short-story version clearly establishes that Tom is reminiscing about the events five years after they have occurred. The perspectives created for the two "narrators" are then comparable in the distancing they provide, but whereas Tom looks at the past from the point of view of an adult who has survived it, the poet of Crane's work looks at it through the eyes of the child who is still undergoing the events.

41. Paul, p. 125.

42. In his essay "On A Streetcar Named Success" (1947), rpt. in *Where I Live*, p. 22.

43. Paul, p. 129.

44. As the speaker in the poem is "conscripted" to the "shadows' glow" of the decanters (*Poems*. p. 92), Tom is "conscripted" by the collection of small animals in at least two ways: first, as one whose vulnerability the glass menagerie symbolically represents, along with that of all the other characters; and second, as a brother reminded literally on every street corner of the small menagerie and its owner.

45. Lewis, p. 193.

46. *Steps Must Be Gentle: A Dramatic Reading for Two Performers* was published first in New York, Targ Editions, 1980. It was reprinted in *The Theatre of Tennessee Williams*, VI (New York, 1981), 315–327. All quotations of the play are from the latter edition; page references appear parenthetically in my text.

47. The uncharacteristic absence of a specific setting and the impression that the communication between the characters is exclusively verbal may be the playwright's attempt to suggest that this is a parapsychological contact such as those the poet's mother claimed to have established repeatedly with her dead son through the ministrations of a spirit medium. On this aspect, see Unterecker, p. 17.

48. The short play shows us a Williams who is thoroughly acquainted with Crane's poetry, as attested by the various quotations and allusions. But if 1947 is indeed the date of composition, as Stephen S. Stanton tentatively suggested in *The Tennessee Williams Newsletter*, 2 (Spring 1980), 63, then the work also reveals a surprisingly early as well as thorough familiarity with Hart Crane's biography. Indeed, Williams must have been aware, beyond the information he could gather from Horton's account of 1937, of the difficult last years of Mrs. Crane; in the interview with Cecil Brown he even mentions that Grace Hart Crane had sent him the poet's fan as a memento (290). But it is equally clear that Williams has added stage directions to the 1980 version published by Targ, since he calls attention there, on the first page, to "my homage to Crane as printed on the slipcover of my Caedmon Records recording of a reading I gave of his poetry in the 60's." It is quite likely that he similarly revised portions of the dialogue to include fragments of the correspondence to which only Mrs. Crane could have provided access in 1947. Passages from the letters edited by Thomas S.W. Lewis (New York and London, 1974) and quoted extensively in Unterecker's *Voyager* are incorporated verbatim in the play. Grace's statement that "I sold my beautiful diamonds for a song" (*Steps*, 325) is quoted from a letter of justification written long after her son's death to Sam Loveman, one of the poet's intimate friends. Williams's familiarity with the material is obvious also from his tinkering with the evidence for dramatic purposes. The telegram Grace sent Hart to announce his grandmother's death in reality read: "Mother passed away tonight. Funeral here. Advise

later. Grace" (Unterecker, pp. 554–555). By omitting the word "later," Williams makes it sound as if Grace expected Hart to advise her promptly on a course of action. And indeed, the character in the play reproaches her son at length for not reacting as the telegram instructed him to. In fact, Hart immediately wired condolences and flowers from New York, following these with a long, compassionate letter (mentioned in Unterecker, p. 555). Williams thus bends reality again when Grace says to Hart in the play: "If you replied, the letter does not survive." These discrepancies clearly indicate that in the process of fashioning his story Williams works as a dramatist rather than a chronicler.

49. From a letter of 24 February 1942 to Windham it is clear that Williams was reading *Moby Dick*, and he discusses incidents from *Billy Budd* in a letter of 25 March 1946 (*Letters*, pp. 25, 186).

50. *Letters*, p. 184.

51. Lewis, p. 351.

52. L. S. Dembo, *Hart Crane's Sanskrit Charge: A Study of the Bridge* (Ithaca, N.Y., 1960), p. 117.

53. The play contains a number of these puns, possibly in imitation of Crane. They are not all particularly felicitous, as, for example, in the exchange in which Hart says: "I appealed to father ... to make some provision for your—welfare, Grace"; and the mother replies: "—I wonder if what you confessed in California, that obscene confession of your sexual nature hasn't a little to do with so much of such well-demonstrated grace of the heart in you, Hart" (326). The puns on their respective names are too obvious, and the syntax too belabored, to establish—as is presumably intended—that Grace is about to acknowledge the important role she has unwittingly played in her son's homosexuality.

54. I know of no other place in the Williams published canon where homosexuality, defined as "a way of life imposed on me like a prison sentence" (*Steps*, 322), is presented more honestly and simply. There is nothing of the melodramatic effect associated with Allen Grey in *A Streetcar Named Desire*, Skipper in *Cat on a Hot Tin Roof*, or Baron de Charlus in *Camino Real*; or of the devil-may-care exuberance of the letters or the *Memoirs*. The declaration has a ring of authentic feeling, coupled with a characteristically Williamsian will to endure, that makes this resignation of a broken creature to the inevitable totally convincing.

55. *Suddenly Last Summer* was first presented as part of a double bill with *Something Unspoken*—a one-act play in which the main character is named Grace—under the collective title *Garden District*, an echo of another Crane poem, "Garden Abstract." The associations with Crane are too numerous to be mere coincidence.

56. "The Hart Crane image, which has possessed Williams's imagination since his youth ... has now [i.e., at the time of *Suddenly Last Summer*] become a frightening picture of the romantic corrupted in his search for purity" (*Tennessee Williams* [Austin, Tex., 1969], p. 35).

57. *The Theatre of Tennessee Williams*, III (New York, 1971), 343–423 All quotations are from this edition; page references appear parenthetically in my text.

58. What is identification as far as Violet and Grace are concerned becomes bondage in the perspective presented by Catharine, who views Mrs. Venable as keeping Sebastian unduly attached to her by "that string of pearls that old mothers hold their sons by like a—sort of a—sort of—*umbilical* cord, long—*after* ..." (409).

59. In my article "Oedipus in New Orleans: Autobiography and Myth in *Suddenly Last Summer*," *Revue des Langues Vivantes*, U.S. Bicentennial Issue (1976), 53–63. I argued that

part of the structure of *Suddenly Last Summer* reproduced the Oedipus myth as dramatized by Sophocles and interpreted it as a variation of a solar myth. I suggested also that a missing link in the mythical structure was to be found in *I Rise in Flame Cried the Phoenix*, the play on D.H. Lawrence's last days in St. Paul de Vence. Now, from the perspective of *Steps Must Be Gentle*, it becomes clear that much of Crane's biography and, indirectly, of Williams's, went into the making of *Suddenly Last Summer*. Besides the clearest biographical reference, the prefrontal lobotomy that Mrs. Venable wants performed on Catharine, the name Venable was also borrowed from real life, as pointed out by Leavitt (p. 119), as was the name Wingfield in the earlier *Glass Menagerie* (*Letters*, p. 135). This evidence, incidentally, does not preclude the possibility that these names were chosen for the symbolic values that commentators have detected in them.

60. In this connection, see Drewey Wayne Gunn, *American and British Writers in Mexico, 1556–1973* (Austin, 1974).

61. Felicia Hardison Londré, *Tennessee Williams* (New York, 1979), p. 132.

62. *The Theatre of Tennessee Williams*, II (New York, 1971), 262.

DAVID CASTRONOVO

The Major Full-Length Plays:
Visions of Survival

After seeing a production of *Our Town* in 1969, a young girl from Harlem commented to a *New York Times* reporter that she was unable to identify with the characters and situations.[1] Grover's Corners, New Hampshire, was a completely alien place and its people were in no way relevant to her concerns. Such a response is not singular or especially unsympathetic. From its first tryouts in Princeton prior to the original New York production in 1938, the play has met with significant critical and popular resistance. If it isn't the distance of the urban audience from Wilder's small-town setting and values, it is a matter of contemporary sensibility or fear of sentimentality, or unease about the play's obsession with mortality, or lack of familiarity with unconventional theatrical forms. New York audiences did not immediately take to a play with no scenery and a last act that was set in a graveyard. Mary McCarthy, writing for *Partisan Review*, was favorable in her reactions, but somewhat ashamed that she liked the play. "Could this mean that there was something the matter with me? Was I starting to sell out?"[2] Miss McCarthy's review was careful to take shots at the scene between Emily and George: "Young love was never so baldly and tritely gauche" as this. She also made sure that readers of *Partisan* knew that *Our Town* was "not a play in the accepted sense of the term. It is essentially lyric, not dramatic." With this comment she was able to set the play apart from great modern dramas of movement and characterization like *Six Characters in Search of an Author* or

From *Thornton Wilder.* ©1986 by the Ungar Publishing Company.

Miss Julie: she could like the play without acknowledging that it was fully a play. On an emotional level, Eleanor Roosevelt also responded ambivalently—"Yes, *Our Town* was original and interesting. No, it was not an enjoyable evening in the theatre."[3] She was "moved" and "depressed" beyond words. Edmund Wilson's reaction was similarly complicated: Wilder remarks in a letter that Wilson was "so moved that you found yourself trying to make out a case against it ever since" (January 31, 1938). Wilson's later pronouncement (letter to Wilder, June 20, 1940) that *Our Town* was "certainly one of the few first-rate American plays" is far less revealing about his emotional reaction than the earlier response. Wilder's play, in short, had its difficulties with general Broadway audiences, with intellectuals, and with prominent people of taste and moral sensitivity. For every Brooks Atkinson who enthusiastically found "a profound, strange, unworldly significance"[4] in the play, there was an uncomfortable Mary McCarthy.

The barriers that stand between us and *Our Town* are even more formidable than those of 1938. McCarthy of course was writing as a literary modern in sympathy with the anti-Stalinist left: the commitment to experiment of the *Partisan Review* might have drawn her toward the lyric innovation of Wilder's work, but behind her reaction was an uneasiness with Wilder's sentimental situations. Other progressives of 1938, perhaps even Mrs. Roosevelt, were struck by Wilder's essentially tragic view of human potential: despite what we aspire to, we are always unaware of life around us and of the value of our most simple moments. We must face death in order to see. Such an informing theme could only cause the liberal, progressive mind to recoil. After more than forty years, audiences have accumulated attitudes, convictions, tastes, and experiences that set them farther apart than ever. Distrust of WASP America's values, the sexual revolution, feminism, fear of America's complacency, the resistance of many Americans to marriage and family life, the distrust of group mentalities, the rise of ethnic literatures, the general loosening of restraints on language and conduct: such obstacles have wedged their way between us and Wilder's drama. As a scene unfolds— for example, Mrs. Gibbs being gently chastised by her husband for staying out so late at choir practice—the way we live now occupies the stage beside the players, mocking them and pointing up their limitations as fully developed men and women in the modern world.

Many of the roads that lead us to the drama of mid-century seem to be in better shape than the Wilder road: O'Neill and Williams deal with obsession, sexual passion, illness, and torment. Miller deals with broken American dreams. But Wilder employs the notations of an essentially stable and happy society. To reach his work, we must pay more attention to the situations and themes that he created for people such as ourselves: *Our Town* has our themes, our fears, our confusion; Wilder built the play so that every scene has something to reach us. Our problem has been that whereas other American playwrights have offered encounters with desolation and the tragic isolation of tormented people—the themes of the great modernists and indeed of Wilder himself in his first two novels—Wilder's 1938 play is about another area of our struggle: the essentially ordinary, uncomplicated, yet terrifying battle to realize fully our own ordinary existences. Such a subject obviously is more difficult to present than the more visceral situations that many great contemporary writers have dealt with; but Wilder's style and form are what force the concerns of the play to become familiar truths charged with new vision.

His style and the design in the play produce the effects of American folk art: in setting, dialogue, and structure, the play comes before the audience like a late nineteenth-century painting depicting the customs, colors, and destinies of ordinary lives. Whereas O'Neill and Williams give resonance to their characters by exploring hidden motivations and desires, Wilder directs us to the bright surface and the overall pattern of his people's existences. Essentially plotless, the three acts are rooted in theme rather than dramatic movement. We do not so much wait for events or develop curiosity about characters; instead we are made to stand away from the tableau and contemplate three large aspects of earthly existence: daily life, love and marriage, death. As many folk artists do, Wilder positions us at some distance from his subjects: the audience even needs a stage manager to take us into the town and back to 1901. Like the folk artist, Wilder does not care much about verisimilitude, accurate perspective in drawing characters, and shading: "reality" does not require subtlety or many-layered characters or ingenuity of plot. Quoting Molière, Wilder said that for the theater all he needed "was a platform and a passion or two."[5]

This attitude toward his art can best be understood if we look at Wilder's plot ingredients and observe their affinities to folk art.[6] Act I is packed with natural scenery, social usages, material things, and typical encounters. The sky lightens and the "morning star gets wonderful bright." The town is presented building by building, and then the Gibbses and Webbs are shown in the foreground. Like figures in a typical folk painting, however, the two families are not drawn with careful perspective, and they are no more or no less important than the life that surrounds them in Grover's Corners. They are in the midst of the town and the universe, absorbing and emblemizing social and cosmic concerns. The stage manager dismisses people with, "Thank you, ladies. Thank you very much" just as the folk painter avoids focusing: Wilder's manager switches our attention from Mrs. Gibbs and Mrs. Webb to Professor Willard and his discourse on the natural history of the town. Soon social life and politics are surveyed; the act closes with a cosmic framing of the material. Jane Crofut, Rebecca Webb's friend, received a letter from her minister: after the address the envelope reads—"The United States of America; Continent of North America; Western Hemisphere; The Earth; The Solar System; The Universe; The Mind of God." Rebecca marvels that the postman "brought it just the same." This closing line—with its reminder that the most ordinary address in an average town has a clear relationship to the cosmic order—is Wilder's way of practicing the folk-painter's craft: Grover's Corners lies flat before us, open to the hills and firmament. Every person, object, feeling, and idea takes its place in the tableau of existence. If Wilder had taken the route of probing Mr. Webb's psyche, he would have ruined the simple design of his composition. Act I, in its multifariousness and plenitude, stands as a kind of celebratory offering to the universe, a playwright's highly colored, two-dimensional rendering of living.

Act II is called "Love and Marriage" and takes place in 1904. Once again, it does not appeal to our desire for complex shading and perspective. Character motivation is very simply presented: Emily has always liked George, then has her doubts about him because he is self-centered, and finally feels his capacity for remorse and development. George's motivation for redirecting his life and staying in Grover's Corners after high school is equally direct and simple: "I think that once you've found a person that you're very fond of ... I mean a person who's fond of you, too, and likes you enough to be interested in your character ... well, I think that's just as important as college is, and even more so." This is all that Wilder uses to set the act in motion: no ambivalence, no social complications, no disturbances. The primary colors of human love, however, do not preclude the black terror that seizes George before his wedding. He cries out against the pressures and publicness of getting married. Emily's response to the wedding day is no less plaintive; why, she wonders, can't she remain as she is? This apparently awkward doubling of fears and sorrows is the kind of strategy that has made Wilder seem hopelessly out of touch with modern men and women. Indeed, if we are looking for what Yeats called "the fury and mire of human veins" we have come to the wrong playwright; it is not that Wilder's lovers have no passion. It is simply that their creator has risen above their individuality and sought to measure them against time and the universe. What counts in the historical and cosmic sense is that they are two more acceptors of a destiny that connects them with most of humanity: "M ... marries N ... millions of them," the stage manager comments at the end of the act. Hardly a romantic, Wilder directs us to the complete unadorned design of the human sequence. "The cottage, the go-cart, the Sunday-afternoon drives in the Ford, the first rheumatism, the grandchildren, the second rheumatism, the deathbed, the reading of the will." There is no mist of feeling, no religious sentiment, no attempt to assign high significance to the procession of events: if audiences find Act II touching—and if some people are moved to tears—the cause is certainly not in any overwriting and pleading for response. Wilder's language is almost bone dry. The stage manager's comments set the mood. As a man who has married two hundred couples, he still has his doubts about one of Grover's Corners' most cherished institutions.

Act III is about death and has the form of a memorial folk painting: like many pictures from the nineteenth century that memorialized famous or obscure men and women, Wilder's act brings in scenes from a life—in this case Emily's is featured—and surrounds the central figure with the routines and rituals of ordinary, rather than extraordinary, existence. A typical "important" memorial piece—for instance, the death of George Washington—is filled with references to valor and public deeds; a more modest person's life has the notation of his simple good works. Emily's death, and by extension the deaths of Mrs. Gibbs and lesser characters, is placed in the context of the quotidian. Newly arrived in the graveyard on the hill, the young woman at first refuses to accept her fate and yearns to reexperience the texture of her life. Any day will do; but once she returns to earth on her twelfth birthday, the details of existence—people's voices, a parent's youthful appearance, food and coffee, the gift of a postcard album—are overpowering. Through a clever ironic twist that both prevents the scene from being conventionally sentimental and also forces insight on the audience, Wilder has Emily refusing to mourn or regret. Instead, she throws the burden of loss and blindness on the audience, on the living people who never "realize life while they live it." This very short scene is both birthday and funeral—actually a grim, hard look at the spectacle of human beings, adorned by Wilder with folk motifs: habitual comings and goings, Howie Newsome, the paperboy on his route, breakfast being served. These details have had the curious effect of making some audiences find *Our Town* a cozy vision of New Hampshire life. Looked at in relationship to their structural function—the building up of a dense, ordinary, casual, and unfelt reality to stand against the cosmic order—they are chilling. Like Ivan Ilyich's curtain-hanging (which brings on his fatal illness) or his tickets for the Sarah Bernhardt tragedy (which he can't attend because he is dying), the Wilder folk objects and motifs are frightening fixtures of our lives that once gave pleasure but can only stand in Act III for all the blindness of human existence. After having presented us with this striking fusion of folk art and existential dread, Wilder regrettably mars the last scene with hokum about stars and human aspirations. While this does complete the pattern in Act I where the "Wonderful bright morning star" opens the first scene, it also insists on a kind of message that the experience of the play does not support: only the earth, among the planets and stars, "is straining away, straining away all the time to make something of itself."

This kind of didacticism is disconsonant with and unworthy of Wilder's most fully realized scenes. The fact is that Grover's Corners hardly strains for anything: it isn't very progressive or cultured or enlightened or interesting. Culturally, there is *Robinson Crusoe*, the Bible, Handel's *Largo*, and Whistler's Mother—"those are just about as far as we go." Mrs. Gibbs has cooked thousands of meals. George aspires no higher than—perhaps not as high as—his father. "Straining" to be civilized and to make oneself into something is singularly absent from the play's action. Wilder has instead built up something far less sententious in his three acts: rather than give us yet another American story of social aspiration and the love of democratic vistas, he has used American ordinariness to embody the ardors and terrors of human existence. Tolstoy said of his existential protagonist Ivan Ilyich, "Ivan's life was most simple and most ordinary and therefore most terrible." Wilder would only add "wonderful" in summing up his own characters' lives.

Wilder had a very definite sense that his play was being manhandled by its first director, Jed Harris: the flavoring and style of Wilder's brand of folk art were in danger of being reduced to the level of calendar art. Harris insisted that the language of certain scenes be simplified—that poetry be sacrificed in the interests of movement and stagecraft. Later on, other changes in the play—having children cutely corrected by ever-scolding, kindly parents—made the production look like the worst kind of ersatz Americana. Wilder was infuriated that his cosmic drama was being brought down to the level of Norman Rockwell's small-town scene painting. Never a provincial, he was disturbed to find that his artful use of folk motifs could be translated into such vulgar stage forms. The folk-art techniques that he worked with were actually quite different from the flood of pictures and stories produced by local-color artists offering Americans souvenirs of New England. Wilder, of course, was not a "genuine primitive" artist: an accomplished adapter of Proustian motifs in *The Cabala* and *The Bridge*, he couldn't ever hope to have the innocence of the natural storyteller. At the same time he was not the meretricious sort of artist who fed off folk motifs and invested nothing in them. *Our Town* is one of many modern works of literature that employ abstraction, flattening, and distortion: its technique is like that of Hemingway's careful building up of a design from very simple physical details; the emphasis is on reverence for objects in themselves and the sensations that come from perceiving them. Attention to startling aspects of surface—just as Hemingway or Woolf or Picasso attend to physicality—makes *Our Town* a modernist exploration of being rather than a tendentious old-fashioned work that seeks to explain away the mystery of human and nonhuman reality through analysis. Wilder's people in *Our Town* are rarely allowed to move out of their mysterious innocence and become hokey figures who are too sophisticated for their setting and the terms of their dramatic existence. Emily—the young girl who poses the greatest threat to the play by her speechmaking about blindness and the fact that we never "look at one another"—is not allowed to spoil the play. After Emily bursts into lines about what has happened to them as a family—her brother Wally's death, the changes in fourteen years, the fact that her mother is a grandmother—Mrs. Webb answers with the reality of the twelfth birthday on her mind. In the haunting style of *The Long Christmas Dinner*, Wilder makes Mrs. Webb offer the young girl an unnamed present in a yellow paper, "something" from the attic and the family past. The immediacy of life—how we experience it at the time, not how we muse about it—is Wilder's concern. The New Hampshire details are accessible bits of the palpable world that Wilder shapes into a cosmic design: he has little interest in them as quaint reminders of a lost world.

Most of his play was written in a small village in Switzerland, once again reminding us that he is the international artist like Joyce or Hemingway who stands at a distance from his subject, respects its patterns, carefully builds its particulars, but has little interest in creating a New England period piece. The irony, of course, is that a work with great generalizing powers can also be received as a portrait of a specific time and place. Wilder profited in the short run from this irony as audiences began to feel comfortable with the play that was supposedly about small-town American life. But after almost fifty years, the "American" localism is eroding his stature among his contemporaries.

If *Our Town* is to remain alive as an American drama, it must come before us as a play about sensations—about how we receive the concrete news of cold, heat, food, love, joy, and death. In a letter to Edmund Wilson, dated January 31, 1938, Wilder remarked that his play—with its "columns of perspective on the trivialities of Daily Life"—"must be some atavistic dynamite." Since the impact of the play is not obscured by the social problems that muddy many of O'Neill's or Miller's plays or the sexual concerns that are likely to make Williams inaccessible to audiences attuned to a different image of women, Wilder is likely to stand out as an artist with a timeless concern for "Mama's sunflowers. And food and coffee. And new ironed dresses and hot baths ... and sleeping and waking up." Whether audiences will be engaged by Wilder's existential tableau or whether they will prefer fascinating new social and psychological issues is not as yet clear. But one thing is certain in the 1980s: Sam Shepard's *True West*—with its wild parody and disjointed presentation of crazed American dreams—is what occupies the minds of serious theatergoers while *Our Town* has been relegated to television and summer theater. Once said, this should not obscure the claims that the play is likely to have on future audiences. The world of the Gibbses and the Webbs is an antielitist vision of human existence that may appeal to audiences sickened by domination and brutality. Grover's Corners reminds us that affection and family loyalty animate human lives; competition and self-interest—the themes of American life in the 1980s—are overshadowed in *Our Town* by more generous recognitions. Young George's feelings of guilt come from not having helped his mother; Emily's speech about "blindness" proceeds from her own sense that willfulness and vanity have made life a painful memory. Mrs. Gibbs's small savings, which have been accumulated from the sale of an old piece of furniture, do not serve her or give Dr. Gibbs his vacation: yet unknown to Emily and George, the money gives the young couple their start in life. Wilder's interlocking world of feelings and interests is a version of life in a democratic culture to which we are so unused that it may soon become remarkable.

Only months after *Our Town* appeared on the boards in New York, Wilder offered a second full-length play. *The Merchant of Yonkers* is altogether different in style and atmosphere from the earlier work: while the world of Grover's Corners impinges on the cosmos—and uses the abstract techniques of the folk artist to universalize small-town experience—this new play is about society and employs the sparkle of the comedy of manners along with the roughhouse of farce. But for all its buoyancy, *The Merchant* deals with the darker side of human nature-capitalistic greed, exploitation, denial of vital possibilities, and neurosis. Ironically, the play that became *Hello Dolly!* is all about Horace Vandergelder, a sour Protestant businessman, and his success at manipulating those around him; Dolly Levi, the widow of a Viennese lover of life and pleasure, is Vandergelder's comic nemesis. When the Yonkers and Vienna mentalities meet, the clash becomes another one of Wilder's international studies of values. The spirit of Vienna comes to pervade this play just as the spirit of Christmas—what Louis Cazamian has called *la philosphie de Noël*[7]—suffuses many of Dickens's tales: generosity of feeling, spiritual regeneration, the affirmation of pleasure, and the adventure of life give the play the qualities of a nineteenth-century protest against grasping materialism. But the play's date, and the actions of its central character Vandergelder, should remind audiences that Wilder is working through the issues of the American Depression. This is also done as he comically explores the way the capitalistic ethos blights lives and makes the office and the home places of confinement rather than of pleasure and fulfillment.

Horace Vandergelder, a widower who has paid some attention to New York dressmaker Irene Molloy, is not merely the prototypical miser of farce. In Act I he appears as the spokesman for a point of view that had considerable currency during the 1930s: as a good, solid businessman, he preaches about the dangers of wastefulness and extravagance; apprentices and employees such as his clerks, Barnaby and Cornelius—the one an innocent of seventeen, the second a worn-down man of thirty-three—don't know the value of work and have no claim on the private sector for a better life. He believes that almost all the people in the world are spendthrifts and talkers of foolishness. Vandergelder decides to turn the nonsense of love and marriage into a practical deal—if handled correctly, a wife can be transformed into a contented drone who imagines that she has a share in a rich man's prosperity. Vandergelder embarks upon a cautious search for a wife-employee, someone to fulfill his dream of exploitation mixed with "a little risk and adventure." "Marriage," he reasons, "is a bribe to make a housekeeper think she's a householder." The crudity of this theory of relationships is a parody of the way the hard-bitten capitalist of the thirties (and indeed of the eighties) regarded those who own nothing but their labor. Wives and employees have to be made to feel part of the economy. "Did you ever watch an ant carry a burden twice its size? What excitement! What patience." In trying to work through his plans for manipulating those around him, he comes up against recalcitrant human nature: discontented workers like Barnaby and Cornelius who want to have a fling in New York; a niece who wants to marry an insolvent artist; and Dolly, a witty and charming busybody who isn't satisfied with the world as the Vandergelders have made it. Dolly, like some interfering and generous spirit, is anti-laissez-faire. "Nature is never completely satisfactory and must be corrected" is certainly a line that chills Vandergelder's sort. And money, Dolly argues, should not be "idle, frozen." "I don't like the thought of it lying in great piles, useless, motionless." Dolly believes in money as a resource for people rather than as a mechanism for asserting power. "It should be flowing down among the people, through dressmakers and restaurants and cabmen, setting up a little business here, and furnishing a good time there." Dolly too is a manipulator—and Act I ends as she talks Vandergelder into coming to New York to dine with the woman of his dreams. Dolly has it in mind to make New York a happier place—"more like Vienna and less like a collection of nervous and tired ants." Vandergelder's vision of the patient ant is comically threatened even before he goes on his ill-fated "little adventure."

Act II carries along and embroiders the themes of exploitation and generosity, manipulation and unencumbered pleasure. Mrs. Molloy and her young apprentice Minnie are trapped in their shop just as Horace and his apprentices are trapped in their Yonkers store. Mrs. Molloy has developed a disillusioned attitude toward life, and intends to marry Horace for material reasons. Like Horace, she yearns for something more—some of the "wickedness" that milliners are supposed to enjoy. She is ripe for the arrival of the two apprentices and for the kindly practical joke that Dolly has in store. In the course of the act, Cornelius and Barnaby hide from Vandergelder, accidentally provide the impression that Mrs. Molloy is "wicked," and cause the merchant to stalk out with Mrs. Levi. Dolly has meanwhile altered "nature" and the reality of economics a bit by giving out the fiction that Cornelius is a bon vivant. Now that she is freed of the practical entanglement with a man she doesn't love, Irene Molloy is prepared for a night out—at the expense of Cornelius, now baffled and intoxicated by a "woman's world" and in possession of a bit more than a dollar. But Cornelius and Barnaby have made a life-availing pact in Act I—to have a good meal, to be in danger, to spend all their money, and not to return to Yonkers until they've kissed girls.

In Act III the complications mount as all the characters collide at the Harmonia Gardens Restaurant. Vandergelder is supposed to meet the fictitious Ernestina Simple, a model of thrift and beauty; Cornelius and Barnaby are treating Mrs. Molloy and Minnie; Dolly is setting up Vandergelder for herself, the niece Ermegarde and her boyfriend are dining upstairs. In the farcical tradition, most of the relationships are temporarily short-circuited: Vandergelder, in particular, escapes Dolly, and the niece and the artist are still in Vandergelder's power.

Cornelius and Barnaby are fired from their positions—this time they encounter Vandergelder's wrath when he discovers them dancing in drag. Thematically, two important points have been reached. During the evening's scuffle, Vandergelder has lost his purse—and Cornelius has had his night out at the miser's expense. Such comic disbursement—another kind of generosity—is central to the play's meaning. But Vandergelder without a purse is still not a Scrooge ready to celebrate Christmas. Dolly predicts his future: the man who is friendless, living with a housekeeper who can prepare his meals for a dollar a day. "You'll spend your last days listening at keyholes, for fear someone's cheating you." Yet even this idea of the unlived life is not enough to bring him around.

Act IV functions like a mechanical toy: it wraps up the problem and disentangles the miseries with little reference to human psychology. Vandergelder snaps out of his miserly groove and makes Cornelius his partner. Lovers are united; money is spent; greed vanishes in the dizzying atmosphere of newly found pleasure and adventure. The most believable events concern Dolly herself—once a desolate woman sitting with her Bible and hearing the bell strike at Trinity Church, she has now chosen to live among "fools" (to use Vandergelder's term) and to find some comfort and pleasure by marrying and transforming Vandergelder. Once like the dead leaf that fell from her Bible, she is now able to rejoin the human race. The privatized lives of the play—Vandergelder communing with his economic fantasies, his two employees living in innocence of life's adventure, Dolly in her room, Mrs. Molloy and Minnie shut out from pleasure, Ermegarde's aunt, Miss Van Huysen, in her lonely New York house—are propelled toward one another by an author who has now made comic capital out of his 1920s theme of the unlived life. The play's positive energy is wonderfully distilled in the line of a minor character: "Everybody's always talking about people breaking into houses, ma'am; but there are more people in the world who want to break out of houses, that's what I always say." The remark not only contains the meaning of the play's resolution; it also brings forward a theme from Wilder's early career: he has not finished his dealings with private desolation and the suffering of people enclosed by culture and neurosis. *The Skin of Our Teeth* is the next phase; *Theophilus North* the last.

For a play that has earned a reputation as a trivial farce, *The Merchant of Yonkers* offers a clever assessment of life in a competitive society. It does so, however, in the joking, slapstick manner of the commercial theater; it is also equipped, it should be added, with Freudian and Marxist insights. Bubbling out of this farcical evening is a series of observations about isolation, neurotic self-involvement, and the waste of human potential. Cornelius is a thirty-three-year-old man who has never tasted life; Dolly herself was almost the victim of isolation; Miss Van Huysen sees the young lovers' plight in the terms of her own imprisoning existence. On the socioeconomic side, Wilder employs the reasoning of Marx in *The Economic and Philosophic Manuscripts of 1844*—money is a universal solvent in bourgeois society; it dissolves and alters all human relationships.[8] A little of it, as Dolly keeps reminding us, can create a world of pleasure; the lack of it—or the Vandergelderian accumulation of it—stunts lives. Instead of presenting a cynical or bitter character, Wilder has managed to offer Dolly as a buoyant, worldly-wise woman whose major social mission is to get the juices of the capitalist system flowing. Put in Wilder's terms, the language that Dolly uses to describe money, wealth is like manure: it should be spread around to help make young things grow. Wilder has adopted the thinking of nineteenth-century writers like Dickens, Ruskin, and Marx—money is a waste product, Dickens's "dust" and Ruskin's gift of the dust, which makes society develop. Dolly's outlook, in its final form, is essentially one of compromise and accommodation to capitalist culture—like a New Deal planner, she saves Vandergelder from destructive greed and directs the flow of his money for the public good. Part social planner, part psychological counselor, Dolly is Wilder's image of contemporary survival—getting along in this world comes through taking an imaginative chance. The expansive projects of the human spirit—adventure, playing hunches, going to New York—are what save the lives in the play.

This farce, charged with social meaning, is an altogether more modest achievement than *The Skin of Our Teeth*. The new play, which reached Broadway in wartime, is Wilder's multicolored, many-styled exploration of endurance and survival; the austerely rendered routines of Grover's Corners and the bouncy adventures of Dolly in New York both lack the craftsmanly ingenuity, the imaginative steeplechasing, and the emotional variousness of this latest three-act play. The windup-toy quality of characters like Vandergelder has also been displaced by a more satisfying and penetrating investigation of people's problems and moods.

Measuring Wilder's progress as a dramatist inevitably involves placing *The Skin of Our Teeth* beside *Our Town*: the works invite comparison not only because of their ambitiousness but more importantly because of strong thematic amities. Both concern American families struggling with implacable fate and their own smallness: Emily and George and their parents and Mr. and Mrs. Antrobus and their children experience joy and dread as they contend not only with the localized social problems of American life, but more importantly with the churnings of the universe. The macrocosmic references in both plays—to planets, vast numbers, ideas that hover around mortal lives—are an unmistakable sign that Wilder remains obsessed by the ways ordinary lives in Grover's Corners or Excelsior, New Jersey, take their place in a universal design. But for all this similarity in cosmic subject matter, there is a very considerable difference in the dramatic visions of the plays. The last act of *Our Town* takes place in a graveyard—its epiphanies are tragic, but its affirmations about stars and striving are so much inauthentic rhetoric grafted onto a great play. Unfortunately for those who seek easy contrasts with *The Skin of Our Teeth*, the later play—for all its brio and broad humor—is not essentially comic, although a wide variety of comic and humorous strategies are used in the very serious, emotionally wrenching drama about the struggle to transcend the disasters of nature, human society, and the warped human self. Act III situates the family in a war-ravaged home with Gladys as an unwed mother, Henry filled with fascistic rage, and Sabina anxious to become a good self-absorbed American citizen ready for a peacetime prosperity of movies and fun. Mr. Antrobus is ready to start putting the world together again, but he is old and tired and has had many setbacks. This is hardly comic—and in its matter-of-fact look at what men and women wind up with, it is hardly the complacent vision that repelled Mary McCarthy when she reviewed the play.[9] *The Skin of Our Teeth* is not about the fat of the land: what's in view for man is grinding struggle, close calls with total destruction, and the permanent fact of human violence and selfishness.

This theme of human struggle and limited achievement comes to us in the form of three loosely constructed, elliptical acts. Never a writer of well-made plays, Wilder has now brought his own episodic technique to a pitch of dizzy perfection. From his *Journals* we learn that Wilder considered that he was "shattering the ossified conventions" of realistic drama in order to let his "generalized beings" emerge.[10]

Act I, set in Excelsior, New Jersey, has about as much logic and verisimilitude as a vaudeville skit. Using the Brechtian strategy of screen projections and announcements, Wilder surveys the "News Events of the World." Mostly the reports concern the extreme cold, the wall of ice moving south, and the scene in the home of George Antrobus. It is six o'clock and "the master not home yet"; Sabina—the sexy maid who sometimes steps out of her part to complain about the play—is parodying the chitchat that often opens a realistic well-made play: "If anything happened to him, we would certainly be inconsolable and have to move into a less desirable residential district." The dramatic movement—never Wilder's strong point—involves waiting for Antrobus, contending with the cold, disciplining a dinosaur and a mastodon, receiving Antrobus's messages about surviving ("burn everything except Shakespeare"), and living in a typical bickering American family; Maggie Antrobus—unlike her inventive, intellectual, progressive husband—is instinctual and practical. Her children, Henry and Gladys, are emblems of violence and sexuality: the boy has obviously killed his brother with a stone; the girl has trouble keeping her dress down. When their father arrives home—

with a face like that of a Keystone Cop, a tendency to pinch Sabina, and a line of insults that sounds like W. C. Fields, the plot moves a bit more swiftly. He asks the dinosaur to leave and receives Homer and Moses into the house. As the act ends, the family of man is trying to conserve its ideas and knowledge—including the alphabet and arithmetic; it has also accepted "the refugees"—the Greek poet and the Hebrew lawgiver. The fire of civilization is alive, and members of the audience are asked to pass up chairs to keep it going.

Act II has the glitz of Atlantic City and the continuing problem of Mr. Antrobus dealing with the disasters of terrestrial life, the fact of his own sexuality, and the gnawing obligations of a father and husband. Once again, in the style of Brecht's epic theater, an announcer comments on screen projections—"Fun at the Reach" and the events of the convocation of "the Ancient and Honorable Order of Mammals." The plot is jumpier than ever—Miss Lily Sabina Fairweather, Miss Atlantic City 1942, tries to seduce Antrobus; a fortune-teller squawks about coming rains; Mrs. Antrobus bickers with the children, champions the idea of the family, and protests against Antrobus's breaking of his marriage promise; Antrobus, ashamed of himself at last, shepherds his flock and an assortment of animals into a boat.

Dealing with the effects of war, Act III is a powerful ending to this play about surviving. The wild and often inspired stage gimmickry of the first two acts has given way to the darkened stage and the ravaged Antrobus home. The emotions become more concentrated, the actions and efforts seem less scattered, the people's situations reach us as both tragedy and the inevitable business of men and women enduring. A play that seemed to be in revolt against realistic character representation, psychological probing, and the fine shadings of nineteenth-century drama, explodes into a moving exploration of personalities as they face the modern world. Deeply affected by the suffering of the war, the family members come into focus as human beings rather than emblems. Henry, the linchpin of this act about war and violence, explains himself for the first time and becomes more than a stick figure. Resentful about having "anybody over me" he has turned himself into a fascist as a way of mastering the authorities—his father, especially—who oppressed him. His truculence, fierce selfishness, and horrible individualism make him both a believable neurotic and a distillation of brutal resentment. Sabina, the temptress who has competed with Mrs. Antrobus for the attention of George, also comes alive as an individual. Driven to depression and cynicism by the hardship of the war, she pronounces that people "have a right to grab what they can find." As "just an ordinary girl" who doesn't mind dealing in black-market goods to pay for a night at the movies, she represents Wilder's honest appraisal of what suffering often does to people. Antrobus—the

principle of light, reason, and progress in the play—also has his moments of depression. He yearns for simple relief. "Just a desire to settle down; to slip into the old grooves and keep the neighbors from walking over my lawn." But somehow a pile of old tattered books, brought to life by passages from Spinoza, Plato, and Aristotle delivered by stand-in actors, rekindles the desire "to start building." Self-interest, complacency, despair, and violence coexist with intellectual aspirations and energies to begin again: although outnumbered by ordinarily self-involved and extraordinarily violent people, Antrobus can still go on. Despite the fact that the play ends, as it began, with "the world at sixes and sevens," there is still the principle of the family in Mrs. Antrobus's words and the desire to create the future from the past in Mr. Antrobus's reverence for Plato and technology.

The styles of this play are as various as modern literature and the twentieth-century stage. Not at all austere or carefully crafted, the drama is a brilliant jumble of Pirandello, Joyce, and epic theater.

Once again Wilder employs the manner, and the basic outlook, of *Six Characters in Search of an Author*. Sabina and Henry, particularly, make us aware that they are performing, that their parts are not entirely to their liking, and that they want to convey something about themselves that the theater does not have the means to express. Just as Pirandello's actors distort the story of a tragic family, Wilder's script does not always allow Sabina to tell about her truths or Henry to explain his real-life motivations. Like Pirandello's agonized daughter-figure, Henry insists on the brutal truth of his situation and interrupts the flow of the action to cry out against the false representation that he is given by the playwright. The management of the stage business in *The Skin of Our Teeth* is another reminder of Pirandello's theater. The awkward, clumsy matter of props and their arrangement leads us back to *Six Characters* and its arguments about where people should stand, what a room was like, and how people should look. Wilder delights in offering us not only a drama of survival, but also the laborious process of making a play—the scaffolding of a work of art is just as much his subject as the work itself. The stops and starts, the interruptions and localized quarrels of the actors, the puncturing of the whole theatrical illusion by the reality of actors who have become sick from some food and need to be replaced: such ploys carry through Wilder's theme of struggle and endurance, but also suggest the impact of Pirandello's artfully disordered dramas. Wilder's debt to Pirandello does not end with stage technique. The vision of the play— Antrobus beginning again and the family ready "to go on for ages and ages yet"—has most often been traced to Joyce's *Finnegans Wake*: Wilder himself acknowledged this partial debt in the midst of the brouhaha about his "plagiarism" (as noted in chapter 1). Other influences were overlooked. Pirandello's tragic and tormented family in Six Characters goes offstage only to find another theater in which to play out its drama: in a mood of guarded optimism, this is precisely what the Antrobus family is about to do. Sabina reports that they are on their way.

The Skin of Our Teeth also becomes a more enjoyable and intelligible theatrical experience when it is placed beside Bertolt Brecht's epic-theater works. The staging, character presentation, themes, and generalizing power bear an important relationship to Brecht's experiments in the 1930s.[11] Without having to argue for direct influences, one still can see a great deal about Wilder's techniques and idea by placing them in apposition to a work like *Mother Courage*. Since both plays take place in time of war, employ epic exaggeration, explore violence and selfishness, and take an unadorned look at what suffering does to people, it is not unreasonable to view them together. *Mother Courage* was also written three years before *The Skin of Our Teeth*, a fact that is not without significance considering Wilder's close touch with the currents of twentieth-century literature. Yet whether he was influenced directly or not, the affinities are strong. As pieces of stagecraft, both plays employ a large historical sweep and present material in a nonrealistic manner; Brecht's play of the Thirty Years War and Wilder's play of civilization's disaster both reach for large generalizations about man's durability and defects. The works do this essentially didactic job by means of screen projections, announcers, jagged episodic plots, and characters who are often stereotypical or emblematic. Wilder's third act overcomes Brecht's relentless detachment from his characters, but even here—as we sympathize with Sabina and Henry—we are not in a theater where the individual psyche is the main concern. Wilder is more involved with the process of learning, the hope of progress, and the impediments in human nature and culture than with the individuality of his people. In this he is one with Brecht, a writer who studies the harshness of civilization and the brutality of ordinary folk. Sabina's selfish, compromising, essentially amoral view of the human struggle for survival is like nothing so much as Mother Courage's matter-of-fact attitude toward suffering and willingness to hitch up her wagon and do business after her children are dead. Wilder has humanized and intellectualized this savage world, but he essentially works with its terrifying ingredients. Even Antrobus, the beacon light of the three acts, is tainted by the lust, a cynicism, cheapness, and hypocrisy that Brecht saw as the central features of bourgeois life. While Antrobus brings his noble and selfish impulses into a unity, he is still like Humanity as described by Brecht in *Saint Joan of the Stockyards*:

Humanity! Two souls abide
Within thy breast!
Do not set either one aside:
To live with both is best!
Be torn apart with constant care!
Be two in one! Be here, be there!
Hold the low one, hold the high one—
Hold the straight one, hold the sly one—
Hold the pair![12]

During the period when Wilder was working on *The Skin of Our Teeth*, the influence of *Finnegans Wake* was also taking effect on his vision. In his correspondence with Edmund Wilson in 1940 and 1941 Wilder gave his own version of the Joyce connection and offered a perspective on his imagination that is more wide-ranging than Robinson and Campbell's detective work. Wilder explained to Wilson that the *Wake* was a book with "a figure in the carpet": the design, he argued, was to be discovered in Joyce's anal eroticism; the great conundrum of modern literature was all about "order, neatness, single-minded economy of means."[13] Whether or not this is a reductive interpretation of Joyce, the "discovery" tells us something about Wilder's mind, points to his own career as a preserver of other people's motifs, and suggests a possible explanation for his constant borrowings in *The Skin*. Wilder claimed that he felt a joyous "relief"[14] as he understood Joyce's psychic and literary strategies; each interpreter of these remarks (and of Wilder's *Wake* obsessions) will have to decide what they are revealing. But the present study of Wilder's imagination offers this material as another example of his loving accumulation of ideas and patterns. The letters are a way of coming to terms with his own nature.

Writing to Wilson, Wilder spoke of the *Wake* as embodying "the neurotic's frenzy to tell and not tell."[15] Tell what? the reader might ask. Once again, this remark might be turned on Wilder's own work-in-progress: there are at least two of Wilder's recurring anxieties in the new play—resentment and guilt felt by a son *and* fear of civilization's destruction. His play, Wilder told Wilson, was meant to dramatize "the end of the world in comic strip."[16] On one level the description matched Joyce's remarks that *Finnegans Wake* is "a farce of dustiny." But Wilder's readers cannot help recalling the disaster of *The Bridge*, the end of the patrician world in *The Cabala*, the declining pagan world in *The Woman of Andros*. *The Skin of Our Teeth* may be seen as both a Joyce-burdened work and the latest version of Wilder's anxieties about violence and the collapse of Western culture.

The folk-style of *Our Town*, the social parable of *The Merchant of Yonkers*, and the rich suggestiveness and borrowing of *The Skin of Our Teeth* are three forms of expression that Wilder developed to convey the struggle of people enduring the churnings of the cosmos and the conflicts of civilization. The three plays offer guarded affirmations about man's strivings: growth and insight are abundantly available in Wilder's theater and make it altogether unlike the visions of other major American playwrights.

NOTES

1. Goldstone, p. 140.

2. Mary McCarthy, "Class Angles and a Wilder Classic," *Sights and Spectacles* (New York: Farrar, Straus and Cudahy, 1956), pp. 27–29.

3. Quoted by Linda Simon, p. 144.

4. Ibid., p. 143. Wilder's 1938 letter is in the Beinecke Collection; Wilson's 1940 letter is in *Letters on Literature and Politics 1912–1972*, edited by Elena Wilson, foreword by Leon Edel, introduction by Daniel Aaron (New York: Farrar, Straus and Giroux, 1977), p. 185.

5. Wilder, "Prefaces to *Three Plays: Our Town, The Skin of Our Teeth, The Matchmaker*," in *American Characteristics and Other Essays*, p. 109.

6. See Jane Kallir, *The Folk Art Tradition* (New York: The Viking Press, 1981). This fine treatment presents the international view of the folk-art phenomenon. For a more analytic treatment of the folk style see Jean Lipman and Alice Winchester, *The Flowering of American Folk Art (1776–1876)* (New York: The Viking Press, 1974). Lipman and Winchester study the motifs of the folk artist, show how folk painters were not involved with the quaint and the nostalgic, and analyze the use of sharpened colors and simplified forms. They also deal with the fact that folk painters did not paint from nature—just as Wilder did not strive for realistic representation.

7. Louis Cazamian, *The Social Novel in England, 1830–1850: Dickens, Mrs. Gaskell, Disraeli, Kingsley* (London: Routledge and Kegan Paul, 1973).

8. Karl Marx, *The Economic and Philosophic Manuscripts of 1844*, 7th ed., Dirk Struik, trans. Martin Milligan (New York; International Publisher, 1964), pp. 165–170.

9. Mary McCarthy, "The Skin of Our Teeth," *Sights and Spectacles*, pp. 53–56.

10. *Journals*, p. 22.

11. See also Douglas Wixon, Jr., "The Dramatic Techniques of Thornton Wilder and Bertolt Brecht," *Modern Drama*, XV, no. 2 (September 1972), pp. 112–124. This informative essay gives special attention to the anti-illusionist theater of Brecht and Wilder; it argues that Wilder employed Brechtian techniques from 1931 onward. The article does not explore the thematic affinities of the two writers.

12. *Seven Plays* (Brecht), ed. Eric Bentley (New York: Grove Press, 1961).

13. Letter to Edmund Wilson (January 13, 1940), Beinecke Library.

14. Letter to Edmund Wilson (June 15, 1940), Beinecke Library.

15. Ibid.

16. Letter to Edmund Wilson (June 26, 1940), Beinecke Library.

ROBERT A. MARTIN

Arthur Miller:
Public Issues, Private Tensions

"The American Dream is the largely unacknowledged screen in front of which all American writing plays itself out—the screen of the perfectibility of man. Whoever is writing in the United States is using the American Dream as an ironical pole of his story."[1]

—Arthur Miller

During a prolonged period of silence between *A View From the Bridge* in 1956 and *After the Fall* in 1964, Arthur Miller's dramatic vision underwent a major transition. From a focus on the inherent conflict between the individual and society that characterizes his earlier plays, with *After the Fall* Miller began to explore themes primarily concerned with a personal search for forgiveness, salvation, and a reluctant recognition of the forces that threaten to destroy his protagonist's sense of dignity and to diminish his humanity. The transition has been nowhere more obvious than in the two volumes of his *Collected Plays*,[2] which suggest a shift from primarily social causation in Volume One to a concern with the effects of public issues but presented through the refracted tense of a disengaged private sensibility in Volume Two. Although Miller has continued to explore the social and private ramifications of the 1930's Depression as a sociological reference point in such later plays as *The Price*, *The American Clock*, and in portions of *After the Fall*, his highest ambitions, have resided dramatically in the plays dealing

From *Studies in the Literary Imagination*. 21, no.2 (Fall 1988). © 1988 by the Department of English, Georgia State University.

with more universal themes and events as in *After the Fall, Incident at Vichy, The Creation of the World, Playing For Time,* and *The Archbishop's Ceiling.* Although these later plays have received the highest critical acclaim in Europe, they have never received the level of critical acceptance in the United States that one would expect for the mature work of a major playwright. To Miller, the plays of Volume Two apparently speak to a different audience that, for his purposes, has disappeared.

> When I began writing, when Tennessee Williams began writing, we shared the illusion that we were talking to everybody. Both of us wrote for the man on the street. So consequently the architecture of our plays, the embrace of our plays, their breadth, was in accordance with that conception. It was the very opposite of an elitist theatre, the very opposite of an intellectual theatre.[3]

In the earlier plays of Volume One, Miller posed a major dramatic question that reflected both the public issue and the private tension between family members that result in a betrayal of either a legal or social aspect of the American Dream. "In all my plays," he remarked in 1947, "I try to take settings and dramatic situations from life which involve real questions of right and wrong. Then I set out, rather implacably and in the most realistic situations I can find, the moral dilemma and try to point a real, though hard, path out. I don't see how you can write anything decent without using the question of right and wrong."[4] Miller has also defined the issues of his earlier plays as the dislocation of the family that results when public and private issues threaten to disrupt its essential unity, tradition, and harmony. In "The Family in Modern Drama," for one of several examples, Miller speculated on the nature of "great plays" as having a precise involvement between the public and the private spheres:

> Now I should like to make the bald statement that all plays we call great, let alone those we call serious, are ultimately involved with some aped of a single problem" It's this: How may a main make of be outside world a home? How and in what ways must he struggle, what must he strive to change and overcome within himself and outside himself if he is to find the safety, the surroundings of love, the ease of sod, the sense of identity and honor which, evidently, all men have connected in their memories with the idea of family?[5]

If we apply these pragmatically theoretical precepts to the plays of Volume One in terms of the major dramatic question and philosophical questions of the protagonists in each play, we find miller's philosophical intent parallels almost exactly what his audiences have found in watching the plays; that is, that Miller has built into each play an unavoidable recognition that the issues of public and private conflicts are socially and legally intertwined and irreducible beyond the point of free will and moral choice. Thus stated in many essays on drama and theatre, Miller asks a question of each play to which the audience already knows the sociologically correct and morally imperative answer. The major dramatic question in *All My Sons* becomes "Is Joe Keller guilty of shipping out defective engine heads that resulted in the deaths of twenty pilots?" *Resolution*: He is guilty and chooses suicide rather than to face his guilt and lose his son. In *Salesman* the question becomes "Will Willy Loman kill himself has Linda, Biff, and Happy suspect) because he is a failure in the eyes of his family?" *Resolution*: He does kill himself, not because he has failed to achieve his own dreams, but because he wants to put Biff ahead of Bernard again. In both *All My Sons* and *Salesman*, the issues of materialistic success versus the success of fatherhood are constructed so that nothing but death can result from the tensions that result since they are, philosophically at least, irreconcilable. In *The Crucible* the question is presented without the complication of the father–son relation, but with the complication of a historical precedent arising from the 1950's parallel between McCarthyism and witchcraft. The question now becomes one of conscience: "Will John Proctor hang rather than confess publicly to witchcraft and adultery?" *Resolution*: He will and does to preserve his name and identity as a man of conscience. *A View From the Bridge* is a more complicated play than critics have generally acknowledged, but follows structurally and philosophically upon the themes of betrayal through a violation of the Sicilian code of death to informers. "Will Eddie Carbone turn in Marco to the immigration authorities to save his name and to save Catherine for himself? *Resolution*: He does and is willing to die to vindicate his "honor" in front of the entire neighborhood for *polis* in the Greek sense of the community—the entire society). In brief, the four plays I have been discussing here illustrate Miller's dramatic strategy of combining public and private issues to arrest the audience's attention on the fundamental moral issue of the plays.

Never one to write plays, as an exercise in craftsmanship, Miller has consistently avoided issues that are entirely "social" or that result in "problem plays" of the contemporary moment. He has, in fact, made clear his case against critics and for his merger of public and private conflicts as thematically coherent paradigms. In "The shadows of the Gods" (1958) Miller had come to the point where he believed that the theatre in America was "narrowing its vision year by year, it is repeating well what it has done well before." As if to emphasize the point further by expanding his role as writer-critic-intellectual, Miller clarified his view of the relationship between man and society. Interestingly, Miller's idea differs radically from that of Eugene O'Neill, who stated that he was not interested in the relation between man and man, but only in "the relation between man and God."[6] For Miller, however, the social relationship is critical to the kind of theatre he is writing for.

> I can hear already my critics complaining that I am asking for a return to what they call problem plays. That criticism is important only because it tells something important about the critic. It means that he can only conceive of man as a private entity, and his social relations as something thrown at him, something "affecting" him only when he is conscious of society. I hope I have made one thing clear to this point—and it is that society is inside man and man is inside society, and you cannot even create a truthfully drawn psychological entity on the stage until you understand his social relations and their power to make him what he is and to prevent him from being what he is not. The fish is in the water and the water is in the fish.[7]

With the exception of *A Memory of Two Mondays*, all of Miller's early plays end with the death of the protagonists in situations of the crisis that results from a total commitment to one's chosen image of oneself, of who and what they are I the world they live in, whether that world is in Brooklyn or Salem. "There's nothing like death," Miller stated in a *Paris Review* interview in 1966. "Dying isn't like it, you know. There's no substitute for the impact on the mind of the spectacle of death. And there's no possibility, it seems to me, of speaking of tragedy without it."[8] As a playwright, then, whose reputation has rested firmly on the bedrock of realism and as a private citizen who has always been involved in liberal causes, Miller's shift away from death as a resolution and toward a more abstract, contemplative, and retrospective viewpoint in his later plays has led him into new territories of his dramatic imagination that am unfamiliar to audiences and critics alike. He has, perhaps unwittingly, strayed into territories that are essentially European in attitude and intellect—a territory unbiased by American audiences who are still groping for a connection between themselves, their society, and their fragmented culture. Even the most casual reading of Miller's later plays in Volume Two reveal that his vision has darkened, his philosophical disquietude has deepened, and his belief in the possibility of social redemption through an act of individual commitment has progressively diminished. In the early plays, Miller attempted to answer specific questions of who is guilty and why, what circumstances might have misled a character such as Joe Keller to commit a crime against his society, or why Willy Loman feels compelled to commit suicide in order to be a success. In the later plays the law is either corrupt, as in *Incident at Vichy* and *The Archbishop's Ceiling*, or the protagonist such as Quentin in *After the Fall* is no longer able to see the value of personal or social commitment. "It is that Law," Miller has said, "which, we believe, defines us as men,"[9] in his Introduction to Volume One. And as if to define the new direction his plays after 1956 will take, he has Quentin tell the Listener in the first few lines of *After the Fall*, "I think now my disaster really began. when I looked up one day—and the bench was empty. No judge in sight."[10]

Miller's approach to writing a play—at least up to *After the Fall*—has always; been to ask, "What do I mean? What am I trying to say?" This analytical self-probing has paid off handsomely when Miller was dealing with subjects with which his audience could identify. The specific moral gravity of his early plays lend themselves precisely to these questions because they lead to conclusions both dramatic and thematic that are based on reasonable alternatives. Joe Keller knows exactly what he has to conceal; Willy Loman knows exactly what is troubling Biff; and John Proctor knows exactly why Abigail would like nothing better than to see his wife, Elizabeth, hanged for a witch. Eddie Carbone may not have the same degree of insight into his mixed motives as do his dramatic predecessors, but, he knows exactly what he must do to remove Rodolpho from his home and neighborhood. And he does it.

Miller's thematic shift in his later plays derives from a change in the nature of the questions he is now asking himself. Instead of "What do I mean? What am I trying to say?" Miller now asks himself, "What is real? What is reality? On what basis does one dare make a commitment to another person?"[11] Clues to such a shift lie scattered about everywhere in Miller's work even before *After the Fall*. As early as 1960 with *The Misfits*, the absoluteness of Miller's social and moral imperatives may have started to dissolve. As Roslyn asks Gay Langland, "Oh, Gay, what is there? Do you know? What A there that stays?" we see for the first time in Miller's work a major character who, although uncertain, clearly poses the alternative of a compromise rather than a confrontation. "God knows," Gay replies,

"Everything I ever see was comin' or goin' away. Same as you. Maybe the only thing is ... the knowin'. Cause I do know you now, Roslyn, I do know you. Maybe that's, all the peace there is or can be."[12] Such a statement of reconciliation by any of Miller's earlier protagonists would have been literally impossible only four years previously. And the setting of the film—the American West—is finally itself an illusion. The remote canyons full of wild mustangs, new hopes, and old dreams that day, Guido, and Pence are searching for turn out to be merely empty. What is real for these misfit cowboys is only a memory from the American past that cannot possibly be fulfilled or sustained in the reality of the present.

The most visible hint of Miller's changing vision of man and his society, however, occurs in the closing moments of *After the Fall*. Quentin ("struck" as Miller's acting cue suggests) by the force of his accumulated experience, suddenly turns away from Holga and proclaims, "Is the knowing all? To know, and even happily, that we meet unblessed; not in some garden of wax fruit and painted trees, that lie of Eden, but after, after the Fall, after many, many deaths. Is the knowing all?"[13] For Gay Langland, knowing was enough; but for Quentin it poses a dilemma: even as he discovers some particle of truth to live by, he can't believe that the betrayal—by friends, parents, wives, himself—is real. "God," he exclaims, "why is betrayal the only truth that sticks?"[14] By the end of the play, Quentin can only ask the ultimate question—does he dare commit himself to Holga after all his past commitments have turned into disasters? Miller's answer is a qualified "yes," but implies by indirection that all relationships are impermanent at best, and that the commitment made in the name of love may be the greatest illusion of all. Quentin, therefore—unlike Miller's earlier protagonists—can walk away from a conflict, but only with the precarious piece of knowledge that for him there is no innocence left and we truly meet each other "unblessed."

In many ways, *Incident at Vichy* is a continuation of *After the Fall* in its theme of universal guilt and responsibility. Like *The Crucible* historically, Vichy has a certain amount of authentic and existential angst attached to it because of its origins in the Holocaust and with World War II to background, but with the reverberations of those events dramatized more directly. In this play, Miller's public issues and private tensions are represented on a much wider scale through the psychiatrist, LeDuc—representative of reason and sanity—who (contrary to Miller's approach in *Fall*) convinces Von Berg, a prince, that the nature of man is inherently evil, Von Berg hands his pass to freedom to LeDuc, who accepts it, and walks away, but who does so only with an excruciating awareness of his own guilt and complicity. "I wasn't asking you to do this," LeDuc tells Von Berg. "You don't owe me this."[15] The situation is pure Sartrean and asks the question, "What is reality in the face of the absurd?" Von Berg is Miller's true existential hero, an extension of Chris Keller's idealism ("Once and for all you can know there's a universe of people outside and you're responsible to it, and unless you know that, you threw away your son because that's why he died"[16]) and John Proctor's mighty conscience ("How may I live without my name? I have given you my soul; leave me my name"[17]). Von Berg is also the one character in the later plays who fits Miller's definition in the *Collected Plays* Introduction of 1956:

> For I understand the symbolic meaning of a character and his career to consist of the kind of commitment he makes to life or refuses to make, the kind of challenge he accepts and the kind he can pass by. I take it that if one could know enough about a human being one could discover some conflict, some value, some challenge, however major or minor, which he cannot find it in himself to walk away from or turn his back on.[18]

And even here, Von Bug's aristocratic status will most likely save him From death in a prison. Miller's point in *Vichy*, however, is not that the Holocaust could have happened so easily, but that it could so easily happen again.

The Price (1968), although seemingly a return to the conventions of realism, contains elements of a questionable reality. As the central issue of a son's betrayal by his father emerges to constitute the private, tension as well as the major issue of the play, the moment of recognition between the boundaries of public issues and private outrage (the family again) emerges in a new construction. The moment unites past and present as Victor Franz, a policeman, learns from his brother Walter, a wealthy surgeon, that their father had lied to him about the family's finances. While Victor had committed himself to supporting his father for the remainder of his life, and in the process sacrificed his own family's economic welfare, he now learns that his father actually had $4000 all during the time Victor says "we were eating garbage here."

VICTOR: Why didn't you tell me he had that kind of money?
WALTER: But I did when you came: to me for the loan.
VICTOR: To "Ask Dad?"
WALTER: Yes!
VICTOR: But would I have come to you if I had the faintest idea

he had four thousand dollars under his ass? It was meaningless to say that to me."[19]

The price that Victor pays is a lifetime of diminishment, disillusionment, and economic deprivation. For Walter, who did not help his father at all, the unreality of Victor's life compared with his own simply reflects the inner hollowness of the family relationships. To Victor's claim that he kept the family from "falling apart," Walter replies, "what fell apart? What was here to fall apart? Was there ever any love here? When he needed her, she vomited. And when you needed him, he laughed. What was unbearable is not that it all fell apart, it was that there was never anything here."[20] At the end of *The Price* both brothers walk away from their past and each other with little more than a fragmentary awareness of the failed reality of their lives. Such is the real price, Miller asserts, socially and personally, of misplaced commitments; such is the price of failing to distinguish between what is real and what is reality. What is real in the play for Miller is his dramatic retelling of the effect of the 1930's Depression on the lives of Americans caught between the dream of Gatsby's mythical "fresh green breast of the new world," as viewed by the generation of the 1920's, and the reality of the nightmare that ushered in the 1930's. For Miller, the water is still in the fish and the fish in the water.

The final play I would like to discuss here is *The Archbishop's Ceiling* (1977), a play that Miller at one time believed was "the best thing I ever wrote."[21] For Miller, the play was "a dramatic meditation on the impact of immense state power upon human identity and the common concept of what is real and illusory in a group of writers living in a small European capitol today."[22] The setting is an apartment in a former Archbishop's palace in which, under an ornate ceiling that may or may not contain hidden microphones, four acquaintances gather to discuss the political problems faced by one of the group, a dissident writer, who is trying to decide whether he should attempt to emigrate to the West. They not only suspect that the ceiling is bugged, but that one of their number—Marcus—may in some way be involved with the authorities and is about to betray them. As Christopher Bigsby has noted in the Methuen edition's *Afterword*, "They meet in the conviction—never fully confirmed—that they are being overheard. In other words, they are turned into actors and their lives into theatre; but there is, finally, no evidence for the existence of the audience before whom they take themselves to be performing."[23] The level of unrelieved anxiety and private tensions that Miller creates in the play, along with the apparent lack of a perceivable reality, leads the audience to Kafka's castle, in which neither God nor man nor the state can absolutely be known to reside. Beyond the political and public issues of freedom of speech, thought, and action (which the critics took to be the central issue of the play), resides Miller's unstated but nevertheless underlying assumption that the nature of political reality is, in fact, the unreal, a world in which not only anything can probably happen, but probably will. At the end of the play, a knock is heard at the door. Sigmund, the dissident novelist, is presumably about to be arrested. He turns to Maya, an actress and his former mistress, to ask forgiveness, and then to Adrian, an American writer, to whom he says, "Is quite simple. We are ridiculous people now. And when we try to escape it, we are ridiculous too."[24]

In Miller's later plays commitment is not something one dies for, it is something that one survives for. If in the early plays public issues and private tensions were closely joined, in the later plays they are overshadowed with an introspective, philosophical, and existential angst that the earlier protagonists did not have to contend with. If we do indeed, as Miller seems to be saying in play after play, "meet unblessed," it becomes a point of new departure in his plays in which contemporary mankind—socially and individually—stands poised on the edge of an abyss in which everything and nothing exist simultaneously. And if Miller has taken a dramatic and philosophical leap—as I believe he has—beyond "real questions of right and wrong" into questions of "what is real, what is reality," the critics and audiences in the American theatre seem unable or unwilling to follow. Neither of which possibilities has lessened his ideals of truth and social justice, nor the optimism that Miller feels for the future. In his recently published autobiography, *Timebends*, he has noted once again his affection and respect for the American political guarantees in the Bill of Rights following an encounter with Alexei Surkov, head of the Soviet Writer's Union, concerning the possibility of Soviet writers joining PEN and changing the organization's constitution and voting procedures. "The miraculous rationalism of the American Bill of Rights suddenly seemed incredible, coming as it did from man's mendacious mind. America moved me all over again—it was an amazing place, the idea of it astounding."[25]

NOTES

1. Matthew C. Roudané, "An Interview with Arthur Miller," in *Conversations with Arthur Miller*, Matthew C. Roudané, ed. (Jackson and London: University Press of Mississippi, 1987), p. 361.

2. Arthur Miller, *Arthur Miller's Collected Plays*, Vols. 1 and 2 (New York: Viking, 1957, 1981).

3. Mark Lamas, "An Afternoon with Arthur Miller," in *Conversations with Arthur Miller*, Matthew C. Roudané, ed., pp. 382–83.

4. *A Treasury of the Theatre*, John Gassner, ed. (New York: Simon and Schuster, 1950), p. 1061.

5. "The Family in American Drama" in *The Theater Essays of Arthur Miller*, Robert A. Martin, ed. (New York: Viking, 1978), p. 73, Hereafter noted as *Theatre Essays*.

6. Eugene O'Neill, "On Man and God," in *O'Neill and His Plays*, Oscar Cargill, ed. (New York: New York University Press, 1961), p, 115.

7. "The Shadows of the Gods" in *Theatre Essays*, p. 185.

8. Olga Carlisle and Rose Styron, "Arthur Miller: An Interview" in *Theatre Essays*, pp. 266–67.

9. Introduction to *The Collected Plays of Arthur Miller*, Vol. I in *Theatre Essays*, p. 149.

10. *Arthur Miller's Collected Plays*, Vol, 2, p. 129.

11. Arthur Miller to Robert A. Martin in conversation, October 1985 at Miller's home in Connecticut.

12. *Collected Plays*, Vol. 2, p. 123.

13. *After the Fall, Collected Plays*, Vol. 2, p. 24.

14. *Ibid.*, p. 202.

15. *Incident at Vichy* in *Collected Plays*, Vol. 2, p. 290.

16. *All My Sons* in *Collected Plays*, Vol. 1, p. 127.

17. *The Crucible* in *Collected Plays*, Vol. 1, p. 328.

18. Introduction to *Collected Plays* in *Theater Essays*, p. 118.

19. *The Price* in *Collected Plays*, Vol. 2, p. 364.

20. *Ibid.*, p. 368.

21. Arthur Miller to Robert A. Martin in conversation, June 1983 at Miller's home in Connecticut.

22. *New York Times*, May 11, 1977, p. 8.

23. Christopher Bigsby, "Afterword" to *The Archbishop's Ceiling* (London: Methuen London Ltd., 1984), p. 92.

24. *Ibid.*, p. 90.

25. *Timebends: A Life* (New York: Grove Press, 1987), p. 583.

ANNE DEAN

Sexual Perversity in Chicago

Like most of Mamet's plays, *Sexual Perversity in Chicago* is set in a desensitized society. The characters inhabit a cheap and fraudulent world in which standards decline daily and sexual intimacy seems to have become public property. Language is often used shoddily and obscenities are commonplace—their sexual connotations have, through overuse, become dulled, rather like their users' consciousnesses. Human relationships have become attenuated to the point at which men and women view each other as little more than media-created stereotypes, and millions of people watch television soap operas sincerely believing that their convoluted plots reflect real life.

In the mid-1970s when the play was written, what Mamet calls the "jejeune super-sophistication"[1] of the American populace was at its height. The "Swinging Sixties" had come and gone and, in their place, was a cynical, rather detached society that plundered the most negative aspects of the previous decade's sexual revolution, emphasizing promiscuity and irresponsibility to the detriment of its emotional sanity. Because of the dominating influence of all things sexual, erotica flourished, pornography boomed, and sex could be found in the unlikeliest of places. It was—indeed, it still is—used to sell clothes, food, cars, books, and toothpaste. Such an emphasis upon the nonemotional aspects of sexuality was bound, sooner or later, to result in a deleterious blunting of the nation's consciousness. This is

From *David Mamet: Language as Dramatic Action.* © 1990 by Associated University Presses, Inc.

precisely what has happened to the four young people portrayed in Mamet's play. For them, sex really has become a dirty word, a sniggering pastime for the easily bored. Rather than fulfilling its original function as an integral part of an emotional relationship, sex is for them little more than a cheap thrill, something that men "do" to women and for which women should be grateful.

Mamet's view of such a society is bleak; his characters are alienated in every sense of the word. Alienation, as Marx observed, is descriptive of more than people's sense of estrangement from the result of their labors. Marx wrote, "What is true of man's relationship to his work, to the product of his work, and to himself, is also true of his relationship to other men, to their labor, and to the objects of their labor ... each man is alienated from others, and ... each of the others is likewise alienated from human life."[2] As a result of this sense of alienation, human relations come to rest on what Christopher Bigsby describes as "an exploitation that is not necessarily of itself material but is derived from a world in which exchange value is a primary mechanism. One individual approaches another with a tainted bargain, an offer of relationship now corrupted by the values of the market ... people become commodities, objects."[3]

The characters in *Sexual Perversity in Chicago* are, in common with many others in Mamet's drama, emotionally adrift in a world where the second-rate has been accepted as the norm. They occasionally glimpse the possibility of something other than the tawdry lives they endure, but these momentary revelations have no chance of taking root in the febrile atmosphere in which they exist. With no real moral base upon which to pin their ideas, their lives are shapeless, distorted, and corrupt. As Richard Eder points out,

> the characters speak as if calling for help out of a deep well. Each is isolated, without real identity. They talk to find it—"I speak, therefore I am"—and the comic and touching involution of their language is the evidence of their isolation and tracklessness.... Their world is full of.... lessons learned but learned of the unreasonable ferocity, the lack of shape or instruction of middle American life.[4]

Sexual Perversity in Chicago is replete with dialogue powered by a pulsatingly neurotic energy. Its urban rhythms are merciless and relentless; its movement is conveyed by Mamet's rapid sentence structure and the fast-paced episodes. The frenetic verbal affrays that the characters indulge in are their way of concealing the vacuum that exists at the root of their lives; the abandon with which they bounce wisecracks and platitudes off one another only partially conceals their desperation. So long as they can continue to joke, criticize, and fantasize, they can delude themselves that they are happy.

Structured in swift, short scenes that rise, like dirty jokes, to punchlines, the play examines the void at the heart of contemporary sexual relationships. Life for Mamet's characters is as shallow as the fictional lives of their soap opera heroes and incorporates many aspects of an obscene joke; their exploits are crude, debased, and usually over very quickly. The form and shape of the play are themselves reminiscent of such jokes, and so the very structure of the piece enacts its meaning. The parallel is carried one stage further with Mamet's Bernie constantly spouting his elaborate and ludicrous sexual fantasies. These are reported to Danny as fact, but are little more than routine dirty stories that have been opened out into mini-dramas in which Bernie himself is the chief protagonist. Sex dominates all their conversations, just as work dominates those of the salesmen in *Glengarry Glen Ross*. Such characters have only one subject at their disposal and they must discuss it exhaustively in an effort to conceal their insecurity and loneliness. Their relentless bragging is intended to impress, but underneath the cool bravado lies a desperate vulnerability. Mamet has commented upon this aspect of the work: "Voltaire said words were invented to hide feelings. That's what the play is about."[5]

Bernie is an excellent example of a man who uses language to conceal his insecurity. He urges Danny to view women as he does—as sexual objects that can be picked up and discarded at random. He does his very best to impress his friend with his callous insouciance and contemptuous reductivism but, in fact, he is terrified of women. There is no evidence to suggest that he has ever had a satisfactory relationship, in spite of all his masculine posturing. Bernie is, literally, "all talk." In order to assuage his fears, he constantly reduces women to the most basic physical level. For him, they can be succinctly summed up in the following crude jingle:

Tits and Ass. Tits and Ass. Tits and Ass. Tits and Ass. Blah de Bloo. Blah de Bloo. Blah de Bloo. Blah de Bloo. *(Pause.)* Huh? (scene 30, p. 47)

The opposite sex is thus described in purely sexual terms, which are debased further still by occurring alongside a string of nonsense words designed to convey Bernie's apparent casual contempt. By saying the words aloud, he can wield his spurious power over women. However, his final "Huh?" suggests his weakness and need for approbation and concurrence from an easily swayed friend.

In *Sexual Perversity in Chicago*, Mamet looks at the ways in which language can contribute to the formation of sexist attitudes. His characters employ a kind of subtle linguistic coercion as a means of influencing and persuading their companions to concur with their way of thinking. Consequently, barriers are erected that are then exceedingly difficult to penetrate. Bernie's relentless chauvinism filters through to Danny, who is influenced by and in awe of his ostensibly suave friend. As a result, he eventually becomes as coarse and offensive as his mentor. Mamet points out that the play is much concerned with

> how what we say influences what we think. The words that Bernie Litko says to Danny influence his behavior; you know, that women are broads, that they're there to exploit. And the words that Joan says to her friend Deborah: men are problematical creatures which are necessary to have a relationship with because that's what society says, but it never really works out. It is nothing but a schlep, a misery constantly.[6]

Partly because of the pressures of language exerted by their companions and partly through cultural fiats, any relationship formed between Mamet's male and female characters is doomed to failure. The men are unwilling—or unable—to view women as anything other than sex slaves and receptacles for their pleasure and, not surprisingly, the women regard men as natural enemies and emotional cripples. The reductive and crude exploitative images of women that are daily emblazoned across tabloid newspapers and broadcasted in countless films and television programs have perverted the perception of their audience. In such a society, women have only two choices: they can try to emulate the ideal feminine stereotype pushed forward by the media and craved by unimaginative men like Bernie and Danny, or they can turn to feminism with a vengeance. Those who choose the former are satirized by Tom Wolfe in his essay, "The Woman Who Had Everything." In this work, Wolfe writes of the trouble to which some women will go in an effort to conform to a popular (and desirable) stereotype:

> Women [engage in a ceaseless quest to] make themselves irresistibly attractive to the men of New York ... coiffeurs ... The eternal search for better eyelashes! Off to Deirdre's or some such

place, on Madison Avenue—moth-cut eyelashes? Square-cut
eyelashes? mink eye-lashes? ... Or off to somewhere for the
perfect Patti-nail application, $25 for both hands, $2.50 a finger,
false fingernails ... [then] the skin ... that purple light business at
Don Lee's Hair Specialist Studio...[7]

Desirability often depends therefore upon as much artificial assistance
as can reasonably be applied—and at a price. Wolfe exposes the obsession
with public myths of beauty and sexuality for the absurdity it undoubtedly is.
Good sense and dignity are overridden by a desperate need to conform.

Although women are without question the most offensively exploited
of the sexes, men do not escape the pressures of the media. They, too, must
manufacture a false image and endeavor to live up to it in order to attract the
equally false objects of their desire. It is little wonder that love should so
infrequently enter such relationships; they are superficial in the extreme,
with both parties acting out a fantasy ideal of what they imagine the other
craves. Mamet blames the mass media for much misery and heartache,
observing that *Sexual Perversity in Chicago* is, "unfortunately, tales from my
life."[8] He explains,

My sex life was ruined by the popular media. It took a lot of
getting over. There are a lot of people in my situation. The myths
around us, destroying our lives, such a great capacity to destroy
our lives.... You have to sleep with every woman that you see,
have a new car every two years—sheer, utter nonsense. Men who
never have to deal with it, are never really forced to deal with it,
deal with it by getting colitis, anxiety attacks and by killing
themselves.[9]

Certainly Bernie seems to be desperately trying to live up to a
stereotype; his adopted persona suggests that he is something of a "super-
stud." What is so tragic about a man like Bernie is that he is, at base, painfully
aware of his own inadequacy and fear, and that is why he must behave in the
overtly masculine fashion that has become his trademark.

The "perversity" of the title is not, as one critic ironically observes, "a
misprint for perversion"[10] but is entirely intentional. Mamet's characters are
indeed perverse, but not in the sense that might be expected—although one
of them does observe that "nobody does it normally any more" (scene 1, p.
13). The perversity Mamet has in mind emanates from his characters'
diminished perception of each other, their lack of understanding, and the

cold, inhumane manner in which they conduct their lives. What is crucially missing is any real sense of value beyond the material, or an awareness of any need unrelated to immediate sexual satisfaction.

Sexual Perversity in Chicago was voted the best Chicago play of 1974 and, in 1975, won an Obie for its off-Broadway production. There have been a number of productions of the work, both in the United States and England and, in 1986, a filmed version was released under the title of *About Last Night.*

The first scene sets the tone for the play: it is fast, funny, and outrageous. In this episode, Bernie lovingly outlines for Danny the details of a ludicrously unlikely story about a recent "erotic" exploit. Bernie's tale is something of a tour-de-force of sexual fantasy, and the longest and most involved of a number of stories he relates throughout the play. What is ironic is that he wants Danny to believe every word he utters. This hymn to sexual excess is hypnotic not only for Danny but for Bernie as well; so involved does he become in the sheer force of his narrative that he appears to believe it himself. This early conversation establishes Bernie as the character with the "knowledge" and Danny as his eager ingénu and is reminiscent of the power plays of language frequently found in the work of Harold Pinter:

> DANNY: So how'd you do last night?
> BERNIE: Are you kidding me?
> DANNY: Yeah?
> BERNIE: Are you fucking kidding me?
> DANNY: Yeah?
> BERNIE: Are you pulling my leg?
> DANNY: So?
> BERNIE: So tits out to here so.
> DANNY: Yeah?
> BERNIE: Twenty, a couple years old.
> DANNY: You gotta be fooling.
> BERNIE: Nope.
> DANNY: You devil.
> BERNIE: You think she hadn't been around?
> DANNY: Yeah?
> BERNIE: She hadn't gone the route?
> DANNY: She knew the route, huh?
> BERNIE: Are you fucking kidding me?
> DANNY: Yeah?
> BERNIE: She *wrote* the route. (scene 1, p. 7)

Bernie's responses to Danny's initial questions are intended by him to be rhetorical; answering a question with another question is his way of emphasizing just how incredible a time he actually enjoyed the previous evening. He works Danny up into a kind of verbal frenzy merely by refusing to give him anything other than strongly implied hints of sexual success. Mamet captures perfectly the grammatical anarchy of idiomatic conversation in the repetition of "building" words like "so" and "yeah" and the abbreviation of a sentence such as "Twenty, a couple years old." The age of the girl is left totally ambiguous, which is just as well since, shortly after its initial mention, it moves from about eighteen to over twenty-five, depending upon whether Bernie currently favors the idea of corrupted naïveté or well-seasoned maturity. Bernie encourages Danny's lasciviousness through his carefully constructed routine; Danny's breathless "Yeah?" increases in intensity until one can almost hear his jaw drop open in erotic anticipation. Exactly why Danny finds it difficult to believe that the girl should have been "Twenty, a couple years old" is unclear. His incredulity is possibly due to the fact that Bernie's success with such a young woman seems unlikely; although Bernie's age is unstated, it is clear that he is considerably older than his friend. Perhaps the woman's age, referred to by Bernie, most potently symbolizes female sexual rapacity for the two men. Or perhaps Danny's incredulity is his way of encouraging Bernie into new areas of excess.

In an effort to make his fantasy sound as realistic as possible, Bernie takes pains to establish the correct location and timing. Danny enjoys the detail, no matter how irrelevant, and incites his friend's erotic imagination still further by uttering neat, monosyllabic asides that will not interrupt the flow of things too much:

DANNY: So tell me.
BERNIE: So okay, so where am I?
DANNY: When?
BERNIE: Last night, two-thirty.
DANNY: So two-thirty, you're probably over at Yak-Zies.
BERNIE: Left Yak-zies at one.
DANNY: So you're probably over at Grunts.
BERNIE: They only got a two o'clock license.
DANNY: So you're probably over at the Commonwealth.
BERNIE: So, okay, so I'm over at the Commonwealth, in the pancake house off the lobby, and I'm working on a stack of those raisin and nut jobs ...
DANNY: They're good.

BERNIE: ... and I'm reading the paper, and I'm reading, and I'm
    casing the pancake house, and the usual shot, am I right?
DANNY: Right.
BERNIE: So who walks in over to the cash register but this chick.
DANNY: Right.
BERNIE: Nineteen, twenty-year old chick ...
DANNY: Who we're talking about.
BERNIE: ... and she wants a pack of Viceroys.
DANNY: I can believe that ... Was she a pro? (scene 1, pp. 8–9)

Bernie still plays cat and mouse, keeping Danny in suspense until the last possible moment. He wants to paint a picture of the events that will accurately reflect his "experience" in all its glory and he makes Danny work for the trifles he offers. Bernie creates an atmosphere of Yuppie-style establishments, where neon lights and potted palms endeavor to give some class to what are, essentially, late-night pickup joints. The slightly sleazy sounding bar and restaurant names add to the aura of Bernie's sexual adventure: "Yak-Zies" and, especially, the onomatapoeiac "Grunts." Danny's responses to the more prosaic aspects of Bernie's tale add immeasurably both to the humor of the scene and to our understanding of him. The banality of his reactions is absolutely hilarious. Despite Bernie's linguistic game of suspense and titillation, which both men clearly relish, Danny unfathomably wishes to hear even mundane details. Whatever the input, he exhibits no impatience and enjoys the opportunity to comment on (and become vicariously involved in?) Bernie's "adventure."

Danny is also obsessed with establishing if the girl was, in fact, "a pro" (pp. 9–10 and 14), that is, a prostitute. At regular intervals, he repeats the question: "Was she a pro?" as if this fact would somehow add to the spiciness of Bernie's tale. As far as Bernie's fantasy is concerned, this information is— at least for his present purposes—irrelevant. He has not yet made up his mind whether she should be a sexually voracious virgin who has been deranged by his charms, or a hard-nosed trouper to whom such exploits are routine. He stalls Danny's tireless questions by responding with variations on the theme of "Well, at this point we don't know" and "So, at this point, we don't know. Pro, semi-pro, Betty Co-Ed from College, regular young broad, it's anybody's ballgame" (scene 1, p. 9).

As Bernie's story progresses to the ridiculous point at which the girl dons a World War II flak suit before allowing him to make love to her, so Danny's ingenuousness similarly reaches new heights:

BERNIE: ... From under the bed she pulls this suitcase, and from
    out of the suitcase comes this World War Two Flak suit.
DANNY: They're hard to find.
BERNIE: Zip, zip, zip, and she gets into the Flak suit and we get
down on the bed.
DANNY: What are you doing?
BERNIE: Fucking.
DANNY: She's in the Flak suit?
BERNIE: Right.
DANNY: How do you get in?
BERNIE: How do you think I get in? She leaves the zipper open.
(scene 1, pp. 11–12)

Bernie is clearly getting carried away with his fantasy. He no longer wishes to hear
Danny's questions and inane remarks, but wants to get on with the action. As
Bernie moves further and further into the ecstasies of libidinous fantasy, Danny
remains down-to-earth, questioning details that had at first acted as spurs to give
the story depth and realism, but now serve only as interruptions and irritations.

The fantasy eventually ends with Bernie's "recollection" that the girl
telephoned her friend during their lovemaking, asking her to make "airplane noises"
over the telephone, and then set fire to the hotel room in an orgy of abandon:

BERNIE: ... Humping and bumping, and she's screaming "Red dog
    One to Red dog Squadron" ... all of a sudden she screams
    "Wait." She wriggles out, leans under the bed, and she pulls
    out this five gallon jerrycan.... she splashes the mother all over
    the walls, whips a fuckin' Zippo out of the Flak suit, and
    WHOOSH, the whole room is in flames. So the whole fuckin'
    joint is going up in smoke, the telephone is going "Rat Tat
    Tat," the broad jumps back on the bed and yells "Now, give it
    to me *now* for the Love of Christ." *(Pause.)* So I look at the
    broad ... and I figure ... fuck this nonsense. I grab my clothes,
    I peel a saw-buck off my wad, as I make the door I fling it at
    her. "For cabfare," I yell ... Whole fucking hall is full of smoke,
    above the flames I just make out my broad (she's singing "Off
    we go into the Wild Blue Yonder")....
DANNY: Nobody does it normally anymore.
BERNIE: It's these young broads. They don't know what the fuck
    they want. (scene 1, p. 13)

Bernie concludes his imaginary exploit without his having reached orgasm: it is as if, even within the realms of a dream, to submit to such an action is to acknowledge some form of commitment. As he imagines his "lover" lying amidst the smoke and flames, his fear of and sheer contempt for women become the uppermost emotions in his mind. Rather than complete the sexual act he has begun, he prefers to turn on the girl, flinging money in her face as if to suggest that she is nothing more than a common prostitute and he a disgusted client. For such deep-seated contempt to manifest itself within the safety of a sexual fantasy suggests Bernie's very real sexual problems. He tells Danny that, having set the room aflame and produced her quota of sound effects, the girl begged him to bring her to orgasm. By denying her that satisfaction, Bernie likewise denies himself. His language takes on the coldness of a character like Mickey Spillane's Mike Hammer; his terminology owes more to fictional cops and robbers than to real life. He evidently sees himself as the cool-headed, although rather misogynistic, stud who has been represented by countless film and television heroes. Bernie has been acting all the time, but perhaps nowhere so purposefully as here; he strives to give Danny the impression of his supreme control over the situation and, in so doing, verbally reenacts what has never taken place. By saying the words aloud, Bernie enjoys a frisson of excitement over an event that had only ever existed in his mind.

Bernie's contempt for women is consolidated as he blames the imaginary girl for her perversion: "It's these young broads. They don't know what the fuck they want." This is patently untrue since, if nothing else, the girl in his dream exploit knew *exactly* what she wanted. Symbolically, Mamet has suggested Bernie's inability to have a satisfactory sexual relationship with a woman, and does so within the first few minutes of the play. Finally, Danny finds out if Bernie's "lover" was indeed "a pro":

BERNIE: A pro, Dan ... is how you think about yourself. You see
    my point? ... I'll tell you one thing ... she knew all the pro
    moves. (scene 1, p. 14)

Sexual Perversity in Chicago has much in common with Jules Feiffer's *Carnal Knowledge*, which was filmed in 1971 by Mike Nichols. In fact, Mamet's play has been directly compared with Feiffer's work: in his book, *The Literature of the U.S.A.*, Marshall Walker observes that it is "a set of clever variations on material ... treated in Jules Feiffer's screenplay for Mike Nichols's *Carnal Knowledge*,"[11] and John Elsom likens it to "Feiffer's cartoons, but less acid and more human."[12] *Carnal Knowledge* concerns the changing fortunes of two young men from their college days through to their early forties. The film version was a great success; Jack Nicholson starred as the sexually predatory Jonathan and Art Garfunkel as his more reserved friend, Sandy. Like Bernie, Jonathan spends his time trying to convey a sense of knowing sexual expertise to his eager, and sexually curious, younger friend. Also like Bernie, Jonathan is unable to sustain a satisfactory sexual relationship. At first, in an effort to retain a feeling of superiority over Sandy, he steals Susan, Sandy's girlfriend, and later becomes involved in a love affair with a stereotypical "dumb blonde" who wants to be loved for more than her body. Jonathan is capable of being aroused only by the most buxom—and passive—of women, is incapable of treating them as individuals, and refers to them always in demotic terms that relate to their physical characteristics. Early in the screenplay, Jonathan and Sandy discuss the ideal woman. Like Bernie and Danny, the two men at first differ from one another in their crassness:

> SANDY: You want perfection.
> JONATHAN: What do you want, wise guy?
> SANDY: She just has to be nice. That's all.
> JONATHAN: You don't want her beautiful?
> SANDY: She doesn't have to be beautiful. I'd like her built, though.
> JONATHAN: I'd want mine sexy-looking.
> SANDY: I wouldn't want her to look like a tramp.
> JONATHAN: Sexy doesn't mean she has to look like a tramp.
>   There's a middle ground.... Big tits.
> SANDY: Yeah. But still a virgin.
> JONATHAN: I don't care about that.... I wouldn't mind if she was
>   just a little ahead of me—with those big tits—and knew
>   hundreds of different ways ...[13]

Just as Danny is the character in Mamet's play who actually manages to sustain some kind of sexual relationship, however, brief, so it is the naïve Sandy who first attracts the beautiful—and sexually experimental—Susan. Like Bernie, Jonathan resents the relationship and ignores any emotional involvement that may exist, reducing it always to a sexual level. The truth of the matter is that Jonathan feels excluded. In an effort to put his own "stamp" on the proceedings, he notes how Susan's "tits were too small," how "her legs were great" and (with great generosity!) declares that he "wouldn't kick her out of bed."[14] Bernie, too, realizes that he may be losing his hold over Danny and so tries to influence (and diminish) Danny's view of Deborah:

BERNIE: So what are we doing tomorrow, we going to the beach?
DANNY: I'm seeing Deborah.
BERNIE: Yeah? You getting serious? I mean she seemed like a hell
     of a girl, huh? The little I saw of her. Not too this, not too that
     ... very kind of ... what? *(Pause.)* Well, what the fuck. I only saw
     her for a minute. I mean first impressions of this kind are often
     misleading, huh? So what can you tell from seeing a broad
     one, two, ten times? You're seeing a lot of this broad.... I mean,
     what the fuck, a guy wants to get it on with some broad on a
     more or less stable basis, who is to say him no. *(Pause.)* Alot of
     these broads, you know, you just don't know. You know? I
     mean what with where they've been and all. I mean a young
     woman in today's society ... time she's twenty two-three, you
     don't know *where* the fuck she's been. *(Pause.)* I'm just *talking*
     to you, you understand. (scene 14, pp. 30–31)

Bernie includes Danny in his plans for "the beach" without hesitation; to
admit the possibility that there may be other parties who have a claim on his
friend's time is unthinkable for him. His reaction to the news that Danny is
"seeing Deborah" is to try to diminish Deborah's importance in the scheme
of things while carefully avoiding outright criticism—at least at first. Lest
Danny suspect his motives, Bernie must take care not to appear too jealous
or resentful so he begins by praising Deborah. However, he then moves
rapidly into another phase wherein she becomes just another "broad" who
might have a very dubious sexual history. After his initial statement, "she
seemed like a hell of a girl," he undermines his approach by adding, "The
little I saw of her" and "first impressions ... are ... misleading." He goes on to
infer that men can never know women, even if they meet them on numerous
occasions, thus suggesting that Danny's relationship with Deborah must be
of the most shallow kind. He acknowledges that his friend is "seeing a lot" of
the woman but infers that whatever may be between them can only be sexual.
Bernie gradually moves toward the final phase of his verbal destruction of
Deborah; almost imperceptibly, she has become just another "broad." He
takes on the attitude of an older brother, an experienced and trusted giver of
advice to one who needs assistance; "Alot of these broads, you know, you just
don't know. You know?" He brings Danny, unwillingly or otherwise, into the
conversation, involving him, making him collude with him, never pausing to
allow time for any response. He begins to talk about Deborah as if she were
something dirty, or diseased: "where [she's] been and all." Double standards
are rife here. It is perfectly acceptable for Bernie and Danny to have had

numerous sexual encounters—indeed, they believe this makes them attractive catches—but women are not allowed similar experiences.

Bernie's repetition of "what the fuck" also adds to the coarseness of his innuendo and serves as a means of grounding the conversation at the most basic sexual level. By now, there is the suggestion that Deborah is unworthy of any serious consideration, and is probably not unlike the "pro" in his initial fantasy. This latter insinuation is given further weight by Bernie's echo of the indeterminate age of his "pro"; Deborah, like the fantasy girl, is aged about "twenty two-three." His concluding assertion that he is merely *"talking"* to Danny about Deborah anticipates Moss and Aaronow's notable linguistic distinction between "talking" and "speaking" in *Glengarry Glen Ross.*

Bernie and Jonathan are excellent examples of what Colin Stinton calls the "Teach-like character";[15] both men are, essentially, full of hot air and have very little genuine knowledge to impart, but they nonetheless see themselves as instructors and mentors. Stinton comments upon the specific type of "teaching" that occurs in *Sexual Perversity in Chicago*. He notes that Bernie's "Teach-like quality is really bullshitting ... sexual bullshitting of the type that men usually engage in most. The whole idea of the conquest—this is one of the things that identifies such men in their pathetic little way. The likes of Bernie use this built-in tendency to influence and persuade those around them."[16]

Because of the extremely coarse, sexist language used in the play, Mamet has sometimes been accused of being deliberately outrageous and misogynistic. Although there may be some truth to criticism that the playwright courts outrage, Mamet does not do so in order to score cheap laughs out of obscenity and sexism. Connie Booth, who has appeared in two of Mamet's plays, speaks specifically about the playwright's use of obscene and scatalogical language: "He is anything but arbitrary... . It would be interesting for those who believe his work to be obscene to take out all those words and see just how much their absence would affect both the sense and rhythm of the piece."[17]

As far as accusations of misogyny are concerned, *Sexual Perversity in Chicago* could, in some ways, be viewed as a feminist play in that it is so very critical of its male characters; Mamet examines what he sees as the deplorable state of sexual morality in modern urban America and, in so doing, illuminates inadequacy and ignorance. His female characters are so disenchanted with the men they meet, and so resentful of the pressures put upon them to form heterosexual relationships, that they appear to have retreated into lesbianism!

Colin Stinton asserts that, although Mamet portrays chauvinistic, sexist, or violent men in his plays, it does not mean that he is in some way advocating their behavior:

> A lot of criticism of [Mamet's] work—especially from women— emanates from the rather incredible notion that he is somehow advocating sexist men! If anything, he is calling attention to the fact that there *are* sexist men and this is why they are that way, this is how their minds work. He then subjects these characters to some scrutiny.... Perhaps more than other writers, he takes to heart the maxim that you should only write about what you personally have experienced, and [Mamet's] experience is definitely not having been a woman! ... He feels happier writing from the male viewpoint, but the male viewpoint doesn't have to be a sexist viewpoint. One of the things that is always illuminating is to talk to [Mamet] and to see him in action with his family and you realize what a caring kind of person he is. You begin to see that his plays always deal with the obstacles to the kind of care, kind of love and affection he wishes were there. Some people feel that because he has portrayed the world in this negative, tragic way he is somehow saying that this is how it should be. This is really ridiculous. In fact, what he does is to bemoan the fact that there is not a better world ... he is in fact a feminist writer in that sense because he is very, very critical of males.... He depicts such characters to show up their fragile egos, to show them struggling to find out who they are. He tries to provide some insight into how their minds work.[18]

Similarly, Miranda Richardson believes that

> Mamet is documenting what he has heard other men say. The fact that he *does* it is instructive. He is not suggesting that this is the right way to behave.... He might be writing from his own experiences, but I still enjoy what his experience is. I certainly don't think he's a sexist writer ... he still manages to spark one's imagination, even if there are only ten lines to go on in his script. There's a deep sensitivity in his writing.[19]

Of the allegations of sexism in *Sexual Perversity in Chicago*, Mamet says: "There's a lot of vicious language in the play.... The real vicious language is the insidious thing, calling somebody a little girl or this girl. That's a lot more insidious than calling somebody a vicious whore—which is also insidious but you can deal with it."[20] C. Gerald Fraser notes that Mamet's play is about "the myths that men go through"[21] and that Mamet "credited the Women's Liberation movement with 'turning [his] head around a lot.' He added: 'Women have babies, have the menstrual period, for God's sake, they have something to do with the universe.'"[22]

The women's roles in *Sexual Perversity in Chicago* are quite substantial but, again, it is the male characters who enjoy many of the best lines. Mamet is only too aware of this imbalance and is anxious to correct it and thus alleviate some of the criticism. While writing the play, he remarked, "I kept getting huutzed by the director and the women in the cast, you know, to write parts for women. I said I don't know anything about women, they said 'Well, you better find out, you're getting too old'—so I tried. The fleshier parts are the male parts. I am more around men; I listen to more men being candid than women being candid. It is something I have been trying to do more of."[23]

Colin Stinton feels that those who urge Mamet to write more parts for women are, in some respects, asking for the wrong thing; he believes that the writer goes to such pains to be truthful in his work that if he should begin to try, self-consciously, to write in a women's voice, he may be doomed to falsity and failure. Mamet is concerned about the imbalance of male/female roles in his plays to the extent that during the writing of *The Woods*, Stinton was told (albeit apocryphally) that Mamet had given some of Nick's lines over to Ruth to make their dialogue more even in terms of volume. Stinton said that this was exactly the sort of thing that Mamet would do and that the story is probably absolutely genuine. Similarly, the role of John, the clairvoyant in *The Shawl* was obviously written for a male actor, but since the play has been performed, Mamet has considered changing the homosexual pair at the center of the work to a heterosexual couple. Thus, John could, without much hindrance, become Joanne! Mamet retains some doubts, but it is a mark of his desire to appease criticism that he has considered the transition at all.

From my own reading of Mamet's plays and from comments made by him concerning women, I feel that the school of opinion that brands him sexist is completely wrongheaded. Quite clearly, many of Mamet's male characters are hardly admirable or self-assured; there is little in them to suggest that the writer is in some way condoning their behavior. His female characters, on the other hand, often seem to represent Mamet's own wish that the world were a nicer and more caring place. In *The Woods*, Ruth and Nick try to come to terms with their rather precarious love affair. Their propinquity in the weekend cottage serves to underline Ruth's need for love and affection and Nick's reticence and anxiety. Ruth's main concerns are romance and love, whereas Nick's are far more sexually oriented. For Ruth, sex is important only when it is a part of love; for Nick, love can often be an obstruction to good sex. In *Speed the Plow*, it is the temporary secretary who comes to work for Gould, the film producer, who injects compassion and warmth into a sterile and ruthless environment. Whatever Karen's ultimate motives prove to be, she brings peculiarly feminine vigor and energy to the proceedings, causing the mercenary Gould to reevaluate (at least temporarily) his opinions on what is worthy and what is not. Her idealism and fecund creativity leave their mark on an otherwise barren and arid play.

Deborah and Joan in *Sexual Perversity in Chicago* also appear to be idealistic but, as the play progresses, their disappointment with what they are offered becomes almost tangible. By the end of the work they seem to have concluded that affection is often more genuine and freely forthcoming from members of their own sex, and that the whole fabric of heterosexual pairing is something of a confidence trick. Indeed, Joan laments:

> JOAN: ... and, of course, there exists the very real possibility that the whole thing is nothing other than a mistake of *rather* large magnitude, and that it never *was* supposed to work out.... Well, look at your divorce rate. Look at the incidence of homosexuality ... the number of violent, sex-connected crimes ... all the anti-social behavior that chooses sex as its form of expression, eh? ... physical and mental mutilations we perpetrate on each other, day in, day out ... trying to fit ourselves to a pattern we can neither *understand* (although we pretend to) nor truly afford to *investigate* (although we pretend to).... It's a dirty joke ... the whole godforsaken business. (scene 20, pp. 37–38)

Joan's sentiments are explored further in a short play Mamet wrote in 1977 entitled *All Men Are Whores: An Inquiry;* the female character in that play muses:

> ... What if this undignified and headlong thrusting toward each other's sex is nothing but an oversight or physical malformity? *(Pause.)* Should we not, perhaps, retrain ourselves to revel in the sexual act not as the consummation of pre-destined and regenerate desire, but rather as a two-part affirmation of our need

for solace in extremis.... In a world where nothing works. (scene 17, p. 199)

Exactly how seriously we are meant to take all this is left deliberately unclear. Certainly in Joan's case, Mamet has her spout her ideas as she and Deborah have lunch; Joan frequently undercuts the sobriety of the situation by casual interruptions such as "Are you going to eat your roll? ... This roll is excellent" (scene 20, p. 38) and so on. Deborah responds only intermittently and monosyllabically, twice announcing "I disagree with you" and stating that she is "moving in with Danny." Mamet therefore makes Joan's grave sentiments psychologically questionable; could not there be a suggestion that she is, in fact, jealous of her friend's success with Danny and that her denigration of heterosexuality is little more than resentment? Deborah's disagreement with her friend's ideas is also based on rather ambiguous premises; she has just decided to live with Danny, and so Joan's criticism of the basis of sexual relationships between men and women could be seen as a threat. Her friend's castigation undermines Deborah's security and the reasons for her decision to move in with her lover. It is not, therefore, altogether surprising that she should repeat that she disagrees with Joan—in her present situation, she cannot really afford to do otherwise. There remains the possibility that she secretly agrees with Joan; her silence as her friend rambles on could indicate either concurrence or disapproval. Mamet deliberately leaves the sexual psychology of his female characters ambiguous—and somewhat ambivalent.

In *Sexual Perversity in Chicago*, the characters can conceive of themselves only as sexual beings; the world in which they live forces them to do so. Theirs is a much harsher world than that portrayed in Edward Zwick's cinematic version of the play, *About Last Night* (1986). In the film the director chose to concentrate almost exclusively upon the "romantic" aspects of Danny and Deborah's affair, which completely distorted the meaning and altered the balance of the work. Bernie and Joan were reduced to wise-cracking cyphers who existed on the sidelines of the protagonists' lives. What is intended by Mamet to be a bitterly perceptive satire on contemporary sexual mores became, in the film, little more than a routine Hollywood teenage romance, albeit with a slightly harder edge and a rather more brittle script.

In Mamet's play, the characters' sexual experimentation and hard-edged aggression function as their principal means of expressing their urban neuroses. There is little time for romance or sweet words. Moments of self-perception, or a brief, fleeting acknowledgment of life outside of sex, are undercut by the relentless pragmatics of everyday life. An earlier bout of Joan's lamentations is interrupted by that unavoidable aspect of modern life, the telephone:

> JOAN: It's a puzzle. Our efforts at coming to grips with ourselves
> ... in an attempt to become "more human" (which, in itself is
> an interesting concept). It has to do with an increased ability
> to recognize *clues* ... and the control of energy in the form of
> *lust* ... and *desire* ... (And also in the form of hope). But a *finite*
> puzzle. Whose true solution lies, perhaps, in transcending the
> rules themselves ... and pounding of the fucking pieces into
> place where they DO NOT FIT AT ALL.... Some things
> persist. "Loss" is always possible ... (*Pause. Phone rings.*)
> DEB: I'll take it in the other room. (scene 13, pp. 29–30)

When Mamet's characters indulge in philosophical theory, their language inevitably takes on a heightened, linguistically more sophisticated tone. It is as though they have moved beyond their usual limited range of discourse into another sphere of understanding; there is a "textbook" literalness in what they have to say. Joan speaks as she seldom does at such times—her streetwise banter is suddenly replaced by careful phrasing and elevated terminology—and only once does a familiar obscenity intrude. But this speech is unnatural; it is contrived, pretentious, and didactic. Joan tries to sound authoritative, impressive, and in command of what she avers but there remains a sense that Mamet is also satirizing this level of awareness. Like the rest of his characters' conversation, Joan's is artificial—although in a more educated way. That Mamet constantly undercuts high-flown sentiments with crass banalities or ringing telephones is perhaps his way of suggesting that *nothing* these people can say is truly authentic; it is all the manufacture of a false society.

Joan and Deborah share an apartment and are, apparently, close friends. Whether their relationship is of a platonic or a sexual nature is unclear, but Mamet does drop the occasional hint that their friendship may be at least partly lesbian. For example, when Deborah first meets Danny, she announces that she is "a Lesbian" (scene 5, p. 18), although later she refutes this claim, choosing to imply that although she has had "some Lesbianic experiences.... and ... enjoyed them" (scene 7, pp. 20–21) she is, in fact, happily heterosexual. In any case, the friendship between Joan and Deborah seems to be warm and genuine, if a little overpossessive on Joan's part. What is noticeable, both about Joan in her reaction to Danny, and Bernie in his opinion of Deborah is that both parties are jealous of any outside involvement. As Christopher Bigsby notes, they "value only the apparently simple, undemanding and essentially adolescent camaraderie of the same sex,"[24] viewing members of the opposite sex as an intrusion upon their privacy. On both sides, each appears to possess an element of protective concern for his or her friend's welfare; each sees sexual involvement leading inevitably to pain and unhappiness and as something to be avoided on anything other than the most casual basis. The following exchange takes place between Deborah and Joan when the former has been seeing rather a lot of her new boyfriend:

> JOAN: So what's he like?
> DEB: Who?
> JOAN: Whoever you haven't been home, I haven't seen you in two days that you've been seeing.
> DEB: Did you miss me?
> JOAN: No. Your plants died. *(Pause.)* I'm kidding. What's his name?
> DEB: Danny.
> JOAN: What's he do?
> DEB: He works in the Loop.
> JOAN: How wonderful for him.
> DEB: He's an assistant Office Manager.
> JOAN: That's nice, a job with a little upward mobility.
> DEB: Don't be like that, Joan.
> JOAN: I'm sorry. I don't know what got into me.
> DEB: How are things at school?
> JOAN: Swell. Life in the Primary Grades is a real picnic. (scene 8, pp. 21–22)

From her opening question, it is clear that Joan will in no way be persuaded that the intrusive Danny could possibly be a worthy lover for her friend. In that initial query is an aggressive hard-boiled bitterness, which is not concealed by the question's commonplaceness. The tone of the question is one that invites a response of denigration rather than approval and Joan's edginess and barely suppressed sarcasm establish her mood for the rest of the scene. An actress playing Joan's part could interpret her mood in several ways: she could be hurt, bitter, resentful, aggressive, chiding, or even playful. As always with Mamet's work, great sensitivity to the text is required if all the nuances and subtleties are to be exploited. It would be only too easy to portray

Joan as an unsympathetic harpy who is intent upon destroying her friend's relationships. This would, indeed, be a great shame since Mamet has written the part with sensitivity and understanding for the character's emotional position. Although Joan *does* resent Danny's involvement with Deborah, it is important to be aware of her vulnerability and the reasons for her resentment. Joan has found a good and kind friend in Deborah and is understandably loath to lose her to someone who might be a harmful influence.

Joan's convoluted but brilliantly authentic sentence: "Whoever you haven't been home, I haven't seen you in two days that you've been seeing" has been described by Ross Wetzsteon as "the utter clarity of total grammatical chaos."[25] Such language owes something to that heard in Woody Allen films, particularly those that chronicle the increasing incidence of urban neurosis such as *Play it Again, Sam, Annie Hall,* and *Manhattan.* The idiom is purely American, with no concessions made toward "good" English. As Jack Shepherd has observed, Mamet "is so in touch with the way American people talk that he often doesn't use any discernible English grammar."[26] Thus, sentences are relentlessly broken up midway, tenses are confused, and grammatical accuracy is the least priority. It is all ostensibly very naturalistic but, as Shepherd has also observed, "in [Mamet's] text ... everything that is written is *intended* ... it is never just there for the sake of it."[27]

Through Joan's convolutions and inconsistencies, Mamet suggests so much about her state of mind. His inspired use of anarchic rhythms is another way in which he extracts every ounce of humor from a situation. Joan's defensive sarcasm—"Your plants died" immediately followed by "I'm kidding"—serves to illustrate her adopted veneer of urban toughness, which can be so easily shattered when she finds herself cornered and in a vulnerable position. Despite her assertion that she is "kidding," she goes on to denigrate Danny's job as a pathetic one for a man to hold and, finally, having failed to elicit any criticism from Deborah, seems to blame her for the fact that "Life in the Primary Grades is a real picnic." It is clear from the tone that it is anything *but!* Joan suggests that her life is tormented and fraught with problems enough as a kindergarten teacher, without Deborah adding to her misery by keeping away from home. Cleverly and insidiously, Joan manages to make Deborah feel guilty for her actions. In Joan's eyes, the selfishness is not her own but that of her gadabout friend.

Bernie is as wounded as Joan by his friend's love affair. As he tells imaginary "buddies" at the gym all about Danny's relationship (about which, presumably, Danny had told him in confidence), Bernie takes on once again the role of seasoned mentor and advisor:

BERNIE: So the kid asks me "Bernie, Blah, blah, blah, blah, blah, blah, blah, blah, blah. The broad *this*, the broad *that*, blah, blah, blah, blah." Right? So I tell him, "Dan, Dan, you think I don't know what you're feeling, I don't know what you're going through? You think about the broad, you *this*, you *that*, you think I don't know that?" So he tells me, "Bernie," he says, "I think I love her." *(Pause.)* Twenty eight years old. So I tell him, "Dan, Dan, I can *advise*, I can *counsel*, I can speak to you out of my *experience* ... but in the final analysis, you are on your own. *(Pause.)* If you want my *opinion*, however, you are pussy-whipped." (I call 'em like I see 'em. I wouldn't say it if it wasn't so.) So what does he know at that age, huh? Sell his soul for a little eating pussy, and who can blame him: But mark my words. One, two more weeks, he'll do the right thing by the broad *(Pause.)* And drop her like a fucking hot potato. (scene 19, p. 37)

Bernie establishes the avuncular tone that he will use to denigrate Danny's relationship with Deborah in the opening words of this speech: he calls Danny "the kid" and suggests that Danny's reliance upon his advice is far from unusual. Bernie's dismissal of the seriousness of Danny's affair moves from his claim that he, too, has felt exactly the same way to his contention that Danny is "pussy-whipped." En route, he has condescendingly sneered that a mere boy (of twenty-eight!) could entertain such feelings and has wasted no time in repeating, over and over, that Deborah is nothing more than a broad. There is something pathetic in Bernie's assumption that Danny could not know he was in love "at that age"; after all, twenty-eight is an age by which many men are already married with a family. Bernie tries to make Danny sound like a lovelorn child—"Bernie ... I think I love her"—and negates Danny's sentimental outburst by once again reducing the relationship to the crudest level. He implies that Danny is ready to "sell his soul for a little eating pussy," rushing his words and abbreviating his sentence in an effort to emphasize the absurdity of Danny being "in love." He immediately follows this coarse statement with a phrase that accurately sums up his phony "macho" bonhomie: "and who can blame him". With studied, casual conceit, Bernie implies that he has, himself, been similarly misguided; the folly of youth is rejected in knowing maturity. The underlinings emphasize those words that Bernie feels are most relevant and important to his argument. For him, they are the essence of friendship but, as he pointedly remarks, "in the final analysis"—a sly dig by Mamet at a dreadful Yuppietype cliché—Danny must make his own decisions. The false effort Bernie makes to sound fair and reasonable and, above all, *sympathetic* to his friend's plight, is both appalling and irresistibly funny.

At the end of his speech, Bernie suddenly changes tack. He announces that Danny will "do the right thing by the broad" by dropping her like "a fucking hot potato." In his mind, this is precisely what Danny will do; all he needs is some careful prodding and manipulation. Subtlety is not one of Bernie's strong points. After he has rid his and Danny's relationship of the offensive Deborah, things can be the same again between the two friends. There has been no mention that Deborah is being somehow exploited or used by Danny—quite the opposite. However, in order to give his story a well-rounded and equitable conclusion, Bernie chooses to imply that she would, in fact, be far better off without Danny, who will soon see the error of his ways.

It is significant that Bernie should begin his destruction of his friend's affair with a string of nonsense words. Again and again, Mamet's frightened characters lapse into nonsense language when under pressure, and Bernie is no exception. He chooses to forsake normal speech on more than one occasion in the play and each time he does so he undermines the seriousness of his subject. His reductive chant, already quoted elsewhere, takes its rhythms from nonsense words: "Blah de Bloo. Blah de Bloo. Blah de Bloo. Blah de Bloo" (scene 30, p. 47). The "Tits and Ass," which makes up the rest of the litany is, therefore, reduced to similar meaninglessness. In *Glengarry Glen Ross*, Richard Roma refers to the couple to whom Levene has just sold $82,000 worth of land as "Harriett and blah blah Nyborg" (act 2, p. 38) and in *American Buffalo*, Teach pretends that he is not angry with Grace and Ruthie because he has lost a large sum of money at cards, choosing to affect a world-weary tone of selfless resignation:

> TEACH: These things happen, I'm not saying that they don't ...
>   and yeah, yeah, yeah, I know I lost a bundle at the game and
>   blah blah blah. (act 1, p. 15)

In *The Squirrels*, Arthur responds to Edmond's question about the sense of a particular passage in one of the plays they are writing with a stream of repetition, making gibberish of the words he speaks:

> EDMOND: What does this mean?
> ARTHUR: Meaning? Meaning?
> EDMOND: Yes.

ARTHUR: Ah, meaning! Meaning meaning meaning meaning
    meaning. Meaning meaning meaning. You ask me about
    meaning and I respond with gibberish ... (episode 1, p. 23)

Roma's description of Mr. Nyborg as "blah blah" suggests his contempt for and sheer disinterest in the unfortunate man; as far as the ruthless salesman is concerned, Mr. Nyborg is now completely irrelevant. Teach's concluding "blah blah blah" takes up the rhythm he sets up in the preceding "yeah yeah yeah" and is intended to convey his detached emotional stance in the matter. It fails miserably. Arthur's repetition of "meaning" is a desperate attempt at ironic humor; both men are supposedly creative writers but are struggling with a banal story. To conceal his very real sense of impotence, Arthur chooses to joke about it, masking his loss of control in self-deprecating irony in an effort to appear self-effacing and sardonic. It is clear from these random examples that gibberish can be utilized in a most versatile manner; in Mamet's drama, even nonsense can speak volumes.

    A number of scenes in *Sexual Perversity in Chicago* are set in night clubs and bars; the one-night stand and casual barroom encounter are obviously familiar occurrences for the individuals dramatized here. In particular, the frequenting of singles bars—those peculiarly horrible inventions of the fake friendly American culture of excess—has become a way of life. In a book that among other things, outlines the contemporary sexual mores of New Yorkers, Stephen Brook recalls a visit to "Rascals," a singles bar on First Avenue:

> This is real singles territory, and lone wolves scour this stretch of the East Side for prey.... Opposite the crowded bar, a ... gutsy-voiced female lead belted out old Stones and Motown numbers. I bought a drink and stood about feeling foolish, then left.[28]

Early in *Sexual Perversity in Chicago*, Mamet satirizes the kind of encounter that can take place in such establishments. Bernie tries to pick up Joan as she sits alone in the bar, and he becomes very hostile indeed when she makes it clear to him that she is not interested:

BERNIE: How would you like some company. *(Pause.)* What if I
    was to sit down here? What would that do for you, huh?
JOAN: No, I don't think so, no....
BERNIE: ... So here I am. I'm just in town for a one-day layover,
    and I happen to find myself in this bar. So, so far so good.

> What am I going to do? I could lounge alone and lonely and
> stare into my drink, or I could take the bull by the horn and
> make an effort to enjoy myself ...
> JOAN: Are you making this up?
> BERNIE: So hold on. So I see you seated at this table and I say
> to myself, "Doug McKenzie, there is a young woman," I say to
> myself, "What is she doing here?", and I think she is here for
> the same reasons as I. To enjoy herself, and, perhaps to meet
> provocative people. *(Pause.)* I'm a meteorologist for T.W.A. ...
> (scene 3, pp. 14–15)

Bernie carries on in this vein for some time, lying about his name and his job,
trying to make his life sound romantic and thrilling until, finally, Joan has
heard enough:

> JOAN: Can I tell you something?
> BERNIE: You bet.
> JOAN: Forgive me if I'm being too personal ... but I do not find you
> sexually attractive. *(Pause.)*
> BERNIE: What is that, some new kind of line? Huh, I mean, not
> that I mind what you think, if that's what you think ... but ...
> that's a fucking rotten thing to say.
> JOAN: I'll live.
> BERNIE: All kidding aside ... lookit, I'm a fucking professional,
> huh? My life is a bunch of having to make split-second
> decisions.... You think I don't have better things to do....
> nowhere cunt.... You're a grown woman, behave like it for
> chrissakes.... I mean what the fuck do you think society is, just
> a bunch of rules strung together for your personal pleasure?
> Cockteaser.... You got a lot of fuckin' nerve. (scene 3, pp.
> 16–17)

Bernie completely ignores Joan's assertion that she would not, in fact, be
interested in his company, preferring to launch into his elaborate, supposedly
sexy routine. His line is an extraordinary amalgam of lies, patronage, and
soap-opera bravado. It is interesting to note that he uses a typical WASP
name, rather than admit to his own very ethnic name, Bernie Litko. In his
fantasy projection of himself, Bernie not only takes on another man's job but
also another man's name—one that may be more acceptable to a woman who
might, just possibly, be class conscious or even anti-Semitic. He also

emphasizes the temporariness of his "fling" by stating that he is "just in town for a one-day layover." Mamet's use of the term "layover" rather than "stopover" adds a suggestive subtext to Bernie's opening gambit, as does his statement that he acted on impulse when he saw her, taking the "bull by the horn." The use of the word "horn" in the singular, rather than in the more familiar plural, is surely intended as a phallic quip.

Bernie cannot allow even the smallest detail of his story to slip; even when Joan wounds his ego with the news that she doesn't find him "sexually attractive," he stubbornly hangs on to his fantasy about being a high-flying meteorologist. This, like the rest of his spiel, is an integral part of the act. Cut to the quick by her remark, his rhetoric becomes more and more vicious. He alternates obscenities with biting sarcasm until, finally, he resorts to something that Mamet's characters often rely upon when under pressure: he cites civic rules of conduct. Bernie appears to be under the impression that the "bunch of rules" that apply to his own "personal pleasure" should in no way extend to Joan.

Just as the salesmen in *Glengarry Glen Ross* see themselves only in terms of their jobs, so Bernie views himself purely in terms of a sexual athlete, no matter how absurd this may seem. He has built up for himself a fantasy world that is quite as powerful as that invented by George and Martha in Edward Albee's *Who's Afraid of Virginia Woolf?* or by Susan in Alan Ayckbourn's *Woman in Mind*. Joan's remark that Bernie is not sexually inviting to her is more than a mere insult to such a man; it is tantamount to negating his existence. She has punctured his dream and devastated his self-image. Bernie's violent reaction and frightening aggression is, therefore, understandable. His predicament is reminiscent of that of the Vicomte de Valmont in Christopher Hampton's adaptation of de Laclos's *Les Liaisons Dangereuses;* when the Vicomte's sexual reputation and vanity are threatened, he crumbles. He has become so much a part of his assumed persona that the real man beneath the sophisticated exterior hardly exists. Rather than risk exposure of his essential vulnerability, he decides to give up the love of his life and to accept death. So it is with Bernie, although his dilemma is dramatized in considerably less romantic and expansive terms. As the abuse tumbles out and his grammar collapses, Bernie's agony is almost tangible; he does all he can to crush the woman who has, in a sense, murdered him with words.

After his singular lack of success with Joan, Bernie's first reaction is to advise Danny to behave in exactly the same way! His manner of speaking is infused with the nonchalance of one who has just enjoyed runaway success with his quarry:

> BERNIE: The main thing, Dan.... The main thing about *broads*....
> Is two things: One: The Way to Get Laid is to Treat 'Em Like
> Shit.... and Two: Nothing ... *nothing* makes you so attractive to
> the opposite sex as getting your rocks off on a regular basis.
> (scene 4, pp. 17–18)

Bernie's linguistic slip in the first two lines suggests his haste to communicate
his great knowledge to Danny. At first, it is enough to suggest the "main
thing" but then he recalls that there are, in fact, "two things." Bernie has
clearly learned little from his encounter with Joan—in fact, the whole
incident seems to have receded to the back of his mind or been hastily
reconstituted into a success story of which he can be proud. His dictum for
success with women is echoed in *Lakeboat*. In that play, too, the men are
lonely and ignorant, spending most of their time talking about encounters
that have probably never taken place. In a moment of pedagogic fervour,
Fred tells Dale how to succeed sexually with women, and exactly reproduces
Bernie's advice:

> FRED: ... my uncle, who is over, is conversing with me one night
> and as men will do, we start talking about sex. He tells a story.
> I tell *My* story. This takes him aback. "What?" he says, "The
> way to get laid is to treat them like shit." Now you just stop for
> a moment and think on that. You've heard it before and you'll
> hear it again but there is more to it than meets the eye. Listen:
> THE WAY TO GET LAID IS TO TREAT THEM LIKE
> SHIT. Truer words have never been spoken. And this has been
> tested by better men than you or me. (scene 10, pp. 54–55)

Fred's recipe for success is lamentable. To give it further weight, he imbues
his speech with a number of well-worn, risible clichés and platitudes, which
he fondly believes will consolidate its truth. *Lakeboat* is a play without a single
female character; there is certainly more than a suggestion that all the
fantasizing and bragging is little more than a means of disguising latent
homosexuality—or, at least, the kind of homosexuality that can develop in an
all-male environment. In a short work written by Mamet to be performed as
a companion piece to the 1979 revival of *Sexual Perversity in Chicago*, the
following, very telling, line is included: "Our most cherished illusions—what
are they but hastily constructed cofferdams restraining homosexual panic?"
(*Sermon*, p. 157).

A number of critics have commented upon the distinct possibility that

Bernie could be homosexual. Certainly, his insistent and overemphatic displays of masculinity seem to suggest this. When questioned on the topic, he reacts in a rather panicky way, at first stating that an early childhood experience with a pervert in a cinema could have ruined him for life and, moments later, countering this with, "A kid laughs these things off. You forget, you go on living" (scene 17, p. 36). The level of hatred he displays toward such men also has a touch too much hysteria about it; he viciously decries a homosexual sales assistant as "a fucking fruit" (scene 17, p. 33) and the man in the cinema as a "faggot queer" (ibid., p. 35).

Underneath their sardonic acceptance of the world as it is, and their rare insights into the cause of their anxiety, Mamet's characters are achingly lonely. Without exception, they seek affection but are unable to sustain relationships based upon emotion. Deborah and Danny enjoy some moments of tenderness but outside pressures eventually force them to declare their love affair null and void, and to negate the experience as a waste. Neither of them has a good word for the other once the relationship has been dissolved; perhaps to acknowledge that genuine feelings were ever present is somehow to admit weakness. However, the need for love and the expression of love persist.

A character in *All Men Are Whores: An Inquiry* sums up the overwhelming feeling of powerlessness and abandonment felt by so many of Mamet's individuals:

> Our concept of time is predicated upon our understanding of death.
> Time pases solely because death ends time. Our understanding of death is arrived at, in the main, because of the nature of sexual reproduction.
> Organisms which reproduce through fission do not "die."
> The stream of life, the continuation of the germ plasm, is unbroken.
> Clearly.
> Just as it is in the case of man.
> But much less apparently so in our case. For we are sentient.
> We are conscious of ourselves, and conscious of the schism in our sexuality.
> And so we perceive time. *(Pause.)* And so we will do anything for some affection. (scene 1, p. 185)

Later in the play, the same character laments the lack of true affection in the world:

Where are our mothers, now? Where are they?.... In cities where we kill for comfort—for a moment of reprieve from our adulterated lives—for fellow-feeling *(Pause.)* (I have eyelashes, too ...)
....One moment of release.
....We have no connection.
....Our life is garbage.

We take comfort in our work and cruelty. We love the manicurist and the nurse for they hold hands with us. Where is our mother now? We woo with condoms and a ferry ride; the world around us crumples into chemicals, we stand intractable, and wait for someone competent to take us 'cross the street. (scene 16, p. 197)

The need for affection is sensitively spelled out in *Sexual Perversity in Chicago* when Danny, unsure of his position with Deborah in the latter stages of their relationship, presses for a response to his questions in the middle of the night:

DANNY: Deborah. Deb? Deb? You up? *(Pause.)* You sleeping? *(Pause.)* I can't sleep. *(Pause.)* You asleep? *(Pause.)* Huh? *(Pause.)* You sleeping, Deb? *(Pause.)* What are you thinking about? *(Pause.)* Deb? *(Pause.)* Did I wake you up? (scene 26, p. 43)

Although it is plain that Deborah is sleeping, Danny childishly insists upon awakening her. The short, simple sentences are indicative of the insecurity he feels; their brevity and repetition bring some form of comfort to one who craves assurance. Merely by hearing the words spoken aloud, Danny is afforded some solace; Deborah's stillness must, at all costs, be broken.

A little earlier in the play, Danny defends Bernie to "an imaginary co-worker" who has presumably criticized his friend. Aware that his love affair may soon be over, Danny holds on steadfastly to the reality of his friendship with Bernie:

DANNY: ... I know what you're saying, and I'm telling you I don't like you badmouthing the guy, who happens to be a friend of mine. So just let me tell my story, okay? So the other day we're up on six and it's past five and I'm late, and I'm having some troubles with my chick ... and I push the button and the elevator doesn't come, and it doesn't come, and it doesn't come, so I lean back and I kick the shit out of it three or four times.... And *he*, he puts his arm around my shoulder and he calms me down and he says, "Dan, Dan ... don't go looking for affection from inanimate objects." *(Pause.)* Huh? So I don't want to hear you badmouthing Bernie Litko. (scene 25, p. 43)

Mamet manages to incorporate a great deal of urban despair into this one, short speech. Danny's defense of Bernie is quite ludicrous, given the set of circumstances he describes. At first glance, it is difficult to understand why Bernie's advice should have inspired such loyalty—especially to the extent that it is cited as a shining example of friendship—but if the language is analyzed, various aspects emerge. In the loveless world he inhabits, *any* constant, unswerving, *steady* manifestation of kindness is lifeblood to Danny; it is immaterial how this kindness presents itself. As he viciously attacks the elevator door (probably fantasizing that it is, in fact, Deborah) Bernie calms him down by suggesting that he should not seek affection from "inanimate objects." This is a strange statement, but one that nevertheless communicates affection to the wretched Danny. There are two ways of looking at Bernie's advice. The first—and less interesting—is that one must not expect elevators to work upon command. The society in which Bernie and Danny live is a mechanized and complex one, and mechanical objects often malfunction. It is, therefore, futile to expect "affection" (or cooperation) from such objects. The second—and most likely—possibility is that Bernie somehow regards Deborah as just such an "inanimate object" and suspects that deep down, Danny probably agrees with him. She doesn't "function" properly; she has caused great difficulties for both men; she has interrupted the natural, easy flow of their lives and is, therefore, less than human. As a good, caring friend, Bernie endeavors to convince Danny that he, alone, is worthy of Danny's love and trust; Deborah is a very poor substitute indeed. This information appears to be subliminally communicated to Danny because his defense of Bernie exceeds any other display of affection that can be found in the work.

As Danny and Deborah's affair crumbles, each vies for the last word during their many arguments. It is their growing impatience with and lack of tolerance for their partner's position that prompts them into endless verbal sparring. They both use black, sardonic humor and cruel remarks to upstage one another and their quickfire dialogue temporarily disguises the emptiness that lies just beyond their words:

> DANNY: ... You know very well if there's any shampoo or not.
> You're making me be ridiculous about this. *(Pause.)* You wash
> yourself too much anyway. If you really *used* all that shit they
> tell you in *Cosmopolitan* (And you *do*) you'd be washing yourself
> from morning til night. Pouring derivatives on yourself all day
> long.
> DEB: Will you love me when I'm old?
> DANNY: If you can manage to look eighteen, yes.
> DEB: Now, that's very telling. (scene 23, p. 41)

The sheer pettiness of this is a well-observed and painfully accurate reflection of the absurdity of many arguments between the sexes. Danny blames Deborah for making him "be ridiculous" about the existence of shampoo; in a neat jump, he shifts the responsibility. His sarcasm is meant to chasten, but its only effect is to further enrage Deborah, who responds with cynical and platitudinous remarks. Danny ridicules her need to keep up with all the beauty hints in *Cosmopolitan*, at the same time requiring her to "look eighteen" even when she's old. Since this is both unrealistic and absurd, it compounds the superficiality of their love and underlines the all-embracing obsession with physical attractiveness to the exclusion of all else.

The couple's linguistic battle for supremacy continues in a similar vein:

> DANNY: I love your breasts.
> DEB: "Thank you" *(Pause.)* Is that right?
> DANNY: Fuck you. (scene 23, p. 42)

Deborah's parody of the stereotyped response expected from a docile woman prompts Danny to lash back with a coarse expletive. When the pair eventually does break up, the verbal recriminations reach an almost frightening level of intensity:

> DANNY: Cunt.
> DEB: That's very good. "Cunt", good. Get it out. Let it all out.
> DANNY: You cunt.
> DEB: We've established that.
> DANNY: I try.
> DEB: You try and try.... You're trying to understand women and
> I'm confusing you with information. "Cunt" won't do it.
> "Fuck" won't do it. No more magic. (scene 28, p. 46)

A desperate sarcasm pervades these lines. Deborah's assertion that Danny is trying to understand feminine psychology by way of means that in no way *involve* him is at once brilliantly funny and painfully true. As Colin Stinton remarks, "Mamet captures so accurately the tension which builds up in situations like this; Danny pretends that he wants to understand Deborah but, deep inside, he can't really be bothered. He wants to learn painlessly, by a kind of osmosis, not by having to make any effort!"[29] Danny now seems to be as insensitive as his influential friend; although he must be aware that Deborah is deeply hurt by their arguments, the only way he can respond to her self-defense is to call her a "cunt." Communication between them having reached such a nadir, it is little wonder that Deborah should reflect that there is simply "no more magic." Nothing either of them can say could inject life into what is now moribund and wretched. Whatever romance once existed has dissolved, and the sexual attraction that once passed for true love has been reconstituted into something fetid and obscene.

Throughout the play, Bernie and Danny reduce the women they encounter to purely physical dimensions, but this activity reaches its apotheosis in the final scene when they lie on the beach, admiring or deriding the women who pass by them. This episode, more forcefully than any other, underscores their sheer inability to perceive women as people. It is vulgar, tragic, and very funny. Bernie draws Danny's attention to what is presumably a well-endowed woman:

> BERNIE: Hey! Don't look behind you.
> DANNY: Yeah?
> BERNIE: Whatever you do, don't look behind you.
> DANNY: Where?
> BERNIE: Right behind you, about ten feet behind you to your right.
> DANNY: Yeah?
> BERNIE: I'm telling you.
> DANNY: *(Looks.)* Get the fuck *outta* here!
> BERNIE: Can I pick 'em?
> DANNY: Bernie ...
> BERNIE: Is the radar in fine shape?
> DANNY: ... I gotta say ...
> BERNIE: ... *Oh* yeah ...
> DANNY: ... that you can *pick* 'em. (scene 34, p. 51)

This echoes the rhythms of the opening scene, in which Bernie and Danny feed on each other's enthusiasm, but there has been a definite change. Danny is less the eager pupil to Bernie's teacher than a wised-up accomplice in lechery. Bernie may still be the man with "the radar," but Danny is rapidly catching up to him. Mamet utilizes the mock-irony of remarks like, "Whatever you do, don't look behind you," to suggest the renewed camaraderie between the two men. As the words are uttered, it is clear that Bernie wants Danny to do exactly the opposite! It is *essential* for Danny to "look behind" to see the object of Bernie's disbelief. He even issues exact directions. Both men use humor as a means of boosting morale and confirming their macho bravado—thoroughly enjoying their "game." This idyllic pastime is suddenly shattered, however, when Bernie's behavior takes a strange and unnerving turn. As they criticize the women around them, he notices one whom he denounces as "something of a pig" (scene 34, p. 54). The presence of this woman on the beach seems to spark something in Bernie and he begins to blame her and the rest of the women for flaunting their assets, beautiful or ugly:

> BERNIE: ... I mean who the fuck do they think they are ... coming out here and just flaunting their bodies all over? ... I come to the beach with a friend to get some sun and watch the action and ... I mean a fellow comes to the beach to sit out in the fucking sun, am I wrong? ... I mean we're talking about recreational fucking space, huh? (scene 34, p. 54)

As Bernie castigates and villifies the women in his midst, his words take on a rather hysterical note. His sentiments are reminiscent of those who would defend an act of rape by suggesting that the victim, after all, "asked for it" by the clothes she wore or by her provocative behavior. Bernie's (low) opinion of women arises, he suggests, through their cheapness and brazenness. He repeats that the only reason for his and Danny's presence on the beach is "to get some sun." This is so blatantly untrue that it becomes a pathetic plea for understanding. That he should refer to the beach as "recreational fucking space" is also deeply telling; Bernie presumably uses the obscenity as an expletive but there is, surely, a sense that he wishes it were a verb instead!

Eventually, Bernie realizes that he has said too much for his own good—and for the good of his image as a suave womanizer. Danny's perplexed question prompts Bernie into defensive action:

> DANNY: Are you feeling alright?
> BERNIE: Well, how do I look, do I look alright?
> DANNY: Sure.

BERNIE: Well, than let's assume that I feel alright, okay.... I mean, how could you feel anything *but* alright, for chrissakes. Will you look at that body? *(Pause.)* What a pair of tits. *(Pause.)* With tits like that, who needs ... anything. (scene 34, pp. 54–55)

Within seconds, Bernie has reverted back to his old routine. He simply cannot afford to let down his "front" in this uncharacteristic way, and his aggression in the phrase, "how do I look, do I look alright?" is a warning to Danny not to probe any further. It is, however, clear that all this bluster and bravado is no more than that; we have briefly seen beneath the surface brittleness into a morass of insecurity and fear.

Bernie's final words, ignorant as they are, manage to speak volumes about the tragic state of his sexuality: "With tits like that, who needs ... anything." By once again diminishing the importance of women to their sexual anatomy, Bernie demonstrates his supreme lack of imagination and his need for fantasy. He plainly requires much more than "tits," but it is highly unlikely that he will ever attain it. Behind the arrogant façade lies a fearful naïveté. Both men hatch plans and exchange ideas about the best ways in which to bed the women they ogle, but their potential success is questionable, to say the least. On a beach full of people, Bernie and Danny remain isolated, solitary. Perhaps more so now than ever, they are on the outside looking in. More bruised by life experience than they had been at the beginning of the play, they appear overwhelmed by a deep-seated bitterness. This is borne out by the final words in the work, which manage to combine arrogance, cruelty, and sarcasm. When a woman passes them, she ignores their greetings:

BERNIE: Hi.
DANNY: Hello there. *(Pause. She walks by.)*
BERNIE: She's probably deaf.
DANNY: She did *look* deaf, didn't she?
BERNIE: Yeah. *(Pause.)*
DANNY: Deaf *bitch.* (scene 34, p. 55)

Bernie's misogyny has apparently influenced Danny to a fatal degree; perhaps he has become a more dangerous type of sexist than his friend. The absurdity of his observation that the girl "did *look* deaf" and his need for corroboration from Bernie—"didn't she?"—suggest that the veil of ignorance and insecurity has, at least partially, been transferred from Bernie to Danny.

Until now, Danny has been portrayed as a fairly normal, if unimaginative young man, but one who was largely without real malice. For him to utter the final, brutal words in a brutal play is Mamet's way of dramatising how fatally Danny has come under Bernie's spell and how he has absorbed the deadening influence of an artificial and sterile society.

Sexual Perversity in Chicago is a very fast—and very black—comedy. The sheer exuberance of the dialogue is compelling, although its vitality is essentially illusory. The characters end the play as they began—confused and vulnerable, and perhaps even more lonely. Friedrich Hebbel once wrote, "Drama shouldn't present new stories but new relationships."[30] In this work, Mamet certainly seems to have fulfilled this requirement. With an accurate ear for the cadences of supposedly sophisticated urban speech and with an acute observation of contemporary sexual mores, he has produced a work that is wholly original and that dramatizes the emptiness of relationships in an empty society. Mamet has devised a play that is absolutely contemporary in its verbal style; the text is a bubbling amalgam of slang, clichés, and what the characters take to be wit, and he invents a linguistic personality for each character that is totally believable. Bernie's false shield of confidence is superbly exposed in the subtext to his aggressive linguistic forays, which have been described as "a combination of whiplash and theatrical swoops"[31] and Danny's ingenuousness and growing dependence on his friend reveals itself in his employment of certain phrases favored by his mentor. Deborah's speech has about it a vitality and innocence that is squashed as the play progresses; she finds only disappointment and frustration in a relationship she believed to be truly loving. Joan is a woman who longs for love but is afraid of it; her language may be cynical and hard but Mamet is able to suggest that under Joan's brittle, sassy linguistic bravado, a subtext of vulnerability and fear remains.

A sharp satire on contemporary sexual mores in the urban America of the 1970s, *Sexual Perversity in Chicago* is also an exposé of what a media-dominated, capitalist-structured society can produce. But finally, Mamet's greatest strength lies not in his persuasiveness as a social critic, nor even in his sensitivity to the plight of human relations: it resides in his superb timing and peerless control over language.

NOTES

1. Mamet, *Writing in Restaurants*, p. 30.
2. Karl Marx cited in Erich Fromm, *Beyond the Chains of Illusion: My Encounter with Marx & Freud* (London: Abacus, Sphere Books, 1980), pp. 46–47.

3. Bigsby, *Contemporary Writers*, p. 50.

4. Eder, "David Mamet's New Realism," p. 40.

5. Fraser, "Mamet's Plays," p. L7.

6. Ibid.

7. Tom Wolfe, *The Kandy-Kolored Tangerine-Flake Streamline Baby* (London: Jonathan Cape, 1981), p. 46.

8. Fraser, "Mamet's Plays," p. L7.

9. Ibid.

10. Peter Stothard, *Plays & Players* 25, no. 5 (February 1978): pp. 30–31.

11. Marshall Walker, *The Literature of the U.S.A.* (London: Macmillan, 1983), p. 194.

12. John Elsom, *The Listener,* 8 December 1977, p. 774.

13. Jules Feiffer, *Carnal Knowledge* (London: Penguin, 1972), pp. 10–12.

14. Ibid., pp. 18–19.

15. Stinton, interview with author, 22 March 1986, National Theatre, London.

16. Ibid.

17. Connie Booth, interview with author, 2 December 1986, Hampstead, London.

18. Stinton, interview with author, 22 March 1986, National Theatre, London.

19. Richardson, interview with author, 8 December 1986, National Theatre, London.

20. Fraser, "Mamet's Plays," p. L7.

21. Ibid.

22. Ibid.

23. Ibid.

24. Bigsby, *Contemporary Writers*, p. 48.

25. Wetzsteon, "New York Letter," (September 1976): pp. 37–39.

26. *The South Bank Show*, London Weekend Television, 20 March 1985.

27. Shepherd, interview with author, 13 March 1986, National Theatre, London.

28. Stephen Brook, *New York Days, New York Nights* (London: Picador, 1985), p. 47.

29. Stinton, interview with author, 22 March 1986, National Theatre, London.

30. Friedrich Hebbel cited in *Playwrights on Playwriting*, ed. Toby Cole (New York: Hill & Wang, 1982), p. 286.

31. Nicholas de Jongh, *The Guardian* 19 March 1984 p. 11.

JANE PALATINI BOWERS

The Play as Lang-scape:
1920 to 1933

Virgil Thomson has suggested that *Four Saints* is about "the working artist's life" as symbolized by the saints. I would say, rather, that *Four Saints* is about the artist at work; the artist is Gertrude Stein and her work is the writing of the play, *Four Saints*. Stein, the writer, is actually a character in her own play. As Richard Bridgman has noted, "almost two-thirds of the text is composed of authorial statement and commentary."[66] Thomson obscured this fact in production by parceling out the authorial commentary to two figures (called "commere" and "compere"), both of whom seem in performance to be stage directors. Even at that, however, they discuss not so much the performance of the play—the stage business—as they do the composition—the business of writing. Thomson divided Gertrude Stein, but he did not conquer her. Notwithstanding Thomson's alteration of the text, the writer of the play makes her presence felt during performance.

At the beginning of the play Stein maintains a running commentary on the writing process (and progress): self-criticism, self-encouragement, progress reports, plans and preparations for writing, and discussions of the difficulty or ease of writing. She even includes dates to mark the course of her composition: April 1, Easter. The process of composition is as palpable as the procession of Saints in Act 3.

Once the play gets well under way, once Saint Ignatius and Saint Therese begin to speak, Stein does not so much discuss the text that is being

From *"They Watch Me as They Watch This": Gertrude Stein's Metadrama.* © 1991 by the University of Pennsylvania Press.

161

written or urge herself to write more of it, as deal with the written text as a plan for performance. However, it is a plan which is never settled because we are meant to see the writing and the performance as simultaneous acts.

There are a Saint Plan and a Saint Settlement among the cast of characters, and the necessity of planning and settling is brought up at intervals throughout the play, most often when Stein or her saints are having difficulty in deciding how the plan is to be settled. The famous question/refrain—"How many saints are there in it?"—is one of many similar questions: "How many acts are there in it?" "How many nails are there in it?" "How many floors are there in it?" "How many doors?" "How many windows?" and "How much of it is finished?" "It is easy to measure a settlement," says Saint Therese (30). But it is not easy to measure this play because it is never settled.

The question of how many saints are in the play has several answers, all of which skirt the issue:

> Saint Therese. How many saints are there in it.
> Saint Therese. There are very many many saints in it.
> Saint Therese. There are as many saints as there are in it.
> Saint Therese. How many saints are there in it.
> Saint Therese. There are there are there are saints saints in it.
> [Stein then names seven saints, hardly a complete list.]
> Saint Therese. How many saints are there in it.
> Saint Cecilia. How many saints are there in it.
> Saint Therese. There are as many saints as there are in it.
> Saint Cecilia. There are as many saints as there are saints in it. (28)

In the second-to-the-last scene (in which Saint Settlement and Saint Anne say that "there can be two Saint Annes if you like"), Stein writes:

> They have to be.
> They have to be.
> They have to be to see.
> To see to say.
> Laterally they may. (47)

If we see saints, they exist. Accordingly, in the last scene, Stein specifies that the saints ("All Saints") be lined laterally to the left and right of Saint Ignatius for our perusal. As the play ends, we can count the saints and answer one of the questions posed in the text.

As for the number of acts, the title promises us three, but the title, written first, cannot possibly measure the play, which has not yet been written. In fact, the play has four named acts, but there are three first acts, two second acts, two third acts, and one fourth act, making a total of eight acts. The only certainty regarding the number of acts in the play is that which is obvious at the end: "Last Act. / Which is a fact." No matter how many acts there are in it, the play is certain to finish. It is only when the play is finished that we will know how many acts there were in it, just as the number of doors, windows, floors, and nails in a house cannot be ascertained until the building is complete, for even the most carefully laid plans can be changed.

Four Saints is certainly pre-planned. The written text exists, and it is the plan that the performance follows. However, we are made to feel that the plan is being created in our presence, as the performance proceeds. Stein writes the play so that during performance she will seem to be feeding the actors their lines. So, for example, Stein will make a statement, "Who settles a private life," which is then supposed to be echoed by an actor—"Saint Therese. Who settles a private life." This pattern recurs as in: "None to be behind. Enclosure. / Saint Therese. None to be behind. Enclosure" (20); and "To be interested in Saint Therese fortunately. / Saint Therese. To be interested in Saint Therese fortunately" (25); and "Nobody visits more than they do visits them. / Saint Therese. Nobody visits more than they do visits them Saint Therese" (16).

In the last example Saint Therese behaves like the ventriloquist's dummy, who, when instructed, "Say hello, Charlie," says "Hello Charlie." Saint Therese echoes her own name and forces us to accept Stein's instructions, the side text, as part of the performance text. The imposition of the written text on the performance text occurs also with the act/scene divisions of *Four Saints*. It is sometimes accomplished by rhyming a line of spoken text with the scene number, as in:

> Scene X
> When. (31)

or by a syntactical connection of the written text to the performance text, as in:

> Scene VI
> With Seven.
> Scene VII
> With eight.

Scene VIII (42)

Or by a homophonic connection, such as:

Scene One
And seen one. Very likely. (35)

At one point, Stein makes the scenes themselves speakers and makes their speeches rhyme with their names:

Scene eight. To Wait.
Scene one. And. begun.
Scene two. To and to.
Scene three. Happily be.
Scene Four. Attached or.
Scene Five. Sent to derive.
Scene Six. Let it mix.
Scene Seven. Attached eleven.
Scene Eight. To wait. (29)

In all of these examples, an enactor could choose to ignore the connection Stein makes between written notation and spoken text, but the connection is there nonetheless.

Often Stein does not give the enactor a choice. The act/scene announcement is made twice, once in writing and once (sometimes more than once) in performance. For example:

Act One
Saint Therese. Preparing in as you might say.
Saint Therese was pleasing. In as you might say.
Saint Therese Act One.
Saint Therese has begun to be in act one.
Saint Therese and begun.
Saint Therese as sung.
Saint. Therese act one.
Saint Therese and begun.
Saint Therese and sing and sung.
Saint Therese in an act one. Saint Therese questions. (23)

And:

> Scene V
> Many many saints can be left to many many saints scene five left
> to many many saints. (26)

And:

> Scene VII
> One two three four five sin seven scene seven.
> Saint Therese scene seven.
> Saint Therese scene scene seven. (27)

And:

> Scene II
> Would it do if there was a Scene II. (24)

In the last example Stein discusses only the possibility of having a Scene
2. "Would it do?" *Four Saints* abounds in the use of conditionals, adding to
the sense of uncertainty and tentativeness in the play. If a Scene 2 would not
do, would Stein eliminate it? As might be expected, uncertainty is most
intense in the first half of the play. As the play takes shape it leaves fewer
questions unanswered. But in Act 1, almost nothing has been determined.
After a five-page discussion of how Saint Therese and Saint Ignatius are to
appear (whether sitting or standing, moving or still, on the stage or off),
Stein has this to say:

> Saint Ignatius could be in porcelain actually.
> Saint Ignatius could be in porcelain actually while he was
> young and standing.
> Saint Therese could not be young and standing she could be
> sitting.
> Saint Ignatius could be in porcelain actually actually in
> porcelain standing.
> Saint Therese could be admittedly could be in moving seating.
> Saint Therese could be in moving sitting.
> Saint Therese could be.
> Saint Ignatius could be.
> Saint Ignatius could be in porcelain actually in porcelain
> standing. (20)

The prolonged discussion of the disposition of the actors on the stage (which the text does not resolve, but which must of course be resolved in performance) proceeds through a series of contradictory directions. At the beginning of her deliberations, Stein repeats four times that Saint Therese is seated, but following the fourth announcement, Stein immediately contradicts herself: "Saint Therese not seated." This direction is repeated, and then, as if to reconcile the two statements, Stein adds "Saint Therese not seated at once" (16). Presumably, Saint Therese is to begin by standing and is then to sit. "Saint Therese once seated. There are a great many places and persons near together. Saint Therese seated and not surrounded" (16). Once seated, Saint Therese will be isolated from the other performers. The contradiction seems to be resolved. But another apparently insoluble stage direction is introduced. Saint Therese is to be "very nearly half inside and half outside outside the house." Stein specifies that "the garden" too is "outside and inside of the wall." While a garden can quite easily be split in two, a person cannot be so divided. So Saint Therese is neither in nor out, but somewhere in between. Poised on a threshold, she is, as Stein says, "About to be" (16). Then Stein introduces Saint Ignatius, who, she tells us, "could be" and finally "is standing." The positions of the two principal saints seem settled, until Stein launches into a passage which epitomizes the text in process:

> Saint Therese seated and not standing half and half of it and not half and half of it seated and not standing surrounded and not seated and not seated and not standing and not surrounded and not surrounded and not not not seated not seated not seated not surrounded not seated and Saint Ignatius standing standing not seated Saint Therese not standing not standing and Saint Ignatius not standing standing surrounded as if in once yesterday. In place of situations. Saint Therese could be very much interested not only in settlement Saint Settlement and this not with with this wither wither they must be additional. Saint Therese having not commenced. (17)

Saint Therese, who was about to be, has not yet commenced because the question of whether she is to sit or stand has not yet been decided. Because of contradictory directions and conditional suggestions, the writing of the play seems always to be in process. Composition becomes a performance event. The writing of the play appears to be going on before our eyes. At the same time, the unfinished quality of the written text, its very eventfulness, immobilizes the actors and the performance text. Like Saint Therese, who is half in and half out, the performance itself is suspended in a kind of limbo. It consists entirely of preparation, beginning with the narrative which prepares for the play, followed by a play which prepares for a performance, and ending with the only fact, which is the last act.

Even Stein's inspiration for Saint Therese and Saint Ignatius is immobile. Stein explained that she had imagined Saint Therese as being like the photographs she saw in a store window, of a girl becoming a nun—still shots, one following another, the immobilization of a process by dividing it into the frozen moments of its unfolding.[67] Stein refers to this image of Therese's saintly development within the play:

> Saint Therese could be photographed having been dressed like a
> lady and then they taking out her head changed it to a nun and a
> nun a saint and a saint so. (17)

As for Saint Ignatius, he too has been transfixed by Stein's suggestion that he be a porcelain statue, which she later explained referred to an actual figurine, again in a store window, which she imagined to be Saint Ignatius.[68]

Saint Therese, the photograph, and Saint Ignatius, the statue, are represented in a play where even the syntax of the sentences tends toward a kind of suspended animation. The arias for which this opera is famous ("Pigeons on the grass alas," "When this you see remember me," and "wed dead said led") occur in the last quarter of the play. For the most part the play lurches past us with stuttering, choppy, and flat prose. Stein pares her vocabulary to the most ordinary of monosyllables: as, it, be, at, in, not, the, is, an, was, would, out, might, could, if, with, how, they, this, that, hurt, found, like, and make, for example. Most of these words are normally unstressed, and all are too short to be mellifluous.

Repetition, which in *A List* had knit phrases simultaneously to preceding and subsequent phrases, producing a fabric of words united by similarities but always changing through modulation, becomes in *Four Saints* an annoying case of stuttering. The text becomes stalled on phrases, sometimes only for a moment, "he said he said feeling very nearly everything as it had been as if he could be precious be precious to like like it as it had been" (12), sometimes longer:

> Who settles a private life.
> Saint Therese. Who settles a private life.
> Saint Therese. Who settles a private life.

Saint Therese. Who settles a private life.
Saint Therese. Who settles a private life. (16–17)

At one point the phrase "Once in a while" is repeated twenty-six times in succession (30). Many of the sentences in *Four Saints* remind us of a record which has caught the phonograph needle in one groove, or they seem like a kind of mirror writing where the words which come into the text are immediately reflected in reverse order:

Saint Ignatius. Withdrew with with withdrew....
Saint Ignatius. Occurred withdrew.
Saint Ignatius. Withdrew Occurred. (33)

Some sentences pivot around a center, the words held in place by a kind of centrifugal force, of syntax: "Saints all in all Saints" (20). Many passages come to us in stages, like revised compositions where the variations are never erased:

He asked for a distant magpie as if they made a difference.
He asked for a distant magpie as if he asked for a distant magpie as if that made a difference.
He asked as if that made a difference.
He asked for a distant magpie.
He asked for a distant magpie.
As if that made a difference he asked for a distant magpie as if that made a difference. He asked as if that made a difference. A distant magpie. He asked for a distant magpie. He asked for a distant magpie. (37)

Within her stalled sentences Stein minimizes or manipulates grammatical indicators of activity. Verbs are often eliminated and sentences replaced by noun phrases, like the familiar "pigeons on the grass" or like the following:

Saint Therese in a cart drawn by oxen moving around....
Saint Therese in time. (24)

And:

Saint Ignatius and more.
Saint Ignatius with as well....

Saint Ignatius finally....
Saint Ignatius with it just....
Saint Ignatius with it Tuesday. (25)

The preferred verb form is the participle, most often used as a verbal, as in:

Saint Therese unsurrounded by reason of it being so cold that
they stayed away. (24)

Saint Ignatius well bound. (25)

Saint Settlement aroused by the recall of Amsterdam. (29)

The effect of the verbal is to immobilize the subject, the passive recipient of
the action, the inactive center of movement. At one point Stein asks, "What
is the difference between a picture and pictured" (21). The difference is that
the former is a noun and the latter a participial adjective, and further that one
refers to form and the other to content. But both words (noun and verbal)
focus on the immobilized object (the picture) rather than the activity (picture-
making). Even when the participle indicates that the subject is the actor, not
the receiver, it avoids placing the activity in time, as in the following examples:

Saint Therese seated. (17)

Saint Ignatius standing. (17)

Saint Therese advancing. (19)

Saint Therese using a cart with oxen to go about and as well as
if she were there. (24)

The participle pictures the subject in a steady state. Activity, in these
examples, has neither beginning nor end. By using verbs as adjectives, Stein
forces the performance into a series of tableaux, in which action is
transformed into a quality, with no reference to time.

When Stein does refer to time in the play, it is to render it a
meaningless measurement. For instance, memory, which is normally a
present, evocation of a past event or entity, is used in the following passage
with an apparent disregard for its temporal function:

> It is very easy in winter to remember winter spring and summer
> it is very easy in winter to remember spring and winter and
> summer it is very easy in winter to remember summer spring and
> winter it is very easy in winter to remember spring and summer
> and winter. (13)

It is possible in one winter to remember a winter gone by or to compare the
current season to a generalized memory of past winters, but as the passage
stands, it states that one remembers "winter in winter." One cannot
remember something one is "in." Since one must be out of and past winter
in order to remember it, the passage causes temporal confusion.

The following passage presents a temporal impossibility:

> In the morning to be changed from the morning to the morning
> in the morning. A scene of changing from the morning to the
> morning. (25)

Change, like memory, is a function of time. To change is to move from one
form or identity to another, from the past (before the change) to a different
time (after the change). Change cannot occur without the passage of time.
Therefore, there cannot be a change from the morning to the morning. If
time does not change, then nothing can change.

A similar confusion is created by the following statements:

> It is no doubt not at all the following morning that it is very much
> later very much earlier. (29)

> It is to-morrow on arriving at a place to pass before the last. (29)

> Commencing again yesterday. (33)

These instances of temporal confusion are only reflections in miniature of
the larger time warp created by the play itself.

I have said that in *Four Saints* Stein makes the writing process a part of
the performance. In doing this, she blurs the temporal distinction between
writing, planning, and performance. Stein conflates the time of planning
(past), the time of writing (past), the time of rehearsal (past), and the time of
performance (present). She also synchronizes these activities so that they
occur at the same rate of speed. Because the sensual stimuli of performance
(music, action, and speech) move at a faster tempo than the conceptualizing

activities (planning and writing), Stein immobilizes the former in order to accommodate the latter. We feel that all of these activities occur simultaneously in a very slow-moving present.

The Thomson/Grosser arrangement of the text obscured its purpose and meaning by disguising the authorial voice and by ignoring the improvisational illusion that Stein created. Instead, the production of *Four Saints* emphasized the sensuality and musicality of the teat. Of course, the play does have its musical side. As I have already noted, Stein provides a performance text and writes some arias. But Stein never relinquishes her hold on the text, never withdraws, as the playwright usually does. "When this you see," she writes, "Remember me" (47). Even when the written text is allowed to become a song, Stein, the poet, is its singer. We must not ignore the fact that the arias in this opera are passages of unassigned text. Even "Pigeons on the Grass" is a Stein song, although Thomson had Saint Ignatius sing it. This is how the aria appears in the original text:

> Scene II
> Pigeons on the grass alas.
> Pigeons on the grass alas.
> Short longer grass short longer longer shorter yellow grass pigeons large pigeons on the shorter longer yellow grass alas pigeons on the grass.
> If they were not pigeons what were they.
> If they were not pigeons on the grass alas what were they. He had heard of a third and he asked about it it was a magpie in the sky. If a magpie in the sky on the sky can not cry if the pigeon on the grass alas can alas and to pass the pigeon on the grass alas and the magpie in the sky on the sky and to try and to try alas on the grass alas the pigeon on the grass the pigeon on the grass and alas. They might be very well very well very well they might be they might be very well they might be very well very well they might be. (36)

In an interview, Stein explained the genesis of this aria:

> I was walking in the gardens of the Luxembourg in Paris. It was the end of summer the grass was yellow. I was sorry that it was the end of summer and I saw the big fat pigeons in the yellow grass and I said to myself, pigeons on the yellow grass, alas, and I kept on writing pigeons on the grass, alas, short longer grass, short

longer longer shorter yellow grass pigeons large pigeons on the
shorter longer yellow grass, alas pigeons on the grass, and I kept
on writing until I had emptied myself of the emotion.[69]

By incorporating the moment of creation and the improvised product of that
moment into the work to be performed, Stein once again violates the
temporal boundaries between the creation of the written text and its
performance.[70]

NOTES

66. Bridgman, *Stein in Pieces*, 187.
67. Stein, "Plays," 130.
68. Ibid., 130.
69. Gertrude Stein, typescript of a tape-recorded interview with William Lundell for
the National Broadcasting Company, New York, 12 October 1934, YCAL. Stein's memory
is confused here. She finished the manuscript at the end of July, which is not exactly the
end of summer although the grass in this urban park could certainly have been yellow in
July.
70. In addition to being Stein's lament about the yellowing grass and the end of
summer, "alas" is also a pun on Alice. Ulla Dydo, Harriet Chessman, and Neil Schmitz
have all discussed the omnipresence of Alice Toklas in Stein's writing. As Schmitz writes,
"She is addressed, cited, quoted ... [she is] everywhere in Gertrude Stein's text, variously
figured, differently inscribed" (*Of Huck and Alice: Humorous Writing in American Literature*
[Minneapolis: University of Minnesota Press, 1983], 202). By singing in *Four Saints* to
Alice/alas (the witness to the writing and the companion of the writer), Stein further draws
creation and performance together.

JOHN TIMPANE

Filling the Time:
Reading History in the Drama of August Wilson

Do the excluded and the empowered read history differently? This question is brought to mind by the dramatic practice of August Wilson. In his plays, Wilson portrays individual lives in relation to moments of subtle yet decisive historical change. Finding they cannot live without reference to the change, these characters evolve various ways of reading it. Knowing the change and its significance is complicated by their position and their wishes.

In a Wilson drama, history passes in the form not of a progress but of a crisis of reading. In plays such as *Fences* and *Ma Rainey's Black Bottom*, the audience guesses that a historical change has occurred not because they see the *Augenblick* itself—the "durationless instant" that traditional philosophy has found so elusive—but because they can compare the way different characters read their worlds. Despite mounting evidence that an old way of reading is no longer adequate, one or more characters refuse to give it up. Indeed, they cannot give it up. Reading equals a way of life. Character is reading is fate.

Troy Maxson and Ma Rainey construct their identities based on their relation to a particular social and historic change; they would not be where and who they are had not the change occurred. Yet this relation is tragically ironic for both of them: This change, which they personally helped create (Troy in baseball and Ma Rainey in popular music) ultimately disenfranchises them at the same time that it signals expanded opportunities for other people

From *May All Your Fences Have Gates.* © 1994 by the University of Iowa Press.

like them. Not fully knowing, they have sacrificed themselves so that the change can happen. At some level, however, each does know, making necessary some powerful self-deception in order to survive. Knowing the change and their own role in it, they are now forced to deny it. The violence created by the ensuing mental conflict is mostly potential in both plays: the sacrifice has already happened, and each is *post facto* in his or her own life.

Being post facto, Troy and Ma Rainey call on the audience to search for the factum itself, to become readers and to gauge differences in reading. What they read is not only how individual lives are lived and lost but also how we and they read changes in time. That is a complex matter.

SPECIOUS PRESENT, MANUFACTURE PAST

In the first volume of *Principles of Psychology*, William James turns to the question of our consciousness of time. "What," he writes, "is the *original* of our experience of pastness, from whence we get the meaning of the term?"[1] Constantly, we perceive a past time and the events now *in* the past; the question is, from what vantage point do we experience the movement of time—or, more precisely, since time does not move, the change from present to past? These questions lead James to his consideration of the "specious present," called "specious" because it is so vanishingly short—James himself wrote that only its latter boundary should be called the real "present."[2] The specious present was not to be confused with the "conscious present," a larger construct we are constantly building out of sense impressions and memory. James, Bertrand Russell, and others concluded that, in the words of C.W.K. Mundle, "time" itself "is a notion we construct from temporal relations which are sense-given."[3] Like many important mental processes, this construction is continual, lightning-fast, and invisible to the constructor.

And that is the main point—human consciousness of time is a matter of perception, a tissue of memory, expectation, cultural conditioning. Likewise, an audience's sense of the "pastness" and "presentness" of a dramatic situation involves manipulated memories, manufactured expectations, artificial conditioning. With lightning calibrations, an audience constantly triangulates its present situation with the past, present, and likely future situations predicated by the words and actions in the play. Since these events take place in "real" time, we can experience them much as we experience events outside the theater. But since these events predicate fictive realities occurring in a "stage time," we are alienated from them and forced to judge.

An excellent example lies in Wilson's plays, which appeal to the audience's sense of pastness as a dramatic given. Far from being simply "setting," this appeal forces us to become critical readers. Our irrevocable separation from these pasts alienates us from the manner in which Ma Rainey, in 1927 Chicago, or Troy Maxson, in 1957 Pittsburgh, constructs the "present." We learn about their "times" what is normally invisible to us about our own: how much our sense of the present depends on what we want and where we stand, on wishes and position. We learn precisely what is specious about the present.

Michel Foucault has little to say about how we perceive time—and much to say about how we read and write about it. Following Nietzsche's lead, Foucault explored the concept of history as just such a species of reading. Nietzsche saw the traditional European institution called "history" as a lie riddled with circularity, self-interest, and the will to power. He rejected it in favor of "genealogy," a way of reading the past that does not seek to reduce it to a "story" or to explain it in terms that validate the present. Genealogy does not "demonstrate that the past actively exists in the present"; rather, it identifies "the errors, the false appraisals, the faulty calculations" that accrete to form the assemblage of accidents called the past.[4]

Foucault's target is Nietzsche's target: the old idea that historical change is a "flow," somehow "seamless," proceeding inevitably toward that self-fulfilling prophecy, the present moment. In *Archaeology of Knowledge*, Foucault rejected a reading of history concerned with "continuities, transitions, anticipations, and foreshadowings," replacing it with an archaeology that "is much more willing ... to speak of discontinuities, ruptures, gaps, entirely new forms of positivity, and of sudden redistributions."[5] Foucault portrayed his new historical project as being "willing" to acknowledge what the high priests of the old history were "reticent" to speak of—a present composed of fragments, a life created by disjunction rather than by continuities.

A TIME CALLED TOO EARLY

In the prefatorial piece "The Play," Wilson locates *Fences* in a "big-city neighborhood" of an eastern industrial town—probably Pittsburgh—in, 1957. In 1957, "the Milwaukee Braves won the World Series, and the hot winds of change that would make the sixties a turbulent, racing, dangerous, and provocative decade had not yet begun to blow full."[6] The year 1957, as Wilson does not mean us to forget, was the year of Little Rock, when Eisenhower reluctantly ordered regular army paratroops to prevent interference with court-ordered "racial integration at Little Rock Central

High School. That was the year of H.R. 6127, the Civil Rights Act of 1957, passed after virulent debate and filibuster in the Senate. Texas, Tennessee, Delaware, Maryland, and other states were in the throes of court-ordered desegregation; Little Rock stood out because of the prospect that state and federal troops might face each other. The winds of change blew both hot and cold. The possibility of new positivities coexisted with the fact of ancient recalcitrance. Only three weeks before Little Rock, Ku Klux Klan members had castrated a black man outside of Zion, Alabama. And Louis "Satchmo" Armstrong, in a public gesture that attracted both widespread praise and widespread blame, canceled a much-publicized tour of the USSR, saying that "the way they are treating my people in the South, the government can go to hell.... It's getting almost so bad, a colored man hasn't got any country."

In *Fences*, baseball operates metonymically, as a metaphoric stand-in for the troubled changes of 1957. Much of the action takes place just before the Milwaukee Braves' victory over the New York Yankees in the 1957 World Series. That victory signified a year of many changes in baseball, changes that reflected the social upheavals of 1957. One change, very much in progress, was the emergence of the black ballplayer. Black players had played prominent roles in previous World Series—Willie Mays in the 1954 series and Jackie Robinson in the Brooklyn Dodgers' victory over the Yankees in 1955. Milwaukee was the first non-New York team led by a black star to win a World Series. Hank Aaron, the most powerful hitter in baseball history, played alongside Eddie Mathews, white and a great slugger, and alongside three excellent white pitchers: Warren Spahn, Bob Buhl, and Lew Burdette. Because of the quick rise to prominence of Mays, Aaron, Roberto Clemente, and Frank Robinson, the question was no longer whether blacks would play but whether they could become leaders. As the success of the Braves portended, the answer was yes: Aaron led the league in power statistics, hit a home run on the last day of the season to give the Braves the pennant, rampaged through Yankee pitching to give his team the World Series, and won the National League Most Valuable Player Award for 1957.

Yet the Braves were far from being a truly integrated team, and integration was far from complete in baseball. Though blacks had been playing in the major leagues since 1947, it would take until 1959 for each major league team to have at least one black player. Behind the grudging, piecemeal process of integration in sports lies a Foucaultian "disjunction"— World War II—and a resultant "redistribution": the postwar move west. Hard times in postwar Boston meant dwindling patronage for the Boston Braves, so the team moved west to Milwaukee in 1953. In 1957, the Dodgers left Brooklyn for Los Angeles, and the New York Giants left for San

Francisco. In so doing, these teams mirrored an accelerating westward shift in the center of population. Further, the war probably created new social potential (to this day not completely realized) for women and blacks. For baseball, all this meant new teams, new audiences, and new pressures to tap at last the large pool of talented black players. The National League led in this regard. Indeed, it was not until Frank Robinson was traded from the Cincinnati Reds to the Baltimore Orioles and won the Triple Crown in 1966 that a black player dominated American League pitching the way Mays, Clemente, and Aaron had done in the National League.

Changes in baseball and changes in American life complicate the ability of anyone who, like Troy, bases his assumptions about reality on the facts of a prewar world. In the first scene of *Fences*, Troy pits his reading of things against those of Bono, Rose, and Lyons. Troy intersperses lies with truths, claiming he has seen and contended with Death and the devil. Rose challenges the way Troy presents these tales: "Anything you can't understand, you want to call it the devil", (14). Rose and Bono are a chorus parenthesizing Troy's insistence on his reading:

> ROSE: Times. have changed since you was playing baseball, Troy. That was before the war. Times have changed a lot since then.
> TROY: How in hell they done changed?
> ROSE: They got lots of colored boys' playing ball now. Baseball and football.
> BONO: You right about that, Rose. Times have changed, Troy. You done come along too early.
> TROY: There ought not never have been no time called too early! (9)

James calls the present "a saddle-back ... from which we look in two directions into time."[7] Throughout *Fences*, Troy Maxson straddles this saddle-back, constantly constructing a present selectively out of memory (the past) and desire (the future).

Desire figures most clearly in his conflict with his son, Cory. Troy is affronted by Cory's desire to try out before a college football recruiter from North Carolina. Troy's own sport, and the source of his personal language of metaphors, is baseball; Cory's choice of football galls him. American popular culture has forgotten that integration had come to major league football long before Jackie Robinson signed a baseball contract. Fritz Pollard had played with the Akron Indians beginning in 1919, and black players played professional football until 1933, when the disruption of the Depression made football a whites-only sport for thirteen years.

As with baseball, this redistribution was tied to the postwar westward push. The National Football League (NFL) had originally centered in the Midwest, gradually adding franchises in eastern industrial centers. Longstanding interest in starting a franchise on the West Coast was realized when the Cleveland Rams moved to Los Angeles after the war. A rival league, the All-American Football Conference (AAFC), started up in 1946. Though the two leagues would soon merge, the AAFC forced some innovative moves, including the initiation of western franchises (the Los Angeles Dons and the San Francisco 49ers) and the signing of black players. That same year, the Los Angeles Rams signed Kenny Washington and Woody Strode, and the Cleveland Browns signed Bill Willis and Marion Motley. Motley became a recordbreaking rusher, beginning a strong tradition of black running backs that included Joe Perry, who, while playing for the San Francisco 49ers and Baltimore Colts, broke all rushing records through the 1950s. (His heir-apparent was Jim Brown.) By 1953, a black collegiate running back, J.C. Caroline of the University of Illinois, had broken the hallowed records of "Red" Grange, a white runner of the 1920s and 1930s. By the late 1950s, black athletes had established a prominence in football that at least equaled the standing of Mays, Aaron, and the Robinsons in baseball.[8]

With the stronger tradition of integration, football was on the verge of becoming a truly national sport in 1957. Cory believes, as Troy does not, that a talented black athlete can get a chance. This disagreement emerges when they discuss Roberto Clemente, now in his third year with the local baseball club, the Pittsburgh Pirates.

> TROY: I ain't thinking about the Pirates. Got an all-white team. Got that boy ... that Puerto Rican boy ... Clemente. Don't even half-play him. That boy could be something if they give him a chance. Play him one day and sit him on the bench the next.
>
> CORY: He gets a lot of chances to play.
>
> TROY: I'm talking about playing regular. Playing every day so you can get your timing. That's what I'm talking about.
>
> CORY: They got some white guys on the team that don't play every day. You can't play everybody at the same time.
>
> TROY: If they got a white fellow sitting on the bench ... you can bet your last dollar he can't play! The colored guy got to be twice as good before he get on the team. That's why I

don't want you to get all tied up in them sports. Man on
the team and what it get him? They got colored on the
team and don't use them. Same as not having them. All
them teams the same.

CORY: The Braves got Hank Aaron and Wes Covington. Hank
Aaron hit two home runs today. That makes forty-three.

TROY: Hank Aaron ain't nobody. (33–34)

Far beyond baseball, the ulterior difference here is over whether a change
has occurred in American society. Generational differences indicate a
difference in reading. All Cory knows are the achievements of Aaron (who
would hit forty-four home runs in 1957), Covington, and Clemente; these
seem incontrovertible evidence that his dreams have a foundation.

What Troy knows is his own frustration as a great player in the Negro
Leagues. His success was also his self-sacrifice: The Negro Leagues began to
die as soon as black players began to be accepted in numbers into
professional baseball.[9] What killed Troy's career was, ironically, the *advent* of
integrated baseball. Although he is clearly aware of these facts, and clearly
damaged by them, Troy insists that history is continuous, that what was once
true is still true. Cory assumes that what is true is new—that there is now a
new form of positivity, a sudden redistribution—and this assumption on
Cory's part outrages his father. For one the gap signifies the death he
constantly pits himself against, and for the other it signifies a life in the
future, liberated from his father's limitations. Granted, Troy's knowing
dictum that "the colored guy got to be twice as good before he get on the
team" was quite true in 1957 and is still a widely shared perception today. But
Cory is not arguing that his chance is likely; he is arguing that it is possible.

Troy gives many names to his resistance. Compassion is one. As he says
to Rose, "I got sense enough not to let my boy get hurt over playing no
sports" (39). Jealousy is another. Cory is getting a chance while he is still
young, whereas even in 1947 Troy was "too old to play in the major leagues"
(39). Both these "reasons" are versions of his resistance to reading the change
that is making Clemente and Aaron into national heroes. Both Troy's
compassion for his son and his jealousy of him are ways to deny his own
death.

Here, we may remember one of Foucault's more disturbing claims: that
the traditional view of history as a seamless continuity really disguised the
quest to construct the self as authoritative, continuous, integrated, and
eternal. In *Archaeology of Knowledge* he pictures the outraged author crying,
"'Must I suppose that in my discourse I can have no survival? And that in

speaking I am not banishing my death, but actually establishing it?'"[10] For Troy, to acknowledge the possibility of Cory's success is to acknowledge that his own time has passed. Thus his repression of a fact that would have been available to any avid baseball fan in Pittsburgh—that Roberto Clemente really is getting a chance to play. Clemente had 543 at-bats in 1956 and 451 in 1957.[11] Thus his claim that Aaron is "nobody." Note the extreme care with which Wilson has placed the action of the third act: quite late in September 1957, seemingly to show that reality takes no heed of Troy's judgments. Aaron would win the home-run and runs-batted-in titles, earning him the Most Valuable Player Award. Clemente would go on to 3,000 hits and the Hall of Fame.

LEFTOVERS

Like Troy Maxson, Ma Rainey refuses in order to survive. As one of the first great prominent black female jazz singers to sing with a band, Ma, like Troy, bestrides a moment of disjunction between a present way and a past way.[12] Ma Rainey was the first female blues singer to enjoy widespread popularity through recording: from 1923 to 1929, she recorded almost one hundred sides. Her innovation was to pitch the blues against a large-band accompaniment. She sang a style of "down-home" blues in which the vocal line closely followed the accompaniment. Her style carried many of the trappings of its Southern sideshow past—including the "tent call" at the beginning of a tune, a convention that the stuttering Sylvester is called on to reproduce in the studio.

Recording was both ascent and eclipse. Though quite popular in the South, Ma's records did not move as well in the Northern cities, and her popularity faded before the rise of Bessie Smith. Six years younger than Rainey, Smith began recording the same year, in 1923. Smith practiced a different style of blues vocal—one in which the vocal line was freed from the accompaniment. This simple difference allowed for greater expressive possibilities for the singer—and the public bought it. Twentieth-century popular music would follow Smith's line rather than Rainey's; in the innovations of the former lay the origins of scat singing, jazz, and soul.

It is worth remembering that both singers had very short careers. Ma Rainey recorded for only six years and quit music in 1933. Bessie Smith made her last recording that year and died four years later in a car crash. Rainey died, completely forgotten, in 1939. It is Smith who is remembered today, with Rainey recorded chiefly as a practitioner of a dead branch of music.[13]

Ma Rainey, like Troy Maxson, is an unrecorded great, a leftover of history, a richer subject of reading.

Ma Rainey's Black Bottom is set in 1927, just past the peak of Ma Rainey's success. Sturdyvant and Irvin already are warning Ma of Smith's rise, and Ma recognizes this specter by denying it: "Bessie what? Ain't nobody thinking about Bessie. I taught Bessie. She ain't doing nothing but imitating me. What I care about Bessie? I don't care if she sell a million records. She got her people and I got mine. I don't care what nobody else do. Ma was the *first* and don't you forget it!" (64). Irvin and Sturdyvant are quite aware of the gap in styles and how it is hurting Ma's salability. In a variety of dishonest ways, Irvin tries to get Ma to record "Moonshine Blues," a Bessie Smith hit. When Ma refuses, he tries to get her to record "Black Bottom," not in her arrangement (with the stuttering Sylvester as tent caller) but in Levee's: "Ma, that's what the people want now. They want something they can dance to. Times are changing. Levee's arrangement gives the people what they want" (51). When Ma stands firm, Levee nevertheless insists on improvising over the tune. His clash with Ma Rainey finally names the gap over which they have been at war:

> MA RAINEY: Levee ... what is that you doing? Why you playing all them notes? You play ten notes for every one you supposed to play. It don't call for that.
> LEVEE: You supposed to improvise on the theme. That's what I was doing.
> MA RAINEY: You supposed to play the song the way I sing it. The way everybody else play it. You ain't supposed to go off and play what you want.
> LEVEE: I was playing the song. I was playing it the way I felt it.
> (84)

Just as with Troy and Cory, the ulterior clash here is over whether there has or has not been a gap.

Among the many gaps and disjunctions here, two stand out. The first is the gap between an oral time, in which performance was indissolubly linked to the artist's presence, and an aural time, in which performance could be reproduced (or so claimed the supply side) via the technological innovation of recording. Few histories are less continuous, less rational than this one. Each of the formative discoveries, by Bell, Edison, Berliner, included a large number of accidents, experiments, and leaps of intuition.

More interesting than these technological changes are the shifts they occasioned in the conception of performance. Irvin, Sturdyvant, and Levee are more than comfortable in the new age—but their reading of this change is very different, and the difference allows us to measure Levee's tragedy. Levee stands for a new way to play but an old way to think of performance. He embraces the legitimacy of recording, yet he assumes that in recording his songs he is extending his personality, banishing his death. This becomes clear whenever he speaks about his songs and his band: "I'm gonna get me a band and make me some records. I done give Mr. Sturdyvant some of my songs I wrote and he say he's gonna let me record them when I get my band together.... But everybody can't play like I do. Everybody can't have their own band" (19). Slow Drag, Cutler, and Toledo realize how things really stand: They are work for hire, not artists, as Levee pretends, and their best chance for survival lies in playing as they are told. As Slow Drag puts it, "When the time comes to go up there and record them songs ... I just wanna go up there and do it" (17). They see Levee's assumption that "I got time coming to me" as an obvious self-deception. As his stories about himself show, he has been broken by his contact with the white man.

Toledo, in his elusive philosophical manner, attempts to teach Levee with his parable of history as a stew and African Americans as "leftovers": "See, we's the leftovers. The colored man is the leftovers. Now, what's the colored man gonna do with himself?—That's what we waiting to find out. But first we gotta know we's the leftovers.... But we don't know that we been took and made history out of" (47). Toledo's metaphor portrays history not as linear but as a process full of waste and discontinuity. Levee, conversely, is arguing for the continuity and perpetuity of the self. Refusing to recognize the limits of his own talent or the social limits imposed on him, he is trying to construct a romance of a meritocracy in which he will be surely rewarded. As the older musicians point out, this conflicts with what Levy himself knows about his past and present—that his choices are limited and ruin is always near.

But Levee insists that recording preserves the old personal ties between performer and audience; he forgets that recording renders each invisible and unknown to the other. He tries to ignore Sturdyvant's viewpoint, in which Levee's music, far from being an extended personal contract, is product that changes hands for money, a business transaction driven by the irrational needs of the public for music and sex. When the band finally finishes the date, Irvin chortles, "Good! Wonderful! We have that, boys" (84). The proprietary capitalism in his chosen phrase, the "having" of a recording in order to sell it, shows how his assumptions differ from Levee's. Sturdyvant's success as a seller of records depends on the sustained anonymity of the actual performers. Sturdyvant not only assents to the establishment of their deaths through recording, he actively promotes it. Ma Rainey the person must be erased in favor of the superior selling potency of her "name"; now that Bessie Smith is on the rise, even Ma Rainey's "name" is endangered.

Ma is far less naive than Levee about the nature of recording. She places such a value on presence in performance that she considers recording to be a kind of prostitution: "They don't care nothing about me. All they want is my voice.... As soon as they get my voice down on them recording machines, then it's just like if I'd be some whore and they roll over and put their pants on" (64). This and other comments suggest that for Ma Rainey, live performance is more authentic than recording. The "blues" is a way of learning, a deeply personal thing that needs to be performed to be understood: "You don't sing to feel better. You sing because that's a way of understanding life" (66). It's interesting that singing is, itself, a way of reading.

Yet hers is a losing game, as all the players know. Although imperious (hilariously so) and assertive, Ma as much as admits that with each move she is aiding in her own eclipse. She has decided that, if she is a whore, she had better be well paid. In this, she is different from Troy, less insistent on the continuity of self. She is aware that by signing away her commercial rights to her records she is relinquishing control, and so she holds the moment off as long as she can. When at last she does sign the papers, she covers up for her loss of power by reversing it: "You tell Sturdyvant ... one more mistake like that and I can make my records someplace else" (88). Though Levee is impressed by Ma's attitude ("As soon as I get my band together and make them records ... I'm gonna be like Ma and tell the white man just what he can do" [78]), Cutler and Slow Drag know that Ma's "difficult star" act is simply a way to milk the last drop of power from a completely circumscribed situation. As Slow Drag puts it, "You let her go down to one of them white-folks' hotels and see how big she is" (78).

Ma and the older musicians are thus assenting more or less consciously to their own exploitation. This is what Levee cannot forgive them for, even as he himself does it. In selling records that bring the illusion of Ma into every buyer's home, Irvin and Sturdyvant are actually selling the fact of her absence. They will profit from that absence in every copy of "Ma Rainey's Black Bottom" they sell. In signing the release forms, Ma is establishing rather than banishing her death.

A second disjunction, even less rational than that between a time of presence as authenticity and absence as commercial product (the latter captured in the oxymoron "high-fidelity recording"), is that of the difference in styles. There is no complete account of why Ma Rainey sang with her accompaniment and Bessie Smith sang free of it. Both are the blues, and neither is "like" the other. There is no complete account of why the urban-centered "hot" style of playing that would become big-band jazz gained commercial ascendancy over the "down-home" style. (And this was no binary opposition; there were many other styles vying for the public's dollar, and nearly all of them have utterly perished.) Nor can there be a complete account of why the American record buyer endorsed the freer style—and has consistently continued to do so down to the present. (The obvious answers—that this expressed the "American spirit," that in preferring this kind of singing, record buyers were expressing their own aspirations to personal freedom—are so true that they are banal.)

Levee's destruction does not so much prefigure Ma's eclipse as it prefigures the sacrifice of all the black performers. When Sturdyvant attempts to pay him for the songs, thus making clear his death as author, Levee is left to plead for the special case of his self. "You got to hear *me* play them, Mr. Sturdyvant! You ain't heard *me* play them.... I'd set them down in the people's lap!" (90–91).

And that reminds us of how classical a Wilson drama really is. For what is this tragic inability to change readings other than the protagonist's *hamartia*, that error in judgment emanating from what is most admirable? Ma Rainey refuses to acknowledge that a shift has taken place in the way jazz is performed and recorded. Although she knows that other ways of singing are passing her up, Rainey maintains her demands that things be done *her* way, the way they have always been done. Troy in *Fences* refuses to allow Cory to play football, in part because he fears that his son *will be allowed to play* as he himself was not. To allow Cory to play would be to acknowledge the inadequacy of his way of reading the world. His refusal has tragic consequences for both Troy and Cory. Cory sees the missed opportunity with the recruiter as "the one chance I had" (57), which, as far as football is concerned, appears to be true. He finds his way into the army and is faced with the burden of learning not to hate his father. At the end of the play, Cory states that he will not reenlist, but, chillingly, it is 1965, the year of great changes in American society and in Indochina. What we are encouraged to see as admirable in both Ma Rainey and Troy Maxson—their insistence on their right to assert themselves in the ambit of their experience (even if that experience is mean, shabby, or poor)—also produces their blindness to the change in time. As it does for Oedipus, the failure to shift readings renders them noble and tragic.

In this respect, Wilson's drama closely follows Aristotelian precepts.

Dramatic irony issues from the audience's ability to mark the historical shift that the protagonist insists on denying. We guess that Cory at least might get a chance to play if Troy would let him; from what Sturdyvant, Irvin, Ma, and Levee say, we know that a change in popular music threatens to end Ma's career. Troy's tragedy is that he refuses to allow his son to have a future; he insists on the past as present. Cory tells him so: "Just cause you didn't have a chance! You just scared I'm gonna be better than you, that's all" (58). Ma's tragedy is that, being obsolete, she cannot see that she is obsolete. Levee's tragedy is related but different: he has embraced the new paradigm—of a new jazz, a new way for a black man to be—but cannot be part of it himself. His is the Moses complex.

WHAT HAPPENS ELSEWHERE

Audiences are invited to compare their own readings with those of the characters onstage. That comparison registers a difference, and that difference is what tells us that history has "passed." Note that we do not directly view the change—rather, we realize that a shift *must have happened elsewhere* to enable this difference in readings to exist. Again, Wilson has set these plays at junctures of decisive change in African American history—Chicago in 1927, Pittsburgh in 1957—to sharpen the disparity between our readings and those of the characters. From our privileged perspective, we may well know that "hot" jazz took off in urban centers in the 1920s; we may well know that black athletes were beginning a great tradition in the mid-1950s. A Wilson play presents us with a gradient of readings (Troy-Rosa-Cory, Irvin-Cutler-Ma-Levee), with which we may triangulate our own readings, our own good, better, and best guesses.

I mentioned that in these plays we see not the moment itself passing but rather evidence of a shift that has occurred elsewhere. I don't wish to suggest that such shifts, in a parlance I have always found arrogant, "always occur elsewhere." In fact, they don't. A great shift in the history of American music occurred on a December night in 1939, at "a chili house on Seventh Avenue between 139th and 140th Streets." Saxophonist Charlie Parker had become increasingly "bored with the stereotyped changes" in the jazz of that period. His frustration had arisen from being able to hear something different but not being able to play it. "That night, I was working over 'Cherokee,' and, as I did, I found that by using the higher intervals of a chord as a melody line and backing them with appropriately related changes I could play the thing I'd been hearing. I came alive."[14]

Among other things, Parker found an improvisational technique through which he could imply passing chords not actually stated by his accompaniment.[15] Parker thus discovered a novel approach to melody and harmony that made possible the creation of bebop, "cool" jazz, and late-century jazz. To be sure, despite the fact that he was there for the change, much about Parker's discovery was clearly out of his control—as he says, he "finds" a new way to play. Parker once told the guitarist Jimmy Raney that "sometimes I look at my fingers and I'm surprised that it's me playing."[16] While acknowledging what was out-of-control in Parker's discovery, we must, out of decency, find a way to acknowledge that Parker was there for the change; in part, he was the change.

For the rest of us, however, that historic change in American music did indeed happen elsewhere—and still happens, nearly every time we hear a contemporary tune. For most people, as for Wilson's tragic characters, great historic changes occur in other minds, are spoken on other lips—and they must either accept these changes or not. Ma Rainey is being left behind because people are buying and dancing to Bessie Smith's records. Cory's chances in football are better than his father's in baseball because of Kenny Washington, Hank Aaron, and Roberto Clemente. Because of the way things are, these characters are condemned to a predicament of relation in regard to the origin of change. This origin they themselves cannot know or find. If we are like Troy, Ma Rainey, and Levee, our tragedy lies in our inability to be there for the change itself. Yet that shift is our fait accompli, what we cannot change or avoid. It is precisely the *anangke* before which, according to Sophocles, "even the gods give way." Knowing is complicated by our position (the Mother of the Blues, for instance; former Negro League baseball great, for instance) and our wishes (to be treated as an authoritative figure, to be continuous and eternal).

These plays suggest that we read history for self-advantage. It is to Cory's advantage that he reads history as discontinuous, as much as it is to Troy's to read history as continuous. Ma Rainey, Levee, Cutler, Irvin, Sturdyvant—each character adopts a reading that best serves his or her wishes and position. It would be a naive reader who assumed that, given his or her own experience, either Troy or Ma Rainey would value "political awareness" over personal survival. Neither does, and neither takes any comfort in having contributed to the new possibilities that may exist for others. Survivor's guilt is clear in both, but so are fear and resentment at having been sacrificed. The rise to prominence of the jazz singer and the black athlete do not change the facts about the future. To paraphrase Walter Benjamin, we might say that the future is an emptiness that it will take human labor and suffering to fill.

And so to the answer to our opening question. The excluded and the empowered *do* read history differently. Indeed, they cannot but do so, since so much of reading consists of position and wishes, of constructing and projecting. As Nietzsche and Foucault imply, empowerment leads to a history that assumes empowerment: a way of reading that begs the question, rationalizes what it assumes out of sheer privilege. The empowered read history as a "fullness" of time. As Wilson's art construes the question, exclusion leads to other voices, other ways of reading. The excluded often read history as an emptiness that must be filled. The highest praise Ma Rainey receives is from Toledo: "You fill it up with something the people can't be without, Ma.... You fill up the emptiness in a way ain't nobody ever thought of doing before" (68). History for the excluded is non-linear, non-rational. That is why, as of this writing, American culture may be the first in which so many kinds of history are being written by the losers. For more than two centuries, African American writers have helped build up an alternative model of history: not an authoritative presentation of "what really happened," but an array of readings that challenge the dominant way.

And this suggests much about African American history, which, far from being a smooth, uninterrupted progress, a "flow," has proceeded by bursts, leaps, shifts, disjunctions, tragic, disagreements, the total experience of a group of peoples sharing a diaspora into various fates that have included oppression and exclusion. There have been many positions, many competing wishes (assimilation, radicalism, the Bumpies, the Black Middle Class), many good, better, and best guesses. There will be more. To see African American history as a great river running up to the present is to deny the true richness, tragedy, and achievement in that history. To read it—as Foucault suggests we read anything, and as August Wilson's powerful imagination portrays it—as a series of painful, inevitable rents in what we thought we knew, is to achieve a greater terror, a richer, purer compassion.

NOTES

1. James, *Principles of Psychology*, p. 507.

2. Neither the term nor the concept of the "specious present" was James's invention. In his essay he credits its originator, E.R. Clay. I am grateful to Ralph Slaght for his insights on this topic.

3. Mundle, "Consciousness of Time," p. 138.

4. Foucault, *Language, Counter-Memory, Practice*, p. 146.

5. Foucault, *Archaeology of Knowledge*, pp. 169–70.

6. Richards; Introduction, pp. vii, xviii.

7. James, *Principles of Psychology*, p. 574.

8. For a more detailed discussion about the vexed issue of integration in professional football, see Ocania Chalk, *Pioneers of Black Sport* (New York: Dodd, Mead, 1975).

9. Black professional baseball players referred variously to these organizations as "the Negro League(s)," "the League," and "the Negro Major Leagues" to differentiate them from the white major leagues, black minor leagues such as the Texas Negro League, and the numerous private barnstorming teams of the period. The Negro Leagues have been better represented in literary treatment than in scholarly research. Part of the problem is the scarcity of materials; few teams could afford the printed programs, team brochures, and team magazines common in the white majors. The best work on the Negro Leagues has thus been done by scholars who have interviewed players, recovered sports reports from the black press of the period, and tracked down personal memorabilia. This work includes John Holway's *Voices from the Great Black Baseball Leagues* (New York: Dodd, Mead, 1975), biographies such as William Brashler's *Josh Gibson: A Life in the Negro Leagues* (New York: Harper and Row, 1978) and Art Rust Jr.'s *"Get That Nigger Off the Field!"* (New York: Delacourt, 1976), and the work of John Lomax. An excellent study of its kind is Janet Bruce, *The Kansas City Monarchs: Champions of Black Baseball* (Lawrence: University Press of Kansas, 1985). Information also appears in the autobiographies of Negro League greats, such as Leroy "Satchel" Paige's *Maybe I'll Pitch Forever* (Garden City, N.Y.: Doubleday, 1962) and Jackie Robinson's *I Never Had It Made* (New York: G. P. Putnam's Sons, 1972). A good, though glamorizing, early overview is A. S. "Doc" Young's *Great Negro Baseball Stars and How They Made It to the Major Leagues* (New York: A. S. Barnes, 1953). Later studies, such as Effa Manley and Leon Herbert Hardwick's *Negro Baseball ... Before Integration* (Chicago: Adams, 1976) and Quincy Trouppe's *Twenty Years Too Soon* (Los Angeles: S & S Enterprises, 1977), focus more steadily on the social undercurrents that sustained and eventually killed the Negro Leagues. The two best overviews, Robert Peterson's *Only the Ball Was White* (Englewood Cliffs, N.J.: Prentice-Hall, 1970) and Donn Rogosin's *Invisible Men: Life in Baseball's Negro Leagues* (New York: Atheneum, 1983), are (perhaps unavoidably) anecdotal in nature, and, while both are furnished with statistics and players lists, neither has a bibliography.

It is worth noting that the "death" of the Negro Leagues was a relative matter. The most prestigious of the Negro Leagues, the Negro National League, was in operation, on and off, between 1920 and 1948. Jackie Robinson's signing prompted many Negro League players to sign minor league contracts with the white major leagues. The National Negro League's prestige plummeted, attendance and gate earnings declined drastically and almost immediately, and the league was dead within two years. (It is interesting also to note that some teams unsuccessfully petitioned the white major leagues to be accepted into the minors.) The Negro American League, however, was in continuous operation between 1937 and 1960; after Robinson's signing, it too was promptly drained of its best players. As the play makes clear, Troy Maxson was already past his prime by 1947, and although many black players (notably Luke Easter and Satchel Paige) lied about their age to protect their marketability, players were not even recruited unless they were standouts and willing to accept ill treatment from fans and management. This last "requirement" is surely lacking in Troy's case.

10. Foucault, *Archaeology of Knowledge*, p. 210.

11. Neft and Cohen, *Sports Encyclopedia*, pp. 309, 312.

12. The blues is one of the most thoroughly documented of American cultural inventions. On Ma Rainey herself, the best scholarly study is Sandra R. Lieb, *Mother of the*

Blues: A Study of Ma Rainey (Amherst: University of Massachusetts Press, 1981); on the place of women in the history of the blues, see Chris Albertson, *Bessie* (New York: Stein and Day, 1972); Daphne Duval Harrison, *Black Pearls: Blues Queens of the 1920s* (New Brunswick, N.J.: Rutgers University Press, 1988); and Hettie Jones, *Big Star Fallin' Mama: Five Women in Black Music* (New York: Viking, 1974). Interesting comparisons of the style of the early female blues singers appear in Paul Oliver, *Blues Fell This Morning* (Cambridge: Cambridge University Press, 1990). An important study of the "down-home" style of blues is Jeff Titon, *Early Downhome Blues: A Musical and Cultural Analysis* (Urbana: University of Illinois Press, 1977). Many good studies now exist of the myriad regional blues styles. These include Bruce Bastin, *Red River Blues: The Blues Tradition in the Southeast* (Urbana: University of Illinois Press, 1986) and William P. Ferris, *Blues from the Delta* (New York: Da Capo, 1984). One of the best overviews of blues history is Robert Palmer, *Deep Blues* (Harmondsworth: Penguin, 1981). Two more are Paul Oliver, *The Blues Tradition* (New York: Oak Publications, 1970) and *The Story of the Blues* (Philadelphia: Chilton, 1973). Two good discographies are John Godrich and Robert Dixon, *Blues and Gospel Records 1902–1942* (London: Storyville, 1969), and Paul Oliver, ed., *The Blackwell Guide to Blues Records* (Oxford: Blackwell, 1989). An excellent bibliography is Mary L. Hart, Brenda M. Eagles, and Lisa N. Howorth, *The Blues: A Bibliographical Guide* (New York: Garland, 1989), and the standard biographical reference is Sheldon Harris, *Blues Who's Who* (New Rochelle, New York: Arlington House, 1979). Important readings include Houston Baker, *Blues, Ideology, and Afro American Literature: A Vernacular Theory* (Chicago: University of Chicago Press, 1984); Samuel Barclay Charters, *The Roots of the Blues: An African Search* (Boston: M. Boyars, 1981); and Mary Ellison, *Extensions of the Blues* (New York: Riverrun, 1989).

13. The transitional nature of Ma Rainey's career bears some note. She began as a traveling tent show singer with her husband's group, the Rabbit Foot Minstrels. Thus she did not, in fact, grow up in the blues tradition at all, being seduced to it only after hearing a "strange and poignant" [her words] blues song sung by a young girl in 1904. In 1910, the Rabbit Foot Minstrels took on young Bessie Smith for awhile; Smith was later to disclaim having been influenced by the elder singer. Rainey was probably bisexual (Oliver, *Blues Fell This Morning*, p. 100); she had a reputation for avid pursuit of young men and women alike. This sheds some interesting light on the reference to Dussie Mae as "Ma's girl." Finally, Rainey's retirement from recording was not caused solely by the rise of Bessie Smith. In fact, Rainey retired in order to stay at home and tend sick family members. It is clear, however, that the triumph of Smith's style was a decisive one.

14. Shapiro and Hentoff, *Hear Me Talking to Ya*, p. 354.

15. Harrison, *Charlie Parker*, pp. 31–32.

16. Reisner, *Bird*, pp. 190–91.

WORKS CITED

Foucault, Michel. *Archaeology of Knowledge.* Translated by A.M. Sheridan Smith. New York: Pantheon, 1972.
———. *Language, Counter-Memory, Practice.* Edited by Donald F. Bouchard. Translated by Donald F. Bouchard and Sherry Simon. Ithaca: Cornell University Press, 1977.
Harrison, Max. *Charlie Parker.* New York: A.S. Barnes, 1961.

James, William. *Principles of Psychology*. Edited by Frederick H. Burkhardt. Vol. 1. Cambridge: Harvard University Press, 1981.

Mundle, C.W.K. "Time, Consciousness of." *Encyclopedia of Philosophy*. Edited by Paul Edwards. Vol. 8. New York: Macmillan, 1967.

Neft, David S., and Richard M. Cohen. *The Sports Encyclopedia: Baseball*. New York: St. Martin's Press, 1989.

Reisner, Robert G. *Bird: The Legend of Charlie Parker*. New York: Da Capo, 1975.
Richards, Lloyd. Introduction to *Fences*, by August Wilson, pp. vii–viii. New York: New American Library, Plume, 1986.

Shapiro, Nat, and Nat Hentoff. *Hear Me Talking to Ya*. New York: Dover, 1955.

Wilson, August. *Fences*. New York: New American Library, Plume, 1986.

———. *Three Plays*. Pittsburgh: University of Pittsburgh Press, 1991.

MICHAEL L. QUINN

Anti-Theatricality and American Ideology: Mamet's Performative Realism

David Mamet's dramatic writing, for all its apparent seriousness, and the artistic enthusiasm its effects have aroused, has not been very thoroughly explained.[1] That it seems conventionally realistic helps to make it seem familiar, and some of the best criticism of Mamet has been an attempt to recuperate the value of an artistically fluent and culturally sensitive realism.[2] But from the standpoint of meaning, Mamet's apparent lack of a representational strategy—that is, his realism—tends to make his work seem even more opaque. Simple representational realistic explanations of Mamet are too easy, if the vividness of the dramatic effect and the intensity of the intellectual controversies that the plays have aroused are also to be taken seriously by poststructuralist critics. I argue that Mamet's plays use a specific realistic rhetoric to strike a deep but somewhat inaccessible chord in American intellectuals—inaccessible because the critics themselves often participate in the same ideological processes that form the matrix of Mamet's work.[3] Realism is not in this case representational but expressive, focusing on performed actions rather than mimesis, and making judgments of truth a matter of active construction rather than of comparison with an *a priori* reality. As Mamet notes in his own essay on the subject, "In discarding the armor of realism, he or she [the artist] accepts the responsibility of making every choice in light of specific meaning, of making every choice assertive rather than protective."[4]

From *Realism and the American Dramatic Tradition*, edited by William W. Demastes. © 1996 by University of Alabama Press.

Mamet's self-proclaimed iconoclasm is a kind of doctrine informed by a system of ritualized liberal dissent in which membership in the national tradition depends upon a declared rejection of the current state of cultural affairs. The principal theorist of this perspective is Sacvan Bercovitch, who points out not only how this pattern manifests itself in a set of texts from the Puritans through the foundational documents of American government to the New England Renaissance, but also how this narrative of American Puritan culture is a deliberate creation of twentieth-century literary historians like Perry Miller and F.O. Matthiessen.[5] Perhaps the crucial figure in this tradition is Emerson, who "had decided, on reconsidering the attacks on individualism, that the remedy was not to abandon it, but to draw out its potential,"[6] that is, the link between individual self-creation and the collective creation of American community. Bercovitch points out that such a closure is virtually impossible, but in working through its visionary demands, American artists have used this political paradox as a basis for constantly renewed visions of authentic American creativity. Bercovitch's thesis also points out how Dennis Carroll's reading of Mamet as an artist of "dichotomy" and "paradox," cohering "in the personality he projects" can be joined with C.W.E. Bigsby's attempts to locate Mamet within an American cultural landscape.[7]

In theatrical history, this pattern of community formation through dissent—the rejection of American culture in the name of American values—is very common. (Consider, for example, the Group Theatre.) Such a cultural pattern, applied in an analysis of Mamet's favorite ideas and artistic techniques, can help to establish a critical context for understanding Mamet's work while also explaining something about his embattled but enthusiastic reception. Americans, like anyone working in the context of a naturalized ideology, often find it very difficult to undertake a culturally based analysis of their own literature; what passes for such criticism usually tends to participate in the politics of empowering denunciation, not theorizing its own implication in the pattern. In Mamet's case, the ideologically effective aspects of dramatic construction are often simply taken for something bold, hardheaded, and realistic, rather than as gestures in a standard romantic ritual of American intellectual culture.

Only a few steps are necessary for a writer like Mamet to position himself in the role of a dissenting, revolutionary artist with a unique perspective. One of the first steps is to identify some orthodoxy that can be decried as ruinous, or perhaps un-American. In Mamet's case, this orthodoxy tends to follow the pattern outlined by his intellectual hero, Thorstein Veblen, of excoriating a greedy bourgeoisie—the class that requires conformity to a way of doing business and administering justice that serves those in power, and ruins the life of the ordinary man.[8] In theatre history, this kind of dissent usually finds its object in Broadway.[9] The decadent commercial theatre is then indicted in a vituperative jeremiad—laden with the rhetoric of the pulpit—which also often outlines a visionary path to redemption through the restoration of neglected moral values: truth, authenticity, selfless commitment to art, reason, etc.[10] In Mamet's case, such public comments are easy to find, especially in his essays and speeches. In "Decadence," for example, he decries the corruption of what he sees as the current dominance of a "theater of good intentions":

> We are in the midst of a vogue for the truly decadent in art— for that which is destructive rather than regenerative, self- referential rather than outward—looking, elitist rather than popular. This decadent art is elitist because it cannot stand on its merits as a work of personal creation. Instead it appeals to a prejudice or predilection held mutually with the audience.
>
> This appeal is political, and stems from the political urge, which is the urge to control the actions of others. It is in direct opposition to the artistic urge, which is to express oneself regardless of the consequences. I cite "performance art," "women's writing" ... badges proclaiming a position.
>
> Plays which deal with the unassailable investigate nothing and express nothing save the desire to investigate nothing.
>
> It is incontrovertible that deaf people are people, too; that homosexuals are people, too; that it is unfortunate to be deprived of a full and happy life by illness or accident; that it is sobering to grow old.
>
> These events ... equally befall the Good and the Bad individual. They are not the result of conscious choice and so do not bear on the character of the individual. They are not the fit subject of drama, as they do not deal with the human capacity for choice. Rather than uniting the audience in a universal experience, they are invidious. They split the audience into two camps; those who like the play and those who hate homosexuals (deaf people, old people, paraplegics, etc.).[11]

Mamet's grouping of banal social realists and the formalist avant-garde may have seemed in 1986 like an unlikely orthodoxy, though it has been repeated often in recent years in denunciations of the "politically correct."[12] What matters for ritual purposes, though, is merely Mamet's ability to construct the current scene as moribund, in a kind of statement that is not argued but rather performed. J.L. Austin would call such a ritualized statement an "illocutionary speech act," a kind of "performative" speech that constitutes some state of affairs through linguistic action; other examples would be things like promises, oaths, and declarations, including the political documents that form the bases of governments.[13] Despite Mamet's often acute consciousness of ritual behaviors, especially within the American contexts of holidays and masculine activities, he does not seem particularly sensitive to his own use of the jeremiad as a tool for his political empowerment.

The second requirement for Bercovitch's ritual of dissent is the construction of a unique individuality, a narrative of genesis and personal growth. Mamet's exceptionalist character is again constructed most clearly in his essays: in personal reflections, descriptions of his unhappy childhood at home, the idealizing influence of Old Chicago, his part-time jobs, his Slavic-Jewish heritage, and comments on the unique progress of his career. In one of the notes from *The Cabin* on Chicago radio, Mamet shows considerable cultural awareness about constructing his personality in this creative political context: "The idea in the air was that culture was what we, the people, did. The idea was—and is—that we were *surrounded* by culture. It was not alien to us. It was what the people did and thought and sang and wrote about. The idea was the particularly Chicagoan admixture of the populist and the intellectual. The model, the Hutchins model, the Chicago model of the European freethinker, was an autodidact: a man or woman who so loved the world around him or her that he or she was moved to investigate it further—either by creating works of art or by appreciating those works."[14]

Many of the exceptional characteristics that Mamet claims for himself, which have found expression in his plays, are tied to one aspect or another of what seem to be perfectly ordinary experiences. Yet the conviction remains in Mamet that the unique combination of experiences—the history of choices and conditions that produces his artistic consciousness—is solely his own, as fully individual as are his inherent human talents. This approach to identity is not representational but expressive; people constitute themselves not by thinking of themselves as copies but rather by thinking of themselves as constituted through actions based in their innate desires and qualities. These actions can then take on a pronounced cultural charge. For example, Mamet often seems so fully identified with the Chicago of the past that his nostalgia strains credibility; though born in 1947, he writes with an acute consciousness of his own "aging," and as if he were himself present at crucial cultural moments like the 1934 Century of Progress Exhibition. Mamet, then, claims exceptional status primarily because he thinks of himself as though he has come from an earlier time: the grittier, more inventive, and more communal Chicago before 1968, the time between Al Capone and Richard Daley (when Chicago writers like Carl Sandburg routinely claimed to represent America, too, by embodying its energy or its history of bootstrap immigrant prosperity). The absurdity of Mamet's wish for this subjectivity only emphasizes its constructed quality, which is even more evident when he folds into it—sometimes even in messianic terms—the ideal of the autodidact and the romantic writer. The title of his second book of essays, *Some Freaks*, is Mamet's way of identifying those individuals, like himself, who are leaders because they "do not fit the norm."[15] Mamet's *Chicago* is as fully laden with American ideology as was the New England of Henry David Thoreau, whom Mamet imitates in his Vermont cabin.

Typically the American narrative of dissent ushers in a new vision of community, often a political ideal retrieved through personal struggle or travel to a strange place. Mamet treats his ordinary experiences, in French Canada, in a neighborhood pool hall, or at a part-time job, as if they were such struggles or journeys; in any case, they supposedly offered life lessons. In Mamet's life today this ideal community might be Cabot, Vermont, the village where he sometimes lives and writes, or the neighborhood of his Boston row house, before the area was ruined by division into rental units. In Mamet's version of theatre history, such an ideal scene might be something like the Group Theatre's retreat, or the long day in the Slavyansky Bazaar when the Moscow Art Theatre was conceived. But Mamet's broader political vision is never quite so concretely stated; it seems to be conventionally Jeffersonian, though perhaps even more nearly Rousseauian: an American community where politicians tell the truth, friendship is sacred, simple customs are cherished, and men can be men.[16] This sort of sustaining vision underlies many of the plays like an ideological subtext, a wish tacitly shared among sympathetic characters. Yet Mamet's *America* is rarely dramatized as a place that might actually exist; rather, Mamet's realism is a coming to terms with the difficulty—even the impossibility—of living such ideals.[17]

If the artist and the American individual are free to constitute themselves, to create their visions through the simple action of declaring or performing them, of acting them out, then the negative aspect of Mamet's realism, its paradoxical ideological unveiling, is the dramatic debunking of such constitutive gestures as mistakes of confidence, as willful illusions that the current state of the world cannot sustain. Realism in this context is not a scientific avant-garde, nor even, as Mamet himself notes, is it quite a "scenic truth" in the same way as it was for Stanislavsky; rather, the realistic attitude becomes a skeptical, often physical control on dreams of a better life.[18] This is not exactly the same kind of realism that Jonas Barish would call an "anti-theatrical prejudice," though Mamet often indicts the theatrical when it is abused as a rhetoric of deception in everyday life.[19] Mamet's constant concern in his writings on the theatre, and in his explanations of his style, is with *action*, which he theorizes as a constitutive, authentic movement of the mind and body, as opposed to a less vital, static or mimetic way of living and showing life. In this regard the Method actor is even, for Mamet, an emblem of virtuous life: "When, once again, actors are cherished and rewarded who bring to the stage or the screen generosity, desire, *organic life*, actions performed freely—without desire for reward or fear of either censure or misunderstanding—that will be one of the first signs that the tide of our introverted, unhappy time has turned and that we are once again eager and prepared to look at ourselves."[20] To the extent that Mamet's theatre of action is an attempt not merely to *represent* but actually to *constitute* his vision of a better life, the theatre has special powers. Theatre in such a view does not consciously imitate poetry, but the enactment of vital dialogue might attempt to perform the poetry of life. Theatricality exists in this case in a strange double bind; it can express the truth of things and events, but it can also be used to hide that truth through fantasies or lies. Such an emphasis on action may explain Mamet's preference for a small group of loyal performers, which keeps offstage dramatic intrigue at a minimum.

Consequently the theatrical act within Mamet's work is also, most often, an act of everyday deception, a risky move to create an illusive advantage. Mamet's theatre constitutes an orthodox, illusively realistic world of the play, full of lies, and then these must eventually come undone in an even "more real" scene of social debunking, physical constraint and/or theatrical undercutting. There are a few basic kinds of theatrical scenes in Mamet's work, and these are usually central to what is at stake in the drama. Once these are outlined, I think the anti-theatrical, ideological flow of Mamet's realistic writing will be fairly clear—a dissenting American anti-theatricality, designed to affirm his characters' self-constitutive, performative actions but also to reveal the destructiveness of lies.

THE BUSINESS SCAM

Probably the most famous kind of theatricality within Mamet's dramas, continuing through the filmscript for *Hoffa*, concerns the intrigues of businessmen, whether their purposes are within or, most often, outside of the laws of commerce.[21] In the former case, Mamet seems to criticize the conventional structure of capitalism from the top down; those with the most power and money tend to be able to create situations in which those with the least must scheme for an advantage. When these same ordinary people choose to live outside the law, Mamet's implied criticism falls more directly on the illusions they produce to dupe their victims. In *American Buffalo*, Donny Dubrow is poised on the brink of such a choice. He begins his scheme with Bobby to steal the coin collection as a kind of fantasy, a way of working together with his protégé on an imaginary project that seems to promise more than the poor prospects of his own junk store. Teach forces the scenario, taking the play of theft seriously, and consequently obliging Donny to betray his friend for the sake of the plan.

Glengarry Glen Ross similarly makes financial desperation over into a problem of identity, but it carries the deception two steps further. Shelly "The Machine" Levene built his good name on his ability to close real estate deals, but by the time the action of the play begins, he has failed to maintain the sales record that his self-esteem and his livelihood require. In the first scene Levene asks the office manager, Williamson, to accept a bribe so that he can get better client lists and begin to make more actual sales. Williamson refuses. The second scene does not include Levene, but in it Moss proposes to Aaronow the robbery scam that Levene will eventually enact. The third scene, the shortest of the first act, is an exemplary performance by the most successful agent, Roma, showing how the ordinary business of Levene's firm, the sale of swampland in Florida to gullible investors, requires a rhetorically intense and emotionally exhausting confidence game. In the second act Levene has already robbed the office of its client list and in the meantime believes he has convinced an unsuspecting buyer into signing for "eight units of Mountain View"; he thinks he has reclaimed his identity, but he must sustain himself by performing his own innocence as the break-in is being investigated. In a crucial play-within-a-play scene with Roma, Levene shows the audience that he can still pitch a scam, the two managing to improvise a scene that is designed to put a client off until his check has cleared the bank. As Roma tells Levene, "That shit you were slinging on my guy today was so good ... it ... it was, and, excuse me, 'cause it isn't even my place to say it. It was admirable ... it was the old stuff."[22] It is after playing the old game with Roma, and defending the game itself, that Levene eventually lets slip his crucial knowledge of the contract he saw during the break-in—a lapse of concentration in his double game that causes him to get caught in the robbery scam. A second revelation, that his supposed sale was to a legally incompetent client, only compounds his failure. Levene's performances, as a salesman and an actor in fraud, are what constitute his identity, but when he pushes the illusion a step too far, threatening the profit structure of the business, his whole world comes down around him. Realism in this play is a matter of listening closely, following cues and sustaining the illusion of a seamless performance; when the theatrical self breaks down, reality is felt most acutely by Levene as an absence of achievement, for which he must pay with suffering.

The obverse of *Glengarry Glen Ross* is *House of Games*, Mamet's film about a con game designed to bilk a fortune from a wealthy psychologist, Margaret Ford. After an opening sequence suggesting that psychoanalysis is itself an elaborate scam, Margaret goes to aid a troubled client by confronting Mike, the lender of the con artists, at the *House of Games*, a gambling room. She is quickly drawn in, ends up teamed with Mike in a poker game, and guarantees his bet; when he loses, she is about to write a check when she notices that the winning player's gun is a water pistol. The first plan to bilk her is revealed. The primary problem for Margaret in the film is the problem of depth, of how many layers of playing a scam might involve, and how many of them she is supposed to see through; the criminals here are performers, who can show or conceal the act of their own playing, so long as they are the only ones who know the limit of the play. The first play with the water pistol, like so many others, turns out to be a setup for the big sting on Margaret, in which she fronts eighty thousand dollars to Mike to replace money supposedly borrowed from the mob and lost. Margaret is sufficiently fascinated by Mike's con games to play with him, to be seduced by him, and to be so hurt by his ultimate betrayal that she murders him. In the end it is Mike who does not know the real limit of playing; when she threatens to shoot him, he calls her bluff, only to discover that the threat was real. Even then he will not stop playing, saying after the second shot, "Thank you, sir, may I have another?"[23]

The world in *House of Games* is as completely theatricalized as in the best modern metadramas, and the problem of authentic action within it becomes the problem of which reality to affirm, which of the performances to accept as true. What Margaret understands, which Mike does not, is that death—not just cash, and not realistic illusion—is only a limit of intentional performance for the one who dies; with his dying breath Mike pleads that he himself never *killed* anyone. In a world so full of lies, the metaphysical distinction is mere hairsplitting. Evil characters, as well as good ones, are constituted by their performances, and Margaret Ford, renowned psychologist, is no exception in Mamet's world. The thrust of realism in such a context, as with *The Verdict* or *The Postman Always Rings Twice*, may be the apparently simple matter of finding out the lie, finding out the theatrical pretense, though this may also eventually involve breaking down the characters' fictions through courtroom melodrama, placing speech under the additional obligations of an oath.

HIDING OUT/UNDERCOVER

Often the theatrical game is not very elaborate in Mamet's work, just a matter of personal preservation through improvisation, or simple flight from a previous life. This latter is the context for Mamet's *Reunion*, in which a daughter seeks out the father who abandoned her and attempts to establish a relationship with him. Bernie, the father, has simply dropped out of his past relationships, drinking and occasionally trying to start again with a new family, which he eventually must leave. By the end of the play Carol, the daughter, seems to have persuaded him to forgive himself and to take a small role in her life that will help to ease her own loneliness.

In *Lakeboat* one of the crew members, Giuliani, is lost, and the remaining fellows invent an elaborate crime story about his adventures, his disappearance, and eventual death, when in fact he had simply overslept and missed the boat. Another character on the boat, Dale, is a sophomore English literature major, simply putting in time on a summer job until he can go back to school; a figure for the author, he becomes an audience for the narratives the crew members tell, allowing them to authenticate themselves while simultaneously reminding the audience, through his presence, that the play is based on the similar experiences of a young Mamet.

The most unusual of the plays that involve hiding out is probably *Lone Canoe*, the musical drama of a stranded English explorer from the early nineteenth century, living with the Athabascan tribe in the Canadian wilderness. More in tune with James Fenimore Cooper than with Emerson, this odd little play's hero, Fairfax, takes an Indian wife but is then discovered by a rescue party. Asked to return to England to explain the fate of his earlier party, Fairfax agrees to leave when a fight occurs between the explorers and natives; the tribal shaman wounds the man who led the English party, Van Brandt, and is in turn wounded by Fairfax. The party leaves, and while they wander through the lake country, Van Brandt dies. His journal reveals that he, not Fairfax, is wanted in England, so Fairfax returns to a forgiving tribe, ready to face a food shortage with the native community. This play draws out the common Rousseauian fantasy of the noble savage and the cultured man who discovers virtuous life in a simpler society. From a theatrical standpoint the plot is virtually transparent; Fairfax is free to choose who he will be by choosing which culture to belong to, and he chooses the more authentic, honest, and virtuous group of people. Fairfax rejects English society because he finds its values exemplified completely by the "natural" community of the Athabascans.

LYING ABOUT LOVE

In the politics of self-creation, one of the most dangerous acts is to give oneself over into dialogue, to admit a relation to another; such relations must, like the created self, be constituted sincerely, in declarations of genuine affection. Consequently Mamet's characters are reluctant to love one another, reluctant to admit it when they do, and apt to be extremely sensitive—hurt, angry, or morally outraged—when they are romantically deceived. It is the seduction more than the money that inspires Margaret Ford to kill her deceiver in *House of Games*, and similar dramas of intimacy are played out elsewhere in Mamet's work.

The early paradigm statement of this anxiety about honesty in relationships is surely *Sexual Perversity in Chicago*. The primary dramatic relationship in the play is between Danny and Deborah, as they struggle to establish their intimacy while simultaneously maintaining the personal identities and friendships that predate their relationship. Love, as a kind of contractual performance, is thus potentially transforming, even in a situation in which both fear of commitment and emotional honesty are obviously ideological, that is, "in Chicago." When Danny confesses his love, and Deborah asks him if love frightens him, he answers that it does; her response, "It's only words. I don't think you should be frightened by words," ignores the performative significance of the declaration, as if it were the same kind of speech as her earlier statement, "I'm a Lesbian," a lie designed to ditch Danny's first proposition. Deborah wants to create a bond hewed on less monumental speech acts, a contact established through the continuity of a dialogue with Danny; their conflict may be a simple difference over communicative preferences, but she, too, seeks authentic declarations:

DANNY: I try.
DEBORAH: You try and try. You are misunderstood and depressed.
DANNY: And you're no help.
DEBORAH: No, I'm a hindrance. You're trying to understand
      women and I'm confusing you with information. "Cunt" won't

do it. "Fuck" won't do it. No more magic. What are you
feeling. Tell me what you're *feeling*. Jerk.[24]

The italics indicate, here as everywhere in Mamet, a certain pressure on the
word that emphasizes its performative significance. Similarly, Danny's curses
merely perform anger and aggression theatrically; they have little referential
value, yet they do work against any bond of shared understanding. The social
alternative to the characters' efforts to constitute romance through authentic
speech is a same-sex friendship, which in *Sexual Perversity in Chicago* is almost
purely ideological, that is, based on a shared litany of what is supposed in the
general culture to be true—in pornography, in child rearing, in casual
observation—rather than what might be the case in any particular
relationship.

The layers of theatricality and speech are more obvious and
contradictory in *The Shawl*. In the first act a supposed clairvoyant, John,
meets with a client and convinces her of his psychic talent. In the next act
John reveals to his lover, Charles, that his gifts of spiritual vision and
prophecy are based on educated guesses, confirmed by the client's wish for
his credibility. What seem to be foundational speech actions—prophetic
statements and observations of obscure truths—are the result of theatrical
technique, and what seems to be dialogue—spiritual contact with the other
world—is not. Yet genuine performative speech acts do exist in the play, as
when Charles delivers an ultimatum to John: that if he does not convince the
client to contest her mother's will and give the money to them, Charles will
leave him. In act three when John's seance seems to be going according to
plan, the photograph that the client brings turns out not to be a photograph
of the mother but rather a test; when John identifies the photograph
incorrectly, he puts the whole scam at risk, and can only redeem it through
the image of a red shawl. This shawl eventually nets John a fee, though
exactly how much the image—a likely guess based on a little simple research
in an archive—will net him is not clear. Finally he must lie once again to the
woman; in order to get his money, he must tell her he truly saw her mother
during the seance. This lie may be a help to the client, and it even seems to
coincide with what she remembers, but for John it is too late since Charles
has already left, unable to accept the limits of John's vision.

Lying about love is less benign in *Oleanna*, where the title derives from
Mamet's choice to write, as he often does, against a literary citation; in this
case the framing texts are a quotation from *The Way of All Flesh* on the limits
of moral vision and a verse from a folk song in which *Oleanna* names an ideal
land, beyond the misery of the real world. The language of this play is the

most fragmentary in Mamet's work—half of a telephone conversation, whole pages of simple phrases that trail off or are interrupted, abrupt and unpredictable changes of topic, etc. It seems to be the case that a confused female student, Carol, unable to understand the course material, gradually becomes frustrated with the male teacher's personal attempts to explain her situation and decides to accuse him of sexual harassment.[25] John's career, marriage, and whole identity eventually turn on her accusations, and by the end of the second short, intense act, he finally becomes violent. Here the quandary of interpreting the play falls upon a choice between two attitudes toward the dynamics of true performance. Was the young woman responding to a sexist situation which, in the final image, is ultimately revealed to the audience as the truth of the teacher's character, or was the teacher forced into a desperate, uncharacteristically violent and hateful act because of the enormity of her false accusations?

Oleanna seems to be written not toward any clear resolution but rather toward what has been called, in various critical arguments, the "proper statement of the question." If real human character exists prior to speech acts and is merely revealed by them, then John would seem to have been harboring criminal thoughts all along, and is perhaps innately guilty of some of the charges. If, however, his character is constituted through performed actions, then his hatred of Carol may be a new aspect of his character, an expression of his suffering and frustration. Similarly, the young woman may always have been constructed as simpleminded, that is, talked down to, in her experiences, like the way she is treated when she asks for help in the first act; her accusation of the teacher may be her new discovery of the power of expressive speech to transform her into a stronger person. Mamet does not presume to decide such conundrums in the play, and seems even to withhold the information that would make the job of interpretation easier for the audience. However, in light of the habit Mamet shows of writing against orthodoxies, and also in view of his often-stated position that women tend to manipulate speech, it would seem that even by problematizing the student's accusation, Mamet is writing against the current social trend toward accepting charges of harassment without material evidence or convincing corroboration; the professor's life has already been shattered, his reputation and character apparently altered, before such questions of evidence have ever been considered. Mamet seems to attack the harassment problem from the traditional Americanist perspective of the presumption of innocence and the burden of proof, and to imply that decisions made before such due process are probably unjust; the real truth in *Oleanna*, like the idea of utopia itself, is ultimately deferred.

FORMAL ILLUSIONS/THE TRUTH OF PERFORMANCE

Mamet also uses perspectives of formal manipulation to reveal theatrical structures. The truth within an illusive dramatic fiction can be revealed as a construction by showing the machinery of illusion making, which Mamet accomplishes not through layered Brechtian techniques but simply by moving the audience's perspective "backstage," showing the action of performance as if it were directed toward some other audience.

The most literal version of this *per angolo* technique occurs in *A Life in the Theatre*, in which scenes in various locations around the backstage of a repertory theater (played toward downstage) alternate with scenes that are supposed to be from actual performances (played toward an upstage drop that looks like a dark theater)—"in effect, a true view from backstage."[26] While the behind-the-scenes action is revealed, the onstage action is shown from a new perspective, in sympathy with the actors' frequent discussions of technique and effect. The play has no story, but the twenty-five scenes cohere in a representative impression of the life of a typical actor. The two characters, one young, one old, gradually reveal their limitations and their depth through everyday actions and their identification with their roles. Mamet's play flirts with the phenomenology of the theatre, with the paradox of acting and the body of the performer, as the characters continue to build their own identities while building fictional roles together. The drama seems to play especially well when the old actor is cast for closure, as an older, somewhat minor star: Denholm Elliot in London or Ellis Rabb in New York. In these cases the backstage scenes in rehearsal, after a show, or at the makeup table achieve a powerful illusion of authenticity and great sentimental appeal.

Another early Mamet play also debunks the performance by emphasizing its technique; in *The Water Engine* the onstage performance is of a radio play, so that the theatrical audience sees what the radio audience would only hear. Mamet is fond of the imaginative appeal of radio drama and originally wrote the play (about a 1934 Chicago inventor of an engine that runs on distilled water) for a national radio performance; in this case the era of the play's setting and the performance form were an interesting American historical match. When *The Water Engine* was produced theatrically, the conceit of the radio performance was simply placed onstage, and the theatrical audience asked to listen to the drama while they watched the spectacle of its studio production. The play's story is almost a fairy tale of good and evil, as the inventor is destroyed by dark figures from the big business world of automobiles and petroleum. By undercutting standard radio and theatrical techniques, Mamet manipulates form to emphasize the role of the imagination, aligning the audience's experience of imagining the play with the creative imagination of the inventor. The play finally appeals to the nostalgic, naive virtues of radio drama and of the simpler era that so many of Mamet's dramas try to recall. Through imaginative performance both actors and audience create the illusion of life in that era, though in this case everyone participates with full consciousness of the illusion.

The other major anti-theatrical play by Mamet is not about the theater *per se* but rather about Hollywood. *Speed-the-Plow*, written for a minimalist stage, is about the appalling ethics and greed involved in the behind-the-scenes manipulations of film producers and specifically about the arbitrary decision they make of which screenplay to produce. In the first scene, two self-described "Old Whores," Bobby Gould and Charlie Fox, celebrate over having attracted a major star to act in a formulaic sex-and-violence prison movie. Their artistic reasons for producing the screenplay are nonexistent, but they have a clear concept of "wealth." Most of the first act dialogue consists of sharing fantasies that money can fulfill. Hollywood, rather than Broadway, is the powerful commercial orthodoxy that the play condemns, while the only artistic alternative *in* the play is a visionary ecological novel, "The Bridge or, Radiation and the Half-Life of Society."

Mamet's 1983 play *Edmond*, however, remains outside the realm of specific indictments, utilizing a natural framework of American dissent and creating a kind of anti-allegory, a puritan cautionary tale in reverse, where transcendence comes not through a pilgrim's progress but through a spiraling fall, a submersion in the criminal underworld. Toby Silverman Zinman has recognized the Jewish background in *The Disappearance of the Jews* and the other Bobby Gould plays.[27] The strange peace of Edmond Burke in his jail cell at the end of the play is the result of an anti-baptism, a negative apotheosis which is still fully spiritual:

> EDMOND: Do you think there's a hell?
> PRISONER: I don't know. (*Pause.*)
> EDMOND: Do you think that we are there?
> PRISONER: I don't know, man. (*Pause.*)
> EDMOND: Do you think that we go somewhere when we die?
> PRISONER: I don't know, man. I like to think so.
> EDMOND: I would, too.
> PRISONER: I sure would like to think so. (*Pause.*)
> EDMOND: Perhaps it's Heaven.
> PRISONER (*Pause.*): I don't know.

EDMOND: I don't know either but perhaps it is. (*Pause.*)
PRISONER: I would like to think so.
EDMOND: I would, too.
(*Pause.*)
Good night. (*Pause.*)
PRISONER: Good night.
(*Edmond gets up, goes over and exchanges a goodnight kiss with the Prisoner. He then returns to his bed and lies down.*)[28]

The ending echoes that of *The Cherry Orchard*, where Firs lies down to await death. But the inexplicable breaking string of Chekhov has been cut from Mamet's adaptation of that moment, just as the spiritual symbolism of Edmond as everyman has been thrown into doubt.[29] By writing against genre, against religious doctrine, and against a canonical realistic text, Mamet again asserts himself by performing acts of artistic dissent.

Mamet's enormous commercial success in recent years brings a certain pressure to bear on his status as a figure of dissent. While still a relatively young writer, in mid-career, he is also one of the few of his generation to have sustained his project, to develop a distinct way of working and writing that meets with consistent acclaim. A recent issue of the *Dramatists Guild Quarterly* sought to acknowledge this status, though some of Mamet's remarks demonstrate a certain discomfort with his acquired intellectual credibility. About playwriting in general, for example, he argues: "It's a craft which has been practiced down through the ages, in the main, by whores like me; people who didn't know how to do anything else and were wandering around in the dark trying to express themselves, who somehow got good at it or got famous at it (perhaps not both) and so persevered. The purpose of literature is not to do good, but to delight us. That's why the writer writes it; it delights him or her to express it, or to be rid of it, and in some way delights the audience, appealing either to their self-esteem or to their prejudices, creating in them a new, happy understanding of the world."[30] As this statement reflects both on Mamet's talent and on his mission, this public declaration is surely a case of false modesty. Yet such self-deprecation is precisely what Mamet's public position requires, if he is going to maintain his status as an American writer, unique like others and therefore capable of critical self-expression.

In the creation of an illusion, whether of reality or of singular selfhood, the primary compositional technique is still to undercut, to construct an excess which, when pared away, seems to reveal the essential. As Mamet summarizes: "The main difference between somebody who wants to be a professional writer and somebody who doesn't is that the former knows how to cut. If you don't know how to cut, if you're a product of some school that didn't teach you that, you're not serious. If you're unwilling to cut viciously, just on the off chance that the audience might beat you to the punch line, you haven't been watching the audience. And if you haven't been watching the audience watching your plays, you're not a playwright."[31] Mamet's remarks are in the context of a public address, in which he was acutely aware of his audience as a community of American writers.

What Mamet tends to universalize, then, might be more carefully considered as a gesture specific to a particular cultural moment, and an expression which requires as its background a relatively stable cultural symbology. From a technical standpoint his primary advances over the old "selective realism" of the Group Theatre generation would seem to be his recognition of performance as a constitutive act, and his ability to dramatize the moments in peoples' lives when their performances seem to come undone, and so I have tried to suggest a working typology of those moments. Viewed through the critical lens of a theory of representation, a debunked illusion is merely one stage in an infinite regression, and reality is always deferred, always subject to a subsequent deconstruction. Yet viewed in the expressivist mode, which is one the deconstructive theorist often—inconsistently—employs, a gesture of undoing takes on the converse quality of having founded something singularly true. In an American culture that values such creative rejections, Mamet's dramas enjoy a remarkable affective power. But since cultures themselves are far from any security as critical absolutes, estimates of Mamet's significance will almost surely continue to change.

NOTES

1. There are four book-length studies of Mamet's work thus far: one reference guide, Nesta Wyn Jones, *File on Mamet*; two general surveys, Dennis Carroll, *David Mamet* (New York: St. Martin's Press, 1987), and C.W.E. Bigsby, *David Mamet* (London: Methuen, 1985); and one treatment of his dialogue, Anne Dean, *David Mamet: Language as Dramatic Action* (Fairleigh Dickinson UP, 1989). No interpretive consensus on the significance of his work has emerged, though Mamet is now read internationally; see Martin Roeder-Zerndt, *Lesen und Zuschauen: David Mamet und das amerikanische Drama und Theatre der 70er Jahre* (Tubingen: Gunter Narr, 1993). My argument here is primarily an extension of the "language as action argument" through speech-act theory into cultural politics.

2. See, for example, William Demastes chapter, "David Mamet's Dis-Integrating Drama," in *Beyond Naturalism: A New Realism in American Theatre* (Westport, Conn.: Greenwood Press, 1988), pp. 67–94. As regards realism in general I suppose I should admit

the undue influence of Roman Jakobson, who thought the term so overfull of conflicting significance that its use was mostly rhetorical; see "On Realism in Art," trans. K. Magassy, in *Readings in Russian Poetics: Formalist and Structuralist Views*, ed. L. Matejka and K. Pomorska, pp. 38–46 (Ann Arbor: Michigan Slavic Studies, 1978).

3. This, among other things, causes many critics to dislike Mamet. Ruby Cohn, in *New American Dramatists, 1960–1980* (New York: Grove, 1982), repeats Edward Albee's observation that Mamet had "a fine ear, but there was as yet no evidence of a fine mind," and then went on to say that Mamet has a mind "so fine that no idea could violate it" (p. 46). Nevertheless, in the revision of her book she cedes to Mamet a major historical role, linking him with Shepard in the final chapter (*New American Dramatists, 1960–1990* [Basingstoke: Macmillan, 1991]).

4. David Mamet, "Realism," in *Writing in Restaurants* (New York: Penguin, 1986), p. 132.

5. See Sacvan Bercovitch, *The Puritan Origins of the American Self* (New Haven: Yale UP, 1975); his *The American Jeremiad* (Madison: U of Wisconsin P, 1978); and Bercovitch, ed. *Ideology and Classic American Literature* (Cambridge: Cambridge UP, 1986).

6. Sacvan Bercovitch, *The Rites of Assent: Transformations in the Symbolic Construction of America* (New York: Routledge, 1993), p. 311.

7. Bigsby comes close to this reading in the late pages of his chapter on Mamet in *A Critical Introduction to Twentieth-Century American Drama*, vol. 3: *Beyond Broadway* (Cambridge: Cambridge UP, 1985), when he argues that Mamet's realism is rooted in a "myth of decline" (p. 288).

8. Thorstein Veblen, *The Theory of the Leisure Class* (New York: Macmillan, 1899).

9. See for example Herbert Blau first book, *The Impossible Theatre: A Manifesto* (New York: Collier, 1964).

10. Theatrical manifestoes have a difficult but continuing history; see for example Mac Wellman, "The Theatre of Good Intentions" *Performing Arts Journal* 8:3 (1984): 59–70; or Daryl Chin, "An Anti-Manifesto," *Drama Review* 27.4 (Winter 1983): 32–37, the latter in a special anniversary issue of manifestoes.

11. Mamet, "Decadence," in *Writing in Restaurants*, p. 58.

12. The construction of political correctness as an orthodoxy even allows conservatives, paradoxically, to grasp the rhetoric of dissent, as is evident in *Culture Wars: Documents from the Recent Controversies in the Arts*, ed. Richard Bolton (New York: New Press, 1992).

13. J.L. Austin, *How to Do Things with Words* (Cambridge: Harvard UP, 1962). The principal historian of politics to use this performative method is Quentin Skinner; for an overview see James Tully, ed., *Meaning and Context: Quentin Skinner and his Critics* (Princeton UP, 1988).

14. David Mamet, "WFMT," *The Cabin: Reminiscence and Diversions* (New York: Turtle Bay, 1992), p. 56.

15. David Mamet, *Some Freaks* (New York: Penguin, 1989), p. 3.

16. Rousseau makes his theory perfectly clear in the "Letter to D'Alembert on the Theatre," *Politics and the Arts*, ed. and trans. Allan Bloom (Ithaca: Cornell UP, 1960); for such a reading of Jefferson see Jay Fliegelman, *Declaring Independence: Jefferson Natural Language and the Culture of Performance* (Palo Alto: Stanford UP, 1993).

17. Mamet theorizes such a shared idealism in relation to the theatre in his "A National Dream Life," in *Writing in Restaurants*, pp. 8–11.

18. See for example his remarks on entropy in "Decay: Some Thoughts for Actors," in *Writing in Restaurants*.

19. Jonas Barish, *The Anti-Theatrical Prejudice* (Berkeley: California UP, 1981).

20. Mamet, "Acting," in *Writing in Restaurants*, p. 129.

21. Henry Schvey, "The Plays of David Mamet: Games of Manipulation and Power," *New Theatre Quarterly* 4.13 (Feb. 1988): 77–89. See also, regarding *American Buffalo*, Thomas King, "Talk as Dramatic Action in *American Buffalo*," *Modern Drama* 34.4 (Dec. 1991): 538–48, and remember that to "buffalo" is to intimidate (Jack Barbera, "Ethical Perversity in America: Some Observations on David Mamet's *American Buffalo*," *Modern Drama* 29.2 [Sept 1981]: 270–75).

22. David Mamet, *Glengarry Glen Ross* (New York: Grove, 1984), p. 105.

23. David Mamet, *House of Games* (New York: Grove, 1985), p. 70.

24. David Mamet, *Sexual Perversity in Chicago and The Duck Variations* (New York: Grove, 1978), pp. 57–58.

25. There is a background for this conflict in Mamet's earlier work; see Pascale Hubert-Leibler, "Dominance and Anguish: The Teacher–Student Relationship in the Plays of David Mamet," *Modern Drama* 31.4 (Dec. 1988): 557–70.

26. David Mamet, *A Life in the Theatre* (New York: Grove, 1978), p. 9.

27. Toby Silverman Zinman, "Jewish Aporia: The Rhythm of Talking in Mamet," *Theatre Journal* 44.2 (May 1992): 207–15. In the same issue Carla McDonough reads *Edmond* in terms of American masculinity rituals ("Every Fear Hides a Wish: Unstable Masculinity in Mamet's Drama," pp. 195–205).

28. David Mamet, *Edmond* (New York: Grove, 1983), pp. 105–6.

29. The sound occurs in act two of Mamet's adaptation but not at the end. Anton Chekhov, *The Cherry Orchard*, adapted by David Mamet from a trans. by Peter Nelles (New York: Grove, 1985). Lue Douthit pointed out this absence to me.

30. Mamet, "Mamet on Playwriting," *Dramatists Guild Quarterly* 30.1 (Spring 1993): 8. Compare Mamet's stature, for example, with that of the playwrights with whom he was first compared in Peter Ventimiglia, "Recent Trends in American Drama: Michael Cristofer, David Mamet, Albert Innaurato," *Journal of American Culture* 1.1 (1978): 195–204.

31. Mamet, "Mamet on Playwriting," p. 12.

STEPHEN J. BOTTOMS

Introduction:
States of Crisis

When Sam Shepard's One-Act Play *States of Shock* premiered in New York in 1991, the title, if not the piece itself, seemed almost to summarize the author's entire output. The phrase, which recurs elsewhere in his work, is an apt description for the arresting, disturbing atmospheres which Shepard's plays so often create onstage. While the subtitle of this book expands the frame of reference somewhat ("shock" being only one of the forms of disorientation experienced by the plays' characters and, indeed, by their audiences), this is nevertheless its starting point. The tensions and contradictions generated by Shepard's writing—whether overt or, in much of his later work, more covert—tend to disrupt any possibility of the theatrical event's being experienced smoothly, and so throw up all kinds of unresolved questions. Although Shepard's work has gone through many phases since he first began writing for Off-Off-Broadway venues in 1964, this instability has been a distinguishing feature throughout.

One way to begin to look at Shepard's theatre is to contrast his approach with that of another major American dramatist of recent years, David Mamet. The two share certain superficial similarities in their concerns with have led to frequent comparisons, but there is a fundamental difference in their approaches. Mamet's is a very taut, precise writing style in which ever scene is pared down to the bone, in the belief that "every time the author leaves in a piece of nonessential prose (beautiful though it may be), he

---

From *The Theatre of Sam Shepard: States of Crisis.* © 1998 by Stephen J. Bottoms.

weakens the structure of the play.... Everything which does not put forward the meaning of the play impedes the meaning of the play."[1] Shepard, however, does not share this conviction that the elements of a play must all be made to serve a dominant, preconceived meaning or "ruling idea." Whereas Mamet rigorously avoids random impulses and linguistic excess, Shepard's writing tends to be dominated by such characteristics, and even his most controlled work defies linear dramatic logic. His is a theatre of fragments, and often of verbal and visual glut, in which disparate elements butt up against each other in abrupt or unsettling juxtapositions, and in which intense, disturbing confrontations are inextricably entwined with a certain wild playfulness and madcap comedy (Shepard's plays are nothing if not funny). This inclusive approach often makes the plays seem unwieldy or somehow incomplete, yet onstage if it also this very "flaw"—the lack of structural or thematic resolution—which makes his best work so provocative. Take, for example, the lingering impact of some of his startling stage images, which so stubbornly resist submitting themselves to unidirectional interpretation as symbols for dramatic themes: green slime dripping from a medicine bundle, a phalanx of popping toasters, a chair hurled across stage on the end of a lasso, a butchered lamb, manic swimming on beds against an all-white background. Similarly, Shepard's musically inspired use of language rhythms can operate to seduce or even bombard audiences, even as the reception of exact syntactic meaning is problematized. The overall effect is neatly summarized by one of Shepard's former collaborators, director Robert Woodruff:

> The plays are almost assaultive, without being hostile, and they're full of holes and contradictions that you just can't fill in.... When an audience leaves one of Sam's plays, they're probably really confused. They've just had several hundred images thrown at them—flash, flash, flash!—and they can't synthesize it all.[2]

However, far from impeding the production of meaning, the plays' roughness tends to open up a proliferation of possible ways in which the individual viewer can read meaning into them. In being unable "to synthesize it all," audience members are required to fill in the gaps for themselves, to draw their own conclusions. As Shepard himself has pithily put it: "Ideas emerge from plays—not the other way around."[3] This is not to say, of course, that Shepard never feeds "ideas" into his writing: indeed, his work is packed with concerns and allusions which reward detailed examination. Yet crucially, these ideas are rarely, if ever, worked through schematically or as a thesis. Rather, they are fed into the work as hints and momentary implications which gradually coalesce into a kind of poetic density. Ideas are thrown up, prompting responses which are frequently contradictory, and this in turn leads to further tensions and ambiguities. Shepard's emphasis is on exploring the way these various thematic fragments relate to and are created by emotional conditions, and he treats each new thought less as an object for intellectual scrutiny than as a trigger for exploring hopes and anxieties. Each of his plays thus represents the fruit of a kind of ongoing dialogue the author seems to be having with himself. The intensity of that dialogue may vary, from agonized, near-hysterical extremes in his most overtly unstable work, to the subtler probing and questioning in his more measured pieces. In each case, though, these texts create such a range of conflicting voices and connotations that they defy any attempt to understand them conclusively according to a single interpretive perspective.

My sense that Shepard is, in various ways, exploring questions which remain unanswered, or even unanswerable, informs my choice of the term "states of crisis." For while elements of crisis, schism, and conflict have always been the staple elements of dramatic action, they have classically been presented within structured narratives. An audience empathizes with the protagonists, looking forward to the ultimate resolution of their struggle while following a through-line of cause-and-effect action, in which each moment is seen to be directly relevant to the past and the future of the play and of the characters' lives. This continues to be the most common form of drama, one championed by writers like Mamet, who is (however idiosyncratically) a confessed neoclassicist. Shepard, by contrast, is an experimentalist whose plays largely ignore such conventions. While they may make use of narrative plots, these are sketchy and unstable at best, their premises frequently lifted directly from familiar sources as if to ironize the idea of plot itself. Likewise, characters tend to be opaque and erratic: their motivations are shrouded in confusion, and such goals as they have almost invariably remain unfulfilled. The plays end not in resolutions but with abrupt anticlimaxes, unexplained images, or the suggestion of tensions continuing indefinitely into the future. They do not restore equilibrium, because in adopting an open-ended, exploratory approach to the writing, Shepard has placed himself in a state of disequilibrium and refuses to depict an arbitrary recovery of balance simply for the sake of convention. "I never know when to end a play," he commented in a 1984 interview: "A resolution isn't an ending; it's a strangulation."[4]

In short, Shepard's plays tend to be structured less as chains of events than as collages or patchworks of colors, sounds, and confrontations: the focus is on what is happening on stage *in the moment*, rather than on the explication of some fictional past or future (although the very uncertainty which consequently surrounds the past is often exploited as a further source of anxiety in the present). And in any given moment, the plays may simultaneously suggest a whole range of immediate tensions. There are relational crises (why are these people stuck with each other? how are they supposed to function together?), identity crises (who am I? how do I create or express myself? do I *have* a self?), existential crises (does it all mean anything anyway?), ontological crises (where are we? what is this reality?), national and cultural crises (what is America? what, if anything, defines us as a nation and can we live with that?), and any number of others. In the following sections of this introduction, I outline the points of tension which are treated with particular emphasis in the subsequent chapters, using this discussion to return, finally, the perhaps the most vital issue of all: the crisis of reception. Confronted with the uneven concoctions that Shepard throws at his audiences, just how is one to respond?

CRISIS IN WRITING

I want to begin unpacking some of the factors which inform Shepard's bewildering aesthetic by proposing that there are at least three different Sam Shepards vying for ascendancy in his writing: the "high" or "romantic" modernist, the "late" modernist, and what I will call the reluctant postmodernist. No doubt there are others too, but the key fault lines seem to me to lie between these positions. Nor should this be surprising, given that Shepard's key formative years as an artist were during the 1960s, a period of cultural upheaval he himself has described as "seething with a radical shift in the American psyche."[5] In the avant-garde atmosphere of the Greenwich Village in which he lived between 1963 and 1971, the last American wave of high modernism (swept in by the '50s innovations of abstract expressionist artists and beat poets) coexisted with the impact of recent European imports like Sartrean existentialism and the theatre of the absurd (often classified in hindsight as late modernism), and with the new depthlessness, repetition, and fragmentation of pop art and its literary equivalents (now seen as the beginnings of postmodernism). The philosophical conflicts among these contending aesthetics also reflected wider cultural changes, as American society began finally to fragment beyond repair into competing subcultures and interest groups, while the traditional faith in the basic decency of the nation and its leaders was fatally undermined by revelations of conspiracies, assassinations, war atrocities, and so forth. Shepard's writing represents an arena in which numerous aspects of the cultural and philosophical upheaval of this and subsequent decades can be seen being played out at the immediate level of personal experience.

Shepard's debt to the lessons of existentialism, and its theatrical manifestation in absurdism, is immediately obvious, and one he continues to acknowledge. As recently as 1994 he was quoted as saying that however unfashionable existentialist through might now be, it remains a vitally necessary tool for asking fundamental questions about the human condition.[6] The sense that his characters are adrift and alone in a universe which is essentially without meaning or rationale is one which recurs as either dominant theme or underlying factor in virtually all of his plays, and points to the continuing influence of the work of Samuel Beckett, one of the very few theatrical examples whom Shepard has acknowledged as important to him. Indeed, without Beckett—and *Waiting for Godot* in particular, which first inspired Shepard as a teenager in California—he would never have begun developing as a playwright in the way he did. It was Beckett who had revolutionized theatre by abandoning wholesale the classical model of dramatic narrative, and established instead the idea of presenting a drama of the existential present which consciously resists conclusive rationalization. Beckett's is perhaps the original dramaturgy of crisis-in-the-moment, evoking on stage an immediate sense of fear or emotional paralysis in the face of life's futility. Shepard followed his example in creating stage figures who are fractured victims of inexplicable circumstance, and who fill the voids of their lives with games, confrontations, and blocks of rhythmic, imagistic language. Moreover, as with *Endgame* or *Waiting for Godot*, Shepard's figures are usually imprisoned spatially as well as temporally, trapped in more or less claustrophobic stage spaces which, for one reason or another, they either cannot or dare not vacate.

Yet where Beckett's work tends to suggest the stark austerity of a sensibility on the edge of self-erasure and silence, Shepard's plays seem characterized by a very American brashness, a yearning for freedom, for wild self-release. Such desires almost invariably prove unrealizable: indeed, the specific inability of America to deliver on its promises of liberty and self-fulfillment is one which Shepard's work exposes in myriad different ways. That does not, however, quench the desire, and the frustration generated by its lack of fulfillment seems central to the sense of entrapment and nightmarish hysteria which informs so many of these plays. Accordingly, Shepard's use of both language and image is more extreme and erratic than Beckett's carefully modulated, muted style. The desire for expansive freedom, moreover, has always been central to Shepard's actual writing process: far from accepting the stark nihilism of Beckett's outlook, he has tended (somewhat contradictorily) to ascribe to the more romantic, high modernist belief that the act of creativity itself might somehow be a source of both liberation and redemptive meaning.

In this respect, the early lessons of nontheatrical influences, including action painting, beat writing, and especially jazz music, have been crucial. Shepard has continued to cherish their key principle of unrestricted spontaneity in the creative process, or pursuing the expression of one's immediate impulses rather than trying to submit oneself to preconceived ideas of structure and content. This kind of free-form creativity has often been seen as offering a way both to express underlying feelings of alienation and angst in relation to the everyday world, and also perhaps to break beyond these to unlock hidden truths from the depths of the psyche. In accordance with this, Shepard has cultivated the use of stream-of-consciousness writing in which the present state of the writer's mind is in some sense the subject of the work. As he told *Time Out* in 1972: "I never know what to say when somebody says what are the plays about. They're about the moment of writing."[7] Shepard's free-form technique is evident in its most raw, undeveloped state in his very earliest plays, but he has continued to practice it, with modifications, throughout his career. He claims, for example, that *True West* (1980) went through thirteen different drafts before he was happy with it, and that each of those drafts was not merely an adjustment of the previous one, but a complete rewrite. He finally stumbled over the inspiration he was searching for "when I heard the voice of Lee speaking very clearly, and then I heard Austin's response. The more I listened, the more the voices came.... *True West* felt like a total improvisation, spinning off itself."[8]

Shepard gave his fullest public account of this improvisational approach in this article "Language, Visualization and the Inner Library," written for *The Drama Review* in 1977, in which his language is saturated with the romantic terminology of high modernism. The writing of each play begins not with a concept, he explains, but with an image or a "voice," often recalled from a state of half-sleep or daydream, which serves as a starting point for a journey into the unknown: "the picture is moving in the mind and being allowed to move more and more freely as you follow it." He equates the process with a state of waking sleep, which helps explain why almost all of his plays, to one degree or another, evoke something of the chaotic randomness of dreams. Shepard even goes so far as to reject the traditional definition of craftsmanship as indicating an ability consciously to shape and hone raw material into a finished product, redefining it instead as the ability to resist the temptation to censor the spontaneous creative impulse: "The extent to which I can actually follow the picture and not intervene with my own two cents worth is where inspiration and craftsmanship hold their real meaning."[9]

Shepard's struggle to ensure that his work is genuinely spontaneous is also evident from various of the unpublished notes and draft material held in archive at Boston University. Take, for example, the self-recriminations which end many of the numerous unfinished (often barely begun) typescripts dating from the mid- to late 1970s. One such, titled "White Slavery," ends after just one page and one line of typed dialogue, beneath which, in handwriting that gets steadily more rapid and illegible, are five repetitions of the same frustrated phrase: "writing's not fast enough." Apparently he felt that his conscious mind was being allowed too much time to intervene with its "two cents worth." Another such piece is aborted after a mere four lines, as a "CENSOR enters in black mortician's suit" and announces, "You're painting yourself into a corner and you haven't even started."[10] (Note the use of painterly terminology: for Shepard, the visual and the verbal are inextricable.)

In the modernist tradition, this desire to open oneself up to free-flowing impulses has often been equated with an attempt to tap into imagery which is universally resonant, on some primal or prerational level of experience, and Shepard has expressed a passionate commitment to this idea. For example, in a revealing 1984 interview with Amy Lippman, he clearly alludes to the Jungian notion of a collective unconscious, the repository of mythic archetypes, which lies at a deeper substratum of the psyche than one's personal unconscious, and which it is the task of the artist to locate:

> Hopefully in writing a play, you can snare emotions that aren't just personal emotions, not just catharsis, not just psychological emotions and feelings that are connected with everybody. Hopefully. It's not true all the time; sometimes it's nothing but self-indulgence. But if you work hard enough toward being true to what you instinctively feel is going down in the play, you might be able to catch that kind of thing. So that suddenly you hook up with feelings that are on a very board scale, [moving] in a direction we all know, regardless of where we come from or who we are.... Those, to me, are mythic emotions.[11]

The word "mythic" is worth highlighting as one of the most overused and underdefined words in Shepard criticism. Reviewers in particular frequently deploy it as a conveniently vague adjective which suggests a certain profundity without actually requiring the writer to explain what he or she means by it. As a result it often also becomes confused with "myth," as in *lie*, and "popular mythology," as in American folk culture. To avoid such confusion, I use such terms sparingly in this book, but it is significant that Shepard's own use of the word is consistent with the high modernist notion of seeking to create art that can generate the kind of unifying human experience which—in the skeptical twentieth century—social conventions and religion are no longer able to provide.

Shepard's concern with achieving some kind of universal resonance in his work also helps explain his fascination with the musicality of language. The idea of using language to approximate something of the rhythmic, sensuous quality of music is a commonplace in modernist writing, largely because music too has been seen as representing a symbolic expression of subconscious desires. In the 1960s, in particular, this idea was pushed to extremes: jazz and rock music were seen by many as having the potential to awaken their listeners to another dimension of experience, to "break on through to the other side" (as The Doors' Jim Morrison famously put it). Shepard was again sympathetic to such notions: in his 1975 journal *The Rolling Thunder Logbook*, he compared Bob Dylan's music wish shamanistic rites in which driving rhythms are used to conjure up the spirit world. Shepard's descriptions of his own work are more modest, but this has not stopped others from making similar claims on his behalf, particularly in respect to his earlier work. In Jack Gelber's 1976 article "The Playwright as Shaman," for example, Shepard is credited with using his emphasis on the immediacy of the theatrical moment to create a form of metaphysical drama, which generates ecstatic states akin to a drug trip or a primitive religious rite.

The problem with such hyperbolic claims is that they entirely ignore the many elements of Shepard's writing which openly contradict them. Over the course of his career, his work has increasingly gravitated toward the postmodernist suspicion that the redemptive impulses of high modernism, the desire to create new unities as a focus for a formless universe, might, in fact be futile. Indeed, even as he has continued to pursue his free-form writing technique, Shepard has periodically admitted that this creative process—far from resulting in liberating expressions of the collective unconscious—has all too often led him toward weary self-repetition. ("You suddenly find yourself doing the same thing over and over again"),[12] or to the dredging up of personal neuroses which should have been left well enough alone: "A lot of those things aren't even worth looking into," he has remarked: "they're like devils. You're causing yourself more trouble ... indulging in thought forms that are destructive."[13] Still more pertinent is his awareness that the very idea of using improvisation to liberate the imagination is to some extent a delusion, since the writer is always constrained within the preexistent, culturally determined structures of thought which he or she has been shaped by. Thus, in *The Rolling Thunder Logbook* he questions the assumption of personal heroes like Dylan and Allen Ginsberg that creativity is a purely instinctive quality—"a God-given stamp at the moment you come sliding from your Mama's thighs." Instead, he insists it Is "a worked-at process," and that as one learns, one is being conditioned: "we're not born with any word language to begin with, [so] there must be a kind of system of thought which a poet gears himself into. Over years."[14]

The logical extension of this is the fear—recurrently visible in the plays themselves—that the instinctive material explored through improvisation might simply be the random regurgitations of an imagination entirely shaped by the culture within which it operates. Often largely composed of fragments of imagery and language drawn from American popular culture, Shepard's writing suggests a sensibility acutely aware of its own colonization by a flashy, violent, and spiritually bankrupt society. This kind of cultural specificity openly contradicts the idea of the plays being equally accessible to "everybody … regardless of where we come from or who we are." (It also, incidentally, diverts form the strictly nonspecific, solipsistic landscapes of Beckettian absurdism.) On occasion, Shepard gone still further than this, exhibiting a patently postmodernist skepticism toward the idea that "mythic" expressions of common human experience are in any way possible in the current cultural climate. In a 1992 interview with Carol Rosen (in which he also refuted Jack Gelber's description of him as a shaman), he stated bluntly:

> Myth in its truest form ahs been demolished. It doesn't exist anymore. All we have is fantasies about it. Or ideas that don't speak to our inner self at all, they just speak to some lame notions about the past. But they don't connect with anything. We've lost touch with the essence of myth.... The same with the Native Americans—they were connected to their ancestors through myth, through prayer, through ritual, through dance, music—all of those forms that lead people into a river of myth. And there was a connecting river, not a fragmented river.
>
> ROSEN: And that's gone.
>
> SHEPARD: It's gone, yes.[15]

This apparent contradiction of the sentiments expressed in the Lippman interview seems to be less the result of a loss of romanticism in the intervening years (the same interview has him pontificating about the existence of angels) than simply a rare case of Shepard's allowing himself to talk publicly about the bleaker, more skeptical side of his outlook. This side, however, finds plentiful expression in the actual texts of his plays, in which his sense of life as a "fragmented river" (a bizarre but curiously apt term in his case, given his use of alternately flowing and disjointed rhythms) is powerfully expressed. Indeed, if Shepard's is a theatre of the present moment, this is a present which has less to do with the ecstatic celebration of metaphysical immanence (which would rely, paradoxically, on a stable sense of one's location in time) than with Frederic Jameson's definition of postmodernity as a schizophrenic condition in which existence seems to have dissolved into a series of fractured presents without coherent relation to past or future.

Yet the deracination of human life and society which this perspective implies offers little to be celebrated, and Shepard is clearly acutely uncomfortable with it. Indeed, his doubts over the validity of his spontaneous approach, and its gravitation toward fragmentation, have periodically led him to seek a greater degree of conscious shaping for his work. For example, in direct contradiction to the scribbled exhortation in "White Slavery" to write faster, Shepard wrote just months later that he felt his freewheeling approach was just too random: "improvisation—in my case—trying to find music through stumbling around. I need more head—I need to bring my head into it more."[16] One manifestation of this desire to create a more reliable structure through greater conscious forethought has been his growing interest in storytelling, an attempt to create a sense of more ordered narrative. This impulse, visible as early as 1967, becomes especially evident in some of his later, more realistic plays. And yet even here, the stories told by the characters, usually in the form of monologues, function simply as isolated fragments within overall narrative structures which remain conspicuous for their lack of stability. There is, to be sure, a degree of deliberate subversion at work here: *True West*, for example, seems quite self-conscious in the way it relates Lee's wildly contrived ideas for a movie scenario to the workings of the play itself. And yet there seems little doubt that Shepard would *like* to find a "story" he could believe in, be it for his plays of for life in general. The problem is that such attempts seem doomed to failure: Aristotle is just too far away. In the past, he noted in a 1984 interview,

> storytelling was a real form, that people felt fit their lives in a way:
> this long thing—beginning, middle and ending—really meant
> something in their lives, and maybe now we're in a time where

that doesn't fit anymore … because everything's so fragmented and broken … And it's a hard pill to swallow, because I really still migrate toward that old classical form, although I can't do it. I've tried over and over again to make this kind of sweeping thing, and it just doesn't … [trails off into silence][17]

Shepard's, then, is a reluctant postmodernism: his work displays a profound unease with contemporary American culture (its slick artificiality, its loss of centeredness, its abandonment or corruption of basic human values), while also demonstrating an awareness that it is not possible to transcend or step outside that cultural condition in order to adopt a critical distance. Moreover, I would suggest that—whether by accident or design— the plays have become gradually more sophisticated in their handling of the kind of disruptive, unresolved formal qualities typical of postmodernist art. As the early, relatively simple stream-of-consciousness playfulness gave way to an increasingly jagged, agitated style, a mounting fear of the total absence of reliable structures became visible. By the mid-1970s, Shepard had grown adept at stealing and subverting the familiar conventions of filmic or dramatic genres so as to undermine the comforting assumptions underlying them: the introduction of detective figures, in particular (reprised as recently as 1994 in *Simpatico*), allowing for mockery of the very notion of piecing the "clues" of experience together into some kind of comprehensible narrative. In the later 1970s and '80s, while based at San Francisco's Magic Theatre, Shepard then began developing an idiosyncratic form of stage realism in a series of family dramas. And while this new interest in conventional form may—to some extent—have been another manifestation of the desire for more stable grounding, it also led him toward an increasingly subtle *de*stabilization of the cozy assumptions of the domestic genre. His is a realism which, in the words of the Magic Theatre's founder, John Lion, confronts the "reality" of "a world that doesn't make sense, can never make sense, will never make sense."[18]

The profound ambivalence of Shepard's writing, his simultaneously romantic and deeply skeptical outlook, is perhaps exhibited most clearly in his periodic tendency to draw on the imagery of traditional myth narratives. In *True West*, for example, his portrayal of complementary but eternally feuding brothers, a pairing whose genealogy runs all the way back to Cain and Abel, reads as an almost too deliberate *quotation* of the Jungian scheme of conscious ego and repressed shadow side which such duos supposedly represent. More ambivalent still is *Buried Child*, with its exploitation of a variety of different myth schemes, from Oedipus to Osiris. As with his use of pop-cultural sources, there is something of the self-consciousness of postmodernist pastiche in these instances, the ironic manipulation of the redundant fragments of ancient stories which have lost their power to affect us in their original form. Yet there is also the sense that these stories might contain lingering truths, that the fragments might still resonate, that such myths—however compromised they may be—are all we have. And that contradiction, suggests John Lion, "is the source of the wild humor in Shepard: this romantic impulse versus the conscious intellectual sense that it's *hokum*. Which of course leads us back to the existential dilemma."[19]

Shepard has continued, throughout his career, to search for new images of coherence, but this struggle to establish some sense of stability seems constantly to be undermined by his own tendency toward doubt, irony, even an implicit self-ridicule. This instinct for self-subversion is perhaps most paradigmatically visible in his ongoing inclination toward setting up binary oppositions within the plays as possible, provisional sources of structure, which are then blurred, contradicted, or even dismantled altogether. In effect, the project on which poststructuralist theorists and some more intellectually oriented postmodernist artists have consciously embarked (see, for example, Jacques Derrida's writings, or Thomas Pynchon's novel *Gravity's Rainbow*, which mercilessly ridicules binary oppositions of all sorts) has been roughly paralleled by Shepard's more instinctive approach. Inside versus Outside, civilization versus nature, subjective versus objective, reality versus fantasy, hero versus villain, exterior personality versus essential self, and even, finally, masculine versus feminine: each of these distinctions is proposed and then problematized in Shepard's work. Structure, grounding, certainty remain helplessly inaccessible.

CRISIS OF IDENTITY

The creative tensions generated by Shepard's open-ended writing style find a localized focus in the tortured question of personal identity, which is arguably his most insistent thematic thread. Nor is the importance of this issue surprising, given that so much of his writing derives from an urge toward exploring the inner self. Crucial to the high modernist concern with spontaneous creativity is the conviction that it enables a pure, authentic self-expression, freed from the censoring tendencies of the conscious personality. By sidestepping the rationalizations and deceptions of the ego, and so confronting—as honestly and unflinchingly as possible—one's subconscious fears and desires, many modern artists have sought to arrive at a kind of true personal speech, a statement of unique identity. Here again (alongside his more universalizing aspirations) Shepard has followed suit: indeed, his entire output can in one sense be seen as representing a kind of Whitmanesque "Song of Myself" as he has sought to explore what he once described as the "huge, mysterious and dangerous territories" within his own psyche. Moreover, this fact in itself appears to be one of the key sources of the sense of crisis which his work so often evokes. The earliest plays, for example, combine a liberating sense of playful freedom with the exploration of an acute underlying fearfulness. And if, as he says, those initial sketches were a means of "breaking the ice with myself," then the later progression of his work often displays something little short of mental warfare. "When it comes right down to it," Shepard has stated, "what you're really listening to in a writer is … his ability to face himself."[20]

The urge toward full self-expression, of course, is predicated on the assumption that there is indeed an authentic inner self to find expression, as distinct from the exterior, socially conditioned personality. By his own admission, Shepard's work periodically appeals to an almost religious sense of some inner essence which one has to discover by stripping away the artificial layers of the everyday persona, or perhaps (in the Jungian formulation) by "individuating" the fractured parts of the mind into the true whole. In a 1984 *New York Times* interview, he explained his conviction that "personality is everything that is false in a human being … everything that's been added onto him and contrived. It seems to me that the struggle all the time is between this sense of falseness and the other haunting sense of what's true—an essential thing that we're born with and tend to lose track of."[21] In an apparent attempt to counteract some amnesia, various of his plays posit fleeting utopian images of the divided mind being made whole, or of old, dead roles being purged through an assortment of rituals.

These gestures, however, never survive unquestioned. For there is also a recurrent fear in Shepard's work that the depth model of interior self within exterior appearance might in fact be a fallacy. Indeed, this is one of the binary oppositions which the plays problematize most insistently. What if there really is no inner self to be "true" to, only roles to invent? What if the very idea of a personal essence is merely a fiction concocted by the surface personality to give itself the stabilizing illusion of depth? The plays repeatedly betray a suspicion that personal identity might consist of no more than the sum of one's culturally imposed layers, and that only through the outward performance of a desired self-image can one achieve any sense of distinct being. Such performativity apparently constitutes the *only* "truth" in a postmodern culture which—according to the interplay of self-legitimating, self-perpetuating "language games."

Much of Shepard's writing seems driven by the tortured and ultimately unresolvable conflict between these incompatible depth and surface models of personal identity, a fact which also sheds an entirely different light on the idea of "facing oneself" through the writing process. For the impression created in these plays is often less that of a writer boldly navigating the depths of his psyche than of someone attempting to make himself up: the fragments of autobiographical detail that so frequently find their way into Shepard's writing are incorporated in much the same way as the borrowings from pop culture—scraps of personal experience which might somehow be rendered meaningful by their reification as art. And while it is always a risky business ascribing the nature of a writer's work to the details of his or her biography, the details of Shepard's peculiarly unsettled background are hard to ignore when considering the plays' recurrent sense of a search for personal stability amid rootlessness and drift. The postwar generation of which he was a part grew up during a time of upheaval in almost every aspect of American life. In his case this was compounded by the fact that his father was a military pilot who was constantly being relocated to different postings. Born at an air force base in Illinois in 1943, Samuel Shepard Rogers VII was moved, as a small child, to places as diverse as South Dakota, Utah, Florida, and even the Pacific island of Guam. His family finally settled near Los Angeles, just as he was due to start high school, but this too only added to Shepard's sense of dislocation: he has spoken of his sense of southern California as a "sort of temporary society ... where nothing is permanent, where everything could be knocked down and it wouldn't be missed. [There's] a feeling of impermanence that comes from that—that you don't' belong to any particular culture."[22] As John Lion has pointedly remarked: "same did not 'deconstruct' personality as some would claim: he was a deconstructed personality."[23]

In this light, Shepard's fascination with the notion of self-invention—which has been as obvious as his simultaneous and somewhat contradictory pursuit of the more traditional notion of self-expression—seems no mere game. At several stages in his career, he has abruptly abandoned an established style of playwriting in favor of something new and untried, and this practice has been mirrored by his tendency to invent new roles for himself in life. From his early gesture of renaming himself on becoming a playwright, through his attempts in the late 1960s to turn himself into a rock star, to his now widely recognized persona as a strong-and-silent-type movie actor, he has demonstrated a certain restlessness with himself, and a determination to use new experiences to turn himself into something new. While he denies any active attempt to manipulate the way he is perceived by the world at large, it is also clear that any writer who publishes a book of ostensibly autobiographical sketches—*Motel Chronicles*—which includes a memoir of his own birth ("I lurched off the bed and dragged my pudgy body toward those two windows") must have a highly developed sense of irony about his public image.[24]

The clearest evidence of Shepard's concern with self-invention is the plays themselves, in which characters relentlessly seek to create and recreate their personal appearances. Many of these figures manipulate an ever-shifting series of roles and masks, thereby suggesting the absence of any underlying sense of self, a kind of schizoid instability. Time and again, they call back on the fact of their immediate, physical presence on stage, and perform for grim survival: it is as if, by placing other characters in the position of receptive observers, they hope to gain some fragile, exterior confirmation of their existence, and so establish themselves as coherent characters. Yet this very reliance on exteriors, this insistent urge for attention, tends to problematize any more "sincere" search for truth which the characters purport to pursue. If there is a Pirandellian dimension to these figures—characters "in search of an author" to give meaning, direction, and coherence to their lives—they tend inexorably toward the performative alternative wittily described by Shepard in one frustrated but telling note to himself: "Six Egomaniacs in Search of an Audience."[25]

From the blurry-edged inhabitants of his earliest plays (who are little more than ciphers, vehicles for the author's wordplay), through the kaleidoscopic fragmentation of the figures in *Angel City* (1976), to the more consistent but obsessively performance-oriented family members in *A Lie of the Mind* (1985), Shepard's plays consistently depict characters with a profound lack of clear direction or "rounded" identity. Moreover, their need constantly to perform themselves into existence meets a further complication in that, far from having an endless multiplicity of possible roles from which to choose, they seem trapped within a distinctly limited range of potential options, victims of deterministic influences which, try as they might, they cannot shake off. This is one of the most vexed and recurrent issues which Shepard's work raises: how much of an independent identity can one ever claim to have, if one's fate is being shaped and channeled, even before the moment of one's birth, by forces entirely beyond one's control? The characters in these plays are plagued by an ongoing terror of "unseen hands" (from government to family to the manipulating control of the author himself), which seem to be conspiring to shape their every action, stripping them of any pretense at autonomy. And yet there is a recurrent sense that their ongoing struggle for self-definition—however futile—is also, paradoxically, its own fulfillment. For Shepard, it seems, we are *both* the victims of determinism *and* the inventors of our selves: another of his key existential questions is how to balance these incompatible "truths."

CRISIS OF MASCULINITY

The contradictions inherent in Shepard's treatment of the theme of identity are perhaps made most starkly apparent in his depiction of gender roles, since the urge towards self-exploration has led him to an obsessive fascination with the question of what it means to be an American male. Many different types of masculine behavior are depicted in these plays, from the adolescent mischievousness of the trickster figures in the earliest plays, through the posturing "heroism" of cowboys and rock stars, to the fathers, sons, and lovers of the family plays: in each case, Shepard appears to be working out some anxiety with regard to the adequacy or acceptability of the masculine attitudes depicted. In particular, the plays repeatedly return to the depiction of a violent and arrogant machismo, which is implicitly located as the source of America's tendency toward personal and societal self-destruction. Through their dramatization of tycoons, gunfighters drifters, visionary artists, and modern-day Fausts, the plays suggest that the still-prevalent frontier myth of the heroic "rugged" individual, demanding independence at all costs, lies at the very root of the ruthless self-aggrandizement which still holds sway at every level of American culture.

As Shepard himself admits, this concern with male violence represents an attempt at a kind of exorcism, at confronting and dealing with attitudes which had been inculcated into him from a very young age: "Machismo may be an evil force," he notes, "but what in fact is it? ... I know what this thing is about because I was a victim of it, it was part of my life, my old man tried to force on me a notion of what it was to be a 'man.' And it destroyed my dad. But you can't avoid facing it."[26] Nor was his father the only source of such indoctrination during his youth. The 1950s was, in America at least, probably the most chauvinistic decade of the century, thanks to a concreted national attempt to reestablish rigid social gender roles after a war which had seen women working in "male" industries, while men were fighting abroad. The popular culture of the period was saturated with strong, dominant men and passive, domesticated women, in western serials, superhero comics, Mike Hammer-style detective fiction, and so forth. Shepard's work owes a great deal to such imagery, as he refracts and distorts it through his ironic and at times self-lacerating perspective.

Yet even as he implicitly critiques such dominant attitudes to gender roles, Shepard himself frequently seems trapped within this same limiting view of masculinity. This seems to be largely because of his continuing insistence on seeking to apprehend certain underlying universals, which results in the contradiction of his own suggestion that machismo is a socially constructed phenomenon. Any definition of "essential maleness" is likely to include many of the characteristics Shepard exposes as potentially dangerous, and indeed at times his work appears to imply that male brutality (and, by extension, female victimization) is an inescapable biological given, repeating itself cyclically through the generations. Thus, while he almost invariably ironizes his portrayal of stereotypes masculinity, via pop culture parody, or the more or less gleeful exposure of his characters' personal inadequacies, he rarely seems able to envisage any kind of serious alternative. Moreover, while his determination to write about what he knows and feels most intimately is entirely understandable, his tendency to focus on the problems of straight white male Americans to such an obsessive extent (provocative as this may be in many respects) means that other character types are almost always marginalized and peripheral figures, when they appear at all. Consequently, they can voice little or nothing that might be seen as positing a way out of the trap that Shepard depicts.

A similar problem has also, incidentally, been evident in the construction of Shepard's public image as a movie star. His playing of roles such as the pioneer test pilot Chuck Yeager in Philip Kaufman's *The Right Stuff* (1983) indicates a certain ironic self-consciousness with regard to his representation of masculinity.[27] So too does his willingness to be photographed in 1984 by Annie Leibovitz (the *Rolling Stone* photographer famed for depicting stars in self-mocking poses) in full "Marlboro Man" cowboy regalia, leaning proudly against a horse. Yet the difficulty with such ironic poses, as has often been pointed out in the fields of film and gender studies in recent years, is that even while placing the traditional role "in quotes," one effectively acknowledges its lingering authority by once again reinscribing it in the popular imagination. This is especially the case if the irony is overlooked.

Shepard seems to have recognized this, and it is notable that after his Oscar nomination for *The Right Stuff*, and the concomitant celebration of him as the "New American Hero," he backed away from playing macho film roles, despite numerous offers. Indeed, between 1983 and 1990 he played only minor supporting roles in films dominated by female stars, often as a mild-mannered husband or boyfriend (the exception being his appearance in the film of his own play, *Food for Love*, in 1985). During the same period he finally brought female characters to the foreground in his writing, in a visible attempt to rethink gender division and escape the trap of binary opposition. This was a goal he came closet to realizing with *A Lie of the Mind*, which goes some way toward proposing a kind of utopian-postmodern vision of gender identity as to some extent fluid, another form of role play. According to this logic, the performing self is perhaps able to reconstruct an ideal identity from a range of possible attributes, both "masculine" and "feminine." Even this play, however, has been attached for portraying most of its female characters (subjected to various forms of violence by the men) as brain-damaged or a-rational. Shepard's writing since then, even while idealizing feminine attributes, has continued to suggest a more or less polarized view of gender division (especially in his 1992 film *Silent Tongue*). It seems, moreover, that brute masculinity, for all his evident abhorrence of it, continues to exercise in powerfully seductive influence over Shepard, as it does over American culture at large. His exploration of gender identity remains fundamentally ambiguous and unresolved.

CRISIS IN PERFORMANCE

If Shepard's writing style and thematic preoccupations have suggested a gradual, if seemingly reluctant, shift toward a postmodernist perspective over the course of his career, much the same could also be said of his attitude toward the realization of his texts in performance. At the outset of his career, he initially sought a strict degree of control over the way in which his work was performed. The introductions to four of his earliest pieces by their original directors in *Five Plays* (1967) afford pointed testimony to his tendency to interfere in the rehearsal process if he disagreed with their decisions, and to insist on getting his own way. The idea of the director and production crew having a degree of creative autonomy themselves, a role in the "authorship" of the final performance, was not one he seemed willing to consider at this point. This attitude was entirely consistent with his early adherence to modernist aesthetics, since for a play even to come close to being a pure expression of the writer's unique, personal vision, the possible distorting influences of actors, directors, and designers must be strictly monitored. Samuel Beckett, as director of many of his own plays, sought to restrict the actor's room for individual initiative to the point, in *Not I*, of having only a single mouth, spotlit on a stage otherwise shrouded in total darkness, jabbering away at a speed which prevented the actor's coloring the delivery with any personal inflections.

The very extremity of such gestures, however, also points up the limitations involved in seeking completely to control the production process from a single authorial standpoint: this is to attempt to deny the fundamentally collaborative nature of theatre as an art form. Shepard's steadily more exploratory attitude to the production process indicates his increasing awareness of this fact. From the late 1960s, far from seeking to follow the Beckettian example of stripping the drama down to bare essentials which he could more easily control, he began playing with a greater variety of elements, often using large casts and adding live music and extravagantly theatrical effects. Simultaneously, he became less belligerent about enforcing his own prescriptions on productions. As his comments at the time make clear, he still had very specific ideas about the kind of impact his plays should have on audiences, but this new openness indicated that he was no longer nearly so cocksure about how that could best be achieved: "I've laid myself open to every kind of production for my plays," he told Richard Schechner in 1973, "in the hope of finding a situation where they'll come to life in the way I vision them. Out of all these hundreds of productions, I've seen maybe five that worked."[28] That year Shepard granted Schechner's Performance Group the rights to present the American premiere of *The Tooth of Crime*, despite severe personal misgivings about what Schechner might do with the play. (While experimenting feely with most other elements of the theatrical event, Shepard has always adhered to the traditional model of frontal staging and a clear separation of stage and audience, and is skeptical about the value of the more overtly avant-garde uses of theatre space pioneered by contemporaries like Schechner.)[29]

In 1974, Shepard made his first tentative attempt at directing one of his own plays, *Geography of a Horse Dreamer*, apparently in the hope of learning more about the dynamics of theatrical rehearsal and performance, so that in the long term he could indeed make his plays "work" in the way he envisioned. This experience, however, taught him that the challenges of the production process itself are far greater than he had previously realized. Subsequently, from the mid-'70s through the early '80s, while playwright-in-residence at the Magic Theatre (which, with its small auditorium and proscenium stage, ideally suited Shepard's preference for an intimate but still separate relationship between stage and audience), he acted almost as an apprentice to Robert Woodruff, who directed most of his major plays during this period, while experimenting with directing some of his own lower-profile pieces. Having finally assumed full directorial control of his plays during the 1980s, he used this position not to reinforce the playwright's authoritarian position as creator-auteur, but to play down the sanctity of his own text, to de-privilege its significance by treating it as simply one element in an interplay of multiple creative inputs. Refusing to provide anything but the loosest instructions to actors, designers, and musicians, he actively encouraged them to bring their own ideas to the production, and functioned more as a facilitator for this collaboration than as director per se. He would even make amendments to the text in response to the way the piece was developing through rehearsal. In effect, the modernist desire for pure authorial presence had by this stage been shed in favor of a more open, dialogic process in which text and performance form a dynamic tension, informing and feeding off each other without either one claiming ultimate precendence.[30] This kind of playful exchange of ideas, in which no prescriptive, singular vision is imposed on the production, represents a distinctively postmodernist directorial approach.

These questions over how best to approach the production process have been mirrored quite closely by arguments about how best to respond to Shepard's work as an audience member. Parallel to the notion of asserting total authorial control over the stage image, there is the high modernist tendency to view the artist as a visionary whose work must be treated as sovereign, rather than being submitted to critical authority and scrutinized for interpretation. That attitude has been bound up with responses to Shepard's work from the beginning: Edward Albee, with a degree of skepticism, noted of *Icarus's Mother* in 1965 that "if we have to ask ourselves what it is [about], then it becomes nothing."[31] Jack Gelber again provided a more evangelical take on the same idea by insisting, in his 1976 article, that the metaphysical qualities of Shepard's work can only be appreciated fully by those willing to surrender themselves to its effects: "One must not ask him to answer questions he hasn't asked."[32] The objections to this attitude are obvious: just because these plays refuse to submit themselves to unidirectional interpretations, is one therefore required to leave one's brain at the door in order to appreciate them? Does this mean that those who do not experience ecstatic release in the plays' presence have somehow spoiled it for themselves by thinking too much?

Interestingly, if Shepard himself ever shared such attitudes, he shed them quite quickly. As is evident from a short article written during his time in England in the early 1970s, in which he reflects on his experience of two very different English audiences, his own attitude to the audience reception of his work is considerably more sophisticated and open-minded than Gelber's. After attending a concert given by the rock group The Who, he describes both his love of the music and his vague sense of discomfort that "everyone looks ecstatic and hypnotized as though the same emotion has put everyone out to lunch." Conversely, he speaks of his worry that *The Tooth of Crime* will not be received well at the Royal Court Theatre, with its tradition of earnest, socially concerned dramas, where audiences, he believes, are conditioned to expect "'significant overtones.' ... Somehow it's got to be analyzed and put in the right perspective." Ideally, he notes, a viewer of his plays would react with neither mindless emotionalism nor reductive intellectualizing: "Somewhere between the Who concert and the Royal Court there must lie another possibility."[33]

It seems to me that Shepard's desire for something "in between" these poles suggests a genuinely progressive position on his part, indicating the need for an *active* engagement with plays which cannot be neatly understood, but should not just be unthinkingly absorbed. The relationship of audience and stage, in other words, is itself a dialogic an nonhierarchical one: the spectator may not be able to interpret a clear statement from the play, but is nevertheless liberated to respond to it in his or her own way, questioning it, perhaps mentally arguing with it in a manner not dissimilar to that pursued by Shepard in the writing process itself. And while he stresses that people should feel free to come at his work "any way they can," it is certainly the case, in my own experience, that the audience members who seem to have drawn most from Shepard's work are those who have actively grappled with the contradictory thoughts and emotions the plays elicit in an attempt to discover their own understanding of their significance.

This is not, however, to suggest that the possible range of audience responses is left as wide open as it is in, say, the visually oriented abstraction of performance art. It seems to me that Shepard's work—alongside that of a few contemporaries such as Maria Irene Fornes—occupies a richly fertile but still relatively unexplored no-man's-land in American theatre, between the normative standards of conventional drama and the almost entirely subjectivized territory of experimental performance. Shepard's use of fragmentary narratives, and his borrowing from familiar generic conventions, means that in most cases audiences are able—and sometimes actively encouraged—to form certain assumptions or expectations about where one of his plays might be going. Yet these are invariably subverted, or thwarted entirely, as the free-flowing style of the work leads off in fresh, unexpected directions. This, in turn, requires the spectator to reconsider his or her perspective, possibly only to have that new position problematized. The resulting sense of crisis, the lack of conclusive resolution, can be distinctly unsettling for audiences. But the necessity to find one's own way through what is happening can also be strangely liberating. Whatever the other problems or shortcomings of his playwriting, this ability to prod and cajole audiences into uncomfortable, exploratory spaces gives Shepard's work a peculiar vitality in a theatre culture where the expected is all too often championed as the correct.

NOTES

1. David Mamet, *Writing in Restaurants* (London, 1988), 26, 132.

2. Robert Woodruff quoted by Michael Vermuelen, "Sam Shepard: Yes, Yes, Yes," *Esquire*, February 1980, 85.

3. Sam Shepard, "Language, Visualization and the Inner Library" (1977), reproduced in Bonnie Marranca (ed.), *American Dreams: The Imagination of Sam Shepard* (New York, 1981), 215.

4. Shepard interviewd by Amy Lippman, "Rhythm and Truths," *American Theatre*, April 1984, 11.

5. From Shepard's Introduction to *The Unseen Hand and Other Plays* (New York, 1986), x.

6. See Michael Almereyda's interview with Shepard, "Sam Shepard: The All-American Cultural Icon at 50," *Arena*, May/June 1994, 65.

7. Shepard interviewed by Naseem Khan, "Free-Form Playwright," *Time Out*, 7–13 July 1972, 31.

8. Shepard interviewed by Stewart McBride, "Sam Shepard," *Christian Sience Monitor*, 23 December 1980, B2.

9. All references in this paragraph from Shepard's "Language ...," 215.

10. These papers held in Boston University's Mugar Memorial Library, Shepard archive, Box 3, File 2 ("White Slavery"), and Box 13, File 2.

11. Limman interview, 9–10.

12. Shepard interview by Kenneth Chubb, "Metaphors, Mad Dogs and Old Time Cowboys" (1974), reprinted in Marranca (ed.), 198.

13. Shepard interviewed by Jennifer Allen, "The Man on the High Horse," *Esquire*, November 1988, 148.

14. Shepard, *The Rolling Thunder Logbook* (New York, 1977), 52. Subsequent references included parenthetically in the text.

15. Shepard interviewed by Carol Rosen, "Silent Tongues," *Village Voice*, 4 August 1992, 36.

16. Notes for January 1978, Boston University archive, Box 4, File 7.

17. Shepard interviewed in "A Long Ride," *Paris, Texas* press kit (ed. Jean Pierre Vincent; Paris, 1984), 16.

18. John Lion, "Rock and Roll Jesus with a Cowboy Mouth," *American Theatre*, April 1984, 8.

19. John Lion in an unpublished interview with the author, 7 August 1996.

20. Vermuelen interview, 86.

21. Shepard interviewed by Michiko Katukani, "Myths, Dreams, Realities—Sam Shepard's America," *New York Times*, 29 January 1984, 2.26. This oppoision of personality and essence is, significantly, consistent with the terminology used by the Russian mystic G.I. Gurdjieff, whose ideas have long been of deep personal importance to Shepard. It is, however, difficult to relate Gurdjieff's often arcane writings to the details of Shepard's actual playwriting, and this is not a connection I shall be pursuing.

22. Chubb interview, 198.

23. Lion, "Rock and Roll Jesus," 8.

24. Shepard, *Motel Chronicles and Hawk Moon* (London, 1985), 45–6. Numerous other pieces in the book display similar automythologizing tendencies.

25. Boston University archive, Box 13, File 7 (1979 notes): "All my dreaming is in vain: a repetition of actors repeating themselves. Six Egomaniacs in Search of an Audience."

26. Shepard quoted in John Dugdale (ed.), *File on Shepard* (London, 1989), 62.

27. In *The Right Stuff*, Shepard (who is known to be afraid of flying) plays the fearless Yeager as unflinchingly cool and manly. This pose is exploited to the point where, in the final scene, he walks unharmed out of a wrecked and burning airplane. "Is that a man?," asks one of the salvage crew. "You're goddamn right it is!" comes the reply.

28. Letter from Shepard to Schechner, cited in the latter's book *Performance Theory* (London, 1988), 76.

29. Cf. Chubb interview, 202. Speaking in 1974, Shepard mercilessly parodies the environmental theatre approach which Schechner had recently applied to *The Tooth of Crime*: "If an audience walks into a building and people are swinging from the rafters and spaghetti's thrown all over them, it doesn't necessarily mean ... that their participation in the play is going to be any closer. In fact it might very well be less so, because of the defences that are put up as soon as that happens."

30. I am indebted to Michael Vanden Heuvel for this concept of a dialogics of production, which he develops in his book *Performing Drama/Dramatizing Performance* (Ann Arbor, 1991).

31. Edward Albee, "Theatre: *Icarus's Mother*," *Village Voice*, 25 November 1965, 19.

32. Jack Gelber, "The Playwright as Shaman," in Marranca (ed.), 47.

33. Shepard, "News Blues," *Time Out*, 31 May—6 June 1974, 17.

ELINOR FUCHS

Fefu and Her Friends:
The View from the Stone

I

In the world of *Fefu and Her Friends*, the men possess the outside world. Fefu's unseen husband Phillip, her brother John, and the gardener Tom walk the grounds "in the fresh air and the sun."[1] The women gather in the house, "in the dark" (13), venturing forth only so far as a garden lawn near the house. There are three breaches of this divided genderscape: Emma's exuberant leap out the door to greet the men, the ominous invasion of dead leaves into Julia's bedroom, and Fefu's catastrophic foray with the gun in the last scene. It is not accidental that it is these three characters who "cross over."

If Fornes genders the out-of-doors male in *Fefu*, she genders the interior, with its depth, penetrability, and comfort—its domestic spaces figured as body parts and inner organs—female.[2] The division between house and grounds is one of several variations on Fefu's parable of the stone, offered early in Part I. The story metaphorically describes a chief organizing pattern of the play.

> Have you ever turned a stone over in damp soil? ... And when you turn it over there are worms crawling on it? ... And it's damp and full of fungus? ... You see, that which is exposed to the exterior ...

From *The Theater of Maria Irene Fornes*, edited by Marc Robinson. © 1999 by the Johns Hopkins University Press.

is smooth and dry and clean. That which is not ... underneath, is slimy and filled with fungus and crawling with worms. It is another life that is parallel to the one we manifest.... If you don't recognize it... (*Whispering*) it eats you. (9)

The stone, Fefu immediately makes clear, is not simply a metaphor for the difference between life and the grave. It is a metaphor for the crucial, characterological difference between men and women. Women, like the undersides of stones, are "loathsome." Phillip, Fefu's husband, thinks so, and Fefu agrees. Men, she says, "are well together." They seek fresh air and the sun. But women are not wholesome; they either chatter to avoid contact or avert their eyes. The closest they can come to feeling wholesome is the stupor they experience in the presence of men (13).

The inner life of *Fefu and Her Friends* is governed by the rule of the stone: Its bright upper side is matched, indeed virtually overwhelmed, by the parallel underside hidden from view. As it is with the out-of-doors and the interior of the house, so is it with the men and women who inhabit those spaces. But by the same rule, the house differs from itself. It is the locus of human warmth and social affirmation, but also the site of human and animal functions that should remain unseen, such as the broken upstairs toilet, or the black cat's explosion of diarrhea in the kitchen.[3]

The community of women may also be divided by the rule of the stone. The ecstatic Emma, who sings hymns to the body, sexuality, the "Divine Urge," and the "glorious light" is the upper side of Julia's horrific depths. It is Emma who, joyously ignoring tragedy, throws herself on Julia's wheelchair lap and begs for a ride. The stone divides women from themselves as well. Julia, who above all the other women "knew so much" and "was afraid of nothing" (15), is the one who is now most shockingly abject. Paralyzed, she suffers hallucinations, more real than life, of being beaten, tortured, and condemned to humiliating recitations about the "stinking" and "revolting" parts of the female body (24). She is viscerally abject in Julia Kristeva's sense of "death infecting life," subject to and of "[t]hese body fluids, this defilement, this shit."[4] Fefu may be the most divided figure of all. She enjoys "being like a man," fixes toilets, and shoots a gun, but is hypnotically pulled toward Julia's female abyss (13).

Viewed through this sickening vortex, the source of all disgust, disease, revulsion, and death is the female body. The underside of the stone, that which is "loathsome," is not just women, as Fefu teasingly asserts early in Part I, but specifically the sexual organs of the female body. The reason Fornes set her play in 1935 was to create women freshly naive to the source of this accepted "truth."[5] "Women are inferior beings," Octavio Paz wrote in *The Labyrinth of Solitude* in 1950. "Their inferiority is constitutional and resides in their sex ... which is a wound that never heals."[6] It is surprising that twenty years of criticism about this play have produced greater attention to the capacity for positive bonding among the group of eight women—itself a kind of bandage over a perennial wound—than to the bottomless negative sublime of Fefu's distaste for the female body, the horrifying bodily images of Julia's hallucinations, and Julia's almost biblical suffering.

While the men discuss the lawnmower, the talk in the house circles back again and again to women's bodies. It begins discreetly. In Part I, which takes place in the living room, the public portion of Fefu's house, the references to female bodies emerge for the most part in veiled allusion and literary device. In addition to the metaphor of the stone, there is the curious reference to Voltairine de Cleyre, the figure on whom Fefu has just recently given the talk that Paula heard and Emma was sorry to miss.

De Cleyre, a late-nineteenth-century American anarchist and feminist, attacked church, state, and the institution of marriage as colluding in the bondage of women. In a tract entitled "Sex Slavery," de Cleyre called the married woman "a bonded slave, who takes her master's name, her master's bread, her master's commands, and serves her master's passion." Contesting the common prejudice of her time, de Cleyre attacked the fictional "Mrs. Grundy" for declaring that women's bodies are "obscene" and should be hidden from view. Young girls, wrote de Cleyre, should swim, climb trees, dress freely, and live fearlessly.[7]

Like Emma Sheridan Fry, the educator of a generation later who is quoted in Part III, de Cleyre emerges from the apparently desultory chatter as a kind of bulwark against the forms of feminine (un)consciousness represented in the play, as if to say that somewhere, in the background of women's history, lay the possibility for a different path. Had Fefu not been in thrall to Phillip, had Julia not been vulnerable to the mysterious accident, they might have been Voltairine de Cleyres. Perhaps Paula could be a Voltairine de Cleyre, but Paula, like Masha in *The Seagull*, is in mourning for her life.

The culminating event of Part I is the description of Julia's accident. Up to this moment, Fefu has seized the stage with her shooting game, her toilet repair, and her playful riffs on the superiority of men to women. Her own superiority as a masculine woman is underscored by her condescending good humor to the more conventional women, Cindy and Christina. By these means, she mostly keeps herself, and the tone of the play, on the sunny side of the stone. But suddenly we enter the nightmare of the body. A young woman arrives in a wheelchair, the victim of an objective event and a subjective state of mind. The most painful details are at this point obscured. We know Julia has a "scar in the brain." There were symptoms of a spinal nerve injury, but no injury. She has "petit mal" (15). She cannot walk. She was not struck by the hunter's shot that left her with a bleeding forehead. From now on in the play, the fearless host Fefu will fear herself "host" to Julia's mysterious female contamination.

One must pause at the surrealistic image: A shot kills a deer, a woman falls with blood on her forehead. Julia is, or was, a deer and a woman, for a strike at one brought down the other. If they were at some level the same being, the deer must be associated with the powers she has lost. For she was once afraid of nothing and wise beyond her young years, Fefu tells us, and now, like Wagner's Klingsor, she is wounded without end.

The traditional iconography of the deer as a purifier of venom, poison, and sin—of the "loathsome" in short—would seem to operate in Fornes's play as well. From ancient times, the deer was thought to leap toward purifying water after devouring the venomous snake, of which it was the antidotal creature. An entry in the Biedermann *Dictionary of Symbolism* figures the deer as an emblem of rebirth because of its capacity to purify venom. In Christian mythology, by extension, the deer becomes the enemy of "the great serpent, the devil" and of "filthy sin." Biedermann points out that the carved reliefs on Christian baptismal fonts for that reason often included representations of deer.[8] Finally Christ himself was linked to the image of the "stricken deer." I will return to this link later, at Julia's final catastrophe.

II

With the announcement to the spectators that they will be divided into four groups, circulating through four locations in Fefu's house to witness the scenes of Part II, the alternate, compensating pattern of the play begins to emerge.[9] We soon learn that there is no correct, linear order in which to perceive the central scenes of the play. Despite the hoary device of the gun of the first scene going off in the last, the dramatic model in *Fefu* will not be linear and progressive, but circulatory and cyclical. The second deep pattern of the play, then, is not, like the "stone," one of binary opposites, but of organic and biological circularity. At the levels of text, dramaturgy, and reception, the play is embodied.

Not content merely to align her spectators and her actors on facing planes, Fornes now welcomes her audience into the very body of Fefu's house. Like the body, and unlike most stage sets, the house has a depth and scale matched to our own offstage bodies. Its rooms are tied to the needs of the body—the kitchen, the stomach; the bedroom, sleep and sex. But beyond such familiar associations, spectators begin to discover something unfamiliar, the specificity of their own bodies in the theater.

In the American Place Theatre production, where I first saw the play, spectators were invited at the beginning of Part II to cross the mainstage living room set and walk through an upstage door. There we found our way to the kitchen on the left, to the lawn at the rear, and to the bedroom up a few steps to the right. (The study scene in this production was played on a side level of the mainstage, bringing one-fourth of the audience back into the auditorium.) With this staging, I was no longer separated from the actors by the ontological divide of theater—the "house" and the stage. Since the actors and I now shared the same "house," their bodies became real bodies instead of the stand-ins for the imagined bodies of characters that most audiences make of actors. Even more remarkable in making me aware of my own body in the theater was the acquiring of new seating companions for each segment: next to me in each scene, new elbows, knees, rates of breathing. I was bodily alive to my environment in more senses than "spectator" or "audience" suggest. In the theater (as Emma says in Part II of people and their genitals at business meetings), spectators do have bodies, they just pretend they don't.

But if Part II reveals the often literally organic concern with bodies and embodiment that is part of *Fefu*'s design, it does so in pieces: Plot, dramaturgy, and the poetry of Fornes's dramatic world—as well as the setting of the house that is their expression—all follow a trajectory from dis- to re-memberment. Part II marks the stage of dismemberment in this process, a centrifugal motion that fragments the audience, cast, and setting, while stories of the individual characters' shatterings are being revealed. It is in this part of the play that Fornes breaks her group of eight women into twos and ones. In the scenes that follow, the talk turns again and again to the dismembered female body.

The eight women of the play fall into three groups, the more conventional heterosexuals, the lesbians, and the three androgynous women, whom Fornes develops as figures with mythic imaginations. Some critics of *Fefu* treat the eight as a chorus united in their experience of men, violence, and fear. Rather, they appear to me to live out distinct trajectories within what Fornes depicts as the wounded world of women. The conventional women, Cindy, Christina, and Sue, lend balance and order to that world. Sue, the treasurer of the group effort rehearsed in Part III, stitches the world together with soup and tea, good cheer and practicality. Of these three, she alone is apparently not uncomfortable in her body, and makes no reference to its needs, longings, or vulnerability, although in Part III we learn she went through an unhealthy episode in college. Sue makes only fleeting appearances in the scenes of Part II.

THE WOMEN IN THE STUDY

Christina, a confessed "conventional," is timid and unimaginative. The two unruly scenes, Fefu's shooting at Phillip in Part I and the anarchic water fight in Part III, flatten her weakly on the sofa, the second time with a pillow over her head for protection. "One can die of fright, you know" (10). Yet only she musters an appropriate level of concern over Fefu's outrageous shooting "game" with Phillip, and about Fefu's keeping lethal weapons in the house. Fefu, she observes, may not be "careful with life" (22).

Christina and Cindy now share a scene in the study, which, with its books and neutral furnishings, is the safest—safest in the sense of the least gender- or sex-encoded—of the four intimate spaces that provide the settings for Part II. In this scene, Christina uneasily discusses Fefu, whose dangerous shooting game had earlier left her "all shreds inside" (13). Cindy, who is closer to Fefu and to Julia in friendship, is also somewhat nearer to them in psychic potential. She reports a disturbing dream populated by male authority figures. At first paternalistically Friendly, and then apparently indifferent, these figures become menacing in a way that mixes seduction and physical threat. A policeman, Cindy relates, "grabbed me and felt my throat from behind with his thumbs while he rubbed my nipples with his pinkies. Then, he pushed me out the door. Then, the young doctor started cursing me" (23).

Cindy is not without resources in this dream. From the height of a balcony she slows down the now furious doctor with the words "Stop and listen to me," and when he does so, she manages to command, "Restrain yourself." Her sister is present as support. Cindy is unable to say what she wants to say, however, which is "Respect me." With the help of a friendly man the two women run to a taxi "before the young man tried to kill me" (23). The dream ends in unresolved panic, with Cindy waking up as the doctor is on the verge of wrenching open the taxi door.

Stacy Wolf suggests that the dominant force in the play is male violence—either fear of it, enactment of it in the background story, or performance of it by Fefu and Cecilia in their masculine aspects.[10] But such a reading does not take account of differences in planes and degrees. Julia suffers hallucinations as real as life and actual physical symptoms, Fefu is visited by daytime terrors of death and alarming portents of infirmity, but Cindy's more complacent imagination only dreams of a malevolent doctor treating her for an indistinct health problem. Cindy's fears are walled off in dreams from which she can awaken. She can use her waking life to counter her nightmares, even as she is capable of making positive efforts to save herself within the dream.

THE WOMEN IN THE KITCHEN

The two lesbians seem not to share the fear and dependency that is particular to heterosexuals in the play, but they also differ from each other. The frosty Cecilia, who at some point in the past jilted Paula, has a shrunken emotional life and speaks in intellectual abstractions. On the other hand, one senses that, more than any of the others, she identifies herself as a woman with a career. Cecilia makes aggressive, even cruel, sexual advances to the still-wounded Paula in the course of the play, but for better or for worse she utters no word of connection to either her body or her feelings. Paula, on the other hand, can be seen as the strongest, and most fully alive, woman in the play.

Fornes distinguishes Paula from the other women in a number of ways. She is the only character from a working-class background, and the only one capable of class analysis, glimpsing her upper-class friends in political and economic dimensions of which they themselves are unaware. Paula expresses no terror of predatory males or the encroachment of a mysterious female malaise, nor does she express, as does Fefu, an envy of the male role in the world. If this comfort with her situation in the world does not leave her immune to suffering, hers is the only suffering in the play that is scaled to a full emotional and sexual life. When Paula speaks of her body, as she does in effect in describing the unraveling of her love affair—the phases undergone "in parts" by the brain, the heart, the body, the mind, the memory—she anchors these successive stages in terms of intimate, lived-in space ("You move your things out of the apartment but the mind stays behind," etc. [27]).

Paula here echoes the structure of the play that sets up a correspondence between body and domicile. However, in Paula's account there is no hint of descent into the basement or foundation, the hell realm of pathological disgust and terror "underneath the stone" that Julia inhabits, Fefu dreads, and Cindy—in her dream effort to take control of her destiny by standing on a balcony—distantly sights and flees. (Fornes's later *The Conduct of Life* again makes such an association by placing Nena, the young girl kept as a sexual slave by the Latin American torturer Orlando, in a basement room of a house whose upper rooms respectably house a wife and a domestic servant.) It is no accident that the scene with the most emotionally complete of the women—and the competent and caring Sue, who is also briefly in this scene—is staged in Fefu's kitchen, the sustaining core, or stomach, as it were, of Fefu's house.

THE WOMEN ON THE LAWN

The other scenes of Part II, those involving Fefu, Emma, and Julia, are set in a less realistic, more symbolic world. Fefu and Emma play croquet on the lawn, in effect on the "clean, dry, and smooth" upper side of the stone. This is the only represented scene that abandons the house for the sunlight and air Fefu associates with men. And they are doing somewhat mannish things for 1930s women: They are talking openly about sex while swinging at croquet balls. As in the other scenes, the talk is of body parts, but these parts are curiously detached from bodies and unmarked by gender. The subject is genitals, and anybody's will do. "Do you think about genitals all the time?" Emma asks. "Each person I see in the street, anywhere at all ... I keep thinking of their genitals.... I think it's odd that everyone has them. Don't you?" (19). Fefu's response is ever so slightly embarrassed, "No. I think it would be odder if they didn't have them." But in her sudden "Oh, Emma, Emma, Emma, Emma," she strikes other notes we had begun to hear in Part I. The tone is affectionately patronizing, like that of an adult speaking to a favorite child. In Part I, Fefu had greeted Emma, "How are you, Emma, my child?" (16). Now she will add, again as if to a child, "You always bring joy to me" (20).

Emma may clean up sex and sexuality all she wants, clean up in the sense of rescuing sex from the slimy side of the stone by imagining a lovers' heaven in which only the most devoted sexual enthusiasts, "religiously delivered" (20) to the act, are admitted. But with the repeated "Emma"s, Fefu may be signaling that Emma is too young, naive, inexperienced, or shallow to understand the dark side of life and the trap of female sexuality. Yet isn't Fefu signaling as well a strand of sexual attraction between the women? Emma is the only one of her visitors Fefu embraces in Part I. Now, at the end of the scene on the lawn comes the stage direction: "Emma kisses Fefu." Fornes may be posing the question, as a kind of grace note here, whether a sexual relationship between two women not afraid, symbolically, to leave the house, yet still heterosexually identified, would result in a refreshing cleansing of the "slime" of conventional sexuality; or whether it would result in adding another layer of confusion to the slime-fungus-worm-filled imaginative space in which their sexuality is culturally inscribed.

Immediately following Emma's ecstatic riff on sexual performance Fefu blurts out a confession: "I am in constant pain." She describes the beginning of a kind of breakdown, evidencing itself—she speaks in quasi-erotic terms—through the disappearance of a "spiritual lubricant" in her life, without which "everything is distorted." Fefu then tells the story of the mangled and diseased black cat who appeared one day in her kitchen, an animal she felt obliged to feed. "One day he came and shat all over my kitchen. Foul diarrhea." Though she fears him, "He still comes and I still feed him" (20).

The relationship with the cat sounds suspiciously like Fefu's relationship with her husband Phillip, but with the roles reversed. In the reversal, Fefu becomes the black cat, in effect her own familiar, haunting herself and Phillip from hell. "I exhaust him"—she explains her tortured marriage to Julia in Part III—"I torment him and I torment myself ... I need him ... I need his touch ... I can't give him up" (39). Just as Phillip (Fefu's first line of the play) "married me to have a constant reminder of how loathsome women are," so Fefu adopted the cat because of his monstrosity. "At first I was repelled by him, but then I thought this is a monster that has been sent to me and I must feed him" (20).

After her disturbing tale about the cat, Fefu goes off to assemble lemonade. Emma is left alone on the lawn, reciting Shakespeare's fourteenth sonnet, dedicated to the gaze of the sonneteer's lover. It is the second of three important moments in the play in which Fornes draws attention to the revelatory force of the human gaze.

But from thine eyes my knowledge I derive.
And, constant stars, in them I read such art
As truth and beauty shall together thrive (20–21)

In Part I, in her comparison of men and women, Fefu had said that women "keep themselves from making contact ... they avert their eyes ... like Orpheus" (13). In Part III, the entire confrontation between Fefu and Julia turns on their ability, or failure, to meet each other's gaze. Here, in the setting of the lawn, which Fornes has ironically established as the realm of the wholesome and the "masculine," Fornes offers the fullest statement of the ideal of direct, unashamed, human exchange. The aspiration, which is really the aspiration to the highest form of human love, is stated in two ways, in the ideal of equal, conscious sexual union, and in the ideal of the silent, profound, speech of the eyes. Emma, in her riff on the "divine registry of sexual performance," and in her own performance of Shakespeare, is thus far the bearer of both messages.

In the play's manner of delicate indirection, the scene hints at a culture of feminine freedom, of women able to leave the house-world that demands entrapment as the price of protection. The implication is not that women must henceforth discuss the new lawnmower, so to speak, but that they internalize a principle of freedom that protects women's minds and spirits, as Fefu tells Christina in Part I. However, this attainment is not within the reach of any of Fornes's women, not even Emma, who is too charmingly blind to the dark side, or Paula, who hurts too much.

The Woman in the Bedroom

Julia's world is the hell to Emma's heaven. In an interview published in *TDR* shortly after *Fefu* was first produced, Fornes described her manner of working on the play. Each day, she explained, she would need to recreate a certain kind of heaven and hell for herself before beginning to write. She would listen to the recordings of the "passionate and sensuous" Cuban singer, Olga Guillot. And she would also read passages from her folder of "sufferings."

> A playwright has a different distance from each script. Some are two feet away, and some are two hundred feet away. *Fefu* was not even two inches away. It is right where I am. That is difficult to do when one feels close. A different kind of delicacy enters into the writing. Each day I had to put myself into the mood to write the play.... Each day I would start the day by reading my old folder ... where I have all my sufferings, personal sufferings: the times when I was in love and not, the times I did badly, all those anguishes which were really very profound.... It was writing for the sake of exorcism. A lot of those things had been in this folder for many years. I had never looked at them. That was where the cockroaches were, so to speak. I would start the day by reading something from that folder.... [I]t would put me into that very, very personal, intimate mood to write. I never before set up any kind of environment to write a play! This was the first time that I did that because the play was different. I had to reinforce the intimacy of the play.[11]

Julia is as deep a portrait of the feminine subterranean "where the cockroaches are" as exists in modern dramatic literature, and its dramaturgy and staging are similarly radical. The scene in the Bedroom moves off the realistic continuum of the play. Julia's problems are not those of the dream (Cindy), the ecstasy (Emma), or the portent (Fefu), where bridges back to the realistic imagination are allowed to stand. In this scene, the bridges are gone for the character, and even for the spectator, on whom Fornes imposes physical and psychic discomfort.

The spectators are not given seats, but stand surrounding the "patient," who lies on her mattress on the floor, wearing a medical gown. We are like medical students at one of the famous lecture-demonstrations, Rembrandt's anatomy lesson perhaps, or Dr. Charcot's medical circus of female hysterics at Saltpêtrière. But there is no Dr. Charcot here to exhibit the patient, place her in what might pass for an objective frame, and assure us that boundaries are in place. The experience of Julia's hallucination melts and slips across boundaries, those between spectator and actor, between character and invisible persecutors, and even between character and spectator. Can we be certain that it is not we, the surrounding audience, to whom Julia is describing her journey through hell? As close observers in an undivided theater space, we have become uneasily implicated in the medical and spiritual experiment that is this character's fate.[12]

Of the four intimate scenes of Part II, the bedroom scene is the only one that is not in the form of a dialogue between women. Though Julia appears to be in intense relationship with her unseen male interrogators, no other character of the play joins her until Sue arrives with soup at the end. Putting Julia's hallucination in the form of soliloquy without an authorized observer or receiver is Fornes's chief means of creating its surreal effect.

This scene is also the only one to depart from realism in its setting. It is a sunny day in late spring or early summer, with cold drinks being served and the new lawnmower under inspection, yet in the Bedroom—stage directions tell us that it is a bare and unpainted storeroom that has been converted into a sleeping room for Julia—there are dead leaves on the floor. The leaves offer a symbolic contrast with the bright lawn of the Emma–Fefu scene. The incursion of the woods into the space of the house ironically recalls Julia's last moment of independence, when, in or near the forest, she was felled by the hunter's shot that killed a deer. Fefu and Emma are capable, within limits, of appropriating the masculine preserves of fresh air and sunshine. Julia, once the most independent of women, who moved as if unimpeded in the male world, is now a captive in the house-world of women, her former freedom reduced to a handful of dead leaves. These leaves expressionistically portend her losing battle with death.

Expecting an expansion on her "folder of sufferings," I asked Fornes how the Julia figure came into being. Fornes's surprising reply was something out of a feminist Brothers Grimm. In the 1960s, she relates, she had been thinking of writing a mystery play about scary, fairy-tale "gremlins" who abduct the spirits of women. At some point this story attached itself to her consciousness-raising group experience in the feminist movement of the 1970s Julia was born of this combination.

> I had thought at some point that I wanted to write a murder mystery. I imagined certain judges, non-existent in flesh and blood, but in my mind they were these little people, with animal-like faces. They had a determination to destroy the desire in women to be intelligent, to be adventurous, to be courageous, to be curious. They abducted the spirit of any woman who dared to break the rule of modesty and discretion, and would take the woman into their world for a trial. They would condemn these women to death, or if the women repented they would be left in a brain-washed state. These "gremlins" were small and vicious like rats, but were more terrifying than Nazis. They were like animals, you could not reach them. Or like squirrels—they had that fast movement. All of that is how I connected the idea of writing a murder mystery with what happened with the feminist movement in the 70s. At the group I could discuss things I thought all my life. These thoughts were maybe in the category of a woman who has short legs. She is conscious of it, but she doesn't think of it all the time. But these thoughts are in the "reserve room" because you think there is something odd about feeling that way, especially when we live in a century when women's freedom is absolute. We have public rights, yet we feel these other things. So it kind of lives in a mysterious place and we don't understand it. Something made its not talk about our feelings of this kind of inferiority. We didn't want to recognize our sense of inferiority.[13]

The overlay of Fornes's personal experience in the women's movement on something akin to a comic-strip playwriting experiment evolved into the complexity of Julia, whose mutilation is both socially imposed and regulated, but also strangely self-generated.[14] It is because Julia both exemplifies and grasps this ambivalent condition of women better than any other character in the play that Fornes once identified her as "the mind of the play—the seer, the visionary."[15]

Fornes places her torture victim in a setting that extends the motif already well established in the play, the body-as-house. The setting is a domestic version of the *locus classicus* of torture described in Elaine Scarry's *The Body in Pain*.

> In torture, the world is reduced to a single room or set of rooms.... The torture room is not just the setting in which the torture occurs.... It is itself literally converted into another weapon, into an agent of pain.... The domestic act of protecting becomes an act of hurting and in hurting, the [room] becomes what it is not, an expression of individual contraction, of the retreat into the most self-absorbed and self-experiencing of human feelings.[16]

Scarry draws the telling contrast that Fornes dramatizes in the four domestic variations that comprise the middle movement of her play.

> In normal contexts, the room, the simplest form of shelter, expresses the most benign potential of human life. It is, on the one hand, an enlargement of the body: it keeps warm and safe the individual it houses in the same way the body encloses and protects the individual within.... But while the room is a magnification of the body, it is simultaneously a miniaturization of the world, of civilization.... It is only when the body is comfortable, when it has ceased to be an obsessive object of perception and concern, that consciousness develops other objects. (40–41)

If I were to put *The Body in Pain* and *Fefu and Her Friends* into conversation with each other, the play might tell the book to get a little gender. It would say that to some of its women the body cannot cease to be an "obsessive object of perception and concern," that such concern is forced back on them by this same "civilization," and that they are not simply protected by their house but crippled in it. Nonetheless, Scarry's distinction between settings that affirm and support life, and those that extinguish it, is valuable in illuminating Julia's radical separation from the organic assurances of normal life.

In three of the four scenes of Part II, the spectators have shared the domestic trials of the play's characters in just such benign settings as Scarry suggests. But in what should be the most intimate of settings, a room intended to shelter sleep and sexual love, the most exposed and defenseless of human acts, Julia hallucinates a scene of physical and psychological annihilation. Though all four scenes develop the motif of female dismemberment, Julia's goes far beyond the others to an imaginative limit that approaches the literature of apocalypse. But the apocalypse here is inward, taking the form that Kristeva calls abjection.[17] Abjection, says Kristeva, is at bottom the appalling process of "death infecting life." Kristeva describes the soul-shaking spectacle of abjection in a meditation on this collapse of boundaries.

> I behold the breaking down of a world that has erased its borders, fainting away.... The body's inside ... shows up in order to compensate for the collapse of the border between inside and outside. It is as if the skin, a fragile container, no longer guaranteed the integrity of one's "own and clean self" but ... gave way before the dejection of its contents. Urine, blood, sperm, excrement then show up.[18]

Julia lucidly reports—resists—succumbs to—the particular horror of this loss of integrity. The narrative is not entirely clear. As I read it, in her hallucination Julia is speaking, and mostly responding, to one or more male interrogators who have trained her in the recitation of a prayer. She is explaining to them, once more in the language of dismemberment, what another set of inquisitors did to her body. These were the implacable judges, who claimed to love her, but threatened to cut her throat if she resisted.

> They clubbed me. They broke my head. They broke my will. They broke my hands. They tore my eyes out. They took my voice away. They didn't do anything to my heart because I didn't bring my heart with me. They clubbed me again ... I never dropped my smile. I smiled to everyone. If I stopped smiling I would get clubbed because they love me. They say they love me. (23–24)

In a grotesque parody of Paula's lament for the love affair that ends "in parts" associated with the higher human functions, the heart, the brain, the mind, the memory. and the body (as if that were just one "part"), Julia reports the instructions of one of her tormentors on how to contain the material enormity of the female body. The "stinking" parts—the genitals, the anus, the mouth, the armpit—"must be kept clean and put away" (24). The bottom is "revolting" and must be kept concealed in a cushion. The worst part of all is a woman's "entrails." "He said that women's entrails are heavier than anything on earth.... Isadora Duncan had entrails, that's why she should not have danced. But she danced and for this reason became crazy" (24). But when Julia in a confident aside defends Duncan (whose dancing was known in part for its new emphasis on gravity, on connection of the lower body with the ground),[19] an unseen interlocutor threatens to slap her face. "She moves her hand as if guarding from a blow" (24).

And now comes the strange language of religious inquisition. To defend herself, Julia hastily mumbles her "prayer." She says she has "repented." She defends Fefu, receives several invisible blows, then says the prayer aloud. The prayer is a catechism of gender that might have been written by Otto Weininger in 1903, directing the believer-in-training in the meaning of the first rule of the universe: "The human being is of the masculine gender."[20] "They say when I believe the prayer I will forget the judges. And when I forget the judges I will believe the prayer. They say ... all women have done it. Why can't I?" (25). Julia's problem, within the dramaturgy of the hallucination, is that of all religious heretics, a refusal of belief. For her resistance, yet also for her failure to resist enough, Julia is sacrificed. *Fefu* finally crystallizes as a feminist Passion Play.

III

If Part I is about gathering, Part II is about dismemberment—in text, dramaturgy, staging, and spectatorship. The "smooth, dry" affirmative level of the characters as social beings enjoying the community of women is undermined by the "loathsome" fantasies and terrors that arise when they are splintered into their own individual existences. In Part III the motion runs the other way, toward reintegration, although at a terrible price, as it will appear. All the characters now return to the group scene of Part I, while the audience returns to the auditorium, enacting its own reunion in a movement that parallels the reassembly onstage. The spectators are beginning to experience in their bodies the motions of dis- and re-memberment that move the play and its characters.

This third part of the play—musical movement is almost more appropriate a term—contains two group scenes with all characters present that formalize in circular tableaux the circular shape of the play. However, in their opposed motions of life and death, growth and decay, these scenes represent yet one more version of Fefu's parable of the stone. In between are the several scene fragments that comprise the joyous rondo of the water fight, as well as the confrontation between Fefu and Julia that precedes the play's mysterious, surreal end.

The first of the group scenes is the women's run-through of their appeal for support of what appears to be a primary school arts project. The women position themselves in a semicircle, then one by one five of them step forward to walk through their parts. Emma, at the center of this performance, just as her ecstatic ideology is at the center of the school program the women are collaborating on, performs her part in a flowing floor-length robe. Paula imitates Emma affectionately, bringing her hands together, opening her arms, and throwing her head back to speak. Ah-ha, it is Isadora Duncan! Or perhaps Duncan doing Delsarte. In the performance within the rehearsal, the speech Emma performs is taken from the writings of Emma Sheridan Fry. Emma does indeed perform with the expressive gestures of a Duncan. It is a layered double or triple image, recalling the turn-of-the-century performing arts theories celebrating "Expression," in which progressive women of the 1930s continued to educate their children.

Emma Sheridan Fry was one of the remarkable arts educators of the first two decades of the twentieth century, teaching children dramatic expression in the same years in which Duncan's reputation was at its height.[21] At the Educational Alliance in New York City, she founded and ran the Children's Educational Theatre. In an influential short book, *Educational Dramatics*, published in 1913 and again in a revised edition in 1917, Fry set forth the vitalistic principles, so close to those of Duncan, which governed her work. The high calling of the dramatic educator, wrote Fry, was not mere preparation for a show, but the development of the entire human being through the cultivation of the Dramatic Instinct, a reflection of the consciousness of God.[22] Fry thought of dramatic expression as Duncan thought of dance expression, as the individual "interconnected with the cosmos." Duncan wrote that the dancer's soul could "merge with the universe" if it was "awakened" to the universal by means of either music or nature.[23] The "environment" of Fry's theory, battering at the gates of the soul to wake it up, was equivalent to Duncan's music or nature.

Fry is the last of the three historical "foremothers" invoked by Fornes's women: Fefu is linked with Voltairine de Cleyre in Part I, Julia with Duncan in Part II, and now Emma with her namesake, Emma Sheridan Fry. The three turn-of-the-century women, models of feminine activity and independence, might be seen as a chorus of resistance to the nightmarish male patrols who perform surveillance on the world of women. (Their representatives in the play are Phillip, who loads the gun, the mysterious hunter who shoots the deer and fells Julia, the malevolent doctor and policeman of Cindy's dream, and Julia's evil interrogators.) Even if their understanding of gender may seem limited by contemporary insights, as the following example from Fry will show, yet these female historical figures would seem to belong among Julia's benign "guardians," figures or faculties that protect women from death.

Fornes adapted Emma's "Environment Knocks at the Gateway" speech from the introduction to Fry's 1917 edition of *Educational Dramatics*. With its celebration of an exuberant surge into life, the speech is the culmination of the Emma-motif in Fornes's composition. Celebrating the Divine, or Eternal, Urge, the speech contemplates no serious barrier to the achievement of what Fry calls the Whole or the All. "What is Civilization?" asks Emma as she quotes Fry, "A circumscribed order in which the whole has not entered" (32).

In the universe of both Emmas, the restraints of civilization can be transcended by those who tap into the ever-present inner energy of the Divine Urge. But both are blind to the worm of gender within the ecstatic drama. Fry teaches that each individual's Divine Urge is locked inside "Center"—the individual's Being, narrowly conceived. Environment, the active principle outside ourselves, batters at Center, striving to be admitted. "Never was a suitor more insistent than Environment ... shouting to be heard," exclaims Emma-quoting-Fry. "And through the ages we sit inside ourselves, deaf, dumb, and blind, and will not stir" (31). Does this not sound suspiciously like Fefu's Part I description of the difference between men and women, the "wholesome" males appropriating the sun and air, "while we sit here in the dark?"

Fornes has Emma repeat the unwitting language in Fry that makes the gender rules of the Environment/Center courtship very clear. Eternal Urge "pushes through the stupor of our senses, making paths to meet the challenging suitor, windows through which to see him, ears through which to hear him. Environment shouting "Where are you?" and Center ... battering at the inside of the wall ... dragging down bars, wrenching gates, prying at port-holes.... The gates are open!" (31–32).

No doubt the "suitor" of Emma's recitation, the external, active principle, is gendered male, while the female partner, eager though she may be to be awakened, is trapped inside the walls of her body/house, unable to see the light. (This love affair of opposites moves toward the extremes of Kokoschka's proto-expressionist one-act play, *Murderer, the Hope of Woman*, written in the same decade in which Fry began her teaching in New York and Duncan had her first triumphal tour of the United States.)

Emma seemed earlier to embody a route to freedom from the curse of Fefu's stone, but here she unconsciously recapitulates it. The "glorious light" she extols, implicitly gendered as a male sun, cannot penetrate Julia's persecutory death-realm. And to Julia, now trained in the ways of that realm, such light is not the result of "life universal" chasing "life individual" out of its dark retreats, but is inborn in fearless women who haven't (yet) noticed that they are "loathsome." The light is inner: It is what such women lose if they "get too smart" (24). "Oh, dear, dear, my dear, they want your light. Your light my dear. Your precious light," moans Julia in imaginary dialogue with Fefu from the depth of her hallucination (25).

It is not possible finally for Emma to wish away the underside of the stone, the slime, worms, and darkness, with a religion of light. Julia's prayer teaches the doctrine of another religion, an enormous machinery of gender-darkness. Like Emma's it is a cosmic system, and like hers, it has its higher universal principle and its lower individual one. In Julia's system, the difference between those planes turns on sex, or more precisely, on projections of male fear onto female sexuality. Man's "spirit is pure," as the prayer insists, but "women's spirit is sexual." "(Women's) sexual feelings remain with them till they die. And they take those feelings with them to the afterlife where they corrupt the heavens, and they are sent to hell where through suffering they may shed those feelings and return to earth as man" (25).

THE SACRIFICE

Throughout the play, Fefu has adopted two more or less unmediated gestures toward the world. She has playfully, even swaggeringly, performed the man, shooting at Phillip, fixing the toilet, and making macho pronouncements about women to scare the "girls," or she collapses into fear and anxiety. Only in the final moments of the play does she attempt to move beyond this alternation. After Julia is seen walking in a scene that may very well be Fefu's own hallucination or a piece of Fornes's domestic surrealism, Fefu confronts her in a new guise, assuming the role of the very Orpheus she prophetically invoked in Part I. Like the gun in the first act that goes off in the last, every vagrant reference in Fornes's seemingly nondirectional text assumes a precise place in a dense poetic structure. So it is in this culminating scene that Fefu attempts the recognition that will "blow the world apart."

As Orpheus, Fefu seeks to break the law of the underworld and the grip of death. She will do this not by sticking to the rules and avoiding Julia's gaze, but by breaking them and actively seeking it. She and death's captive must urgently understand each other, must speak honestly and exchange a fearless gaze in mythic style, the attempt is made three times:

JULIA: What is the matter?

FEFU: I don't know, Julia. Every breath is painful for me. I don't
know. (FEFU *turns* JULIA's *head to look into her eyes.*) I think you
know. (39)

But "Julia looks away," and answers evasively. Fefu describes the trouble with
Phillip: Their relationship is in the second phase described earlier by Paula,
"His body is here but the rest is gone." Fefu tries again.

FEFU: (*She looks into* JULIA's *eyes.*) I look into your eyes and I know
what you see. (JULIA *closes her eyes.*) It's death. (39)

This Eurydice will not join Fefu in rewriting the myth. She pleads
exhaustion even as Fefu demands a response: "What is it you see! ... What is
it you see!" (40). Fefu charges Julia with lack of courage, but a moment later
her own courage fails. "I want to put my mind at rest. I am frightened." With
this confession the roles reverse. Now the stage direction: "JULIA *looks at*
FEFU." And Fefu's surprising response:

FEFU: Don't look at me. (*She covers* JULIA's *eyes with her hand.*) I
lose my courage when you look at me. (40)

The opportunity to "blow the world apart" is lost. Between them, the
women cannot sustain an honest gaze. It is not clear whether it is Julia's
failure to look when asked, or her willingness to look when not asked, that
seals her fate. Whichever it is, she has now passed from being rescued from
death every minute by her "guardians" (among which she had earlier named
eyesight itself [35]), back into the kingdom of death. From there she delivers
a final "blessing" over Fefu, wishing her protection from the shattering
dismemberment that she herself has suffered.

Fefu is a map of the dismembered female body. Julia's account of her
sufferings in Part II may be the most frightening version of this theme, but
it appears again in Paula's account of the death of a love affair, in Emma's
obsession with "genitals," in Cindy's dream about the policeman's menacing
grip on her neck and nipples, in Christina's having been reduced to "all
shreds inside," and in the implications of Fefu's parable of the stone. Now the
last long speech of the play, Julia's blessing of Fefu, repeats the threat of
dismemberment as an *apotropaion*—a ritual charm to ward off evil. As Fefu
cries "Fight!" to the exhausted Julia, Julia makes a last, heroic effort to stitch
her endangered friend back together: "May no harm come to your head ...

May no harm come to your will ... May no harm come to your hands ... May no harm come to your eyes ... May no harm come to your voice ... May no harm come to your heart" (40).

In the famously disputed ending that follows, Fefu takes the gun outside to clean it, fires, and Julia is "struck." The play ends in a circular tableau, the final gathering-in of women. Julia sits center in her wheelchair, her head thrown back with a bloody wound in the forehead. Fefu stands behind her. The other women circle around. It is a group portrait, a final remembering as the lights fade. I believe the ending hints at much more, as I shall develop in a moment.

I am sympathetic to Assunta Bartolomucci Kent's probing questions directed to the liberatory assumptions of many of the readings of this enigmatic, if shocking, ending.[24] To believe that Fefu's shot can symbolically free the women from self-representations as victim is to read Fefu's conflicted character too uncritically, and especially, to weigh Julia's "lucid" (Fornes's word) understanding of how-things-are-for-women too lightly. It molds the eight women into a group identity that erases the differences Fornes has carefully inflected. And it forces on the ending an ideological purity, a sudden lack of what Fornes calls "delicacy" that the play does not support. Finally, behind many of the positive, emancipatory, readings of the ending has been the (excessive) anxiety that without them Fornes would be suspect as a feminist.

I earlier suggested that there were two dominant organizing patterns of the play. Perhaps from them further meaning can be discovered. The codings threaded through the play by the potent images of the upper and hidden sides of the stoic and of the membered and dismembered body are sustained to the end, but they are ultimately lifted entirely out of realism.

It is of course almost overdetermined that Fefu must seize the gun and go out-of-doors to the men in order to find a safe "smooth" place after Julia's incarnation promised an approaching descent into the hell of female dismemberment. And it is similarly determined that the final resolution—the rabbit dead, Julia "dead," the wound on her forehead, the group circled in a gesture of concern and mourning—would once more cast doubt on the efficacy of these same masculine gestures. The hunt, presumably one of the activities in which men are "wholesome" together, nevertheless really kills, as Fefu had already decided in giving it up before this backsliding. (Christina is right: Fefu is not careful with life.) "I'm game," Julia had said earlier with an attempt at gaiety, standing in for the class of women who are "eaten"—Fefu's dark prophecy of Part I.

The ending of the play is a riddle to most readers and spectators. Why, first of all, a rabbit? No one speaks of it in reading *Fefu*, but there is something vaguely disappointing, dare one say almost comic, in Julia's "dying" as a rabbit. One wonders whether Fornes is pulling a rabbit joke out of her playwriting hat. The rabbit has a homely association with reproduction. If it has benefited from its annual appointment with Easter, it is only as the dumb and earthbound manifestation of Easter's regenerative theme. It may be a mark of Julia's decline and weakness that while she earlier fell as a deer, she has now succumbed as a rabbit. The mystery of the rabbit is intensified by the formality and seeming solemnity of the context in which it appears. In Fornes's original published version of the play, with which I am working here, the stage direction has Fefu entering with the dead animal in her arms. She continues to hold the animal in this fashion as she stands behind the prostrate Julia. There is a symbolic dissonance here: The pathetic creature takes its place in a tableau that echoes the iconography of the Pietà.

Like the dead Jesus, Julia has acquired a stigmata-like wound. She has received the bullet hole as saints develop such insignia, by some process of intense and mysterious identification. Julia sits center in her wheelchair, feet forward, body falling back. Like the Madonna in traditional representations of the Pietà, Fefu is positioned behind the sacrificed figure—Fornes is very clear in these directions—and like her, she is holding the sacrificed, in this case Fornes's peculiar sacrificial surrogate, the dead rabbit. Surrounding the mortified body, flanking "Mary," is the familiar circle of mourning women. It is a Passion Play in mythic-domestic double image. As the dying god, Julia becomes heroic, and through an overlay with Christ (the "stricken deer") she has in her martyrdom moved beyond the punishment of gender. "The corpse, seen without God and outside of science, is the utmost of abjection," writes Kristeva.[25] But at the last moment Fornes mysteriously transforms the scene with a touch of "God."

Other associations may be brought to this impacted moment. Perhaps Julia is the dying, dismembered Orpheus, torn apart by women who could not hear his music. The felling of Julia was, if truth be told, not Fefu's doing alone, but a group enterprise. Phillip loaded the bullet, Christina hid the gun but then weakly revealed it again, Julia removed the remaining slug from the gun and dropped it on the floor, yet Cindy was careful to reload it. So whether the women are, as a group, simply the mourners of Julia, or covert collaborators in this second and perhaps fatal "accident" is an unresolved question.

One can read the scene with different emphases, but such a complex, simultaneous image may be distorted by cumbersome linear explication. It speaks through methods unfamiliar in our still realistic theater. Fornes's nonrealism has been called "absurdist" and "metatheatrical,"[26] but I sense she is functioning here as a painter. Fornes was a painter before she was a playwright, and it should not surprise that she sometimes speaks on the stage in the compressed visual language of the painter's art. It is futile to work such stage language for certain meaning. It acquires meaning through context, every detail signifying, nothing excluded, which is no doubt why Fornes directs her own work. In the final scene, Fornes is "painterly" both in creating a stationary tableau and in staging the scene in reference to a high tradition of European religious painting. She may have gone even further, and wickedly combined one of the most sacred motifs of religious painting with a secular tradition that strikes today's museum-goer as vaguely comic— the Dutch genre painting of the seventeenth century in which the trophies of the hunt became the central adornment of the domestic scene. I recall numerous paintings by forgotten painters in which dead rabbits, draped for skinning and cooking, were displayed with deadpan reverence. Fornes may have administered the rabbit to the audience to counter its inflationary appetite for symbols.[27]

Fornes writes a realism that is both underpinned and interrupted by what we could call surrealism. Or in honor of Fornes's Cuban origins, perhaps a more Latin American inflection, magic realism, should be brought into service. The Latin American painter whose work especially illuminates Fornes's in *Fefu* is Frida Kahlo. Just as magical, intensely visualized eruptions—Julia as prey, the Hallucinations, the black cat—break the seemingly realist domestic world of *Fefu*, so Kahlo combines autobiographical and domestic motifs with fantastic, often savage, depictions of psychological and physical suffering. This abrupt combination of discontinuous planes has led to confusion about Fornes's method and intentions. Around Kahlo's work too has swirled a classification debate, some critics agreeing with Breton's enthusiastic embrace of Kahlo as a New World surrealist, and others pointing to the autobiographical and domestic elements as proof of her difference from European surrealists.[28]

Kahlo's imaginative world has strong and sometimes uncanny resonances with the world of *Fefu*. Kahlo depicted herself as a kind of Julia, surrounded by dismembered parts of her own body, identifying herself with animals, religious martyrdom, and images of death. Like a Madonna of suffering, Kahlo represented herself in fierce self-portraits with a "wound" in her forehead, the source of suffering being located, as in Fornes, within and outside the subject. In the 1943 portrait *Thinking About Death* the emblem on the forehead becomes a dark circle containing a skull and crossbones.

Like Julia's bloody circle of a bullet wound, Kahlo's marks are located at the "third eye," the seat of superior, spiritual, vision.

Both in the Fornes of *Fefu* and in Kahlo the gaze or its absence is significant. In Kahlo, the painter's unwavering gaze is often depicted above a broken body, an arresting of affect that deflects sentimentality and encourages critical thought. A particularly striking image of this type is the Kahlo painting most uncannily suggestive of Julia, the *Little Deer* of 1946. This well-known painting depicts a deer pierced with arrows like Saint Sebastian. On its bleeding body is superimposed the painter's head, wearing antlers. Her eyes gaze with steadfast intelligence at the viewer. Julia, as stricken deer and as "lucid" narrator of her own disaster, incorporates both aspects.

Another Kahlo painting that powerfully suggests the nightmare of Julia is one in which it is precisely the subject's averted gaze that reduces her to total abjection. It depicts a naked woman in a room that could be the bedroom setting of Julia's hallucinations. The painting, ironically entitled *Unos Cuantos Piquetitos!* (A Few Small Nips!), shows a woman's body, still wearing a shoe and a rumpled stocking, sprawled on a low hospital-like cot in a windowless and doorless room that is as frighteningly isolated from the outside world as any setting Scarry could imagine for the infliction of physical torture. The only colorful element is the woman's blood, splattered on her body, the sheets, the floor. Like Fornes, who implicates the spectator in Julia's persecution by gathering us into the same cramped physical space she inhabits, Kahlo brings her scene of mutilation into the viewer's world by spilling the blood of the painting out over its wooden frame. In both cases, boundaries "bleed."

Standing over the woman in Kahlo's painting is a fully clothed man in a blood-spattered shirt. His expression is cruel and detached. He has the woman completely in his power. One hand rests easily in his pocket, a menacing detail. The other holds the knife that has chipped away at the woman's face, torso, legs, arms, and breasts as if she were a cheese. The woman's face is turned away and her eyes are closed. But a surrealist element in the painting gives the viewer perspective. The ironic title, *Unos Cuantos Piquetitos*, floats on a ribbon held above the scene by a pair of doves.

The distancing device of the title helps to locate the female perspective of the artist: She is not in masochistic or voyeuristic collusion with the male perpetrator; she criticizes male violence against women as well as male denial or rationalization of that violence. The case of Julia, like the case of the wretched woman in *Piquetitos*, is also double-coded. Julia falls into the "concentrationary universe" of her male judges, yet brings back a clear-eyed, even subversive, report from the abyss. Kahlo has inserted a surrealist element into a scene of brutal realism; Fornes creates a grotesque world of the imagination, then anchors it with characterological realism. In both Kahlo and Fornes, a response of some complexity is mobilized by the layered, often conflicting, representations before us.

We do not finally know what happens at the end of this play, not even whether Julia has actually died, though many critics declare this as a certainty. The pattern of affirmative circularity does not rescue the women from their invisible oppression, nor us from the dilemma of uncertain agency and meaning. The re-membering of the female community has occurred, but the community is nonetheless broken. A message of hope may be taken from the reassembly of dramaturgy, spectators, and characters that drives the play's last movement. (The dismembered Orpheus, after all, was gathered up and restored by women.) But the "recognition scene" that Fefu longs for in her Orpheus speech—the confirmation that the torn fabric of women's existence can be made whole—refuses to take place. There is a hint of religious iconography, but Julia does not finally "die for our sins" and redeem the group. Tragedy and hope circle uneasily and perpetually, and no easy resolutions are possible. The dilemma of gender will not lift like a cloud. Fefu's stone must split or erode, and old fault lines crumble away from long disuse, before the circle of women can find its lull freedom and strength. In this, Fornes is a strict realist.

NOTES

1. Maria Irene Fornes, *Fefu and Her Friends*, in *Wordplays* (New York: PAJ Publications, 1980), 13. All subsequent page references will appear parenthetically in the text.

2. In dictionaries of symbolism and iconography, the house is frequently associated with the body, and especially the female body. See Philip Thompson and Peter Davenport, eds., *The Dictionary of Graphic Images* (New York: St. Martin's, 1980).

3. In *Fornes: Theater in the Present Tense* (Ann Arbor: University of Michigan Press, 1996), Diane Lynn Moroff also notes a discrepancy of tones in the house, locating its source in the difference between what we hear and what we see: We may hear about suffering, but we see a network of supportive relationships.

4. Julia Kristeva, *Powers of Horror: An Essay on Abjection*, trans. Leon S. Roudiez (New York: Columbia University Press, 1982), 3–4.

5. Writing in the *SoHo Weekly News* of January 12, 1978, Fornes states her "affection ... for a kind of world which I feel is closer to the 1930s than any other period ... because it is pre-Freud.... Today there is an automatic disbelieving of everything that is said.... It's implied that there's always some kind of self-deception about an emotion" (38).

6. Octavio Paz, *Labyrinth of Solitude*, trans. Lysander Kemp, Yara Milos, and Rachel Phillips Belash (New York: Grove, 1985), 30. For the purposes of reading Fornes, this

passage is interestingly quoted in Liza Bakewell, "Frida Kahlo: A Contemporary Feminist Reading," *Frontiers* 13, no. 3 (1993): 165–89.

7. "Voltairine de Cleyre," *American Women Writers: A Critical Reference Guide from Colonial Times to the Present*, vol. 1, ed. Lina Mainiero (New York: Frederick Ungar, 1979), 482–83.

8. Hans Biedermann, *Dictionary of Symbolism*, trans. James Hulbert (New York: Facts on File, 1992), 92–93.

9. This seemingly essential structure is abandoned in an alternate version Fornes has recently written to be performed by large theaters in which the breakup of the audience into small groups is impracticable.

10. Stacy Wolf, "Re/Presenting Gender, Re/Presenting Violence: Feminism, Form and the Plays of Maria Irene Fornes," *Theatre Studies* 37 (1992): 17–31.

11. Maria Irene Fornes, "I Write These Messages That Come," *The Drama Review* 21, no. 4 (1977): 26–40, 32–35.

12. W.B. Worthen calls this scene the "shaping vision" of the play. He sees the spectator as standing in for the coercive male "guardians" whose gaze "constructs, enables, and thwarts the women of the stage." "Still Playing Games: Ideology and Performance in the Theater of Maria Irene Fornes," in *Feminine Focus: The New Women Playwrights*, ed. Enoch Brater (New York, Oxford University Press, 1989), 167–85, 177.

13. Telephone interview with the author, August 1997.

14. Fornes is not alone among contemporary women playwrights in creating a composite image of the social-cum-bodily shattering of women. The method appears in Joan Schenkar's *Signs of Life*, in Adrienne Kennedy's *Funnyhouse of a Negro*, and in Rachel Rosenthal's *Pangaean Dreams*. In the latter, Rosenthal appears in a wheelchair, crippled. The action of the piece, an archeological dig to reassemble her own shattered form, was a metaphor for the restoration of the shattered environment, the body of the earth. Barbara Ehrenreich has echoed this entanglement of personal and political, sexual and social, in her introduction to Klaus Theweleit's *Male Fantasies*, in which she writes that male power is predicated on the derogation and suppression not only of the female body but of a wide range of categories men gender "feminine."

15. Fornes, *SoHo Weekly News*.

16. Elaine Scarry, *The Body in Pain: The Making and Unmaking of the World* (New York: Oxford University Press, 1985), 38–39.

17. Kristeva herself notes a connection between apocalyptic literature and a "horror for the feminine." Kristeva, *Powers of Horror*, 205.

18. Ibid., 4, 53.

19. Fredrika Blair, *Isadora: Portrait of the Artist as a Woman* (New York: McGraw-Hill, 1986), 401–2.

20. I am indebted to Katherine Profeta, a student at the Yale School of Drama, for pointing out the similarities between the views of Julia's judges and those of the notorious Weininger, whose 1903 *Geschlecht und Charakter* (*Sex and Character*, 1906) attributed positive energy and morality to the male, and negativity and amorality to the female.

21. For a brief outline of Fry's career, see Beatrice L. Tukesbury, "Emma Sheridan Fry and Educational Dramatics," *Educational Theatre Journal* 16, no. 4 (1964); 341–48.

22. Emma Sheridan Fry, *Educational Dramatics* (New York: Moffat, Yard, 1913).

23. Ann Daly, *Done Into Dance: Isadora Duncan in America* (Bloomington: Indiana University Press, 1995),136–37.

24. Stacy Wolf, Gayle Austin, and Assunta Kent have variously summarized the range of responses to this ending. See Wolf, "Re/Presenting Gender," 27–28. In "The Madwoman in the Spotlight: Plays of Maria Irene Fornes," in *Making a Spectacle: Feminist Essays on Contemporary Women's Theatre*, ed. Lynda Hart (Ann Arbor: University of Michigan Press, 1989), 76–85, Gayle Austin sees Fefu as Julia's "double," who fights, even shoots, rather than give in to "women's predicament" (80). In *Maria Irene Fornes and Her Critics* (Westport, Conn.: Greenwood, 1996), Assunta Bartolomucci Kent critiques the too easy affirmations of Fefu's rash shooting as a "necessary sacrifice" of the "woman-as-victim" (138–40).

25. Kristeva, *Powers of Horror*, 4.

26. These two quasi-formalist readings stand somewhat outside the feminist discussions of the ending. Toby Silverman Zinman claims that Fornes's concluding move is a piece of absurdist theater speaking in "the powerful shorthand of concrete images" and not subject to realist interpretation ("Hen in a Foxhouse: The Absurdist Plays of Maria Irene Fornes," in *Around the Absurd: Essays on Modern and Postmodern Drama*, ed. Enoch Brater and Ruby Cohn [Ann Arbor: University of Michigan Press, 1990], 203–20, 209). Diane Lynn Moroff (*Fornes*) sees the ending, and much of the play, as metatheatrical, in keeping with the play's "deliberate theatricalization of character" (36).

27. Fornes tells the story of the audience's response to the rabbit in the discussion sessions that took place at the American Place Theatre. At each of these, someone would always mention that Fefu made her final entrance holding the black cat in her arms. To counter the creation of this false symbol, Fornes says, she stayed up all one night sewing a new, all-white, rabbit. But at the next audience discussion, a man raised his hand and asked, "Why was the black cat white?" (Author's interview, August 1997). This persistent audience confusion may account for the changed stage direction in the single-edition version of the play (New York: PAJ Publications, 1990). Here Fefu drops the rabbit before taking up her position behind the wheelchair. The result is a somewhat less mysterious and supernatural ending.

28. In her account of Fornes's staging of *Uncle Vanya* in *Directors in Rehearsal* (New York: Routledge, 1992), Susan Letzler Cole quotes Fornes as directing the actor playing Vanya to perform a scene as if he were a "penitent rising from the flames below" (48). When questioned by Cole about this "painterly" staging, Fornes "clarifies that she does not have a particular work of art in mind but that her stage image of the penitent has some resemblance to certain Mexican paintings" (239n. 34).

C . W . E .   B I G S B Y

Tennessee Williams:
The Theatricalising Self

The pre-war world was another country. From the distance of the mid-to late forties and early fifties it seemed secure, reassuring, but in fact the Depression had destroyed one version of America and the Hitler–Stalin pact another. Wartime rhetoric had reinvented small-town America, an amalgam of Thornton Wilder's *Our Town* and *Saturday Evening Post* covers, where old values were preserved and celebrated, a world worth fighting for; now that was already fading into history. William Inge, Carson McCullers and Robert Anderson might continue to place it at the centre of their work, but in doing so showed how bleak it could be until redeemed by an ambiguous love.

And of course, something radical had happened. In Europe 6 million Jews had been systematically put to death. In Japan, the heat of the sun had been replicated by man over two major cities. If Virginia Woolf had suggested that human nature changed in 1910 there were now other dates with greater claim to mark a shift in human affairs. Certainly American notions of the autonomous self, secure and morally inviolable, seemed suddenly more difficult to sustain. The enemy was no longer simple modernity, the inhuman scale, the mechanical rhythms against which Eugene O'Neill and Elmer Rice, Sidney Kingsley and the young Miller and Williams had railed. It was a flaw in the sensibility that made betrayal seem a natural impulse and the self complicit in its own annihilation. It was no longer a case of pitching an integral self against anonymity and social despair for now that self is presented as fragmented and insecure.

From *Modern American Drama, 1945–2000.* © 2000 by Cambridge University Press.

Death of a Salesman and *The Crucible, The Glass Menagerie* and *A Streetcar Named Desire*, seemed to suggest the end of a particular model of America and of individual character. Time seemed to be gathering pace. Basic myths having to do with family and community, civility and responsibility, style and grace had dissolved. The future seemed to offer little more than a bland materialism or a drugged conformity.

The choice was between Happy Loman and Stanley Kowalski. In such circumstances the past had a seductive attraction. So, Willy Loman, in *Death of a Salesman*, is pulled ever more back into the past of his own imagining, before the city encroached on his freedom, before the wire recorder cut across a simple act of human communication, before the automobile threatened his life and the world became such a mystery to him. So, John Proctor, in *The Crucible*, struggles to accommodate himself to a language which no longer speaks his life and to a system which denies him reality. Laura's glass menagerie is frozen. Time is suspended as it will continue to be suspended fur her, as it has been suspended for the woman on whom she was based and who has spent a lifetime in a mental hospital in recoil from the real. Like so many of William Faulkner's characters Laura Wingfield in *The Glass Menagerie* stands as a paradigm of the culture of which she is a part. The world of modernity, the dance hall and the typewriter, is outside of her experience. Vulnerable, she chooses instead a world of myth, symbolised by the glass unicorn. It is a factitious security broken as easily as the unicorn's glass horn. Blanche, too, in *A Streetcar Named Desire*, resists the pull of time, terrified of the first signs of age, aware that something has ended and that it can only be recovered at the level of story, only through the roles that she so desperately performs and which finally offer her no immunity. Insanity, literal or metaphoric, seems to threaten. Williams acknowledges the impossibility of recovering the past. Indeed he accepts the equivocal nature of that past, stained, as it is, by cruelty and corruption. But the future is worse: power without charity, passion without tenderness.

Williams had the romantic's fascination with extreme situations, with the imagination's power to challenge facticity, with the capacity of language to reshape experience, with the self's ability to people the world with visions of itself. He deployed the iconography of the romantic: fading beauty, the death of the young, a dark violence, a redeeming love. Like the romantic he was inclined to blur the edge of the divide between his life and his art. It would be tempting to see his fondness for drink and drugs as yet another aspect of the romantic's twin quest for vision and self-destruction except that in his case it had more to do with terror and despair. It was certainly as a romantic in an unromantic world that he wished to present himself, transfiguring the failed enterprise that is life with noshing more than language and the imagination.

Tennessee Williams's explanation for his career as a dramatist was that he was 'creating imaginary worlds into which I can retreat from the real world because ... I've never made any kind of adjustment to the real world'.[1] It was an honest remark and one that could be applied with equal force to his characters. In one direction such a failure of adjustment may generate neurosis and psychosis; in another, art. And if his characters are indeed pulled towards mental instability they also tend to be artists, literal and symbolic. Blanche turns her life into an art work. Her trunk is full of clothes for the various roles she plays while she transforms the Kowalski apartment with the eye of a theatre director. Laura arranges her menagerie with an artist's touch. Val Xavier is a musician, Chance Wayne an actor. Sebastian, in *Suddenly Last Summer*, and Nonno, in *The Night of the Iguana*, are both poets. But this sense of failed adjustment is not entirely a pose of romantic alienation nor the imagination simply an agent of the self in retreat from the real. The social and political seldom disappear entirely from Williams's work. As he himself remarked,

> I'm not sure I would want to be well-adjusted to things as they are. I would prefer to be racked by desire for things better than they are, even for things which are unattainable, than to be satisfied with things as they are ... I am not satisfied with the present state of things in this country and I'm afraid of complacency about it.[2]

At the beginning of his career he had insisted that 'My interest in social problems is as great as my interest in the theatre ... I try to write all my plays so that they carry some social message along with the story.' He had favoured the one-act form because he 'found it easier to get across a message and with more impact if I made it brief'.[3] Later in his career, and sometimes to the surprise of critics, he was prone to draw political significance from plays which seemed precisely to evade the political. So, while insisting that he had thought *Camino Real* 'a sort of fairy tale or masque' set originally in Mexico and containing elements of Fez, Tangiers and Casablanca, he felt constrained to add that 'Each time I return here [the United States] I sense a further reduction in human liberties, which I guess is reflected in the revisions of the play.'[4] And it is worth recalling that the play was indeed a product of the same year as *The Crucible*. The crushing of the wayward spirit, the artist, the man whose sympathies extend to the dispossessed, the poor, those not dedicated to a material world of acquisition and conformity, had its correlative in an American society wilfully submitting to the corrupt power of Senator Joseph McCarthy.

Williams was aware of his tendency to 'poetize', explaining that that was why he had created so many southern heroines: 'They have a tendency to gild the lily and they speak in a rather florid style which seems to suit no one because I write out of emotion.'[5] Such language, however, is less poetic than effusive. It is a style of speech designed to draw attention to itself, to distort, to deceive. Detached from the reality of experience, it is a mask which conceals a truth which the characters cannot articulate. It is that, doubtless, that contradiction, that irony which is heightened by theatre in which appearance and reality co-exist in the same instant, in which language and action are in conflict and words are placed under a tension which may be felt rather than heard.

His observation that 'poetry doesn't have to be words ... In the theatre it can be situations, it can be silences',[6] is a critical one and in part explains why he was drawn to the theatre. His sets have a metaphoric force, sometimes too literally so. His characters expose their lives through the smallest gesture. Blanche and Stanley, personally confronting one another across a space charged with sexual energy, generate a meaning which does not lie in their words. There is a rhythm to their relationship which creates its own inevitability, its own crescendos and diminuendos.

Williams has said that:

> everything is in flux, everything is in a process of creation. The world is incomplete, it's like an unfinished poem. Maybe the poem will turn into a limerick and maybe it will turn into an epic poem. But it's for all of us to try to complete this poem and the way to complete it is through understanding and patience and tolerance among ourselves.[7]

This sense of incompletion applies equally to his characters who resist being too fully known. As he has suggested, 'Some mystery should be left in the revelations of character in a play, just as a great deal of mystery is always left in the revelation of character in life, even in one's own character to himself.' To define too closely is to accept 'facile definitions which make a play just a play, not a snare for the truth of human experience'.[8] That incompletion is vital to his work. At its best it moves him away from metaphor and towards the symbolic whose essence lies in its inexhaustible significations. And the truth of human experience he sets himself to capture? That has to do with a particular kind of desperate dignity in defeat. His subject, he has said, is human valour and endurance, even arguing that Amanda's courage constitutes the core of *The Glass Menagerie*: 'She's confused, pathetic, even stupid, but everything has got to be all right. She fights to make it that way in the only way she knows how.'[9]

Williams was never interested in realism. Like O'Neill before him he was hostile to an art of surfaces. So he set his face against 'the straight realist play with its genuine frigidaire and authentic ice cubes, its characters that speak exactly as the audience speaks'. This has 'the same virtue of a photographic likeness' and 'Everyone should know nowadays the unimportance of the photographic in art.'[10] There are no sets in a Williams play which merely provide the context for action. They are, without exception, charged with a symbolic function, from the enclosing space of *The Glass Menagerie* and *Streetcar* through to the primal garden of *Suddenly Last Summer*, the collapsing house of *The Kingdom of Earth*, the urban wasteland of *The Red Devil Battery Sign* and the empty theatre of *Outcry*. There is no prop that does not function in terms of character and theme, whether it be a glass animal, a covering over a lamp, an anatomical chart, a liquor glass or a hammock. Williams himself cited the dropping out of the window, by the hotel proprietor, of Casanova's shabby portmanteau of fragile memories in *Camino Real*. This, he suggested, was 'a clearer expression of an idea than you might be able to do with a thousand words'.[11] He might equally have invoked the phonograph-cum-liquor-cabinet in *Cat on a Hot Tin Roof* or the urn of ashes in *The Rose Tattoo*. The fact is that if there was more than a touch of the poet in Tennessee Williams, there was also something of the artist. Certainly he had a strong visual imagination which translated poetic images into practical correlatives in terms of staging.

At the beginning of his career Tennessee Williams saw himself as a radical, creating a series of protest plays for a political theatre group in St. Louis. It was a radicalism that at first was precisely directed. The villains were industrialists, war profiteers, prison officials, those who presided over public squalor. Behind these lay a political and economic system that encouraged corruption and broke the individual on the rack of private profit. Such power as the plays had was generated less by their dramatic force than by the melodrama of daily life which appeared to validate such a Manichaean vision. Despite these origins and a persistent regard for those who lived lives at a tangent to capitalist enterprise, audiences and critics preferred to respond to him as southern gothicist or the mordant poet of dissolution and despair, as an aesthetic bohemian offering a vicarious sexuality. He was certainly all of those things and his vote for the socialist candidate for the presidency (the only vote he ever cast) should not deceive us into the belief that his was an ideological drama, any more than should his appearance on a public platform, thirty years later, to protest the Vietnam war. His radicalism was neither Marxist nor liberal. In a way, indeed, it was profoundly conservative. What he wanted above all was for the individual to be left alone, insulated from the pressure of public event. But he never forgot the cruelties which he dramatised in those early days, cruelties which left the individual a victim of a system resistant to human needs.

It is tempting to suppose that his response to the repressiveness of the public world, his patent alienation, perhaps stemmed from another source. As Arthur Miller suggested,

> If only because he came up at a time when homosexuality was absolutely unacknowledged in a public figure, Williams had to belong to a minority culture and understood in his bones what a brutal menace the majority could be if aroused against him ... Certainly I never regarded him as the sealed-off aesthete he was thought to be. There is a radical politics of the soul as well as of the ballot box and the picket line. If he was not an activist, it was not for lack of a desire for justice, nor did he consider a theatre profoundly involved in society and politics ... somehow unaesthetic or beyond his interest.[12]

But even if his radicalism is better viewed as a celebration of the outcast or the deprived, a sympathy for those discarded by a society for which he anyway had little sympathy, his work reveals a consistent distrust of the wealthy and the powerful, a suspicion of materialism. Although, in stark contrast to Faulkner, scarcely a black face is to be seen in Williams's South, in *Orpheus Descending* and *Sweet Bird of Youth* he made clear his contempt for the racist, his association of bigotry with sterility and death. If, after the 1930s, Williams rarely chose to formulate his sense of oppression in overtly political ways, his portraits of individuals pressed to the margins of social concern, trapped in a diminishing social and psychological spark, are not without ideological significance, for, as Michel Foucault has reminded us, there is a link between space and power.

Many of his early plays—the largely unknown plays of the 1930s tend to be set in claustrophobic and constrictive spaces (a prison in *Not About Nightingales*, the lobby of a flophouse in *Fugitive Kind*, a coal mine and its surroundings in *Candles to the Sun*, a tenement building in *Stairway to the Sky*). In *Fugitive Kind* the city itself becomes both naturalistic trope and coercive presence ('a great implacable force, pressing in upon the shabby room and crowding its fugitive inhabitants back against their last wall').[13] Already, though, he was bending naturalism in the direction of symbolism and there were to be few of his characters who would not find themselves similarly trapped in the suffocating constraints of a small back room, in an asylum, real or metaphorical, or, as one of his characters remarks, inside their own skins, for life. Shannon, the defrocked priest, tied in his hammock in *The Night of the Iguana*, can stand as an image of many of Williams's protagonists.

It would be a mistake, therefore, to regard Williams's radicalism as not only a product of but also contained by the 1930s. His insistence that art is a 'criticism of things as they exist',[14] should be taken entirely seriously. Indeed there is a surprising consistency in the comments that he made about his society from the beginning of his career to its end. In 1945 he commented on the weight of reactionary opinion that descended 'on the head of any artist who speaks out against the current of prescribed ideas', likening investigating committees to Buchenwald. Two years later he insisted that it was no longer safe to enunciate American revolutionary ideals. In 1950 he objected that 'Our contemporary American society seems no longer inclined to hold itself open to very explicit criticism from within.' Faced with the 'all but complete suppression of any dissident voices' the artist was forced to withdraw into 'his own isolated being'.[15] Seven years later (and a year after writing to the State Department to protest the withdrawing of Arthur Miller's passport) he attacked the simplistic dualism of cold war politics, insisting that 'no man has a monopoly of right or virtue any more than a man has a corner on duplicity and evil and so forth',[16] suggesting that failure to acknowledge this fact had bred 'the sort of corruption' which he had 'involuntarily chosen as the basic, allegorical theme' of his plays.

In 1975, speaking in the context of his apocalyptic *The Red Devil Battery Sign*, he placed the moment of corruption in the 1950s: 'The moral decay of America', he insisted, 'really began with the Korean War, way before the Kennedy assassination.' Vietnam, which he described as an 'incomprehensible evil' merely proved that 'this once great and beautiful democracy' had become 'the death merchant of the world'.[17]

By 1978 he had backdated the corruption, seeing Hiroshima and Nagasaki as marking the effective end of civilisation, and while suggesting that 'No rational, grown up artist deludes himself with the notion that his inherent, instinctive rejection of the ideologies of failed governments, or power-combines that mask themselves as governments, will in the least divert these monoliths from a fixed course toward the slag-heap remnants of once towering cities', still insisted that 'there must be somewhere truth to be pursued each day with words that are misunderstood and feared because they are the words of an Artist, which must always remain a word most compatible with the word Revolutionary'.[18] Thus it was that he later insisted that the title of his play *A House Not Meant to Stand* was 'a metaphor for our society in our times' and denounced the 'Me Generation' for its apathy with respect to American involvement in El Salvador and Guatemala and the 'plutocracy' whose power was reinforced under President Nixon. So it is that he asserted, with some justification, that all of his plays 'have a social conscience'. So they do. But the very implacability of history as he presents it suggests the extent to which the artist becomes less a social rebel than a Quixote transforming the real at the level of the imagination. Instead of corruption being a product of recent history it becomes the given against which the artist must rebel. Thus it is that the decay of American idealism is seen as beginning when 'it ceased to be able to exist within its frontiers'.[19] And that, of course, pushed the date back beyond the twentieth century, beyond his own appearance. America's fallen state thus becomes the implacable fact against which the artist must protest and rebel.

Tennessee Williams's plays are not naturalistic. The determinisms which his characters resist are not primarily the produce of physical environment or heredity. They are built into the structure of existence. When, in the 1970s, he wrote *Gnädiges Fräulein* it seemed a belated gesture in the direction of European absurdism. In fact, the absurd was deeply rooted in his sensibility. The irony which governs the lives of his protagonists, whose needs are so patently at odds with their situation, is less a social fact than a metaphysical reality. His characters, too, give birth astride the grave and try to make sense of their abandonment (*Camino Real*, perhaps his most obviously absurdist work, was actually produced in the same year that Beckett's *Waiting for Godot* opened in Paris). But Williams, unlike Beckett, is enough of a romantic to feel heat even in the cold flame of such ironies. Beckett's figures are the uncomprehending products of their situation, drained of substance, alienated even from the language they speak. Williams's characters resist with the only weapons they possess—their imaginations and, on occasion, a vivifying sexuality which sometimes transcends the irony in which it is rooted—the illusion of connectiveness dissolving even as it is proposed, time asserting its hegemony even as it is denied. His is the romantic's sense of doom. That was why he was drawn to F. Scott Fitzgerald, to Hart Crane and to Byron. Jay Gatsby and Dick Diver both tried to remake the world in their own image; both were destroyed by the hard-edged realities of American power, as they were, more profoundly, by the ultimate futility of their attempts to resist natural process and the pull of time. Much the same could be said of Blanche in *A Streetcar Named Desire*, of Laura in *The Glass Menagerie*, of Alma in *Summer and Smoke*, or of Shannon in *The Night of the Iguana*.

Theatrically, he set himself to dissolve the surface of a naturalism whose propositions he denied. What he was after, he insisted, was a plastic theatre, fluid, evanescent, undefined and undefining. His was to be an attempt to find in the style of his theatre an equivalent to that resistance to the given which characterised his protagonists. Thus the set of *The Glass Menagerie*, his first Broadway success which premiered in 1945, was to indicate those 'vast hive-like conglomerations of cellular living units that flower as warty growths in overcrowded urban centres' and which deny a 'fundamentally enslaved section of American society ... fluidity and differentiation'.[20] That set was not created to suggest a social reality that could be modified by political action or radical reform. It was the context for a play having to do with the desperate strategies developed by those whose options have run out. Tom, a writer, returns in memory to a family he had deserted in order to claim his freedom to write. The family consists of his mother, Amanda—voluble, neurotic, surviving on memories and will—and his sister, Laura, whose crippled foot is an image of a damaged spirit in recoil from the real. Tom, as narrator, stands outside this world, literally and figuratively. He is the one who has found an avenue of escape through his art. By summoning the scene into existence he asserts his power over it. And yet what he has achieved is what Jerry, in Edward Albee's *The Zoo Story*, was to call 'solitary free passage'. Indeed, the very fact of his summoning this world into existence demonstrates its continued power over him and the guilt which was later to send Blanche Dubois to her appointment in another tenement in New Orleans. Such solitude, though, is perhaps the price to be paid by the artist, and *The Glass Menagerie*, like others of his plays, is in part a contemplation of the role of the artist. In this case it is a very personal account of his relationship with his own family. Not for nothing is the narrator given the author's own name. Like his character, Williams was all too aware that he had claimed his own freedom at the expense of his mother and sister, Rose, the lobotomy which destroyed her life being performed while he was away at university beginning his career as writer. Even in the context of the play Tom's escape seems too much like his father's desertion of the family to seem like anything but abandonment. As he was to show in *Suddenly Last Summer*, Williams was acutely aware of the degree to which art could be said to serve the self, the extent to which the artist moved himself outside the normal processes of social life.

Williams came to distrust the framing device of the narrator in *The*

Glass Menagerie but it is that which, by introducing another time scale, creates the ironies on which the play depends. It is, indeed, a play in which time becomes a central concern. So, Amanda's present, in which she exists on the margins of society, surviving by pandering to those whose support she needs, is contrasted to a past in which, at least on the level of memory and imagination, she was at the centre of attention. Laura's wilful withdrawal into the child-like world of her menagerie derives its sad irony precisely from the fact that it is a denial of her own maturity, of time. Even her 'gentleman caller' is momentarily forced to confront the discrepancy between the promise of his high school years (recalled by the photograph in a school yearbook) and the reality of his present life. Time has already begun to break these people as their fantasies and dreams are denied by the prosaic facts of economic necessity and natural process alike. Laura seeks immunity by withdrawing into the timeless world of the imagined, Amanda by retreating into a past refashioned to offer consolation. Tom alone seems to have escaped these ironies, at the price of abandoning those whose lives he had shared. But the play itself is the evidence that he has no more escaped that past than have his family. For why else does he summon this world into existence but for the fact that the past continues to exert its power, as the guilt engendered by his abandonment pulls him back to those whose sacrifice he had believed to be the necessary price of his freedom. The play, in other words, is purely reflexive as Williams creates a play about a writer, named after himself, who dramatises his own life in order to exorcise the guilt which is the price he has paid for his freedom.

The metatheatrical element in Williams's work is central. The theatre was not only Williams's avocation, it was his fundamental metaphor. His characters tend to be writers and actors, literal or symbolic, who theatricalise their world in order to be able to survive in it. The theatre is their protection as it was Williams's. What it chiefly protects them from is time:

> It is this continual rush of time ... that deprives our actual lives of so much dignity and meaning, and it is, perhaps more than anything else, the *arrest of time* which has taken place in a completed work of art that gives to certain plays their feeling of depth and significance ... In a play, time is arrested in the sense of being, confined ... The audience can sit back in a comforting dusk to watch a world which is flooded with light and in which emotion and action have a dimension and dignity that they would likewise have in real existence, if only the shattering intrusion of time could be locked out. The great and only possible dignity of

man lies in his power deliberately to choose certain moral values by which to live as steadfastly as if he, too, like a character in a play, were immured against the corrupting rush of time.[21]

Williams's characters inhabit a linguistic universe which privileges the prosaic, the literal, the unambiguous; but they themselves speak another language. They claim the right to detach words from their literal meanings. They deal in ambivalence, the poetic, the allusive, the metaphorical. If at times they spill words recklessly, as Blanche does, in *Streetcar*, this is liable to be a defence against the real. More often they prefer silence, like Val in *Orpheus Descending*, Brick in *Cat on a Hot Tin Roof*, Shannon in *The Night of the Iguana* and Chris in *The Milk Train Doesn't Stop Here Any More*.

In *The Glass Menagerie* Williams is careful to distinguish between the constant flow of chatter from Amanda, a neurotic flood of language with which she seeks to still her fears, and the reticence and finally the silence of her daughter. In some ways speech is suspect. The gentleman caller, who disappoints Laura's hope of another life, is learning the art of public speaking, hoping that this will open up a clear path to power. He believes that language will give him control over a life that otherwise seems to be slipping away from him. There is little to suggest that it will. The only true moment of contact comes at the end of the play when the final scene between mother and daughter is played out as 'through soundproof glass'. Her speech stilled, Amanda suddenly has a 'dignity and tragic beauty'. Her daughter smiles a reply, her stuttering uncertainties calmed. Only the narrator, the poet (in elect the playwright) who summons up this scene, retains access to words, all too aware of their falsity and cruelty. Perhaps that is one reason why the dramatic symbol acquires the significance it does in his work.

For most of his life Tennessee Williams chose to dramatise himself as alienated romantic. A homosexual, at a time when this was illegal and in some states attracted severe penalties, he felt threatened and marginalised. A writer, in a culture which valued art merely as material product, he regarded himself as the victim of other people's ambition. His characters find themselves pressed to the very edge of the social world, face to face with their own desperation and with no resources beyond their powers of self-invention. In a world 'sick with neon', whose basis is identified by the young gentleman caller in *The Glass Menagerie* as 'Knowledge! ... Money! ... Power!', they struggle to survive.

Williams pictures a society on the turn. Not for nothing was Chekhov his favourite playwright. The southern setting of most of his plays suggests a culture whose past is no longer recoverable, except as myth, and whose future represents the threat of dissolution. Language has been evacuated of meaning, ironised by time. History has swept on by. Private illusions and public values are shattered by the quickening pace of a modernity that implies the corruption alike of style and morality. Art alone, it seems, has the power to halt, however momentarily, the rush towards extinction. And for Williams, writing was, indeed, a way of freezing time, of abstracting himself from process. It was a defence equally deployed by his characters who are all compulsive fictionalisers. Having run out of time and space they seek to shore up their lives with fragments of the past, invented or recalled, and elaborate fictions which confer on them a significance they could otherwise never aspire to.

The problem is that unless they can persuade others to join them in their illusions they are thereby condemning themselves to isolation. Safety seems to lie in flight. To rest for a moment is to risk definition, to risk being fully known, to become vulnerable. And yet flight is solitary and as such denies the only other consolation offered to his characters, love; but such relationships carry with them the potential for further pain, as virtually all of his figures discover.

For the most part his characters are without jobs or have simply fled them. Laura, in *The Glass Menagerie*, runs away from her secretarial course, Blanche, in *Streetcar*, is dismissed from her post as teacher, as Shannon, in *The Night of the Iguana*, is from his role first as a priest and then as tour guide. These are not people who work to play their part in the great commercial enterprise of America. They are not mesmerised, as is Miller's Willy Loman, by its dreams of wealth and success, though Maggie in *Cat on a Hot Tin Roof* and Brick in *Sweet Bird of Youth* feel its pull. They are damaged, emotionally, sexually. They are hyper-sensitive to their surroundings. They frequently tread the boundary of insanity, driven towards this territory partly by the callousness of others (as in *Streetcar*, *Suddenly Last Summer*, *The Night of the Iguana*) and partly by their own preference for the fictive, the imaginary, the unreal.

Tennessee Williams's characters resist being incorporated into other people's plots. They distrust alike the causal implications and the temporal logic of narratives which can have only one conclusion for them. They reject the characters offered to them—Blanche, the tramp, Val Xavier, the bum, Brick, the homosexual—and seek to neutralise the plots that threaten to encase them by elaborating their own. Theatrically, his plays reflect this process. Sets dissolve, time is made to reverse itself, lighting softens the hard edges of naturalism. The transforming imaginations of his characters find a correlative in a theatrical style which makes its own assertions about the relative values of the real and the fictive. Sometimes the imagination can be bizarrely destructive—as in *Suddenly Last Summer*—more often it is offered as a transfiguring grace to those discarded by the plot of history and displaced from a narrative of national aggrandisement but still subject to its destructive drive. The structure of his plays reflects this resistance to a national plot which now included investigating committees and a distrust of the deviant. As he asked, somewhat plaintively, 'What choices has the artist, now, but withdrawal into the caverns of isolation?'[22]

Williams's plays are in effect elaborations of the metaphors they enclose: the glass menagerie, the anatomical chart (*Summer and Smoke*), the dried-up fountain (*Camino Real*), the burning rose garden (*Orpheus Descending*), the exotic garden and cannibalism of *Suddenly Last Summer*, the bound priest of *The Night of the Iguana*, the wasteland of *The Red Devil Battery Sign*, the house built over a cavern in *The Rose Tattoo*, or over a flooding river in *Kingdom of Earth*. In a note written in 1943 he had warned himself against an over-reliance on dialogue and committed himself to thinking in more directly visual terms, developing each play through a series of pictures. The note related to a forerunner of *A Streetcar Named Desire* but the commitment to images which crystalised the dramatic essence of a play remained, sometimes debased into crude and obvious metaphors, sometimes elevated into symbols which extended the thematic core of his plays.

The success of his first Broadway play, *The Glass Menagerie*, was considerable. It ran for 561 performances, but the new young playwright was in fact thirty-four years old and very conscious of the pressure of time. As he was later to imply, loss became a central theme. It was certainly a concern of the protagonist of his second great success, *A Streetcar Named Desire*. With an epigraph from Hart Crane which identified the fragility of love, it placed at its centre a woman herself acutely aware of loss and the passage of time, a woman, it seems, in her early thirties. Certainly she spends much of her time trying to conceal what she assumes to be the depredations of time and experience. She (and the world from which she comes) has lost something of her natural grace; her original vivacity has given way to artifice. Her marriage to a homosexual husband had in effect been a logical extension of her desire to aestheticise experience, her preference for style over function. Her entirely natural but cruel exposure of him, besides being the origin of a sense of guilt to be expiated by her own sexual immolation, is itself evidence of that neurotic recoil from the real which is the essence of her life. Indeed, in some sense her choice of this fey young man and of the adolescents with whom she subsequently conducts her empty relationships represents her desire to resist the implications of maturity. She does not want to be part of a world in which actions have consequences and in which the logic of relationship (in her sister Stella's case, courtship, marriage, pregnancy) pulls her into the narrative of history. She wishes to freeze time. It is not hard to see how her life mirrors that of the South, whose myths she in part embraces.

Desire may, as she believes, neutralise death but desire allowed to follow its course leads to death. Blanche needs the sanctuary implied by a relationship but she fears the trap which it represents. Perhaps that is why she is now drawn to another man whose sexuality seems in some way suspect, a mother's boy weak enough, she supposes, to be made to enact the essentially adolescent fantasies which she stage-manages with such care. Meanwhile, the relationship between her sister Stella and her Promethean husband, Stanley, must be destroyed not simply because he threatens to eject her from her last refuge (this he only does when she reveals herself as a threat) but because then the clock will be turned back. The two sisters will become as once they were, inhabiting a world that yields nothing to time, in which, like the South itself, the intrusion of the real can be denied. For the South is no less a conscious fiction, a deliberate construct, than is the life which Blanche attempts to play with true conviction. Blanche's life and the South alike become art objects, admirable for their style, compelling in their artifice but surviving only because they are no longer animate. Blanche enters the play, an actress creating her entrance. Her 'character' consists of a series of performed roles, constructions. 'You should have seen Blanche when she was young', says Stella. She is young no longer. Whatever was natural, whatever was spontaneous, whatever was true seems to have given way to performance. To be is to act; to act is to be. But her audience withdraws its belief—first Stanley, then Mitch, then Stella—and she is left, finally, an actress alone, her performance drained of meaning, inhabiting a world which is now unreal because unsanctioned.

At the other extreme, it seems, stands Stella, pregnant with life, generous in her affections and ready to acknowledge a natural process which pulls her even further from her origins and, by implication, ever closer to her cud. Yet she, too, is forced to a refusal of the real at the end of the play, to a denial of the brute destructiveness of Stanley, a man who represents the forces which have thrust aside the myths of the past. Indeed that denial becomes as essential to her continued survival as Blanche's had to her. As the play's first director, Elia Kazan, recognised, she is doomed, too. Even Stanley now has to live a life hollowed out, attacked at its core.

When Blanche Dubois faces Stanley Kowalski, class and gender are in ambiguous confrontation. For Blanche is powerfully attracted by the social crudity and masculine directness which she simultaneously despises, as

Stanley is fascinated by those very qualities of aristocratic arrogance and neurotic sexuality which he affects to hold in contempt. With echoes of Strindberg's *Miss Julie*, a play Williams had admired as a student, *Streetcar* explores the energy created across the gender and class divide. Like Chekhov's *The Cherry Orchard*, which he similarly admired, it focuses on a culture on the turn, an old world, elegant but reflexive, inward turned and inward turning, in process of surrendering to a new order, lacking the civility of a passing world but lacking, too, its neurotic, enervated products. There is an ambivalence, a doubleness which here, and throughout his career, takes him to the edge of androgyny. It is not merely that male and female are locked in a relationship that breeds cruelty and consolation, meaning and absurdity, in equal parts but that each represents part of a divided sensibility. Though in interview he was prone to celebrate Blanche for her courage in the face of the implacable, her own destructiveness makes her a deeply suspect source of values.

The androgynous had a powerful appeal to Williams. As he remarked, 'the androgynous is a myth ... an ideal. You can seek it but never find it. However, the androgynous is the truest human being.'[23] Its power lies in its denial of definition, its functional ambivalence, its fusion of opposites, its transcendence of barriers. It was partly what drew him to Hart Crane. Gilbert Debusscher has commented on Williams's gloss on Crane's lines (from 'For the Marriage of Faustus and Helen'): 'There is the world dimensional for those untwisted by the love of things irreconcilable.' Acknowledging that it is open to multiple readings, Debusscher asks, 'Could he have meant that his vocation as a poet of extraordinary purity, as well as intensity, was hopelessly at odds with his nighttime search for love in waterfront bars',[24] a contradiction which precisely mirrored Williams's own. The yoking of a gentle, lyrical self to predatory sexual aggression was one he experienced as well as dramatised. His homosexuality, like Crane's, came to stand for him as an image of a revelationary contradiction. When Jessica Tandy, the original Blanche Dubois, objected to the use, for advertising purposes, of Thomas Hart Benton's oil painting of the poker night scene (the cast were to be posed in the same positions as those in the painting, for a *Look Magazine* photograph), a work that stressed the sexuality of Blanche and Stanley, Williams replied:

> I have such a divided nature! Irreconcilably divided. I look at Benton's picture and I see the strong things in it, its immediate appeal to the senses, raw, sensual, dynamic, and I forget the play was really about those things that are opposed to that, the delicate

half-approaches to something much finer. Yes, the painting is only one side of the play, and the Stanley side of it. Perhaps from the painter's point of view that was inevitable. A canvas cannot depict two worlds very easily, or the tragic division of the human spirit, at least not a painter of Benton's realistic type.[25]

But that division equally affects the individual characters. So it was that Kazan said of Brando, 'he is bisexual in the way an artist should be: he sees things both as a man and a woman'. It was that, too, that the critic Eric Bentley detected in his performance: 'Brando has muscular arms, but his eyes give them the lie ... a rather feminine actor overinterpreting a masculine role.'[26] Later in his career Williams was to express satisfaction with the title of his play, *Something Cloudy, Something Clear*, precisely because it expressed 'the two sides of my nature. The side that was obsessively homosexual, compulsively interested in sexuality, and the side that in those days was gentle and understanding and contemplative.'[27]

Blanche may be the representative of a world of elegance and style corrupted by brute materialism but she is also the source of a cruelty which associates her most clearly with the death she seeks to neutralise through desire. Stanley may set his strength against Blanche's desperation but he has what Blanche does not, the ability to survive and dominate. Nor is he without tenderness, as Blanche is capable of a cold callousness. She is history as artifact; he is history as dynamic force.

In *Lady Chatterley's Lover* (originally entitled *Tenderness*) D.H. Lawrence distinguishes between a soulless sexuality, obsessive and self-destructive, and a sexuality which vivifies and regenerates the self through its surrender. Connie Chatterley knows both kinds. In *Streetcar*, Blanche and Stella represent those two opposing interpretations, two poles of experience. But such contradictions are, to Williams, the essence of human existence. As he explained, 'We love and betray each other in not quite the same breath but in two breaths that occur in fairly close sequence.'[28]

Williams's comment about the realism of Thomas Hart Benton, and still more his sense of the inadequacy of the two-dimensional nature of art, is a revealing one. It stands as an implicit claim for the potential of the theatre and for his belief in a drama that pressed beyond realism. *Streetcar* seems to replicate the world of 1920s and 1930s realism. The set appears to make a social statement, as the characters are hemmed in by surrounding tenements, while in the background we glimpse the flow of social life (emphasised still more in the London production). But Williams was not writing *Street Scene* or *Dead End*. His aim was to create a lyric theatre, a poetic theatre in which, as with a poetic image, opposites could be yoked together.

The virtue of the South, for Williams, as also the source of its particular pathos, lay in the fact that it had jumped the rails of history. Its psychological investment was in the past. As the twentieth century rushed away from it, the South became an aesthetic rather than a social fact. This had certain advantages. Taste and style could be retained as primary virtues; the vertiginous dangers that accompany maturity denied as time is frozen and reality transposed into myth. So it is that Faulkner's Quentin, in *The Sound and the Fury*, smashes his watch and seeks to isolate his sister and himself in such a way as to deny her organic need for change. But there is a price to be paid for such a refusal of life. Stasis slides into decay. Time, it appears, can only be denied at the level of the imagination, only sustained by a violence of thought or action rooted in a fear of natural process. So it is that Tennessee Williams's characters are in part the victims of modernity— inviting our sympathy and concern—and in part the enemies of all that is vital and unpredictable. Terrified of death, they become its collaborators imagining, as they do, that the world can be made to align itself to their demands for perfect order. The southern racist insists that the world conform to his will, accommodate itself to a model whose authority lies in its history; Blanche Dubois insists that it respond to her need for a life carefully shaped into art.

The gothic tinge to a number of his plays is an expression of this violence that seeps out of the culture like the juice from a windfall apple. This is a society which has lost its connection with the living tree. Its dissolution is only a matter of time. Blanche, in *Streetcar*, and Laura, in *The Glass Menagerie*, are perfect images of the world that they in part represent. Trapped in psychosis or stranded in an imagined world, they win immunity from time only by stepping into an existence where there is no love as there is no ageing. As Williams remarked, after writing these two plays, 'It appears to me, sometimes, that there are only two kinds of people who live outside what E E Cummings has defined as this "so-called world of ours"—the artist and the insane.'[29] In Williams's world the two are not always separable. They both exist within the shadow of artifice.

What Richard Gray says of Faulkner's language could be said with equal force of Tennessee Williams's. It 'never ceases calling attention to its artificiality. His prose is insistently figurative, intricately playful, as if he were trying to remind us all the time that what he is presenting us with is, finally, a verbal construct.'[30] Language is, indeed, the central device with which his characters seek to shape their worlds. Blanche's mannered prose, her self-conscious archaisms, her strained lyricism is at the heart of her attempt to generate a space which she can inhabit without fear. Like Williams himself she uses language to pull her out of the prosaic, the direct, the implacable. Her allusiveness, her irony, her playful use of French to a man who understands nothing but his own baffled need is an expression of her desire to evade too precise a definition. What she seeks to accomplish in covering the lamp light for fear that it will reveal the truth of her fast-fading youth, she also tries to achieve linguistically. She recasts experience through the words with which she chooses to engage it. She spins images and fantasies linguistically, hoping that these filaments will harden into a cocoon. Inside: the butterfly. Outside: threat. The long series of disasters she has suffered can be denied so long as they have not found their way into her language.

There is no denying Faulkner's love affair with words. His sentences perform arabesques, words tumble out, pile up and finally exhaust themselves in the telling. Working with drama Williams is more constrained. Only his characters can speak and their language is contained and shaped by individual experience. But even so it is those who radically recast language, force it to bear the imprint of their own needs and fantasies, who most clearly carry his sympathy. The poet, not the salesman; the bohemian, not the businessman; the actor, not the politician.

Stanley Kowalski has no past. He comes into existence ready-made and fully known. Directness is his keynote and his virtue. Blanche is quite other. She is the end result of process. She resists the given and denies all definition. An observation from Faulkner's *Requiem far a Nun* applies with equal force to her: 'The past is never dead. It's not even past.' So, the music playing when she forced her young husband to confront his suspect sexuality still plays in her ears as the family history of debauchery seems to be enacted in her own life.

Blanche is deeply narcissistic in a narcissistic culture. She transforms her life into myth, demanding acquiescence in her own mythic inventions. The South itself scarcely does less. Her affairs with young boys and a homosexual husband leave her if not inviolate at least untroubled by consequences. Sex is emptied of its provocative implications. It becomes reflexive.

The myth encloses Blanche. Stella could purge whatever inheritance of guilt she might have received. Blanche cannot. Denying herself or being denied the vivifying effect of marriage to the future, she is trapped in the past. The barren woman condemned to an asylum becomes a perfect image of the South. Why does she seek to transform experience with myth? Because she thereby removes its sting—the sting of death. As Frank

Kermode observed, discussing Eliade's theory of myth: 'Myths take place in a quite different order of time—in *illo tempore* ... Then occurred the events decisive as to the way things are; and the only way to get at *illud tempus* is by ritual re-enactment. But here and now, in *hoc tempore*, we are certain only of the dismal linearity of time.'[31]

Williams has said that:

> I write out of love for the South ... But I can't expect Southerners to realize that my writing about them is an expression of love. It is out of regret for a South that no longer exists that I write of the forces that have destroyed it ... the South had a way of life that I am just old enough to remember—a culture that had grace, elegance ... an inbred culture ... not a society based on money, as in the North. I write out of regret for that ... I write about the South because I think the war between romanticism and the hostility to it is very sharp there.[32]

Inadvertently, in the original production the play became more of a clash between North and South than Williams had intended. In his notebook for the production, Elia Kazan saw Stanley as representing 'the crude forces of violence, insensibility and vulgarity which exist in our South',[33] but because Marlon Brando's accent was incorrigibly northern it became necessary to adjust the slant of the play and even individual lines to make it clear that Stanley came from outside the South. In essence, though, what matters is less his origin than his force as a cold, pragmatic and powerful, if spiritually maimed, future.

The shock of *Streetcar* when it was first staged lay in the fact that, outside of O'Neill's work, this was the first American play in which sexuality was patently at the core of the lives of all its principal characters, a sexuality with the power to redeem or destroy, to compound or negate the forces which bore on those caught in a moment of social change. Familiar enough from *Lady Chatterley's Lover*, then still a banned book and indeed clearly a none too distant inspiration for Williams, it brought a dangerous *frisson* to the public stage. It was, of course, in his sexuality that Williams was most directly menaced by the public world. It is scarcely surprising, therefore, that, besides his faith in a Lawrentian revolutionising of a decadent culture, he should choose to make this the arena in which his plays had their being. With surprising consistency Miller associated sexuality with betrayal and guilt. For Tennessee Williams it was otherwise: betrayal and redemption, torment and consolation. It provided the grammar of his drama.

These ironies intensified in his next play, *Summer and Smoke* (1948), though now they were spelled out with a clarity which obscured their real force. The tension in his work between the physical and the spiritual, in *Streetcar* and elsewhere contained within the sensibility of individual characters, is here flung off in pure form. The gap between the two parts of a riven sensibility is now crudely externalised and the ironic commentary which each constitutes of the other emphasised by a reversal too mechanical to be taken seriously. Although written at the same time as *Streetcar* (opening at Margo Jones's Dallas Theatre in the same year), it lacks its subtlety. There is an echo of Lawrence's image of the mind redeemed by the body but there is too much of the autodidact and the pedagogue to make it theatrically compelling.

John Buchanan is Stanley Kowalski with intellect, a Lawrentian Promethean 'brilliantly and restlessly alive in a stagnant society'. A doctor, he understands the physical basis of experience but is aware, too, of a sense of incompletion, being drawn to Alma Winemiller, whose first name, we are pointedly reminded, is Spanish for soul. She has a distaste for sexuality, which she keeps at a distance by an obscuring language no less than by her evasion of the relationship which might release her from her isolation. In the course of the play she seems to undergo a moral education, realising that the spiritual focus of her life has denied her the vivifying consolation of human relationships. What she fails to understand, however, is the need for a self in which the physical and spiritual combine. As a result the pendulum swings too far and she shows signs of embracing that empty sexuality which had characterised Blanche Dubois's relationship with strangers and the brittle relationship in which Lawrence's Connie Chatterley had engaged before the fulfilment offered by Mellors, a man and a force associated with the natural world. Meanwhile, Buchanan has moved the other way, embracing precisely that arid spirituality which he had once urged Alma to abandon. This simplistic irony is typical of a play in which character is subordinated to symbolic function and the stage is divided into discrete areas representing body, soul and eternity and dominated by a stone angel and an anatomical chart—a naive symbolism which offers a redundant correlative to the play's thematic concerns.

The essence of Laura and Blanche was that they had been simultaneously drawn in two different directions—out into the public world of relationship, of time, of process, and back into a private world where time is suspended and the self must substitute its own imaginings for the causalities and pain of an engagement with the other. In *Summer and Smoke*, *The Rose Tattoo* and *Camino Real* (1953), such tension is relaxed and externalised and as a result immobilised into pure image, *The Rose Tattoo* (1950), in particular, setting out simply to celebrate the Dionysian. One of his few comedies, it was inspired by his relationship with Frank Merlo, whose later death of cancer was to play its part in precipitating Williams's personal and artistic collapse. As a result it has an element of the carnivalesque, the ludic, the celebratory, as passion becomes an unambiguous value. Its energy, though, is too easily dissipated as character is pressed in the direction of comic grotesque.

The central character in *The Rose Tattoo* is a kind of Stanley Kowalski, lacking his cunning and presented with a rival more easily challenged and overcome, since all that stands between him and Serafina, the woman he loves, is the memory of her dead husband, a memory kept alive by an urn containing his ashes. The play, in other words, is a celebration of the life principle. But since the resolution is clear from the very beginning—the characters being wholly unambiguous—when it comes it carries little interest or conviction. In a way he was deliberately working against the assumption and the methods of his earlier success. Aware that *The Glass Menagerie*, *A Streetcar Named Desire* and *Summer and Smoke* had all drawn on the same experiences, he was afraid of falling into a predictable pattern. *The Rose Tattoo* and *Camino Real* in particular were his attempts to break this rhythm. But the generosity and openness of the former, in which all ambiguity is resolved in a sexuality and harmony that are untested and unquestioned, carry far less conviction than do the tensions and ironies of plays in which that ambiguity is definitional and, for their characters, in the end, disabling.

Camino Real was a far more radical effort on his part to challenge his own methods and assumptions. Indeed he liked to think that it was an open challenge to the realistic conventions of the American theatre that would liberate that theatre from its conservatism. As a play it owes something to the comic strip. Locating the action in a kind of spacial and temporal void, he fills the stage with characters from other works by other writers—Camille, Casanova, Don Quixote. These are mostly romantics brought face to face with the fact of death as they find themselves abandoned in a dusty town from which there appears to be no escape. Beyond lies only Terra Incognita, while in the town they are constantly menaced by the street cleaners, the agents of death who patrol the streets in search of victims. The central character is also a fiction, though one defined normally by his absence. Kilroy owed his identity to the name scrawled up by soldiers during the Second World War. 'Kilroy Was Here' was a joke difficult to decode. He was in a sense a gesture of resistance, both heroic and anti-heroic at the same time. The essence of Kilroy was that he could never be seen because he was always in the vanguard, always ahead of the game. He could never be caught.

But in *Camino Real*, as in so many other of Williams's plays, the free spirit is caged. Past tense changes to present. Now Kilroy is here. He has waited too long. He is trapped. From ironic hero he has been turned into eternal clown, a naive victim of experience. Denied the assumption that truth lies in movement, which is to say time, he has to plunder the moment for meaning. But he always learns too slowly to save himself from abuse and degradation. Meanwhile the romantic waifs who inhabit this world sustain their hope in the face of evidence of its fatuity, the absurd victims of their own romantic expectations. They are not without their consolation. The virtue of being trapped in the continuous present (which is the condition and precondition of theatre) is the possibility of connection with others who share the same moment, if not the same apprehension of the moment. But the vice of being trapped in that moment is that there can be no change, no growth. Life becomes aestheticised, theatricalised. So they become, like Vladimir and Estragon in *Waiting for Godot*, clown-like performers, absurd products of their own hopes.

Camino Real reveals a baroque impulse on Williams's part to allow his art to overspill its frame. In the 1960s it became commonplace for actors to invade the audience, thereby potentially, if not actually, redefining the nature of the relationship between audience and performer, underlining the degree to which the audience is implicated in the processes of theatre and the gestures and assumptions of performance. Tennessee Williams was doing this in 1953. It was, he insisted, a play in which he laid claim to a freedom which was equally a central object of his characters and an expression of his own need, as he saw it, to break out of a dramatic style and a thematic concern that had brought him such success but which was threatening to suffocate him. So he stepped not just outside the South but into nowhere.

Not only did he lay aside the figure of the fragile southern woman assailed by the real, he laid aside also the concept of character as a stable function of plot or a single governing imagination. And so characters from other plots settle down for a moment in his house of fiction while Kilroy proves no more substantial or resistant than did Nathanael West's Balso Snell. West, however, felt no inclination to celebrate Balso Snell. Kilroy was too close to Williams's own image of himself as a butt of the gods for him not to feel a certain solidarity and compassion (lapsing into sentimentality). After all, this was to be his portrait of a non-conformist in modern society, an assurance of the bohemian's power to resist his degradation. But there was a paradox nestling at the heart of the play as characters seek a freedom denied by their status as objects of the writer's imagination. If some of them successfully escape the texts which entrap them, but which give them their significance, they do not escape the manipulative power of Williams who releases them from one fictional context only to place them in another. That absurdity works to neutralise the liberating power of carnival. Faced with the terror of Terra Incognita and with the ominous threat of the street cleaners (harbingers and celebrants of death), they cling together seeking in relationship that momentary annulment of absurdity that Williams liked to claim he knew so well in his life and purported to recommend in his work. As Marguerite Gautier (Camille) observes, 'although we've wounded each other time and time again—we stretch out hands to each other in the dark that we can't escape from—we huddle together for some dim communal comfort. But this "love" is "unreal bloodless" like a violet growing in a crevice in the mountain "fertilized by the droppings of carrion birds".'[34] Though such self-conscious rhetoric is not free from the romantic posturing for which she is known it seems to have more conviction than Jacques' reply that 'the violets in the mountains can break the rocks if you believe in them and let them grow'.[35] In Blanche's words, 'It's a Barnum and Bailey world.'

Camino Real was not a success. Critics regretted his abandonment of the poetic realism which they saw as his strength and were largely baffled by characters whose two-dimensionality was celebrated. The tightly controlled dramatic structure of the earlier plays here gave way to a series of loosely related scenes, images and gestures. The critical response left Williams embittered. Believing the play to have freed the American theatre of its commitment to realism, he was depressed by the failure of critics and audiences to respond to what he regarded as its openness of form and thought. Indeed so depressed was he by the failure of both this play and *Summer and Smoke* that he felt himself under pressure and reportedly even considered abandoning his career. Instead he completed his most successful work of the 1950s, *Cat on a Hot Tin Roof* (1955), a play which, apart from anything else, came close to moving his own sexual ambivalence to the centre of attention.

Margaret (Maggie the cat) is married to a former football star, Brick Pollitt, the son of Big Daddy. Big Daddy himself is dying of cancer and the future of his huge estate lies between Brick and his other son, Gooper. Though Brick is the favourite he has produced no sons and seems unlikely to do so, since his relationship with his wife has been seemingly destroyed by doubts about his own sexuality. Suspecting the nature of the relationship between her husband and his friend Skipper, Maggie provokes a sexual confrontation with that friend. His failure to perform leads directly to his death as Blanche's similar exposure of her husband's homosexuality had provoked his suicide. The logic of this situation leaves Brick suspended in self-guilt and doubt. Maggie, therefore, sets out to restore their relationship and thereby, as she sees it, secure the property rightly his, but Brick, now intent on blotting out the memory of his pain through alcohol, refuses the physical relationship she offers, unwilling to face his own ambivalence or the person who had forced affairs to a crisis.

On one level *Cat on a Hot Tin Roof* seems to offer a caustic account of a corrupting capitalism as Big Daddy and his wife plunder Europe of cultural artifacts which mean nothing to them and Gooper and his wife lay plans to seize the assets of a dying man. There is an irony, however, which the play scarcely begins to address. For the logic of the play proposes Brick's redemption through heterosexual intercourse, despite the fact that this is deeply implicated in the processes of capitalist succession. But, then, this represents only one of the paradoxes of a play in which a fiercely acquisitive greed is defeated by a yet more tenacious materialism, social deceit is challenged by a convenient lie, and accommodation to coercive social norms is presented as a value. It is a play in which Williams's social instincts are in evidence as he creates a portrait of a society whose corruption is reflected in the cancer eating away at the man who epitomises its pointless acquisitiveness and fierce egotism—Big Daddy. It is a world in which relationships are deeply implicated in the processes of exchange and transaction. Only that between Brick and Skipper seems to have an idealism which distinguishes it from all others. It is the more surprising, therefore, that the play is resolved by the reestablishnient of a relationship re-forged by Maggie into an agent of capitalist greed. Brick must live with the person who 'raped' his friend as Stella has had to live with Stanley who had raped her sister. Her bold lie—that she is pregnant by a man who in fact shuns physical contact with her—must be transformed into truth if Maggie is to survive and Gooper be defeated.

The social logic of heterosexuality is clear; its moral logic, in the context of this play, less so. The estate had originally been accumulated by two homosexuals whose relationship, Williams pointedly tells us, must have involved 'a tenderness which was uncommon'. Brick's relationship with Skipper seems to have been characterised by a similar quality. To Arthur Miller, Brick has implicitly thrown down a challenge to the values of his society, a challenge which that society, through its representatives, refuses to acknowledge. More seriously, it is a challenge which he implicitly withdraws. In the version offered to director Elia Kazan there was no such accommodation. The play ended with Brick's response to Maggie's declaration of love: 'Wouldn't it be funny if that was true?', an echo of the irony which had concluded Hemingway's novel of mismatched sexuality, *The Sun Also Rises*. In the revised Broadway version the final speech is cut, Brick expresses his admiration for Maggie and her concluding speech is expanded, emphasising her strength and thus the likelihood of reconciliation. Kazan believed that there should be some evidence of a transformation in Brick's attitude in the face of his father's verbal assault. Williams objected that, 'I felt that the moral paralysis of Brick was a root thing in this tragedy, and to show a dramatic progression would obscure the meaning of that tragedy in him.' Nonetheless, he agreed to the changes that Kazan required, thus blurring the moral perspective of the play.

On the other hand, Brick's idealism is not untinged with an adolescent resistance to process. He wants to cling on to the world of college sports and male relationships and when that fails him he turns to alcohol. The crutches on which he hobbles (having injured himself trying to hurdle) are a patent symbol and literal demonstration of his inability to stand on his own two feet. We are offered, in other words, a choice between arrested development and commitment to a corrosive materialism. What Brick is converted to is the need to survive. Maggie the cat has clawed her way up to the point at which she dominates her circumstances. She refuses the role of victim. It is that lesson she passes on to Brick, won back to life or at least to the compromise which is apparently the precondition for life. But that saddles Williams with an ambiguity he is not disposed to examine.

The great strength of *Cat on a Hot Tin Roof* lies in Williams's ability to fuse the psychological, the social and the metaphysical in a play whose realistic set belies its symbolic force. This mansion, like Faulkner's, betokens power made simultaneously substantial and abstract, as religion—in the form of a grasping minister in pursuit of a large bequest—represents a spiritual world corrupted by material values. This is a world in which the denial of reality is a primary concern. The clink of ice in a liquor glass, a record on a phonograph, are means to blot out other sounds, other thoughts. Words are designed to deceive, appearances to mislead. The bed which dominates the opening and closing scenes has been rendered ironic as its literal and symbolic functions have been denied by a man who fears the future it may engender. If Williams was wrong to accede to Kazan's request for changes (though his insistence that Big Daddy should reappear in the second act was doubtless correct) it remains a play whose subtleties go considerably beyond the sexual ambivalence which first attracted concern. For the *New York Times* reviewer, commenting on a 1975 revival, the political corruptions of Watergate had restored its concern with mendacity to its central role in the drama. Beyond the social lie, though, there are other deceits, more profound, more disturbing, which required no Watergate to validate them and which make *Cat on a Hot Tin Roof* the achievement that it is.

The disease from which Big Daddy suffers is uremia, defined as a 'poisoning of the whole system due to the failure of the body to eliminate poisons'. The disease from which his society suffers is essentially the same. Its governing principles are greed and mendacity and Brick, in common with Laura in *The Glass Menagerie*, is ill-equipped to survive. As she is drawn to the child-like mythic world of her glass animals he is attracted to the unproblematic mythic world of his former sporting successes on the football field and the track. When he tries to re-experience that world, however, he breaks his leg, tripped by a high hurdle as he has been immobilised by experience. In the same way the relationship with Skipper had been an attempt to deny process—a process which Big Mama identifies all too clearly: 'Time goes by so fast. Nothin' can outrun it. Death commences too early—almost before you're half acquainted with life—you meet with the other.'[36] The fundamental theme is thus Williams's perennial one, the losing game which we play with time, and the necessity, in Big Mama's words, 'to love each other an' stay together, all of us, just as close as we can'.[37] The irony is that none of the characters has succeeded in negotiating even this limited grace. If truth is in short supply then so too is love untainted by power. In revising the ending of the play Williams deflected irony in the direction of sentimentality, thus losing something of the force of a work whose achievement lay precisely in its refusal to capitulate to such a simple resolution. The incomplete sentences and tentative statements of hope subverted by cynicism now make way, in the revised version, to an overly explicit and over-written speech in which Maggie spells out her redemptive role as Brick expresses his open admiration for her.

In the persons of Maggie and Big Daddy Tennessee Williams created two of the most powerful and original characters in American drama—one seemingly on the edge of death, the other on the edge of life. But the play's epigraph—Dylan Thomas's 'Do not go gentle into that good night ... / Rage, rage against the dying of the light'—should not be seen as applying simply to the man whose roar of pain and terror sounds out with an energy rendered ironic by his circumstances. It applies with equal force to Maggie whose whole being is a resistance movement, a denial, a refusal. If she does not exactly pronounce Melville's 'No, in thunder!' she does pitch her whole self into a battle with the given. What Williams does not explore is the extent of her complicity with the forces she derides—as she exchanges truth for power—or the meaning of the life she is intent on creating by the force of her will and imagination.

Cat on a Hot Tin Roof has more than a little in common with two later works, both of which he was working on when *Cat* was still running on

Broadway. *Orpheus Descending*, a reworking of his earlier disastrous *Battle of Angels*, dramatises a society in which corruption seems endemic and in which a brutal materialism has its sexual correlative. It is a corruption rooted in and exemplified by racism. Essentially the same point is made in *Sweet Bird of Youth* (1959) in which a southern racist takes his vengeance on those who would break out of a hermetic world of greed and power, a world in which sexuality is warped and deformed by those who acknowledge nothing but the authority of their own material needs.

In *Orpheus Descending* Williams dramatises the immolation of a Lawrentian fox set loose in a South dying of its own narcissism. Val Xavier has an animal vitality—a fact redundantly underlined by his snakeskin jacket. Lady, having lost her father to the violence of a group of racists, and her lover, David Cutrere, to a society hostess, marries Jabe Torrence, the owner of a dry goods store. Unbeknown to her, he had been one of her father's killers and now destroys her spirit. Then Val Xavier comes into town. He brings her back to life, a recovery symbolised by her pregnancy. When Jabe Torrence discovers this, however, he murders his wife and frames her lover, who is tortured to death. The only survivor is Carol Cutrere, sister to David, whose resolute bohemianism is a deliberate affront to the southern mores which condemn her.

Written before the Civil Rights movement made such a resolute condemnation of southern bigotry and racism fashionable, the play is as sharply political as anything Williams had written since his days with the Mummers in St. Louis. Indeed, there is an echo of that period in the fact that Carol Cutrere had once protested over the Scottsboro case in which nine black youths had been charged with the rape of two white prostitutes in Scottsboro, Alabama. Bessie Smith's death, purportedly as a consequence of the institutional racism of southern hospitals, is invoked while Lady's father, we are, told, was murdered because of his willingness to serve alcohol to Negroes. In terms of the play, only his women resist—Lady the Sheriff's wife, Vee (an artist), and Carol Cutrere—and they have no social power, any more than does Val. Nor can this Orpheus redeem his Eurydice. The life which he offers her is instantly destroyed. Williams's ironic invocation of one myth is designed to expose another. The South, with its corrupt medievalism, its denial of history, its suspicion of a sexuality which may prove subversive, is dying of its own denials. Its darkness is lit only by the glare of vengeful flames. Death, decay and disease provide the imagery for a play in which refusal becomes a fundamental trope. It is an intransitive society in a double sense. It refuses to abandon its destructive myths and it fears a sexuality which may unite individuals across barriers sustained by prejudice, a sexuality which stands as an image of that natural process and development which is to be evaded not least because it pulls the isolated individual into history. In a perverse way the South inhabits its own destructive metaphor.

Writing in the context of a new production of the play in 1988, Vanessa Redgrave remarked that

> It's about dispossession—of Lady's people from the old country, of negroes, of people like Val who have nothing and no place. It's about racism and intolerance, which leads to a society trying to destroy everything which doesn't fit in with what it says it wants life to be about—leads it to kill Negroes, to kill Jews, and if you're Sicilian and Roman Catholic, you're a wop, and wop comes from guappo which in Neapolitan means thief. The character I play— known as a wop bootlegger's daughter—is automatically therefore a thief.

But to her mind it was a play that had 'long ago stopped being a play about a Southern problem, it's about an American problem, and now a world problem'.

Williams saw his own fictions as challenging the fictions of the state, the myths which had seemingly generated the energy on which America had thrived. Those fictions were to do with authority, power, money, the utility rather than the value of relationships. They had no place for the loser, the bohemian, the artist. But though Val is destroyed, something survives. As Vanessa Redgrave observed of the passing on of the protagonist's snakeskin jacket: 'to the generation that follows, on the shoulders of those who've been destroyed, there are things passed on in the form of scripts, historical documents ... the dead records of living history, that living people need. That's what Tennessee is saying.'[38]

The Negro conjure man is bedecked with talismans; Val's guitar is covered with the inscriptions of black musicians. These texts tell another story, identify another plot not delineated or dramatised here but running like a counter-current to the narrative of a dying civilisation. The Negro conjure man does not speak but utters a Choctaw cry. His magic is from another era, from a time before the world became 'sick with neon'. Then, the country was animated by wildness, now by a systematic cruelty designed to freeze the unpredictable and the vital into an unyielding and unchanging object, an icon to be worshipped. That history of animal vitality is inscribed in Val's snakeskin jacket, handed on at the end of the play to Carol Cutrere who walks out of the play as the Negro conjure man smiles his appreciation. It is hard, though, to take the gesture seriously, as Carol's resistance seems to offer little more than another desperate flight as another legless bird momentarily takes to the air. A girl 'not built for childbearing', she can do nothing to engender change, only to sustain the irony.

Orpheus Descending is not offered as a realistic portrait of the South, for all the anger which crackles through the text. Indeed, the stage directions repeatedly steer director and actors away from realism. We are in a gothic landscape. The images we are offered—darkness, cobwebs, dust, emptiness, dusk, skeleton—all suggest an unreal world, void of life.

On the one hand it is a play in which the gothic politics of the South— with its spectral white-sheeted bigots and dark-skinned unvoiced mystics— move to centre stage; on the other, this is a work in which absurdity is not only a social construct. The southern love affair with sanctioned violence, its desire to wrench experience into line with myth, is a losing game with death, but in that respect it merely reflects a fundamental condition. *Orpheus Descending* is Williams's version of the myth of Sisyphus, his *Waiting for Godot*. Those of his characters who have not chosen to embrace absurdity by enacting its ironies as social policy, killing life wherever it threatens to burst through the arid soil, are its victims through the persistent and self-mocking hope which they embrace. They try to outlive their fate, cling to notions of justice denied by the circumstances of their existence and look for a freedom which is merely another name for solitariness. They wait with no less resolution than Beckett's Vladimir and Estragon and with no more likelihood of a resolution to their questions. As Val observes,

> What does anyone wait for? For something to happen, for anything to happen, to make things make sense ... I was waiting for something like if you ask a question you wait for someone to answer, but you ask the wrong question or you ask the wrong person and the answer don't come. Does everything stop because you don't get the answer? No, it goes right on as if the answer was given, day comes after day and night comes after night, and you're still waiting for someone to answer the question and going on as if the question was answered.

For Val, the true state of the human predicament lies in a sentence of solitary confinement inside our own skins, for life![39] Only two consolations are offered: love and flight. But the commitments of the one conflict with the necessities of the other. When Val speaks of the legless bird that must die if it ever alights he describes himself destroyed by his love for Lady as by his implicit challenge to those trapped by their own past.

Lady seeks to defeat this absurdity by simple resistance—'not to be defeated'. Defeat, though, is woven into the fabric of life in this play. Finally we are left with nothing but the paradox whereby the contingent power of art is pitched against the contingency it attempts to neutralise. So it is, within the play, that the Sheriff's wife, Vee, struggles to come to terms with the anarchic violence which she witnesses by turning it into art: 'Before you started to paint it didn't make sense ... existence didn't make sense.'[40]

The absurd has never been wholly detached from the romantic impulse to pitch art against decay, but where the romantic leaves art its triumph and finds the gulf between experience and representation the source of sentimental regret, the absurdist finds only irony. A distrust of art is built into its central strategies. Indeed, in *Suddenly Last Summer* (called, by Williams, a fable of our times), which followed the relative disaster of *Orpheus Descending*, the writer is purely destructive while sexuality—specifically homosexuality—is seen as compounding the cruelty at large in the world.

Sebastian is a poet who produces only one poem a year, but there is something familiar in Williams's portrait of a writer for whom art is a means of resisting the chaos that menaces him, a chaos partly external and partly at the heart of his own imaginings. If we are back in the familiar morality play in which the rich are corrupt and corrupting, however, this time the principal corrupter is a writer. Sebastian is a homosexual who is eventually destroyed and consumed by those whose company he seeks. His literary talent is faltering. *Suddenly Last Summer* is a play that seems to express a number of private fears having to do with both Williams's sexual identity and his avocation as a writer, and he later admitted that if the play had its roots in a 'developing tension and anger and violence' in the world, it also reflected his 'own steadily increasing tension as a writer and person'.[41] There is, as he admitted, an atmosphere of hysteria in his work. He is drawn to violence, often of the most extreme kind. It is as though he wants to put his characters under maximum stress, not, as in Miller's work, in order to test their authenticity, but to rupture the self, break open an identity exposed as a series of desperate performances. His own explanation for this obsession is his sense of contingency, his morbid fear of death. In a curious way the vivid deaths to which he consigns a number of his characters carry their own grace, not merely because such characters are the victims of a corrupt society but because they thereby refuse the definitional power of that society. *Suddenly Last Summer* is set in part in a mock jungle. Exotic plants frame the action. There is something elemental about this world in which physical need deploys its camouflages and develops its subtle strategies. Sebastian is a homosexual, but to set the stage for his seductions he peoples it with the help of Catherine, the lure who, in her semi-transparent swimsuit, must transform the beach into a place fit for sexual drama.

It is a play in which Williams turns metaphor into reality. Sebastian's need is all-consuming and he is himself duly consumed, literally fed upon by those he would attract. The god he worships is a cruel one and that cruelty is not deflected by his pretences to refinement. The poetry he produces is merely the brittle surface, the patina of culture that conceals the depth of his need and cruelty. It is hard not to see a personal dimension to this play. Certainly Williams's art co-existed with crude appetites which set him cruising the streets for sexual partners. He was acutely aware of a potentially destructive dualism to his sensibility. And there are other personal elements in a play in which Catherine is threatened with the lobotomy actually inflicted on his sister Rose, but then here, and elsewhere, the sensibility of his characters seems always on the point of dissolution. So, too, does the world they inhabit where for the most part power is in the hands of those who represent moral anarchy and whose sexual impotence stands for an apocalyptic potential. In *Sweet Bird of Youth* the southern racist Boss Finley desires his own daughter, an incestuous motif which reflects Freud's association of incest with anarchy. Himself impotent, or so it seems, he urges his daughter into relationships which will serve his political purposes. She, meanwhile, has contracted venereal disease from her lover and is incapable of bearing children while that lover is himself emasculated, at Boss Finley's command, on Easter Sunday.

Sweet Bird of Youth is a bitter play, touched by sentimentality. Chance Wayne, the protagonist, has already sold his soul for the success he equates with fulfilment while the fading movie star, through whom he hopes to advance his career in Hollywood, is also at the end of a personal road. The title of Princess Kosmonopolis is one she invents to console herself for her dwindling public significance. Having invested her whole being in such fictions, in the artificial performances which are the substance of her life no less than her career, she stands cruelly exposed when those performances are no longer observed (a theme which recurs in Williams's work). For a brief moment she finds consolation in her relationship with Chance Wayne, the consolation, Williams remarks, of those who face the firing squad together. When she is unexpectedly reprieved by Hollywood, however, she reinvests her role with energy and conviction, abandoning her lover to his fate. Williams toyed with the idea of allowing Wayne to escape, driving off with the Princess towards Hollywood. It is hard to believe that this would have been anything other than ironic, though, since we have already seen the consequences of inhabiting unreality in the person of the Princess herself.

Sweet Bird of Youth is another indictment of southern bigotry, another portrait of a terminal society trapped in its own myths and blind to the hermetic and incestuous implications of its denial of history. It is also yet another account of the corrupting power of time. So many of Williams's plays take as their protagonists those whose youth has slipped away from them, whose options have run out, whose lives bear the marks of disillusionment, that it becomes more a mannerism than a motif His characters, no less than Beckett's, give birth astride the grave. As Chance Wayne observes, time 'Gnaws away, like a at gnaws at its own foot caught in a trap, and then, with the foot gnawed off and the rat set free, couldn't run, couldn't go, bled and died.'[42] The cruel god of *Suddenly Last Summer* prevails.

This image was one he picked up again in his next work, *The Night of the Iguana* (1961), a play in which a group of individuals, whose lives have run down, come together 'like ... actors in a play which is about to fold on the road, preparing gravely for a performance which may be the last one'.[43] Again the image of a failing theatre and the desperate performances it witnesses becomes a correlative for Williams's sense of a life emptied alike of function and purpose. Here, however, the desperation of his characters, symbolised by an iguana tied to a veranda by its foot—as the play's central character, a defrocked priest and failed tour guide called Shannon, is tied to a hammock in his delirium—is banished by a simple gesture. The artist who creates the symbol dissolves it. The iguana is released, as is Shannon. The severity of Williams's vision is neutralised by a sentimentality which is always a presence in his plays. It is almost as if they reflect a mood swing—the ironies of his early plays being balanced by the comedy of *The Rose Tattoo*, the defeats of *Camino Real* by the victory of *Cat on a Hot Tin Roof*, the murderous traps of *Orpheus Descending* and *Sweet Bird of Youth* by the grace of *The Night of the Iguana*.

But such benign gestures were about to disappear from his work. The 1960s were to prove a personal and artistic debacle. His dependence on drink and drugs led him to the mental hospital and to the violent ward. Committed by his brother, as his sister Rose had once been committed by his mother, he came close to dying. The plays that he produced (*The Milk Train Doesn't Stop Here Any More, Kingdom of Earth, In the Bar of a Tokyo Hotel, The Mutilated, The Frosted Glass Coffin*) were often brutal, apocalyptic and death-centred. He frequently came close to self-parody, a kind of narcissism which reflected his paranoia and self-concern. His talent fed off itself and the effect was a series of shrill, neurotic appeals having to do with the intolerable pressures which threaten to destroy the sensitive, the poetic, the betrayed. Character is represented by little more than idiosyncratic speech patterns and mannered behaviour. Urging the centrality of human contact he created a series of grotesques, animated symbols, whose fate carries neither interest nor conviction. High-camp figures, they spell out their significance with an explicitness which squanders whatever expressive power might lie in action. Self-pitying, these plays moved his own condition to centre stage. Simplistic allegories about the compromises forced by experience and the depredations worked on body and spirit by mortality, they offer little more than attenuated reveries. Gestures at a wider social significance are perfunctory and unconvincing. Occasional lyricism collapses of its own weight, his language hollowed out, rooted in neither character nor situation.

Small Craft Warning (1972), originally, and significantly, called *Confessional*, represented a desperate attempt to recover lost ground but, in certain respects, it, too, proved ill judged. Once again we are in the presence of a group of people whose luck has run out, desperate, lonely, maimed individuals in search of momentary relief. But where once this had proved the substance of powerful drama, now it seemed an ironic echo. There is only a single voice, and that too thin and undifferentiated to command attention. Also, at a time when the mood of the American theatre tended to be confident and celebratory, when sexuality was deployed as an image of freedom and liberation, Williams's bleak dramas of defeat, of sexual depletion and spiritual collapse, seemed largely irrelevant. At a time when community was announced as a social virtue and adapted as a theatrical tactic and theme he chose to stress the collapse of relationship. At a time when the young took centre stage, celebrating the body and asserting their power over history, he focused on the dying, the wounded and the destroyed. The power which he had once been able to draw on from the public suppression of sexuality was now lost to him as its open and joyous expression undermined its subversive power.

The principal exception to this history of decline was the play that he worried away at throughout the sixties and early seventies—the play that most completely expressed his sense of the ambivalent nature of his own resort to theatre. Called *Two Character Play* when it was first produced in 1967, it became, significantly, *Outcry* in the early seventies. It is a play in which he squarely faces the metaphor which underlies so much of his work— the self as actor, society as a series of coercive fictions. The two characters, apparently ex-patients from a mental hospital and now ostensibly actors, play out their lives before an empty auditorium, literally trying to neutralise their fear through performance. The mask is the only reality; nothing is certain. We are, indeed, dealing with the ostensible, the apparent, the seeming. This is Beckett's world. It is governed by an irony which can only be acted out and not transcended. The tension no longer comes, as once it did, from the space which opens up between illusion and the real. Now it is generated by the language itself, brittle, incapable of sustaining communication. The self threatens to dissolve. Even gender roles are unclear, both characters having names which are ambivalent. The blurred identity of androgyny merely underlines the equivocal nature of experience. It is no longer a case of resisting the real with the strategies of the theatre, offering the performed life as a subversion of the real. Now the theatre becomes a governing trope. For Williams, who was trapped in the echo chamber of his own emotions, the play expressed his sense of imprisonment but equally his fear of abandoning familiar structures and beliefs. When one of his characters cries out against the anarchy of improvisation she reflects a fear likewise felt by Williams himself, just as the figure of an old painter huddled in rigor mortis before a blank canvas 'tea kettle boiled dry' reflects the fear of silence which kept him writing and rewriting until the last. At least to act is to convince yourself that you are still alive; to write is to resist a blankness which is no longer that of possibility, but that of nullity. But Williams's characters have a grace or suffer a pain denied to Beckett's. For the most part they know their predicament.

His characters had always been self-conscious actors (sometimes literally, as in *Sweet Bird of Youth*, sometimes figuratively, as in *Streetcar*), playing out their roles in the desperate hope of finding a sympathetic audience, proposing their own theatricalising imagination as a valid opposition to a world which otherwise seemed so prosaic and unyielding; but with *Outcry* this process became central. In this play a brother and sister find themselves in an underground theatre in an unspecified country. The doors are locked so that there is no escape. Apparently abandoned by their company, there is nothing for them to do but speak their lines with diminishing confidence, perform their lives even if that performance has been drained of meaning. The audience, if it ever existed, disappears, leaving them to enact a play, apparently based on their own lives, in an empty theatre. They have no alternative but to continue their performance though, denied an audience, they are denied equally the significance which that audience might have been prepared to grant to that performance. These are no longer figures with a choice. The theatre is the condition of their existence; acting the only verification of their being.

In the late seventies Williams wrote a series of plays in which he revisited his youth: *Vieux Carré* (1977), *A Lovely Sunday for Crève Cœur* (1979) and *Something Cloudy, Something Clear* (1981). A sense of doom seems to hang over them, projected backwards to the 1930s and 1940s. Young hopes and young friends are recalled, though now the irony that surrounds them seems to glow Nothing lasts, nothing, that is, except perhaps the work of art which thereby falsifies the world it offers to portray. His plays had always borne directly on his life, but with the years the degree of refraction lessened until he began to write more and more directly about himself as blighted young poet or debilitated artist for whom writing was a way of denying his mortality. His subject, indeed, had in some essential way always been the artist, and at the end of his life it was to that that he returned with *Clothes for a Summer Hotel* (1980), a play about Scott Fitzgerald, whose own self-image was in many respects so close to Williams's. For Fitzgerald, no less than his creation Gatsby, was his own Platonic creation. It is hard to imagine anyone more dependent on performance than Fitzgerald and Zelda—a fact acknowledged by Williams in a stage direction which insists that, though at times the dialogue which he writes for Zelda might be tentative and though her words might fail to communicate, her 'presentation—performance—must'. Much the same could be said of Williams himself.

Williams was afraid that insanity and creativity derived from the same source. In *Clothes for a Summer Hotel* Zelda Fitzgerald talks of escaping 'into madness or into acts of creation'. The real is unendurable but the alternative carries the threat of dissolution. Towards the end of his career Williams seems to have become increasingly alive to the limits of language. Here Zelda's words blow away in the wind. In a late screenplay, *Secret Places of the Heart*, Janet is a speech therapist who rescued her husband-to-be, Sven, by pulling him into a linguistic world. Her commitment ends his aphasia. But she herself ends up in a mental hospital, separated from her husband, and when he visits her to explain that he will not be returning, making his life with another woman, she becomes catatonic, while he virtually loses the power of speech. Her final reconciliation to her fate is signified by her uttering a single word. In the face of real need, of the limits of experience, language fails. It is, perhaps, what made the theatre such an expressive form for Williams. It is what lies beyond a purely verbal language.

For Tennessee Williams, the social world—the world of power, authority, history, time—is perceived only indefinitely. It is a sense of menace, a corruption, a pressure which bears on the self but is not implicated in that self. That public world is seen only through a peripheral vision; its existence can be presumed to the extent that we see its consequences. Instead, by a trick of perspective, the marginal moves to the centre of our attention. The dispossessed are reinstated, as the artist redresses the balance in their favour. The problem is that the imagination thereby becomes complicit in the absurd. For its gestures imply the possibility of suspending process, of shaping order out of chaos, of winning a reprieve from the very forces whose authority had created the necessity for such imaginings. It is the absurdity which holds his characters in thrall; it is equally the absurdity which his work exemplifies even as it offers to resist it. The desperate fictions of his characters, whose lives have reached their apogee and who can look forward only to a decline whose reality they choose not to confront, are purely contingent. They try to live with compromise, to soften the edges of a reality which they see as threatening. What others may see as lies they cling to as strategies of survival, but when the real exerts its authority they have only two real choices: submission, a kind of martyrdom, as Williams permits them a ritual death; or insanity, as they let go of the world which torments them, and myth, illusion or the lie subsume them completely. They have staged a rearguard action against the implications of their own humanity, and lost. They have struggled to live on the other side of despair. They have aestheticised their lives, becoming themselves fictional constructs. But if that buys them a limited and temporary immunity it does so at the cost of that physical contact which is their only other antidote to the absurd—an antidote, however, which pulls them back into the world which torments them.

In 1960, on the very verge of his vertiginous plunge into the drink and drugs which came close to annihilating his personality, Williams remarked that 'When the work of any kind of creative worker becomes tyrannically obsessive to the point of overshadowing his life, almost taking the place of it, he is in a hazardous situation. His situation is hazardous for the simple reason that the source, the fountainhead of his work, can only be his life.'[44] It was a prophetic remark, for, to a remarkable degree, that proved to be his fate for the best part of two decades as he fed off his own creative fat. In so far as, like their creator, his characters lost their grip on a world against which they could define themselves, they inevitably lost definition. He and they needed resistance. The subversive power of his homosexuality disappeared with its legalising. His sympathy for the poor and disregarded lost conviction as he himself claimed the rewards of fame. Far from being marginalised, the author was frequently feted. He could even buy a limited immunity with alcohol and drugs in a culture which no longer regarded either as particularly deviant. Dramatic attention, meanwhile, had switched elsewhere—to the hyper-realism, the demotic prose, the forceful metaphors of David Mamet and the lyrical, oblique myths of Sam Shepard. The curious accident of his death (he choked to death on the plastic cap of his medication bottle) itself seemed like a casual afterthought of fate.

But there were real signs of recovery at the end as he began self-consciously to explore the mechanisms of his own art and the ironies implicit in an artistic life whose central strategy was a reflection and extension of that adapted by his characters as they worked their way down their personal Camino Real.

Williams did concern himself with moral value. Indeed he insisted that the 'great and only possible dignity of man lies in his power deliberately to choose certain moral values by which to live', adding, interestingly, 'as steadfastly as if he too, like a character in a play, were immured against the corrupting rush of time'.[45] He knew well enough that, as he said, 'there is no way to beat the game of *being* against *non-being*'.[46] How, then, invoke a moral world? The answer is to be found or at least sought in the paradox that lies in an art that seeks to transcend death by mimicking its processes. In stopping time his characters precipitate their own annihilation, but they also force the moment to surrender its meaning. The imagination which lifts them out of the world simultaneously suggests that things can be other than they are. That is what made Williams's therapeutic gestures have the undoubted public power that they do. His plays are all in some fundamental way debates with himself. He is both Tom Wingfield, the poet who escapes, and Laura, the poet trapped in her own inventions; both the spiritual Alma, in *Summer and Smoke*, and the physical John Buchanan; both Val Xavier, in *Orpheus Descending*, who dies, and Carol Cutrere, who lives; both Brick, the defeated, in *Cat on a Hot Tin Roof*, and Maggie, the survivor. But these personal debates became something more. Concerned, as they are, with a divided self; a split between the body and soul, mind and imagination, the death instinct and the life instinct, they claimed and had a relevance beyond Williams's own divided personality.

The British poet and novelist George MacBeth reminds us of Kafka's remark that a good book is an axe for the sea frozen within us and that even the most private of visions may shed light, like a chandelier, into the dark corners of other lives. But, as he insists, it is not any private authority of the grief or the sense of loss or pain which matters: 'that is the fallacy of those who admire their oven sadness too much. One life', after all, 'is much like another. What matters is the shape and pattern provided by the chandelier maker. The light comes from the form, not the substance.'[47] So it proved, for Tennessee Williams.

NOTES

1. Albert J. Devlin, *Conversations with Tennessee Williams* (London, 1986), p. 106.

2. *Ibid.*, p. 90.

3. *Ibid.*, p. 5.

4. *Ibid.*, p. 31.

5. *Ibid.*, p. 99.

6. *Ibid.*

7. *Ibid.*, p. 90.

8. *Ibid.*, p. 37.

9. *Ibid.*, p. 44.

10. *Ibid.*, p. 27.

11. *Ibid.*, p. 32.

12. Arthur Miller, *Timebends* (London, 1987), pp. 180–1.

13. Williams, 'Fugitive Kind'. Typescript in Humanities Research Center, University of Texas, Austin.

14. Tennessee Williams, *Where I Live* (New York, 1978), p. 8.

15. *Ibid.*, p. 35.

16. *Ibid.*, p. 96.

17. *Ibid.*, p. 292.

18. *Ibid.*, pp. 170–1.

19. Devlin, *Conversations with Tennessee Williams*, p. 292.

20. Tennessee Williams, *Four Plays by Tennessee Williams* (London, 1957), p. 1.

21. Tennessee Williams, *Five Plays by Tennessee Williams* (London, 1962), p. 127.

22. Williams, *Where I Live*, pp. 36–7.

23. *Ibid.*, p. 212.

24. Gilbert Debusscher, 'Menagerie, Glass and Wine', in *The Glass Menagerie: A Collection of Critical Essays* (Englewood Cliffs, 1983), p. 34.

25. David Jones, *Great Directors at Work* (Berkeley, 1984), p. 188.

26. *Ibid.*, pp. 150–1.

27. Williams, *Where I Live*, p. 346.

28. *Ibid.*, p. 51.

29. *Ibid.*, p. 49.

30. Richard Gray, *Writing the South* (Cambridge University Press, 1986), p. 178.

31. See in *ibid.*, p. 272.

32. See in *ibid.*, pp. 43–45.

33. Jones, *Great Directors at Work*, p. 144.

34 Williams, *Four Plays*, pp. 288–9.

35. *Ibid.*, p. 289.

36. Williams, *Five Plays*, p. 87.

37. *Ibid.*

38. Vanessa Redgrave, 'The Lady Does What the Lady's Got to Do', *The Independent*, 7 Dec. 1988, p. 21.

39. Williams, *Five Plays*, p. 324.

40. *Ibid.*, p. 338.

41. *The Observer*, 7 Apr. 1957.

42. Tennessee Williams, *Sweet Bird of Youth* (London, 1959), p. 92.

43. Tennessee Williams, *The Night of the Iguana* (London, 1963), p. 44.

44. Williams, *Where I Live*, p. 125.

45. Williams, *Five Plays*, p. 129.

46. *Ibid.*

47. George MacBeth, *A Child of War* (London, 1987), p. 188.

Tony Kushner

1

As an American dramatist, Tony Kushner represents (amidst much else) the confluence of several literary traditions that, to me, seem antithetical to one another: Bertolt Brecht's Marxist stage epics; the lyrical phantasmagorias of Tennessee Williams; Yiddish theater in its long history from the earliest *purimshpil* (Leipzig, 1697) to the exuberant flourishing that was still prevalent in my own youth. A fierce admirer of Kushner's work, I confess an increasing aesthetic aversion to Brecht as I age. Politically I have no differences with Kushner, but for more than a decade now, I have experienced a purely literary anxiety that this dramatist's genius might be so deformed by public concerns that he could dwindle into another Clifford Odets, rather than fulfill his extraordinary gifts by transcending even Tennessee Williams and Thornton Wilder among his American precursors.

Kushner passionately insists that he is a political dramatist, but reading his plays and attending their performance persuade me otherwise. His largest American ancestors are Walt Whitman and Herman Melville, and while *Song of Myself* and *Moby-Dick* are the epics of democracy, their spiritual and metaphysical elements are far more vital than their politics. Brecht's dramas (if they *are* his, rather than Elizabeth Hauptmann's, Margarete Steffin's, and Ruth Berlau's) increasingly threaten to become Period Pieces, just as Clifford

Odets's *Waiting for Lefty* is now nothing but a Period Piece. Kushner's *A Bright Room Called Day* (1985) is a Ronald Reagan Period Piece which depresses me, two decades later, because Reagan now appears virtually harmless in comparison to our astonishing current President, who defies any ironic representation whatsoever. Shakespeare himself could not render George W. Bush dramatically plausible. Nathanael West's Shagpoke Whipple, in *A Cool Million*, cannot match Bush II in blatancy, patriotic religiosity, and bland righteousness. Reality in America has beggared fantasy and one wants to implore Kushner to turn inward, rather than dramatically confront a continuous outrageousness that no stage representation can hope to rival. I need only turn on Fox TV to witness parodistic excess accepted as reality by a majority of my fellow citizens who cared enough to vote. Oscar Wilde, wisely urging art to be perfectly useless, would at this moment be the best of mentors for Tony Kushner.

2

Roy Cohn, to date, is Kushner's best creation, an all but Shakespearean hero-villain. The three versions I have seen of the Kushnerian Cohn were performed by Ron Leibman, F. Murray Abraham, and Al Pacino. All were effective, but Leibman was the best, because he played it with a Yiddish aura of outrageousness and of having been outraged. The only time I recall being moved by Arthur Miller's *Death of a Salesman* was when I saw it in Yiddish translation in 1952, with Joseph Buloff as Loman. I wish that Joseph Wiseman had been young enough to play Roy Cohn. Wiseman was a magnificent Edmund in a terrible *King Lear* I recall seeing in 1950, and later he performed an unforgettable mad Duke in John Webster's *The Duchess of Malfi*. Watching and listening to Leibman flooded me with memories of Wiseman, presumably because both actors played with excess and *sprezzatura*, in a mode I had worshipped in Maurice Schwartz, who perhaps had learned it from Jacob Adler. Kushner, whose superb *A Dybbuk* is undervalued, is a natural throwback to the hyperbolical Yiddish theater where I first saw Shylock, played by Schwartz as hero, not as hero-villain or the farcical bogyman that Shakespeare designed to go Marlowe's Barabas, Jew of Malta, one better.

Kushner is a whirligig of change, unpredictable and unprecedented, except for Tennessee Williams at his strongest. The one time I met Williams (was it in the late Seventies?) he proudly handed me his treasured copy of *The Collected Poems of Hart Crane*, so that I could see he had liberated it from the Washington University of St. Louis Library. We talked about Crane, our mutually favorite poet. I have met Kushner at length primarily in front of a large audience, and so have not been able to ascertain his favorite poet, but surely it must be Walt Whitman, still (in my judgment) the greatest writer brought forth by our Evening Land, the Americas. I delight that *Perestroika* boldly plagiarizes Whitman, just as it is audacious enough to send up Blanch DuBois's: "I have always depended upon the kindness of strangers." But that is High Camp, whereas the employment of the sublime Walt seems to me crucial; since he *is* the Angel Principality of America, despite her inconvenient gender, and her negativity:

> Hiding from Me one place you will find me in another.
> I I I I stop down the road, waiting for you.

That is an Angelic variation upon the very close of *Song of Myself*, substituting "hiding" for "seeking." Just before, this negative version of Whitman has proclaimed: "Forsake the Open Road." What Hart Crane was to Tennessee Williams, a fusion of Whitman and Melville is for Kushner, except that the overwhelmingly personal investment of Williams in Crane is not present in Kushner's veneration of his American fathers, Melville and Whitman. Williams's other prime precursor was D.H. Lawrence, like Melville an evader of homoeroticism.

3

Angels in America, indisputably Kushner's masterwork to date, is accurately described by him as "fantasia." A careful rereading of it demonstrates that Kushner's mastery of controlled phantasmagoria is his highest dramatic gift. Except for Roy Cohn, the double-play has no characters wholly memorable as personalities, fully endowed with individuated voices. The black, gay male nurse Belize has been much praised, but I fear that is mere political correctness. Louie Ironson seems a self-parody on Kushner's part, and the prophet Prior Walter is poignant but scarcely persuasive. The Mormon closet gay and right-wing lawyer, Joe Pitt, is a caricature. Except for Cohn, Kushner's women are stronger, Harper in particular, but then she is at home in fantasy. What carries *Angels in America*, the daemonic Cohn aside, is its extraordinary inventiveness in regard to what might as well be termed the spirit world.

Having been defeated by a stubborn Kushner in a public debate on theatre and religion (March 22, 2004), in New York City, I am only too aware he will continue to insist he is a political dramatist, rather than a theological one, long after I have departed for whatever spirit-world there may be. Not being exactly a devoted Brechtian, I am unable to see how "a relationship of complaint and struggle and pursuit between the human and divine"—Kushner's eloquent characterization of his own Judaism—involves politics. When Kushner declares that "drama without politics is inconceivable," I wonder just how he reads Shakespeare. Those who endeavor to interpret *Hamlet* or *King Lear* or *Macbeth* as political theater lose my interest rather quickly. Is Reagan or Bush II really Kushner's motive for metaphor? No. Kushner has more in common with Kafka than with Brecht, though he does not want to see this. Like his angels, Kushner has filed a suit against God for desertion. God shrewdly has taken on Roy Cohn as his defense attorney and so the angels (and Kushner) are going to lose their case.

4

I have read *Caroline, or Change* in manuscript, but have not seen it performed, and doubtless by now Kushner has revised it anyway. I do not know how much intrinsic relevance it will retain a decade hence, an apprehension I experience also in regard to *Homebody/Kabul*. Kushner hardly is going to agree with me on this, but I think *A Dybbuk* will outlast them both. Social ironies, like political concerns, drive Kushner into the composition of Period Pieces. The dramatic impulse towards phantasmagoria always will be his aesthetic redemption.

Roy Cohn is a hero-villain and a strong individuality. To Kushner, that individuality is one with Cohn's evil. Yet that seems to me Kushner's incessant error. To invoke what ultimately is an Hegelian distinction, singularity *cares* about itself *and others*, while individuality is indifferent, whether to the self or to otherness. Rosalind, in *As You Like It*, is a singularity, as is Falstaff in his plays. Hamlet is an individuality, who loves neither himself nor others, but I can locate nothing political in Hamlet, or in Iago.

Kushner's Roy Cohn is a fascinating blend of singularity and individuality, neither of them a source of his murderous malice. Coleridge mistakenly spoke of Iago's "motiveless malignancy", but Iago, like his disciple, Satan in Milton's *Paradise Lost*, suffers from a Sense of Injured Merit. So, as I read him, does Tony Kushner's Roy Cohn. He wants to have been a major demon like Joe McCarthy, but God has passed him over for promotion. Iago, passed over for Cassio, determines to bring his war-god Othello down to the abyss, to uncreate Othello. Cohn, outraged and outrageous, finds his proper employment only in the afterlife, in the superb (and invariably unperformed) Scene 7 of Act V of *Perestroika*:

As Prior journeys to earth he sees Roy, at a great distance, in Heaven, or Hell or Purgatory—standing waist-deep in a smoldering pit, facing a volcanic, pulsating red light. Underneath, a basso-profundo roar, like a thousand Bessemer furnaces going at once, deep underground.

ROY: Paternity suit? Abandonment? Family court is my particular metier, I'm an absolute fucking demon with Family Law. Just tell me who the judge is, and what kind of jewelry does he like? If it's a jury, it's harder, juries take more talk but sometimes it's worth it, going jury, for what it saves you in bribes. Yes I will represent you, King of the Universe, yes I will sing and eviscerate, I will bully and seduce, I will win for you and make the plaintiffs, those traitors, wish they had never heard the name of ...

(Huge thunderclap.)

ROY: Is it a done deal, are we on? Good, then I gotta start by telling you you ain't got a case here, you're guilty as hell, no question, you have nothing to plead but not to worry, darling, I will make something up.

Is it possible to read this without delighting in Roy Cohn? He *will* win God's case, thus vindicating his entire career, and severely putting into question all Kushnerian dramatic politics. The Messenger, who is the Angel of *A Dybbuk*, at the play's close receives Rabbi Azriel's eloquent charge:

(*Softly*) It doesn't matter. Tell Him that. The more cause He gives to doubt Him. Tell Him that. The deeper delves faith. Though His love becomes only abrasion, derision, excoriation, tell Him, I cling. We cling. He made us, He can never shake us off. We will always find Him out. Promise Him that. We will always find Him, no matter how few there are, tell Him we will find Him. To deliver our complaint.

Kushner, like Azriel, always will deliver his complaint. Pathos, eloquence, fantasia: these never will forsake him. If, as I firmly believe, he yet will surpass Tennessee Williams, it will not be because of his Brechtian faith in the political possibilities of theater.

Chronology

1911	Tennessee Williams born.
1915	Arthur Miller born.
1917	Strike by Actors' Equity closes New York theaters.
1918	First Pulitzer Prize for drama goes to Jesse Lynch Williams for *Why Marry?* Theatre Guild organized.
1920	Eugene O'Neill wins his first Pulitzer for *Beyond the Horizon*.
1921	O'Neill wins his second Pulitzer for *Anna Christie*.
1928	O'Neill wins third Pulitzer for *Strange Interlude*. Edward Albee born.
1931	Group Theater formed; brings Stanislavski methods to U.S.
1932	O'Neill produces *Mourning Becomes Electra*.
1933	O'Neill produces *Ah, Wilderness!*
1934	O'Neill begins twelve-year hiatus from the theater. Lillian Hellman's *The Children's Hour* produced.
1935	Federal Theatre Project begins. Clifford Odets's *Waiting for Lefty* produced.
1938	Thornton Wilder's *Our Town* produced and later wins Pulitzer.
1939	Congress stops Federal Theatre Project. Hellman's *The Little Foxes* produced.

1942	Wilder's *The Skin of Our Teeth* produced and later wins Pulitzer.
1943	Sam Shepard born.
1944	Tennessee Williams's *The Glass Menagerie* produced.
1945	August Wilson born.
1946	O'Neill's *The Iceman Cometh* produced, as well as Miller's *All My Sons*.
1947	Williams's *A Streetcar Named Desire* produced and later wins Pulitzer. David Mamet born.
1949	Arthur Miller's *Death of a Salesman* wins him his first Pulitzer.
1953	O'Neill dies. Miller's *The Crucible* premieres. William Inge's *Picnic* wins Pulitzer. Production of Willams's *Summer and Smoke* begins rise of off-Broadway.
1955	Williams's *Cat on a Hot Tin Roof* produced and later wins Pulitzer. Miller's *A View from the Bridge* produced.
1956	O'Neill's *Long Day's Journey into Night* produced and later wins Pulitzer. Tony Kushner born.
1959	Edward Albee's *The Zoo Story* produced, as well as Lorraine Hansberry's *A Raisin in the Sun*.
1960	Albee's *The American Dream* produced.
1962	Albee's *Who's Afraid of Virginia Woolf?* produced.
1967	Albee's *A Delicate Balance* wins Pulitzer.
1974	David Mamet's *Sexual Perversity in Chicago* produced.
1975	Albee's *Seascape* wins Pulitzer. Thornton Wilder dies.
1979	Sam Shepard's *Buried Child* wins Pulitzer.
1980	Lanford Wilson's *Talley's Folly* wins Pulitzer.
1983	Mamet's *Glengarry Glen Ross* is produced; later wins Pulitzer. Tennessee Williams dies.
1987	August Wilson's *Fences* wins Pulitzer.
1989	Wendy Wasserstein's *The Heidi Chronicles* wins Pulitzer.
1990	August Wilson's *The Piano Lesson* wins Pulitzer.
1991	Neil Simon's *Lost in Yonkers* wins Pulitzer.
1993	Tony Kushner's *Angels in America: Millennium Approaches* wins Pulitzer.
1994	Albee's *Three Tall Women* wins Pulitzer.

Contributors

HAROLD BLOOM is Sterling Professor of the Humanities at Yale University. He is the author of over 20 books, including *Shelley's Mythmaking* (1959), *The Visionary Company* (1961), *Blake's Apocalypse* (1963), *Yeats* (1970), *A Map of Misreading* (1975), *Kabbalah and Criticism* (1975), *Agon: Toward a Theory of Revisionism* (1982), *The American Religion* (1992), *The Western Canon* (1994), and *Omens of Millennium: The Gnosis of Angels, Dreams, and Resurrection* (1996). *The Anxiety of Influence* (1973) sets forth Professor Bloom's provocative theory of the literary relationships between the great writers and their predecessors. His most recent books include *Shakespeare: The Invention of the Human* (1998), a 1998 National Book Award finalist, *How to Read and Why* (2000), *Genius: A Mosaic of One Hundred Exemplary Creative Minds* (2002), *Hamlet: Poem Unlimited* (2003), and *Where Shall Wisdom be Found* (2004). In 1999, Professor Bloom received the prestigious American Academy of Arts and Letters Gold Medal for Criticism, and in 2002 he received the Catalonia International Prize.

LIONEL TRILLING was Professor of English at Columbia University. A critic of literature and culture, his work includes *The Liberal Imagination*, *Eugene O'Neill*, and others.

GERALD WEALES was Professor of English, Emeritus, at the University of Pennsylvania. A drama critic and historian, he authored *Religion in Modern English Drama*, *American Drama Since World War II*, and other titles. He wrote on drama for *Commonweal* and *The Hudson Review*.

ANNE PAOLUCCI is the author of *Pirandello's Theater*, plays, short stories, poems, and a novella. She is the coauthor of a book on Hegel.

LEONARD MOSS was a professor of comparative literature at the State University of New York. He wrote *Excess of Heroism in Tragic Drama* and also wrote on Arthur Miller, Kafka, Milton, and others.

GILBERT DEBUSSCHER has taught English and American Literature at the University of Brussels. He authored *Edward Albee: Tradition and Renewal*.

DAVID CASTRONOVO teaches English at Pace University. He has written and edited books on Edmund Wilson and has published others as well.

ROBERT A. MARTIN has been Professor of English at Michigan State University. He has written *Critical Essays on Tennessee Williams* and edited books on Arthur Miller.

ANNE DEAN has written *Discovery and Invention: The Urban Plays of Lanford Wilson*.

JANE PALATINI BOWERS has taught English. She is the author of *"They Watch Me as They Watch This": Gertrude Stein's Metadrama*, and she has also translated a book.

JOHN TIMPANE has taught English at Lafayette College. He is the coauthor of *Writing Worth Reading*.

MICHAEL L. QUINN was Assistant Professor in Dramatic Theory and Criticism at the University of Washington School of Drama. He wrote articles, reviews, and translations and worked on *The Semiotic Stage: Prague School Theater Theory* and a study of Vaclav Havel's plays.

STEPHEN J. BOTTOMS has taught at the University of Glasgow. He is the author of several titles, including *Theatre of Sam Shepard* and *Albee: Who's Afraid of Virginia Woolf?*

ELINOR FUCHS teaches at the Yale School of Drama and at Columbia University's School of the Arts. She is the author of *The Death of Character:*

Perspectives on Theater after Modernism and the editor of *Plays of the Holocaust: An International Anthology*.

C.W.E. BIGSBY has been Professor of American Studies at the University of East Anglia and has published more than twenty-five books on American theatre, popular culture, and British drama.

Bibliography

Adler, Thomas P. *Mirror on the Stage: The Pulitzer Plays as an Approach to American Drama*. West Lafayette: Purdue University Press, 1987.

Anderson, Maxwell. *Off Broadway: Essays about the Theatre*. New York: Sloane, 1947.

Arnott, Catherine M. *File on Tennessee Williams*. London: Methuen, 1987.

Bartow, Arthur. *The Director's Voice: Twenty-One Interviews*. New York: Theatre Communications Group, 1988.

Bentley, Eric. *The Life of the Drama*. New York: Atheneum, 1964.

———. *What Is Theatre?* New York: Limelight Editions, 1984.

Berkowitz, Gerald M. *American Drama of the Twentieth Century*. London: Longman, 1992.

Bigsby, C.W.E. *A Critical Introduction to Twentieth-Century American Drama*. Cambridge, U.K.: Cambridge University Press, 1984.

Bordman, Gerald. *The Oxford Companion to American Theatre*. New York: Oxford University Press, 1992.

Brinnin, John Malcolm. *The Third Rose: Gertrude Stein and Her World*. Reading, Mass.: Addison-Wesley, 1987.

Brockett, Oscar G. *History of the Theatre*. Boston: Allyn and Bacon, 1999.

Broussard, Louis. *American Drama: Contemporary Allegory from Eugene O'Neill to Tennessee Williams*. Norman: University of Oklahoma Press, 1962.

Brown-Guillory, Elizabeth. *Their Place on Stage: Black Women Playwrights in America*. New York: Praeger, 1988.

Brustein, Robert. *Reimagining American Theatre*. New York: Hill & Wang, 1991.

Cantor, Harold. *Clifford Odets: Playwright-Poet*. Metuchen, N.J.: Scarecrow, 1978.

Clum, John M. *Acting Gay: Male Homosexuality in Modern Drama*. New York: Columbia University Press, 1992.

Cohn, Ruby. *Dialogue in American Drama*. Bloomington: Indiana University Press, 1971.

———. *New American Dramatists, 1960–1980*. New York: Grove, 1982.

———. *New American Dramatists, 1960–1990*. Basingstoke: Macmillan, 1991.

Elam, Keir. *The Semiotics of Theatre and Drama*. London: Methuen, 1980.

Floyd, Virginia. *The Plays of Eugene O'Neill: A New Perspective*. New York: Ungar, 1985.

Freedman, Morris. *American Drama in Social Context*. Carbondale: Southern Illinois University Press, 1971.

Gassner, John. *Directions in Modern Theatre and Drama*. New York: Holt, Rinehart, and Winston, 1966.

Gilman, Richard. *Common and Uncommon Masks: Writings on Theatre 1961–1970*. New York: Vintage Books, 1972.

Gould, Jean. *Modern American Playwrights*. New York: Dodd, Mead, 1966.

Hay, Samuel A. *African American Theatre: An Historical and Critical Analysis*. New York: Cambridge University Press, 1994.

Hill, Errol, ed. *The Theatre of Black Americans: A Collection of Critical Essays*. New York: Applause Books, 1987.

Hughes, Catharine. *American Playwrights, 1945–1975*. London: Pitman, 1976.

Kolin, Phillip C., ed. *American Playwrights since 1945: A Guide to Scholarship, Criticism and Performance*. Westport, Conn.: Greenwood, 1989.

Levine, Ira A. *Left-wing Dramatic Theory in the American Theatre*. Ann Arbor: UMI Research Press, 1985.

Marranca, Bonnie, ed. *American Dreams: The Imagination of Sam Shepard*. New York: PAJ Publications, 1981.

Martine, James J. *Critical Essays on Eugene O'Neill*. Boston: G.K. Hall, 1984.

Orr, John. *Tragic Drama and Modern Society: Studies in the Social and Literary Theory of Drama from 1870 to the Present*. New York: Macmillan, 1981.

Ranald, Margaret Loftus. *The Eugene O'Neill Companion*. Westport, Conn.: Greenwood Press, 1984.

Robinson, Marc. *The Other American Drama*. Cambridge: Cambridge University Press, 1994.

Rogoff, Gordon. *Theatre Is Not Safe: Theatre Criticism 1962–1986*. Evanston, Ill.: Northwestern University Press, 1987.

Schlueter, June, ed. *Feminist Reading of Modern American Drama*. Rutherford, N.J. :Fairleigh Dickinson University Press, 1989.

———. *Modern American Drama: The Female Canon*. Rutherford, N.J.: Fairleigh Dickinson University Press, 1990.

Schroeder, Patrica R. *The Presence of the Past in Modern American Drama*. Rutherford, N.J.: Fairleigh Dickinson University Press, 1989.

Styan, J.L. *Modern Drama in Theory and Practice*, three volumes. Cambridge: Cambridge University Press, 1981.

Szondi, Peter. "Theory of Modern Drama." In *Theory and History of Literature*, volume twenty-nine, edited by Michael Hays. Minneapolis: University of Minnesota Press, 1987.

Wilmeth, Don B., and Tice L. Miller. *Cambridge Guide to American Theatre*. Cambridge: Cambridge University Press, 1993.

Wilson, Garf F.B. *Three Hundred Years of American Drama and Theatre*. Englewood Cliffs, N.J.: Prentice-Hall, 1973.

Worthen, Willliam. *Modern Drama and the Rhetoric of Theater*. Berkeley: University of California Press, 1992.

Acknowledgments

"Eugene O'Neill" by Lionell Trilling. From *Essays in the Modern Drama*, edited by Morris Freedman: pp. 96–103. © 1964 by Lionel Trilling. Reprinted with the permission of the Wylie Agency, Inc.

"Edward Albee: Don't Make Waves" by Gerald Weales. From *The Jumping-Off Place: American Drama in the 1960s:* pp. 24–53. © 1969 by Gerald Weales. Reprinted by permission.

"The Discipline of Arrogance" by Anne Paolucci. From *Tension to Tonic: The Plays of Edward Albee*, 3rd edition, Griffin House Publications, Smyrna, N.Y. 2000: pp 1–13. © 1972 by Southern Illinois University Press. Reprinted by permission.

"The Perspective of a Playwright" by Leonard Moss. From *Arthur Miller*: pp. 91–106. © 1980 G.K. Hall & Co. Reprinted by permission of The Gale Group.

"'Minting Their Separate Wills': Tennessee Williams and Hart Crane" by Gilbert Debusscher. From *Modern Drama* 26, no. 4 (Winter 1983): pp. 455–476. © 1983 by University of Toronto. Reprinted by permission.

"The Major Full-Length Plays: Visions of Survival" by David Castonovo. From *Thornton Wilder*: pp. 83–107. ©1986 by the Ungar Publishing

Company. Reprinted by permission of The Continuum International Publishing Group.

"Arthur Miller: Public Issues, Private Tensions" by Robert A. Martin. From *Studies in the Literary Imagination* 21, no. 2 (Fall 1988): pp. 97–106. © 1988 by the Department of English, Georgia State University. Reprinted by permission.

"Sexual Perversity in Chicago" by Anne Dean. From *David Mamet: Language as Dramatic Action*: pp. 51–84. © 1990 by Associated University Presses. Reprinted by permission.

"The Play as Lang-scape: 1920 to 1933" by Jane Palatini Bowers. From *"They Watch Me as They Watch This": Gertrude Stein's Metadrama*: pp. 50–61. © 1991 the University of Pennsylvania Press. Reprinted by permission of the University of Pennsylvania Press.

"Filling the Time: Reading History in the Drama of August Wilson" by John Timpane. From *May All Your Fences Have Gates*, edited by Alan Nadel: pp. 67–85. © 1994 by the University of Iowa Press. Reprinted by permission.

"Anti-Theatricality and American Ideology: Mamet's Performance Realism" by Michael L. Quinn. From *Realism and the American Dramatic Tradition*, edited by William W. Demastes: p. 235–254. © 1996 by University of Alabama Press. Reprinted by permission.

"Introduction: States of Crisis" by Stephen J. Bottoms. From *The Theatre of Sam Shepard: States of Crisis*: pp. 1–22. © 1998 by Stephen J. Bottoms. Reprinted with permission of Cambridge University Press.

"*Fefu and Her Friends*: The View from the Stone" by Elinor Fuchs. From *The Theater of Maria Irene Fornes*, edited by Marc Robinson: pp. 85–108. © 1999 by the Johns Hopkins University Press. Reprinted by permission of the Johns Hopkins University Press.

"Tennessee Williams: The Theatricalising Self" by C.W.E. Bigsby. From *Modern American Drama, 1945–2000*: pp. 31–68. © 2000 by Cambridge University Press. Reprinted with permission of Cambridge University Press.

Index